Crazy John and the Bishop

CRITICAL CONDITIONS: FIELD DAY ESSAYS AND MONOGRAPHS

Edited by Seamus Deane

Critical Conditions: Field Day Essays

Crazy John and the Bishop

and other Essays on Irish Culture

Terry Eagleton

UNIVERSITY OF NOTRE DAME PRESS
in association with
FIELD DAY

Published in the United States in 1998 by
University of Notre Dame Press
Notre Dame, IN 46556

And in Ireland by
Cork University Press
University College Cork, Ireland

Library of Congress Cataloging-in-Publication Data

Eagleton, Terry, 1943–
  Crazy John and the Bishop and other essays on Irish culture / Terry Eagleton.
        p.   cm. — (Critical conditions : 5)
    Includes bibliographical references and index.
    ISBN 0-268-00832-9 (pbk.)
        1. English literature—Irish authors—History and criticism. 2. National
characteristics, Irish, in literature. 3. Ireland—civilization. I. Title. II. Series.
PR8714.E28 1998
820.9'9415—dc21   98–16340
                                                                                    CIP

For Tadhg Foley and Luke Gibbons

CONTENTS

PREFACE

The following essays are offered for whatever merits they may have, but also to counteract two kinds of narrowness in contemporary Irish cultural studies. The first kind is a question of subject. Scanning the bibliographies, an outsider might be forgiven for concluding that the Irish literary pantheon was populated more or less exclusively by Yeats, Synge, Joyce, Beckett, Flann O'Brien and Northern Irish poetry. Few labourers in the field seem interested in Isaac Butt or Susan Mitchell, George Sigerson or Arthur Clery. I must confess that I have included essays on Yeats and Beckett in this collection; but I have tried to remain as tight-lipped as possible about Joyce, and to retrieve some neglected figures and conceptual subcurrents.

The second kind of narrowness – one of approach – sits oddly with the Great Man bias of the first. Much in Irish cultural studies is shaped nowadays by what one might loosely call a postmodern agenda, which brings into play some vital topics but in doing so tends to sideline other questions of equal importance. It is ironic that a discourse of marginality should have shoved so many other matters brusquely off stage. Religion and education, for example, are at least as weighty matters in Irish cultural history as gender or racial stereotyping, but they happen not to be such favoured items on the postmodern menu, or in North American academia. One cannot coherently insist on the 'otherness' of a culture like Ireland while attending almost exclusively to issues there, however vital they may be to the Irish themselves, which happen to be to the fore at the moment in one's own society. Such parochialism lends a dubious air to one's anti-colonialist protestations. I hope anyway that this book might prise open a little a field which seems to have become rather too tightly bounded.

The other boundary which the book tries to breach is that between textual analysis and intellectual history. The opening essay, on the neglected eighteenth-century poet William Dunkin, aims for a close critical dissection of his writing, and the same applies to the studies of Thomas Moore and W. B. Yeats. Other chapters, however, range rather more widely, exploring cultural concepts of 'benevolence' and 'sensibility' (as in 'The Good-Natured Gael'), or – as in 'Cork and the Carnivalesque' – examining notions of parody, comedy and plagiarism in relation to Irish writing. 'Crazy John and the Bishop' takes Bishop Berkeley and John Toland as its focus, but is really interested in Irish eighteenth-century history of ideas in general, while 'Home and Away' pursues a particular social theme – that of the Irish 'internal émigré' – through a broad span of novelists from Maria Edgeworth to Francis Stuart. A different way of blending the literary and the conceptual can be found in 'Beckett's Paradoxes', which attends to an individual author, but in speculative, quasi-philosophical vein. None of this amounts to a particularly coherent project, even if there are cross-references among the essays and a number of recurrent concerns. What unity the book has, I suppose, lies less in its subject-matter, which is deliberately somewhat eclectic, than in its cultural and political stance – a case which emerges in the chapter on the largely forgotten Irish socialist Frederick Ryan, and in the concluding discussion of the revisionist controversy.

David Berman, Andrew Carpenter, Nur Elmessiri, John Milbank, Manus O'Riordan, David Pierce and Robert Welch all helped with these essays in invaluable ways, and I here record my gratitude to them all.

Terry Eagleton

THE HIDDEN DUNKIN

William Dunkin was at least as fine a poet as many of his English counterparts who have found their assured niche in the eighteenth-century literary canon; indeed he was among the most accomplished English-language poets of eighteenth-century Ireland. But the fact that he spent his life on the wrong side of St George's Channel, along with the current unfashionableness of the neo-classical, have conspired to obscure his remarkable talents. Swift considered Dunkin 'a Gentleman of much Wit and the best English as well as Latin Poet in this Kingdom';[1] and Bryan Coleborne dubs him 'probably the most underrated poet of eighteenth-century Ireland'.[2] On his death, an epitaph in the *Dublin Journal* considered that he would rank with Swift and Pope.[3] But his name is little known even in Irish literary circles today, outside some valuable unpublished scholarship.[4]

Dunkin was born in Dublin in 1709 of an eminent, perhaps patrician family, and gained his MA from Trinity College in 1732, having cut something of a dashing figure there as an undergraduate. He was ordained in 1735 and came under the patronage of Jonathan Swift, who interceded with Trinity to win him a higher annual allowance from the property which his aunt (he was apparently orphaned) had donated to the college for his education and subsequent career. A member of Swift's literary circle and a privileged witness to his will, he served as Latin master at St Michael le Pole school in Dublin, though in 1739 Swift tried unsuccessfully to secure for him the living of Coleraine. As a protégé of the Dean he was plunged in the thick of the Dublin literary wranglings of the day, and was the subject of some peculiarly inept lampoons.[5] In 1746, Lord Chesterfield, Lord Lieutenant and one of Swift's

1. See Harold Williams (ed.), *The Correspondence of Jonathan Swift*, vol. 5 (Oxford, 1965), pp. 85–6.
2. Bryan Coleborne, Introduction to 'Anglo-Irish Verse, 1675–1825, in Seamus Deane (ed), *The Field Day Anthology of Irish Writing* (Derry, 1991), vol. 1, p. 495.
3. See Robert Mahony, *Swift: The Irish Identity* (New Haven and London, 1995), p. 177n.
4. See in particular Bryan Coleborne, 'Jonathan Swift and the Dunces of Dublin', unpublished PhD thesis, National University of Ireland, 1982, and Joseph C. Day, 'William Dunkin: "Best Poet" in the Kingdom? A New Look at his Augustan Burlesque', unpublished MA thesis, National University of Ireland, 1978. I have drawn on both of these works in my account. There are some brief comments on Dunkin's poem *The Parson's Revels* in Roger McHugh, 'Anglo-Irish Poetry 1700–1850', in Seán Lucy (ed.), *Irish Poets in English* (Cork and Dublin, 1973).
5. See *The Funeral Procession of the Chevalier de St Patrick* (Dublin, 1734), and *The Chevalier de St Patrick, Or, The Irish Pretender's Character* (Dublin, 1734), both

cronies, appointed him headmaster of Portora Royal School in Enniskillen, an establishment which was later to produce Oscar Wilde and Samuel Beckett, and he held the post until his death in 1765.

To his contemporaries, Dunkin's best-known work was probably *The Art of Gate-Passing, or The Murphaeid* (1729), the most popular poem in Dublin for generations.[6] Written in Latin – the facing English translation is now suspected not to be Dunkin's own – it is a paean of satiric praise to one Paddy Murphy, under-porter of Trinity College, and so, for a neo-classical poet, a distinctly 'low' subject of composition, however mock-heroically handled. Lowness, however, is in the nature of Dunkin's writing, and he begins *The Murphaeid* with an appeal to James Thomson, whose Muse, as the English translation has it, did not blush 'to sing the sordid plains / And lowly cottages of rural swains'. The mythological Murphy, custodian of the college gate and scourge of errant undergraduates, is presented as a model of the simple-hearted, unambitious Stoic, in a standard Horatian contrast of luxury and frugality. This praise of simplicity is of course conventional enough; but though Dunkin has his tongue in his cheek, his poetry in general really does back the lowly against the mighty, whatever the calculated incongruity with which it deploys high-toned imagery to do so. He is, however, nothing if not protean: his writing, comments Bryan Coleborne, 'combines intellectual and formal discipline with remarkable freedom and flexibility of language'.[7] Thus, having introduced Murphy as a simple-lifer, Dunkin then switches stylistic gear and re-models him as a figure of sublime Gothic terror. The poem is on one level little more than an undergraduate squib, a knockabout, showily erudite effort with a subcurrent of rather callow japery to it; but its linguistic control is nonetheless impressive, and it delivers some scorching satire of the educational establishment.

The Murphaeid's blending of high style and humble subject-matter is a typical feature of burlesque, a form in which Dunkin was well practised. It is a common enough literary mode for its time, but there is something about its mock-seriousness which might be said to speak specifically to Irish conditions. From Swift and Sterne to Joyce, O'Casey, Beckett and Flann O'Brien, the pokerfaced guying of portentous learning is a consistent motif of Anglo-Irish writing. A rhythm of inflation and deflation (literally so in the case of Swift's puffed-up Aeolists), of edifying discourse and crude debunkery, seems peculiarly suited to a society in which a lineage of high learning sits cheek-by-jowl with the dinginess of everyday life. Indeed we shall see in a later chapter how this oscillation lies at the centre of Francis Hutcheson's theory of comedy. Burlesque is a form which can capture the farcical tension between

anonymous. See also *Libel Upon the Dublin Dunces: In an Epistle to Mr William Dunkin* (Dublin, 1734).

---

6.   See, for Dunkin's poetry, *Select Poetical Works* (Dublin, 1769–70), 2 vols, and *The Poetical Works of William Dunkin* (London, 1774).

7.   Deane (ed.), *Field Day Anthology*, vol. 1, p. 396.

well-stocked minds and ill-fed bodies; and Dunkin's persistent resort to it should be placed in this broader historical context, rather than read simply as a particular kind of poetic exercise. If burlesque is a technique, the vision it embodies can often more aptly be termed carnivalesque; and Dunkin's writing at its most vivacious merits this now rather fashionable title.

Some of the most striking effects of neo-classical verse are achieved by what one might call 'overcoding': the pleasurable compacting of a wealth of information into a narrow metrical compass. We shall see something of this in a later chapter in the poetry of Oliver Goldsmith, but Dunkin's verse is equally remarkable for this high-pressured packaging. An art-form which eschews Romantic extravagance, bent as it is upon preserving a purity of diction and a tight metrical scheme; which has at its disposal only a limited tonal range, and which is out to avoid the displeasures of any too brashly innovative effect: such a poetry is forced to make every semantic unit work overtime, dragooning a plurality of perceptions into its heroic couplets without thereby disrupting conventional grammar. In this stringent semiotic economy, each element is forced to pull more than its own weight, so that, as in the poetry of Pope, the slightest syntactical inversion or antithesis becomes almost an image in its own right. What such verse is forced to lose in terms of luxuriant or idiosyncratic imagery, disruptive syntax or dramatic shifts of tone, is recuperated by the delights of economising on the reader's energies, compressing a whole complex action into a single verbal gesture.

Much of this elegant economising is in evidence in Dunkin's *The Poetical Mirror*, a four-book poem couched in blank verse. It is a considerably more ambitious affair than *The Murphaeid*, a piece which, in a venerable Irish literary tradition, says very little in engaging style. Like *The Murphaeid*, however, though on a far grander scale, *The Poetical Mirror* is a daring medley of forms and genres, veering from satire, epic and mock-heroic to pastoral, farce and the grotesque. Like that poem too, it plays off its solemnly elevated style against some obtrusively vulgar content, as in this passage on a poverty-stricken poet with a shilling in his purse:

> Not he voracious with insatiate ears
> Ingulphs new oysters from the distant cry
> ALIVE! ALIVE! impervious to his lips,
> Nor with sagacious nostril snuffs in vain
> The fumes ambrosial of hot mutton-pies,
> Nor melancholy sighs for chearful ale
> With arid lips; but when the beldame night
> With sable mantle overspreads the face
> Of earth, day-widowed, ushered with his friends
> To club-frequented tipling-house he shapes
> His joyful steps, and carolling renews
> The liquid honours of the social board.

This flourishing Miltonic period, sustained over twelve lines with multiple enjambements, is comically askew to its indecorous subject-matter. The stylised 'sable mantle' and self-conscious felicity of 'day-widowed' are rammed incongruously up against the tipling house, so that the stock Augustanism 'The liquid honours of the social board', with its calculatedly mannered abstraction, comes through more as tongue-in-cheek euphemism than as graceful closure. Much the same mock-heroic irony is at work later in the lines 'with sage intent to vend / His curdy venture at Arvonian mart', which refer with arch over-bredness to a peasant trundling his dairy produce to market.

Digressive and episodic in its narrative structure, *The Poetical Mirror* is in effect Ireland's answer to Pope's *Dunciad*, dealing as it does with the tribulations of the minor Dublin literati. Unlike the *Dunciad*, however, Dunkin's work views the Irish equivalent of Grub Street not from the transcendental vantage-point of Reason, but from the standpoint of the impoverished hack himself. In so far, that is, as the poem can be ascribed any consistent narrative standpoint at all: it makes little attempt at artistic unity, as shifting in its focus and preoccupations as it is in its stylistic registers. But the luckless literary drudge is certainly one of its perspectives, handled as he is in much the same jocose, mock-heroic manner as Paddy Murphy. Bailiffs dunning him on behalf of his creditors are the bane of his existence, as he scrambles around his attic to hide from them:

> . . . Arrested with surprise,
> What should I do? or whither turn? aghast
> Amaz'd, confounded, through the mingled mass
> Of ashes, cinders, twice to be reviv'd,
> And slack sulphureous, to the black recess
> Of coal-hole fugitive I slink, and couch
> Reptile, intomb'd beneath the celly gloom.

The dramatic directness of this, with its breathless clauses and abrupt enjambements, is the formal equivalent of its plebeian subject-matter, in which elevated literary epithets like 'sulphureous' and 'celly' struggle vainly against the the coarse naturalism of 'slack' and 'coal-hole'. Both registers, high and low, converge in that weighty, exquisitely placed 'Reptile', an urbane latinism which nonetheless irresistibly suggests the squalid farce of the poet coiling himself anxiously out of sight of his unwelcome visitors.

Much the same blending of satire and mock-heroic invigorates the poem's aggressive portraiture of Dublin aldermen, whose greedy banqueting provokes Dunkin into some plangent pastoral nostalgia:

> What wasteful inroads into mutton-loyns
> Bell-weather'd? what fell havock will they make
> On slaughter'd pigs and lusty chines of beef?
> With fangy teeth shall severally they

Tear tender lambkins with maternal ewes,
Nor quarter give to fatted calves belov'd,
Now doom'd to deviate into various forms
Of animals, and into bipeds rife,
Nor spare thy bird, O Venus; nor the goose
Shall 'scape, alas! their cormoranting rage. . .

As often, Dunkin's tone is here not quite coherent, as poignancy and polemic are unevenly blended. The grand epic style of *The Poetical Mirror* is not the best vehicle for the abrasive satire it contains in plenty, so that the work's medium is occasionally too cumbersome for its message. The effect can accordingly be overstrained, as when the clattering of the aldermen's knives and forks becomes, preposterously, a resounding crash of 'steely forests . . . In harsh encounter'. The line between the mock-heroic and the ham-fistedly grotesque is notably blurred, though 'cormoranting' is a boldly imaginative stroke. Yet Dunkin persists with his pastoral lament in verse which plucks surprisingly fresh energy from the stale poetic convention of innocent Nature served up for the delectation of predatory Man:

Whatever batten in the muddy pools,
Lazy with fenny weed, or those, that coast
The serpent rivers through the winding vales.
Those, that inhabit pleasurable bays,
And briny mansions of the main, or cling
To rocks half-eaten on the sandy shore,
With sundry sauces, dulcet, acid, salt
Glide miscellaneous down their channel throats,
And the crude chaos thickens in their guts.

If 'serpent rivers', 'winding vales ' and 'pleasurable bays' are perfunctory enough gestures, the densely assonantal 'Lazy with fenny weed', and the startlingly abrupt introduction of the sauces (enacting as it does a sudden Fall from innocent Nature to over-indulgent culture), are the devices of a highly accomplished author. And if the penultimate line is embarrassingly maladroit, the line which follows it goes boldly for the kill and just manages to pull it off.

Almost immediately, however, the poem's register shifts again, once more back into low farce. A clumsy servant spills a dish of food over a diner, injuring his forehead in the process:

. . .Indignant welts deform
His honest front protuberant, that o'er
His bristly brows project a gloomy shade,
Horrid and huge, and from the wide canals
Of livid nostrils disemboguing flows
Tartareous ichor. . .

> But a-down his neck
> And shoulders fast an oily deluge runs
> Continuous, and his brawny limbs acquire
> Lard adventitious. With delicious fish
> His bosom spawns; his breeches catch the fry. . .
> and quick the waiters rub
> From his full bosom the superfluous fat,
> The clotted humour, and the pearly drops
> Of grey libation, and their vigour ply
> To bathe his face with purifying streams. . .

This begins uninspiringly enough, with a reach-me-down piece of Gothic monstrosity in the Irish epic tradition; but by the time we reach 'Lard adventitious' – a carnivalesque phrase, one might venture, self-flauntingly yoking together its humble noun and mouth-filling epithet – the verse has begun to take fire. 'His breeches catch the fry' is a pleasingly idiosyncratic stroke of wit, while 'clotted humour' and 'grey libation' couple together the dignified and the everyday in a microcosm of the passage as a whole. Versatile, sinuous and chafingly physical, Dunkin's poetic language at its finest is an impressively resourceful instrument.

The poem then reverts to its pastoral register, in a verse which is stylised and elegant without especial imagistic richness:

> For you the birds in verbal season chant
> Their soft complaints through thick-embower'd groves,
> And airy loves in annual wedlock bind.
> The bees, industrious through the painted meads.
> Incessant roam, and cattle fatten far
> On richest herbage. Patient swains invert
> For you the bosom of untutor'd earth,
> And oxen groan beneath the galling yoke.

The charming conceit of the marrying birds, the oddly scrupulous placing of 'far', the nimble enjambement of the final lines: all this more than counterweighs the neo-classical clichés of 'vernal wood' and 'painted meads', just as the stock image of the last line is offset by the Metaphysical quaintness of the image which proceeds it. (For the swains to invert the earth's bosom is presumably for them to dig.) But the poem then reaches beyond this conventional landscape for a more opulently sensuous note:

> But soft the leaves of Aethiopian woods
> Whiten for you with silky down, the groves
> Of Araby, Sabaean branches glow
> With incense pure, and liquid odours weep.
> Alas! for you the beamy fire of Bards

> Arrays the gardens of Hesperian nymphs
> With rinded gold, and lo! the wedded vine,
> Ungrateful to the pruning hand, for you
> Swells genial, pregnant with the jolly God.

Those groves of Araby and Hesperian nymphs may be familiar neo-classical furniture, but the poise and lyrical relish of these lines, their remarkably limber rhythms and lavish imagery, have a well-nigh Shakespearian resonance. The poetry specifies as much as it dares, without risking a loss of general reference: that beautiful phrase 'Whiten for you with silky down' is unusually delicate and particularised for the poetic genre it inhabits, and the subtle oxymoron of 'liquid odours' enlivens an otherwise stereotyped image. There is a touch of inspiration in the final, intricately complex conceit, as the vine becomes a kind of double adulterer, unfaithful to both the pruner and to Bacchus. This promiscuous vine deserts its wedded partner the pruner, whose ministering hand then takes on erotic connotations, for the drinker himself, while its plump grapes, impregnated by Bacchus, become a belly proffered not for the god's delight, but for that of the reveller. The inspired simplicity of the phrase 'the jolly God' works not least because it carries with it just a hint of oxymoron. Once more, poetic genre is notably unstable: these passages are formally intended as a satire of the hoggish Dublin dignitaries, but their pastoral lyricism rapidly submerges this intention, presenting natural life for its value in itself rather than as pillage for the rich man's table.

All of this culinary extravagance is contrasted with the penury of the poet, which forms the work's major theme. Like much eighteenth-century Anglo-Irish writing, the poem turns out to be about writing. Indeed, in what must be one of the earliest images of hack authorship as sweated industrial labour, it compares the denizens of Grub Street to Birmingham foundry workers:

> . . . As in their murky cells,
> The Birmingham artificers inur'd,
> At bellows this, that over flaming coals,
> Incumbent sweat. These knives embroaden, those
> Point prongy forks. Some hammer by degrees
> The ductile metal into taper swords,
> To which another gives the polished edge;
> Another marries to the sheath, and fits
> The temper'd mischief with resplendent hilts. . .

The lines display Dunkin's artful modulation of sentence-length, along with the neo-classical felicity of 'temper'd mischief'. The chain of deictics – these, those, some, another – is itself almost a rhetorical figure: the point is that this labour is specialised, parcelled out, and for this to happen in the case of writing runs contrary to the humanist ideology which has traditionally sustained it. To deal with the dunces, Dunkin's own style is forced, as it were, to mimic their own lowness:

> But others, pregnant with the Muse, and bald
> Of current cash, and belly-timber void,
> Just in the nick of sickly-teeming time,
> From lofty turrets into bare-fac'd light
> Rush diverse, and itinerant through stews
> And baths fly flocking. Knights and commoners they
> By tribes accost, their bulky works unfold,
> Extol, unbidden without end repeat,
> Cling to the collars of their hearers fast
> With hands Harpeian, pound their passive sides
> With punching elbows, and provoke applause,
> And now from these, and now from those extort.

That 'sickly-teeming time' is a shade too Shakespearian for this stripped, fast-moving verse, though 'bare-fac'd light' does something to redeem it (the light at once exposing the hacks' previously shuttered faces and bare-facedly refusing them privacy). The hungry poet, in a neatly antithetical image,

> . . .rich in tattered regimentals, decks
> Poetic heroes with refulgent arms,
> Flushes with purple, daubs with gold, and sings
> Ceres with empty, Bacchus with dry mouth.

There is an earthy vigour and good humour about Dunkin's poetry which is far removed from the English neo-classical norm of a Pope. *The Dunciad* dabbles in dirt while managing to keep its poetic hands scrupulously clean; Dunkin's language, by contrast, partakes of the grubby materials it mediates, while never relinquishing a formal edge over them. This is the generically unstable, tonally ambivalent writing of a social class considerably less self-assured than their English counterparts, and the insecurity shows through in a certain volatility of viewpoint or digressiveness of structure. As Bryan Coleborne puts it: 'The lack of a secure identity, linked as it was, ironically, to a determination to celebrate life in all its forms, produced verse with a peculiar flavour, full of energy and ambivalence, quite unlike that of eighteenth-century England or Scotland'.[8] Dunkin's writing is copious and animated but sometimes tonally or formally uncertain of itself, the product of a seedy colonial society in which the 'low' was palpable enough to need to be poetically incorporated, rather than remote enough to be thrust aside. It is for this reason that it has a smack of robustness and high spirits about it almost entirely foreign to the writing of, say, John Dryden. Yet counterposing this subversive mischief in *The Poetical Mirror* is a pellucid patriotism, that of a devout adherent of the Williamite settlement, which provides the poem with some of its most finely-wrought passages. Like an unholy hybrid of James Thomson and

8.   In Deane (ed.), *Field Day Anthology,* vol. 1, p. 397.

Brian Merriman, Dunkin is the laureate of British liberty and prosperity as
well as a knockabout satirist and fantasist. King William

> . . .morals gave to peace,
> And into sickles, rural armament,
> And pride of Ceres, beat the deathful blade;
> Then cities half-demolish'd, walls eras'd
> Bade re-arise, and floating forests plow
> The watery waste, to bear Sabacan gums
> And teem with orient gold. . .

The verse resourcefully refreshes the swords-to-ploughshares cliché in a lucid,
deftly turned phrase ('beat the deathful blade'), descends to an Augustan
stock response in 'floating forests', and then goes on in Miltonic vein to
applaud the rout of the Roman Catholics:

> . . .Then lawless fury, sanctify'd misrule
> That rag'd with havoc through Hibernia town,
> And her twin-sister superstition sad,
> And arm'd with snakes imbosom'd, murm'ring fled
> Appalled, and routed to the Stygian shades.

But the poem quickly recovers its genial buoyancy after this fit of sectarian spleen, and unfolds a vision of the *Pax Britannica* as superbly accomplished in technique as it is profoundly unoriginal in content:

> . . .beneath his foster-tree,
> The joyful planter with rewarded hand
> Pluck'd autumn pendant from the woven boughs,
> And undefil'd religion rear'd aloft
> Her awful head. . .
> Hence savage mountains into furrow'd fields
> Are soften'd, miny magazines, conceiv'd
> Long through the bowels of impregnate earth,
> Purge off their dross and into metals melt. . .

> Deep in the bowels of impregnate earth,
> The miny seeds of rigid metals grow,
> Which purg'd by flames are temper'd into shares,
> Inflex, and fitted for the crooked plow.
> The seeded glebe with golden-ear'd increase
> Repays the peasant, nor ungrateful yields
> For bedding chaff, and for her oxen food.
> To forming hands the forest rude affords
> Material pliant, and profusely stores
> The hearth with fewel, and the dome with light.
> The bleating multitudes with fleecy coats

> Spontaneous whiten, whence in heady twirl
> The tufted labour of the spindle swells,
> 'Till by degrees the warpy threads unite,
> Condens'd, embody'd with the lengthy woof,
> And deep infus'd imbibe the Tyrian dye. . .

The masterly simplicity of 'rewarded hand'; the triumphant interlacing of abstract and concrete in 'Pluck'd autumn pendant from the woven boughs', where the elegantly latinate 'autumn pendant' is beautifully counterpoised by the Anglo-Saxonism of 'woven boughs'; the particularised abstraction of 'tufted labour'; the cunning playing off of 'Inflex' against 'crooked': all this can be set against the more ready-made imagery of fleecy coats, golden-ear'd increase and Tyrian dye. There is a particularly choice instance of Dunkin's delicate rhythmic control in the delicately wrought lines 'To forming hands the forest rude affords / Material pliant, and profusely stores / The hearth with fewel, and the dome with light', where syntax and metrical scheme are subtly interwoven.

Satire, farce, epic, mock-heroic, pastoral, panegyric, grotesque, burlesque: *The Poetical Mirror* mingles all of these genres in an exuberant carnival of poetic forms. But its poetic quality is as mixed as its modes, and the poem thus marks a contrast with the sustained inspiration of *The Parson's Revels* (1750), one of the great neglected pieces of eighteenth-century English. This splendid satire, which opens in carnivalesque fashion with lashings of food and drink, centres on a bunch of riotous characters at a ball thrown by a Leitrim squire. Dunkin begins by claiming, mock-grovellingly, that such lowly subject-matter matches his own disinherited condition:

> My ancestors might claim some rank,
> But, as for me, I drew a blank
> From Fortune's wheel, for which I thank
>   My dead aunt:

> Estates with suits are often rife,
> But she would free me from the strife,
> And I was doom'd to be for life
>   A pedant.

'Free me' is nicely sardonic, since Dunkin's aunt apparently relieved him of 'his' estate by selling it to Trinity College, admittedly to defray the costs of his education. A dance is then described in mildly satirical vein:

> Each blithesome damsel shews her shape,
> Enough to burst her stays and tape,
> And bangs the boards: the fiddlers scrape
>   Their cat-guts:

> Brave C——, foe to popish dogs,
> In boots, as cumbersome as clogs,
> Displays his parts, and B—— jogs
> > His fat guts.

But the braggart Captain C—— meets with a mishap while jigging with the parson's wife:

> His trusty spur, when arm'd to kick,
> With which he often us'd to prick
> His palfry, play'd him now a trick
> > Most scurvy:

> It seiz'd her hoop, which made her stop,
> And, in the middle of his hop,
> Quite tumbl'd o'er our hero top-
> > sy turvy.

Dunkin's rhyme scheme is a comic ritual in itself.[9] It isn't only a matter of deliberately maladroit rhyming – scurvy/topsy turvy, from it/vomit, ewe lamb/ per-naculum, mum for't/comfort, and the like – but the way in which the three rhyming lines of each verse set up a seamless continuity then abruptly dislocated by the final tacked-on phrase, which comes after a slight dramatic hiatus in which the reader has just enough time to wonder what monstrously over-ingenious effect is about to be perpetrated. However solemn or exalted the particular rhyme word, its brief trisyllabic lilt, coming after three sets of iambic tetrameters, is inevitably bathetic. These superadded phrases, almost afterthoughts, are too laconic to bear the weight of meaning which the overall rhythm unavoidably throws upon them, and this is itself a comic device. They are textually marooned moments, part of the stanza yet external to it, and this sets up in the reader the faint pleasurable tension of feeling that they both complete each stanzaic unit yet are also lamely superfluous gestures, stitched incongruously on to a three-liner which is already achieved enough in itself. The poem thus reaps the witty effect of having a double closure to each of its units, which are sometimes entirely at odds with each other and sometimes (as in 'top-sy turvy') clumsily elided. Each stanza ends on an emphatic note which is also, structurally speaking, an anti-climax; and the effect is heightened by the way in which the reader has to carry over in her mind from one verse to another a phrase which seems clinching and definitive, yet is humorously disproportionate to what it supposedly brings to a head.

9.   The rhyme scheme is rare, though Andrew Carpenter draws my attention to its use by the English Restoration poet Alexander Radcliffe in 'The Ramble', a bawdy piece which rhymes 'Clitoris' with 'Tell Stories' and 'Very true 'tis' with 'Their Cutis'. See Harold Love (ed.), The Penguin Book of Restoration Verse (London, 1968), pp. 14–19.

When the final rhyming phrase is intended as a rhetorical flourish, its position in the verse ensures that it will be ludicrously undercut:

> In bonds and books I have some pelf—
> But, Sir, this poor poetic elf
> May hang his harp up, and himself,
> on one tree.

> My mind, from public business freed,
> Should moralise on what I read—
> But O my country, O my bleed-
> ing country!

Or the rhyming phrases may be even more pedantically laboured, as in these suavely wrought lines about a blind Irish poet:

> As ladies fair, of taste refin'd,
> Their petted linnets often blind
> To make them sing the sweeter, kind-
> ly cruel;

> To strike his mind with visions bright,
> And give his hearers more delight,
> Melpomene depriv'd of sight
> This jewel.

Occasionally the final rhyming phrase is a masterpiece of feebleness, a triumph of non-inspiration:

> His voice was brazen, deep, and such,
> As well-accorded with High-dutch,
> Or Attic Irish, and his touch
> Was pliant;

> Dubourg to him was but a fool;
> He played melodious without rule,
> And sung the feats of Fin Macool,
> The giant.

Elsewhere the effect is one of solemn grotesquerie, as the final, starkly isolated words of the stanza thud with a *gravitas* they simultaneously deflate:

> While C—— and B—— round the chairs,
> As mad as any dancing bears,
> Bestir their hams, and some say, theirs
> Were limber:

> Sir George, though brave as Scanderbeg,
> Was not so pliable Greg,

    Yet hopp'd on his adopted leg
                    Of timber.

The diplomatic euphemism of that 'adopted' is one of the poem's many masterly strokes.

The company assembled at the revels, as befits such multicultural, carnivalesque occasions, are an ideologically mixed bunch:

    In equal wise the Parson had
    Some sober folks, and many mad,
    Some humoursome, and some as sad
                    as Smedley.

    The world, he knew, from long conviction,
    Was all made up of contradiction.
    And so he chose without restriction
                    A medley.

There is the parish priest Fegan, fleecer of his laity and phoney intellectual, who speaks an atrocious, well-nigh unintelligible Hiberno-English:

    Quoth he, 'I am vwell boarn and brid,
    Shur Teague O'Regan vwash my hid,
    Aldough, deer joay, I never rid
                    Your Nhomars;

    Yit Fegan can confabulaat
    In Frinch and Laatin, dher mey faat,
    And hild a Teshis at dhe graaat
                    Shaint Omars.

The poem's language then thickens into the macaronic, a familiar carnivalesque mode, as Fegan jabbers away in a grotesque, Hiberno-English-inflected Latin:

    Shed, shee jam mavish dishputare
    Pugnish, quam lagishe pugnare,
    Tantundem dat, praesheptor chare,
                    Tanteedhem.

Murphy, another puffed-up professional Gael, vaunts his illustrious ancestry:

    About O Neal he kept a pother.
    For why, he was his foster-brother,
    Begotten on a base-born mother,
                    A spinster;

    But, though reduc'd to live by strings,
    Greater than great O Neal he brings

> His father's blood from antient kings
>> Of Leinster.

The well-bred Sir George, by contrast, is more preoccupied with contemporary culture, and is not slow to parade the fact before his doubtless uncomprehending colleagues:

> We scarce discover in an age
> A single genius for the stage
> The most accomplish'd must engage
>> A faction;

> I hate the rants of Dryden's rhyme;
> Old Shakespear was, (I grant) sublime,
> But broke all unities of time,
>> And action.

Oaf, the zealous Presbyterian, aloofly withdraws from the swinish company, to be clinically dissected by the poet like a piece of architecture:

> Philosophers will argue, whether
> The whole (suppose it were a feather)
> Do differ from the parts together,
>> Compounded;

> But view him over from the sole
> Of arctic foot to noddle-pole,
> And all the parts become the whole
>> Of round-head.

> His capitol, though batter'd oft,
> Was fortify'd, and stood aloft,
> To guard his brains, that were as soft,
>> As jelly:

> The sacred way, his mouth of cod
> Convey'd, officious at his nod
> His victims to that household god,
>> His belly.

Crab the Quaker, a predictably less sectarian type, explains in splendidly crafted religious cant his theological motives for condescending to accept a drink:

> Quoth Crab, the Quaker, who had sat
> Beneath the pent-house of his hat,
> Thine arguments come in so pat,
>> And pithy,

Albeit I renounce thy clan,
And convenants, mine inward man
Now moveth me to cup, and can
                    It with thee. . .

The grape is good, and eke the juice
Thereof was made for human use,
Which thus ye toss about profuse
                    So merrily.

Then, brethren, fit ye round the Board,
And fill your cups with one accord,
It is the creature of the Lord,
                    Yea verily—

It is, appropriately, the pious Crab who benevolently assists a colleague whose hand is shaking too violently to raise his glass:

Quoth C————e, who was over-shotten,
My throttle, yet as dry, as cotton,
Could tipple, but my hand has gotten
                    The palsy.

Quoth Crab, good fellowship instilling,
Assist him, neighbours, in his filling,
The flesh is weak, but spirit willing,
                    And ready.

The satirical tone of *The Parson's Revels* is for the most part affable and emollient, as its bunch of zealots, parasites and braggarts sink their sectarian differences in boozing and banqueting. The good-humoured Dunkin has little of the belligerence of a Swift or the svelte malice of a Pope, just as he lacks for the most part their chiasmic dexterity and antithetical poise. Technically, the piece is a triumph, mischievously playing off its blandly ritualised stanzaic form against the boisterousness of its content. The poem's language is at once convivial and tightly disciplined, neither elaborate nor idiomatic, as in this unshowy but deftly modulated description of feasting:

In spring, or summer, at your ease,
You feast on bacon, beans, and pease:
The pullet, kid, or pig, to please
                    Your mind, falls.

At Michaelmas on geese you dine,
Pluck mellow pears, and pippins fine,
And treat your friends, or fatten swine,
                    With windfalls.

'Falls', meaning 'is killed', is a superbly tactful gesture, at once gracious and ironically evasive.

Much of the rest of Dunkin's writing is competent but unremarkable neo-classical stuff, just but colourless, as in his panegyric to 'Publicola', a public-spirited nobleman:

> As undeceiving, undeceiv'd he pries
> Quick through the knave's and parasite's disguise;
> Nor less indignant of the mean and proud,
> Explores true merit through the sablest cloud.
> Prompt are his hands, and anxious is his breath
> To counsel, soothe, and succour the distress'd.
> His converse flowing from a gentle mind,
> And humour, temper'd with a taste refin'd,
> A rich repast for Attic ears afford,
> And dignify the hospitable board.

This is an urbane performance in a mode whose sincerity it doesn't make sense to inquire after. The discernment of true merit, as opposed to being fawned on by two-faced chancers, is a constant theme of Dunkin's writing, inspired in part, one imagines, by his experience of the sycophants who surrounded his own patron. 'An Epistle to Atticus' drives home the point in rather 'lower' style, illustrated by some astute imagery:

> The sound of vessels, you confess,
> Assures us of their emptiness;
> And from the same identic cause
> We presently detect their flaws.
> The tryal answers well on glasses,
> Yet flattery for candour passes;
> Or how should sages be the tools
> Of servile sycophants, and fools;
> While with aversion they despise
> The men of truth and undisguise,
> As dainty ladies hug an ape,
> Yet startle at a human shape?

The same note is sounded in 'An Epistle to R–B–T N–G–T', which lashes the camp-followers who have deserted Swift in his declining years, and ends, movingly, with a plea to his mentor's Maker to 'Irradiate his benight'd mind' in 'The bright republic of the bless'd'. There can be few more gracious ways of wishing someone dead. Dunkin is a supple, remarkably versatile poet, with a voice which ranges from the lifeless idealisations of 'The Lover's Web' to the vigorous colloquialism of 'A Poet's Prayer'. It is surely time that his impressive *oeuvre* was reintroduced to the world.

CRAZY JOHN AND THE BISHOP

Bishop Berkeley said to his girl, Flo
'Fix your beadies on this thing below
To assuage my deep fears
For it just disappears
*   When there's no one observing it grow.'*[1]

'There was no hill or wood in all the land', writes Austin Clarke in his novel *The Singing-Men at Cashel,* 'which had not been remembered in poetry. Had not those great teachers of the past taught that matter was as holy as the mind, that hill and wood were an external manifestation of the immortal regions?'[2] One is tempted to detect here a relation between the Irish tradition of *dinnshenchas,* or place-name lore, and the idealist epistemology of the greatest Irish philosopher, for whom what looks like matter is in fact rather more like what James Joyce will later call an epiphany. For Berkeley, things are at one with their presence to their perceivers, *res* and *signum* identical, the world one sublimely intricate discourse in which God enunciates himself and utters forth his darkly unfathomable substance. Berkeley's animism has a range of sources in philosophical antiquity, but as the Clarke quotation intimates, one of them may well be Gaelic. The Irish novelist James Stephens writes in Berkeleyan style in *The Demi-Gods* of the moon, stars and clouds as the 'thoughts made visible' of the divine mind.

Just as Berkeley himself was Anglo-Irish, so his philosophy might be read as a combination of English empiricist epistemology and Irish spiritualistic ontology, the latter providing a solution of kinds to some of the problems of the former. In the end, Berkeley returns a theological answer to a philosophical question, a move which cannot easily be philosophically faulted, and which reveals the sovereignty of both politics and theology in eighteenth-century Ireland over even such apparently secular matters as perception, cognition, sensation and the like.[3] If this is a political as well as theological stance,

1. Thanks to Alan Wall for the loan of this limerick, which appears in his novel *Bless the Thief* (London, 1997).
2. Austin Clarke, *The Singing-Men at Cashel* (London, 1936), p. 276.
3. See David Berman and Andrew Carpenter, 'Eighteenth-Century Irish Writing', in Seamus Deane (ed), *The Field Day Anthology of Irish Writing* (Derry, 1992), vol. 1, pp. 760–1. This eighteenth-century interweaving of politics and religion posed a problem for Catholic apologists, who wished to convince their Protestant masters that while they might be religiously dissident, they were nonetheless politically docile. See C. D. A. Leighton, *Catholics in a Protestant Kingdom* (Dublin, 1994), especially Part 2, ch. 5.

it is because it is meant among other things to combat a socially subversive scepticism. If the deity is the ground of all being, the reason why there is anything at all rather than just nothing, then what looks to the philosophical realists and empiricists like a realm of autonomous material objects must actually be God's own idiom, a celestial script which lays bare the grammar of his ceaseless self-communication. As Berkeley puts it in *Siris*: 'As the natural connexion of signs with the things signified is regular and constant, it forms a sort of Rational Discourse . . . Therefore, the phaenomena of nature . . . do form not only a magnificent spectacle, but also a most coherent, entertaining, and instructive Discourse. . . .'[4] The language of Nature is at once rational, aesthetic and rhetorical.

Reflecting on Berkeley's transcendence of the *res/signum* distinction, the theologian John Milbank writes of this textual view of the world, in which creation becomes a kind of semiosis and substance accordingly drops out, as a kind of '"perfect" writing in which the words themselves constitute the surface on which they are written'.[5] There is nothing here 'behind' appearances, no determinate substratum, since what sustains these appearances for Berkeley is the infinitely indeterminate power of the godhead. One might claim similarly that for Jacques Derrida there is nothing 'behind' writing, no realist bedrock to it, since what keeps this utterance afloat is just the inexhaustible force of *écriture*, in which the 'depth' of writing is inscribed on its own surface.[6] Just as for Derrida there is nothing outside textuality, which is to say no worldly element untainted by its complex implication with others, so for Berkeley 'it becomes impossible to say that (things) are anything "beyond" the implicatory network of signs which encompasses our whole practical inhabitation of the world'.[7]

Knowledge for Berkeley is not, as the empiricists would have it, a causal relation between the two mysteriously incommensurable realms of mind and matter, but 'occurs in the single medium of "ideas" or signs, and can be no further explicated than as the reading of signs according to conventions'.[8] For

4.   Alexander Campbell Fraser (ed.), *The Works of George Berkeley, DD* (Oxford, 1871), p. 460. All page references to this work will subsequently be given in parentheses after quotations.
5.   John Milbank, *The Word Made Strange* (Oxford, 1997), p. 98.
6.   The analogy, like any other, is limited. Derrida is not, to be sure, an idealist; indeed – though he would wish to deconstruct the idealism/materialism antithesis itself – what is arguably most scandalous about his doctrine of the signifier is precisely its materialism, its insistence that the foundation of all ideality is to be found in inherently meaningless material marks. It is noteworthy that James Joyce was much taken by the notion that a mere twenty-six alphabetical marks could generate a potential infinity of signifying units. Berkeley himself remarks in his *Principles of Human Knowledge* on how 'a few original ideas may be made to signify a great number of effects and actions' (*Works*, vol. 1, p. 190).
7.   ibid, p. 98.
8.   ibid, p. 98.

Berkeley as for the post-structuralists (though the differences between them are immense), we cannot catapult ourselves outside that vast web of significations which is creation to know an object in all its splendid isolation, since to know is itself to signify. And if substance has thus dropped out, so also has cognitive or semantic determinacy, since knowledge must now become the (potentially infinite) explication of this labyrinthine text rather than a once-and-for-all event. Nouns for Berkeley, so Milbank points out, do not denominate discrete sensory particulars but signify only in their concrete articulations. 'Words have become rules organizing action, not correlates of "things" ';[9] and this pragmatic rather than representational semiotics, resonant of the later Wittgenstein rather than the earlier,[10] involves a certain indeterminacy or polyvalence of meaning.

For Berkeley, then, as much as for his great Irish philosophical predecessor John Scottus Eriugena,[11] the sensible universe itself, as the expressive symbol of its creator's unsearchable depths, must itself finally elude all rigorous determination. For both thinkers, what we call the world is a 'self-referential labyrinth of signs'[12] which can no more be closed off than the perpetual event of interpretation itself. In Berkeley's pre-modern, anthropocentric, alluringly non-alienated universe, objects exist only in so far as they are (in Heideggerian phrase) 'to hand', given over to us, fashioned for the practical service of humanity, as creation itself for St Paul was fashioned from all eternity through the human Word. To hold that *esse est percipi* then bears an oblique relation to Heidegger's claim that Being is the mystery of the world's being so radically accessible to us in the first place, its primordial readability or bound-upness with us, and that this non-substance of Being is what opens up all particular beings. Being and nothingness are close kin for both thinkers; indeed Berkeley seems to regard this as a distinctively Irish mode of thought, recording in his commonplace book that 'The mathematicians talk of what they call a point, this they say is not altogether nothing nor is it downright somthing [sic], now we Irish men are apt to think something & nothing near neighbours.'[13] The epistemology of modernity, by contrast, is a good deal more bleakly disenchanted, as objects turn their backs aloofly on the very subjects who have produced them, withholding from us their noumenal essences as surely as the commodity is insolently indifferent to any particular

---

9.   ibid, p. 99.
10. See Anthony Flew, 'Was Berkeley a Precursor of Wittgenstein?', in W. B. Todd (ed.), *Hume and the Enlightenment* (Edinburgh, 1974).
11. For a brief account of Eriugena, see Terry Eagleton, 'The Irish Sublime', *Religion and Literature*, vol. 28, nos. 2–3 (Summer–Autumn, 1996). For a much fuller treatment, see Dermot Moran, *The Philosophy of John Scottus Eriugena* (Cambridge, 1989).
12. Milbank, *The Word made Strange*, p. 101.
13. Berkeley, *Philosophical Commentaries* (London, 1944), p. 124.

consumer.[14] We are here in the realm of the Lacanian symbolic, in which the object no longer depends upon me for its existence, as opposed to the Berkeleyan imaginary, in which it is still flatteringly possible to imagine that without our vivifying presence the world itself would crumble to nothing.

Indeed Berkeley playfully indulges just such a Lacanian fantasy of the world being fashioned for him personally in an off-duty essay entitled 'Pleasures, Natural and Fantastical', in which he contrasts those who own objects but don't enjoy them with his own relishing, and hence 'possession' of them, as a sort of visual consumer:

> The various objects that compose the world were by nature formed to delight our senses . . . Hence it is usual with me to consider myself as having a natural property in every object that administers pleasure to me . . . I have a property in the gay part of all the gilt chariots I meet, which I regard as amusements designed to delight my eyes, and the imagination of those kind people who sit in them gaily attired only to please me . . . Upon the same principle, I have discovered that I am the natural proprietor of all the diamond necklaces, the crosses, stars, brocades, and embroidered clothes which I see at a play or birthnight, as giving more natural delight to the spectator than to those that wear them . . . In a word, all that I desire is the use of things, let who will have the keeping of them. By which maxim I am grown one of the richest men in Great Britain; with this difference, that I am not a prey to my own cares, or the envy of others.[15]

If Berkeley does not have the *words* 'use-value' and 'exchange-value', his traditionalist Tory suspicion of possessive individualism would seem to involve the concepts.[16] In a kind of ludic parody of his own epistemology, all things

14.   For a re-reading of the philosophy of modernity in terms of the commodity form, see Georg Lukács, 'Reification and the Consciousness of the Proletariat', in *History and Class Consciousness* (Cambridge, Mass., 1971).

15.   *Works*, vol. 3, pp. 160–1. Fredric Jameson discusses the Lacanian imaginary in explicitly Berkeleyan terms, as a space 'which swarms with bodies and forms... [which] carry their specularity upon themselves like a color they wear or the texture of their surface. In this – the indifferentiation of their *esse* from a *percipi* which does not know a *percipiens* – these bodies of the Imaginary exemplify the very logic of mirror images . . .' ('Imaginary and Symbolic in Lacan', *Yale French Studies*, nos. 55/56, 1977). A fable similar to Berkeley's crops up in Oliver Goldsmith's *Citizen of the World,* in which a poor man thanks a Chinese mandarin for the gift of having let him look at the jewels on his dress – which, says the poor man, is all the use the mandarin can have for them himself. See Arthur Friedman (ed.), *Collected Works of Oliver Goldsmith* (Oxford, 1966), vol. 2, p. 267.

16.   G. J. Warnock comments that Berkeley 'was fortunate in being free from political prejudices' (*Berkeley*, Harmondsworth, 1953, p. 214), thus committing a double error: Berkeley was by no means free of political prejudice, and there is nothing necessarily fortunate in such freedom in any case.

have their being in his sensuous savouring of them, as an aesthetic relation to the world comes to usurp a utilitarian one. The self-delighting passivity of this consumerist *flâneur* is a fantasy image of Berkeley's passive perceiving subject. If true possession consists in untrammelled enjoyment, and if the anxieties of actual proprietorship inevitably diminish this pleasure, then it follows that only non-owners can be true possessors. As James Stephens writes in *The Demi-Gods*: 'the person who has nothing may look upon the world as his inheritance, while the person who has something has seldom anything but that'.

Siris, Berkeley's arcane philosophical treatise on tar water, is the most flamboyantly 'textual' of all his writings, and indeed bears more than a passing resemblance to the supreme Irish specimen of that mode, Laurence Sterne's *Tristram Shandy*, the first part of which was to appear some fourteen years after Berkeley's treatise. Indeed Berkeley's original plan for his *Principles of Human Knowledge* involved a Shandyean coverage of the entire field of philosophical, scientific and mathematical inquiry, all of it based on the founding principle of *esse est percipi* or *percipere*.[17] The audacious metaphysical extravagance of *Siris*, in which the humble concoction of tar-water is solemnly hymned as a universal panacea for human ailments, is a thoroughly Shandyean project, as eccentric, obsessive and hobby-horsical as any of Walter Shandy's maniacal schemes. (It also has more than a smack of that other Irish madhouse of Reason, Swift's Laputa, in which scientists extract vital forces from cucumbers.)[18] In fact the chronically ailing Sterne was himself a devotee of tar-water, writing that 'it has been of infinite service to me'.[19] He was also, as it happens, an enthusiast for nothingness, remarking in *Tristram Shandy* that he has great respect for it, 'considering what worse things there are in the world' (vol. 9, ch. 25). Just as the crazed rationalist Walter Shandy is a compulsive system-builder mesmerised by first principles, locked into a paranoid world in which everything is portentously symbolic of everything else, so *Siris*, with equally elaborate pedantry, is in hot pursuit of the key to all mythologies or the founding principle of reality. Both works are curiously modernist in their multiple, fragmented, decentred way,[20] and *Siris* stands at the fountainhead of a distinguished modern tradition of 'anti-philosophy', all

17.   See Warnock, *Berkeley*, p. 21.
18.   In an unwittingly entertaining piece of pseudo-Freudianism, J. O. Wisdom thinks that Berkeley believed that he was poisoned, which is perhaps what 'matter' unconsciously signifies in his work, and that tar-water was his way of purging himself. See his *The Unconscious Origin of Berkeley's Philosophy* (London, 1953), ch. 14.
19.   Lewis Percy Curtis (ed.), *Letters of Laurence Sterne* (Oxford, 1935), p. 84.
20.   J. O. Urmston sees *Siris* as a 'Gothic' curiosity which 'would seem to have strayed from some much later or much earlier period' (*Berkeley*, Oxford, 1982, p. 223). For a valuable literary analysis of the work, see Peter Walmsley, *The Rhetoric of Berkeley's Philosophy* (Cambridge, 1990), Part 4.

the way from Kierkegaard and Nietzsche to Heidegger, Adorno, Benjamin, Wittgenstein and Derrida, which can say what it means only by inventing a whole new style of philosophical writing. Berkeley writes in his essay 'Primary Visitation Charge' that philosophy must deploy persuasive rhetorical strategies, creeping up on the reader as though by chance, 'while that which looks like design is guarded against'.[21] Sterne, for his part, is so mock-solicitous not to deceive the reader by imposing a design on his narrative that he refuses to edit the tale at all and thus ends up bamboozling the reader entirely, in a deft demonstration that non-designing is itself a kind of design. Berkeley presses through the logic of empiricism to the point where he abolishes its underlying 'material substance' and so leaves it in tatters, just as Sterne pushes literary realism to such baroque extremes that it disintegrates in his hands.

Both Walter Shandy and the Berkeley of *Siris* are out to promote the ancient doctrines of cosmic order, universal correspondences and textual totality against the materialist, mechanistic moderns – a position represented in Sterne's case by the jaundiced empiricism of Walter's son Tristram, whose helpless subjection to sheer matter and happenstance can be read as a crafty form of Oedipal vengeance on the determinist fantasies of his father. Walter holds to a motivated theory of the sign, and *Siris*, as we have seen, believes in a 'natural connexion' between sign and referent. For both works, this unity of sign and thing is also a fruitful concordance of mind and matter: Walter the tyrannical rationalist wants the sensible world to reflect the structure of the mind, while Berkeley the idealist grasps it as luminously expressive of spirit. In the words of the eighteenth-century Irish theologian Peter Browne, both men oppose those dualists who speak 'as if (spirit) thought and reasoned *in* the body, and not together *with* any part of it, as if the body were a mere case or place of residence for it'.[22] It follows for both philosophers that a minor material upset can wreak havoc in the realm of *Geist*: Walter's grandiose plans for his offspring are thrown disastrously awry by a chain of trivial domestic accidents, while Berkeley remarks in *Siris* that '(s)mall imperceptible irritations of the minutest fibres or filaments, caused by the pungent salts of wines and sauces, do so shake and disturb the microcosms of high livers, as often to raise tempests in courts and senates' (396). Both men are eager to discipline the body – in Walter's case, Tristram's, in Berkeley's the bodies of the intemperate and overbred – in order to render it a fit medium for the spirit. And since *Siris* as a literary work caters for both body and soul, urging the therapeutic virtues of tar-water in its opening sections while spiritually edifying the reader in its later ones, it stands, formally speaking, as an image of the anti-dualist philosophy it seeks to promote.[23] '(T)he operations of the mind',

21.   *Works*, vol. 3, p. 189.
22.   Peter Browne, *The Procedure, Extent, and Limits of Human Understanding* (Dublin, 1728), p. 149.
23.   A. D. Ritchie points out that there was a dearth of doctors in rural Ireland in Berkeley's day, so that *Siris* is among other things a practical act of charity. See

Berkeley writes in his Introduction, in what might well be a quotation from Walter Shandy, 'so far depend on the right tone or good condition of its instrument, that anything which greatly contributes to preserve or recover the health of the body is well worth the attention of the mind' (365). *Tristram Shandy* opens with the farcical business of its hero's future spiritual life being blighted by the scattering of his father's 'animal spirits' at the moment of conception, and no work more mischievously entangles the spiritual with the material.

The difference between the literary anti-realist Sterne and the philosophical anti-realist Berkeley would seem that the latter succeeds in his project where the former fails. For *Tristram Shandy* is a lamentably, hilariously self-deconstructing enterprise, in which the more you pile text upon text to totalise a recalcitrant world and lay bare its founding origins and principles, the more this great spawning of significations comes to pulverise meaning and thwart all intelligibility, jamming the narrative and hopelessly decentring the reader. To pursue the logic of representation, to tighten the problematic bond between material signifier and ideal signified by anxiously explicating every iota of possible meaning and forestalling every conceivable misreading, is to load representational discourse with a weight under which it buckles and all but collapses. Literary realism, almost before it has properly emerged in English letters, is unmasked as a megalomaniac fantasy by a Tipperary author half-strange to that metropolitan culture. It is this uncontrollable discourse – this infinite mesh of other possible words which each of Tristram's utterances draws inexorably in its wake – which constitutes the 'unconscious' that unravels his efforts to centre himself in speech.

Tristram is out to identify the sources of his own writing, the primordial psychic wounding for which it figures as a form of displacement and revenge; but since he can only do this from *within* writing, his project is as doomed and self-contradictory as all autobiography, which to tell the whole truth of the subject would need to include its present act of writing within the history it is writing about. The autobiographical subject would also need to stop living while he was writing in order to keep abreast of himself, which is why the writing and the written Tristrams can never be identical, divided as they are by the very discourse which seeks to bring them together. The traumatic moment of Tristram's entry into the symbolic order of castration cannot be reproduced within that order, any more than the eye can capture itself within the field of vision. It can be alluded to only in the very form of the symbolic, in its infinite play of absence and difference. Writing, to be sure, has a ground; but since that ground can only ever figure within it in the displaced form of signification, it dissolves at the very point of articulation. So it is that Tristram

his *George Berkeley: An Appraisal* (Manchester, 1967), p. 162. It is the absence of midwives in Tristram Shandy's rural Yorkshire which results in the bungling of his birth.

will never come to represent what constituted him as a subject, since its repression is the very condition of his representing. Likewise Uncle Toby, who constructs a material model of his own past just as his nephew fashions a life-history, will never come to pinpoint the precise moment of his genital mutilation, which was never a 'moment' in the first place. The relations between body and soul, signifier and signified, remain stubbornly ineffable for all their embarrassing intimacy; and Sterne's paradigm of this puzzle is nothing less than the book itself, at once material object and impalpable meaning. By what Cartesian miracle can black marks on white sheets become the bearers of significance? It is, perhaps, a question more likely to bemuse a traditionally oral culture, in which writing figures as supplement rather than source, than one like England in which writing has by now become thoroughly naturalised.

Siris, too, is much troubled by the idea of making an exalted discourse on metaphysical matters available in 'physical books' (479), which are then accessible to the 'vulgar' for whom the sensible is the only measure of reality. Oliver Goldsmith comments in an essay on Berkeley that '(h)is treatise on tar-water rendered him more popular than any of his preceding productions, at the same time as it was the most whimsical of them all'.[24] In Berkeley's hands, Sterne's philosophical conundrum becomes a kind of political contradiction, as the high-minded bishop finds himself ineluctably casting divine pearls before sensual swine. This, however, is a contradiction incarnate in the very nature of a literary text, which cannot fully determine its own reception; and Berkeley consoles himself a little nervously with the hypothesis that, just as his essay has been tracing the 'insensible transitions' up the Chain of Being from tar-water to the Trinity, so this thematic material can become a *performative* matter too, a question of the moral efficacy of his work in weaning the averagely sensual reader away from his fleshly preoccupations and nudging him tactfully, imperceptibly, towards higher things. The content of the text, in other words, is also a political or rhetorical form, as the substantive becomes the strategic. Even Berkeley's esoteric reflections on tar-water turn out to be political, concerned with dispelling the spleen which makes slaves of free nations. True to his own epistemological lights, the most fine-drawn lucubrations are geared to pragmatic ends. (*Tristram Shandy*, so its author informs us, is also written against the spleen, and the comic philosophy of Shandyism is made to sound like a kind of tar-water.[25]) Despite this public-spiritedness, however, *Siris* ends with an elegiac reminder of Plato's advice to Dionysius not

24.　Arthur Friedman (ed.), *Collected Works of Oliver Goldsmith* (Oxford, 1966), vol. 3, p. 39.
25.　'. . . 'tis wrote, an' please your worship, against the spleen; in order, by a more frequent and a more convulsive elevation and depression of the diaphragm, and the succussations of the intercostal and abdominal muscles in laughter, to drive the *gall* and other *bitter juices* from the gall-bladder, liver, and sweet-bread of his majesty's subjects, with all the inimicitious passions which belong to them,

to allow the divine mysteries to fall into the hands of the common herd, a goal best secured by not writing at all. Just as the too-fleshly Tristram betrays the rational projects of his father, so the carnal body of writing will always be faithless to its ghostly essence. But whereas Tristram is chained to signification like a slave to his oar, shuttled from one empty signifier to another, Berkeley eludes the prison-house of language precisely by seeing the material world *as* language, thus bridging the chasm between *res* and *signum* into which the hapless Tristram tumbles, and viewing creation as God's own self-generating, self-founding literary artefact.

Both *Siris* and *Tristram Shandy* turn upon bathos, one of the most persistent tropes of Irish writing. To be pitched between the sublime and the ridiculous is hardly an unfamiliar rhythm in a culture where life is at once meagre and metaphysical. Walter Shandy's recondite notions fall foul of broken window straps, verbal blunders, bungling medics, while *Siris* contains sentences like 'I never knew anything so good for the stomach as tar-water' along with remarks about ethereal fire and the history of the ancient Persians. But whereas Sterne mischievously plays off the humdrum against the high-falutin', Berkeley's intention is to track the minute gradations from the one to the other within a frame of universal order. That chain of being is obliquely alluded to in the chain-like title of his work, which reads 'A Chain of Philosophical Reflexions and Inquiries concerning the Virtues of Tar-water, and divers other Subjects connected together and arising from one another'. The question is whether the work really does display the organic coherence this title claims for it, thus enacting performatively in the form of its text the internal correspondences it discerns in the world, or whether it sails closer to a set of Shandyesque digressions. (Though if Sterne's novel is indeed a set of digressions, exactly what it is digressing from becomes a question worth pondering.) In Shandyesque style, a good two-thirds of *Siris* is not about tar-water at all, and the 'chain' of the title is ambiguous: chains may be tightly linked but nevertheless hang slack, lead nowhere or wind pointlessly round in circles. 'Siris' means 'chain' in Greek but the Nile in ancient Egyptian, so that this chain is a peculiarly fluid, elusive one. Once the Great Chain of Being is horizontalised as discourse, it is in danger of lapsing into infinite regress or metonymic displacement. Indeed, if we are to credit David Berman's bold hypothesis that tar-water is 'drinkable God', or (as one might say) potable Prime Mover, then the highest and humblest links of the chain form a circle rather than a hierarchy.[26] In fact Berkeley ends his essay by wondering whether its argument has been coherent: 'It may, therefore, be pardoned if this rude Essay doth, by insensible

---

down into their duodenums' (vol. 4, ch. 22). In Sterne's case, the therapy in question is humour.

26.   See David Berman, *George Berkeley* (Oxford, 1994), p. 173. Berkeley's celebrated pronouncement that he wished to 'think with the learned but speak with the vulgar' can be seen as a linking of the two ends of the *social* hierarchy.

transitions, draw the reader into remote inquiries and speculations, that were not, perhaps, thought of either by him or by the author at first setting out' (479–80). Unlike God's universe, the end of this particular artefact was almost certainly not immanent in its origins. 'Insensible' transitions can mean tactfully managed ones, but also carry a hint of 'not obvious'; indeed the major structural transition of the book, from its mundane reflections on tar-water to its more abstruse speculations, is far from plain.

Berkeley's search for the founding principle of the cosmos may prove more fruitful than Tristram's hunt for the grounds and origins of his own subject-hood, but it is not without its difficulties either. The chief problem is that what seems to be offered in *Siris* as a pure, singular bedrock of reality turns out often enough to be impure, multiple or derivative. This is partly because we are not really being offered a singular 'underlying' principle at all: if the world is a text, then it has neither depths nor surfaces, and its animating force or medium, like the Nietzschean will to power, is less 'beneath' it than co-extensive with its being, the very form of its content, which is one reason why it is hard to isolate it as a determinate essence. At the same time, Berkeley can no more free himself entirely from the essentialist paradigm than the rest of us, and is to be found in *Siris* implicitly questioning the whole notion of foundations by offering us instances of them which never quite work out. The work's argument thus betrays an intriguing tension between world-as-text and world-as-hierarchy, finding itself making new starts, curving back upon itself, repeating with a difference, recycling one element into another, failing to disentangle interwoven threads and pressing up against the very bounds of interpretability, at the same moment that it affirms its faith in universal order, first principles, privileged rankings. This tension is evident in the fact that if the book does indeed ascend triumphantly from tar-water to the Trinity, *how* it does this is never transparently obvious. The 'horizontal' chain of argument is never quite homologous with a 'vertical' Chain of Being. As an Anglican divine, Berkeley places his faith in a foundation – God – who is no-thing at all, the vanishing point of all substance, the infinite abyss which sustains creation in being. And this aporia of the foundation then infiltrates his text in the form of a search for the elemental stuff of the cosmos which continually dismantles itself, so that it is only in this performative contradiction that the truth of the matter can be shown, as opposed to being said.

In fact the work builds into itself a remarkable series of false bottoms. The first candidate for such a metaphysical ground appears to be acid: 'a fine subtle substance pervading the whole terraqueous globe' (410). But acid is always hybridised, found 'joined to some sulphur' (411), and so can hardly provide a singular foundation. In any case, it seems to be a form of salt, and this, 'the pure salt, salt the principle, is itself similar and uniform, but never found alone' (411). Berkeley will later be found arguing, confusingly, that both acid and sulphur 'are at bottom one and the same thing, to wit, pure fire or aether'

(438). Air next briefly emerges as a more promising universal principle, as 'a general agent, not only exerting its own, but calling forth the qualities or powers of all other bodies' (414). But the fact that it evokes these other powers means that it is constituted by them, and so is an impure, heterogeneous medium, 'a mass of numberless different principles' (415), 'no distinct element, but a mass or mixture of things the most heterogeneous and even opposite to each other' (417). There is, then, 'no such thing as the pure simple element of air' (418); and there is in any case some 'latent vivifying spirit dispersed throughout the air' (415), which strikes air itself instantly secondary, a medium rather than a primal source.

What is more fundamental than air is fire or 'aether', which is indeed what Berkeley takes to be the animating force of creation. 'There is no effect in nature, great, marvellous, or terrible, but proceeds from fire' (421). Air, then, is put firmly in its place, deriving its power wholly from fire; but even fire cannot be unreservedly identified as the essence of the cosmos. For one thing, the fire Berkeley has in mind is not what he quaintly dubs 'culinary' (i.e. common-or-garden) fire, but a finer sort of fire altogether, a 'pure', invisible 'fire, aether, or substance of light' which is the cause and ground of common fire, as it is of all other phenomena. And though he describes it as 'pure', he also regards it as composite, 'contain(ing) parts of different kinds, that are impressed with different forces. . .' (422). Besides, the text appears to equate fire, light and 'aether' as alternative names for the same originary power, an equation which, since it is nowhere fully unpacked, runs the risk of delivering us no less than three founding principles rather than one. And if fire turns out to be a somewhat heterogeneous ground of being, so too does light, 'a medium consisting of heterogeneous parts, differing from each other in divers qualities that appear to sense, and not improbably having many original properties, attractions, repulsions, and motions, the laws and natures whereof are indiscernible to us, otherwise than in their remote effects' (449). There is, then, an epistemological problem too: light/fire is confidently advanced as the quicksilver stuff of creation, but exactly because it is so mercurial we actually know bafflingly little of its nature. And just as there are two brands of fire, mundane and ethereal, so, at least for Plotinus, there are two modes of light, one more fundamental than the other.

Even the most refined fire, however, turns out to be a kind of false bottom as well. For one thing, the fact that it is imperceptible means that it requires a supplement in order to act effectively: it 'only becomes sensible as it is joined with some other principle, which serves as a vehicle for it' (433). If fire remains purely self-identical, it is struck impotent; if it is to act, it must submit to being mongrelised. But fire is less than primary in another sense too: for the pious Berkeley it can only in the end be an instrument of the true mover of all things, which is the divine mind. There is, after all, something even more unimpeachably foundational than fire, and that is force or power, which resides only in the mind of God. Fire has no capacity to act of its own:

it is simply the medium in which the Almighty inscribes 'the bright and lively signatures' of his mind (427). And since God is omnipotent, able to work upon his world directly, he does not strictly speaking have need of this fiery instrument at all, in which case this purported first principle is struck even more arbitrary and contingent. Once more, the message turns out to be a mere medium; indeed Berkeley quotes Galen as claiming that fire or aether provides a corporeal vehicle for the actions of the incorporeal soul, a move which certainly robs it of its *a priori* status. Elsewhere he notes that 'According to the ancients, soul serveth for a vehicle to intellect. . ., and light and fire for a vehicle to the soul; and, in like manner, air may be supposed a vehicle to fire. . .' (437). 'The Platonic philosophers', he comments, 'do wonderfully refine upon light, and soar very high: from coal to flame; from flame to light; from this visible light to the occult light of the celestial or mundane soul, which they suppose to pervade and agitate the substance of the universe by its vigorous and expansive motion' (441). Each apparent ground turns out to be resting squarely upon another for its ontological support. From time to time, Berkeley will wield Occam's razor and cut a superfluous bedrock away: Newton holds that aether is more primordial than light, but Berkeley himself believes the two elements to be identical. But the general drift of *Siris* is to proliferate foundations rather than to purge them, precisely because what it is in pursuit of is not in the substantialist sense a 'foundation' at all.

Aether, light and fire, then, are in essence all one – in which case, perplexingly, they are also acids, since the particles of acids, like those of aether, attract each other with the greatest force. Acids might thus appear more foundational than fire or light, though Berkeley equivocates here, claiming that the particles of aether 'are acids, or constitute the acid', which fudges the question of priority. Once again, we seem to be landed with too many grounds, each of them indifferently exchangeable with the others: 'alkali . . . is a caustic; caustics are fire; therefore acid is fire; therefore aether is fire; and if fire, light' (447). The Chain of Being would appear to be rapidly involuting upon itself, garbling distinctions rather than enforcing them. As far as the kind of first principles promoted by mechanical materialism go, Berkeley considers that the Newtonian law of attraction and repulsion is a definite improvement on competing candidates: 'Nature seems better known and explained by attractions and repulsions, than by those other mechanical principles of size, figure, and the like. . .' (455). But this corporeal force in turn stands in need of an incorporeal underpinning; and in case we imagine that this might be the soul, Berkeley is quick to point out that this is no foundation either, since the force in question acts upon the soul rather than emanating from it. It is not itself a power which can be figured, slipping as it does through the net of language: '. . .what these forces are, which are supposed to be lodged in bodies, to be impressed on bodies, to be multiplied, divided, and communicated from one body to another, and which seem to animate bodies like abstract spirits, or souls, hath been found very difficult, not to say impossible, for thinking men to conceive and explain. . .' (458). Once again, we seem to have located the ultimate stuff of the cosmos only to lose it in that very act, as this sublimely protean force gives the slip to representation. It is as though what can be known cannot by that token serve as a foundation, whereas whatever can furnish one is by definition beyond our cognition. At times for Berkeley the aether or vital spirit of the world would seem to be relegated from primary to secondary status, becoming a medium of communication between the soul and the material world; at other times this vital force acts only by being joined with an intelligence. Surveying his ancient authorities, he finds that for some of them God has given the world both a mind and a soul, whereas others include both in the word 'soul', and suppose the soul of the world to be God. It is not clear either, as one potential grounding principle again opens out into another, whether the soul of the world has a distinct mind of its own, or is directed by a superior one.

What appears, then, as an orderly progression of levels or instances, hier-archically subordinated to each other, figures also in *Siris* as a kind of cease-lessly self-deconstructive motion, in which every so-called first principle can be prised open like a Russian doll to reveal within it some further force or ele-ment, until in a sort of *mise-en-abîme* of microcosms within microcosms one arrives, just a hairsbreadth this side of vanishing-point, at a mechanism so exquisitely deft and delicate as to be effectively invisible. The finest instance of this regress in Irish prose can be found in Flann O'Brien's novel *The Third Policeman*, in which Policeman MacCruiskeen fashions a series of chests one inside the other, the last five so microscopic as to be, like the tools he employs in making them, invisible even to the most powerful magnifying glass. 'The one I am making now', MacCruiskeen remarks to the narrator, 'is nearly as small as nothing. Number One (of the chests) would hold a million of them at the same time and there would be room left for a pair of woman's horse-breeches if they were rolled up. The dear knows when it will stop and termi-nate.'[27] 'It is unmentionable', comments the narrator with courteous admiration, to which MacCruiskeen, evidently a specialist in sublimity, replies: 'Very nearly.'

Edmund Burke saw smallness in terms of the beautiful, the very opposite of the sublime;[28] but that which is minute to the point of invisibility becomes formless and unrepresentable, and so is an inverted image of sublime immen-sity. It is hardly surprising, then, that Berkeley was fascinated by micro-scopes,[29] or that the metaphysically-minded Sergeant of O'Brien's novel

---

27.   Flann O'Brien, *The Third Policeman* (London, 1967, reprinted 1993), pp. 76–7.

28.   See Edmund Burke, *Philosophical Enquiry into the Origin of our Ideas of the Sub-lime and the Beautiful* (London, 1958), pp. 113–14.

29.   See Genevieve Brykman, 'Microscopes and Philosophical Method in Berkeley', in Colin M. Turbayne (ed.), *Berkeley: Critical and Interpretive Essays* (Manches-ter, 1982). The microscope, Brykman remarks, 'makes polished and homoge-

should emerge as a devout Berkeleyan or disciple of Eriugena, believing as he does that '(e)verything is composed of small particles of itself and they are fly-ing around in concentric circles and arcs and segments and innumerable other geometric figures too numerous to mention collectively, never standing still or resting but spinning away and darting hither and thither and back again, and all the time on the go. These diminutive gentlemen are called atoms' (86). One might dub this style of seeing a kind of Irish anti-epic, given that genre's delight in the larger-than-life, in warriors with nostrils as capa-cious as caverns and beards in which the woodlark might nest. The Irish sagas are also much concerned with shape-changing, and a good deal of Irish writ-ing, as Swift's Lilliputians and Brobdingnagians would suggest, has a trick of alternately magnifying and deflating in an oscillation not far removed from bathos. Running as a subtext throughout O'Brien's novel is an account of the philosophy of the French *savant* de Selby,[30] who holds among other edifying doctrines that darkness is simply an accumulation of '"black air", i.e. a stain-ing of the atmosphere due to volcanic eruptions too fine to be seen with the naked eye and also to certain "regrettable" industrial activities involving coal-tar products and vegetable dyes' (120). What we call sleep is no more than a succession of fainting fits brought on by semi-asphyxiation by this noxious compound, various quantities of which de Selby has actually succeeded in bottling. Though too much need not be made of the allusion to coal-tar, it is not hard to detect echoes of Berkeley in this materialisation of the immater-ial. It is, incidentally, one of Swift's most recurrent rhetorical devices too.

The very form of *Siris* enacts something of MacCruiskeen's microcosms, since what connects its opening disquisition on tar-water with its later flights of metaphysical fancy is just the fact that the animal spirits stimulated by tar-water are to the human body what aether or fire or light are to the universe as a whole. As befits such a 'textual' work, its linkages are more formal than sub-stantive, as a reflection on one kind of promiscuous but unifying medium – the power of tar-water to cure so many distempers – gives rise, more as trope than as logical argument, to analogous speculations on the cohering yet differ-entiating force of aether. 'Extracting [tar-water's] virtues from cold water' (369) becomes a kind of metaphor of the philosophic business of extracting the ani-mating substance of the world, and the first part of *Siris* explores the affinities between various substances associated with tar – resin, balm, oil, turpentine,

neous objects disappear, revealing heterogeneous particles and wrinkles' (p. 76) – a suitable analogue of Berkeley's immaterialism, or indeed of his decon-structive or *mise-en-abîme* procedure in *Siris*. Berkeley thought short-sighted-ness, which compels us to scrutinise the object more closely, an aid to philosophy.

30.   Some footnote allusions to de Selby's work can be found in Herbert McCabe, OP, *Law, Love and Language* (London, 1968).

pitch, amber and the like – in a way which grasps them as so many refine-
ments, distillations or derivations of one another. This is formally homologous
to the way that the book's later conjectures put into circulation various cosmic
principles which turn out often enough to be derived from, exchangeable with
or substitutable for one another. Oil is the vehicle of spirit, yet spirit consists
of 'salts and phlegm'; tar-water is resin but also a soap and a vinegar: the same
hunt for origins, precedents, derivations, hierarchies, breaking open one system to find its own microcosmic replica folded mysteriously within it, is at
work in this more humbly material segment of the work too. The whole discourse of the text, in short, is a kind of thematisation of the formal devices of
metaphor, metonymy, synecdoche, equivalence and allied figures, a set of
rhetorical strategies appropriate enough for an author for whom substance,
philosophically speaking, comes down to a set of perceptual forms or pragmatic moves. Form and content in *Siris*, true to its author's immaterialist epistemology, are as intimately allied as body and spirit, so that what the work
speaks of – that intangible medium of fire, light or aether which both unifies
and distinguishes – serves at the same time as an oblique description of its own
rhetorical procedures, in which figuratively self-conscious propositions discriminate and draw together, identify and analogise in the same gesture:

> Some modern writers inform us that tar flows from the trunks of pines and firs,
> when they are very old, through incisions made in the bark near the root; that
> pitch is tar inspissated; and both are the oil of the tree grown thick and ripened
> with age and sun. The trees, like old men, being unable to perspire, and their
> secretory ducts obstructed, they are, as one may say, choked and stuffed with
> their own juice. (371)

> [The vivifying spirit of air] gives and preserves a proper tone to the vessels: this
> elastic fluid promotes all secretions; its oscillations keep every part in motion;
> it pervades and actuates the whole animal system, producing great variety of
> effects, and even opposite in different parts, cooling at the same time and heat-
> ing, distending and contracting, coagulating and resolving, giving and taking,
> sustaining life and impairing it, pressing without and expanding within, abrad-
> ing some parts, at the same time insinuating and supplying others, producing
> various vibrations in the fibres and ferments in the fluids; all which must needs
> ensue from such a subtle, active, heterogeneous, and elastic fluid. (416)

It is not for nothing that John Milbank detects a parallel between Berkeley's
'foundational' medium of light as a 'medium of difference' and 'the process of
natural *semiosis* itself'.[31] *Siris*, he considers, wants to avoid at once a sheer
contingency of difference and a rationally determined unity, so that its resort
to an arcane, allusive, aesthetic mode of discourse – the aesthetic being a
mode of conceiving unity and difference altogether otherwise – can be read
as a formal solution to a substantive philosophical problem.

31.   Milbank, *The Word Made Strange*, p. 102.

The passages quoted above are redolent of the extraordinary sensuous texture of the tar-water sections of *Siris,* their sense of the universe as some pulsating organism whose intricate interchange of energies are those of a work of art, and which Berkeley's rhetorical antitheses, recursions, parallelisms and chiasmuses are alone capable of capturing. The more 'textual' the world appears, as some ineffably complex imbrication of juices, forces, fluids, saps, vapours, salts, fumes and spirits, the more densely capillary waxes the essay's own language. The body of the text becomes the metaphor or mimetic medium of its spirit, as though style were the 'animal spirits' which enabled its fruitful interaction of topics, and this in turn becomes microcosmic of its author's metaphysic. *Siris* is thus, in Austinian terms, constative and performative together, incarnating its own propositions in its form and rhetorical address. Berkeley's teeming, pullulating universe can be given shape only in an answerably cornucopian text – though whether the world and our discourse upon it do in fact consort so harmoniously together is momentarily questioned by an allusion to Themistius, for whom, so Berkeley informs us, any simple or indivisible unity is always constituted by an act of mind, and indeed by the words or signs accompanying it. If unity really is a product of the inherently differential medium of language, then *Siris* has once more unwittingly deconstructed its own faith in first or indivisible principles.

What seems most quaint to the modern reader is just how the metaphysical biochemistry of Berkeley's discourse on tar-water hovers at some undecidable point between the corporeal and the incorporeal. Acids are shaped like daggers and alkalis like sheaths, so that, 'moving in the same liquor, the daggers run into the sheaths fitted to receive them with such violence as to raise that effervescence observed in the mixture of acids and alkalis' (412). There is a kind of ghostly hydraulics at work throughout the text, the aim of which is to concretise the impalpable without dispelling its finally fathomless complexities, reducing to a sensuous image that which defeats the eye:

> . . .as fluids are moved through the vessels of animal bodies by the systole and diastole of the heart, the alternate expansion and condensation of the air, and the oscillations in the membranes and tunics of the vessels – even so, by means of air expanded and contracted in the tracheae or vessels made up of elastic fibres, the sap is propelled through the arterial tubes of a plant, and the vegetable juices, as they are rarified by heat or condensed by cold, will either ascend and evaporate into air, or descend in the form of a gross liquor. (377)

Yet for all this rhetorical labour, 'the *ens primum* or *scintilla spirituosa,* as it is called, of plants [is] a thing so fine and fugacious as to escape our nicest search' (381). In this Chinese-boxes creation, there appears no end to unlocking one structure only to find it pregnant with another. Even the particles of elemental fire 'are known to be heterogeneous, and, for aught we know, may some of them be organised, and, notwithstanding their wonderful minuteness, contain original seeds which, being formed and sown in a proper matrix, do gradually unfold and manifest themselves, still growing to a just proportion of the species' (473). That 'wonderful minuteness' is pure O'Brien. Even the 'elemental' fire may secrete whole other worlds within its atoms, in which case it is hard to see how it can earn its keep as a foundation.

The problem is that Siris really confronts two different antagonists: those sceptics, atheists and empiricists who would deny a grounding to the world, and those mechanical philosophers for whom that grounding is all too crassly material. Berkeley must affirm the reality of such a foundation in the teeth of the former party, but in the same gesture retrieve it from the vulgar reductionism of the latter. It is these reductionists who he dubs in his Alciphron 'minute philosophers', whose impulse is merely to diminish. Berkeley's conservative impulse to order, which necessitates a knowable foundation to things, is thus somewhat at odds with his conservative devotion to mystery, which requires that this foundation defeats any simple act of cognition. In a similar way, his desire to identify the unifying principle of reality contravenes his more radical suspicions of the whole notion of a metaphysical substratum. Ultimate truths must be hermetic, to preserve them from the grossness of the physicists and the grubby paws of the populace: '. . . although the general known laws of motion are to be deemed mechanical', Berkeley writes, 'yet peculiar motions of the insensible parts, and peculiar properties depending thereon, are occult and specific' (454). Yet those truths must not be so entirely occulted as to leave us disarmed in the face of the sceptics. This political dilemma is reflected in the very existence of philosophical writing, since such writing is the medium of sacred truths yet is promiscuously available to everyone by virtue of the book. In this sense, the book resembles the universe, which is similarly a set of enigmatic hieroglyphs which are nonetheless in principle accessible to all. It is, then, not only the form of the *text* which enacts Berkeley's concerns, but the material fact of the book itself.

Foundations must be corporeal, as light for Berkeley is corporeal; but the materiality in question, as with the resurrected body, must be so exquisitely delicate and refined as to figure in effect as a sort of ideality.[32] It is a version of the aporia of foundations in general, which must be in some sense determinate, yet

32.   If Berkeley's view of the aether in Siris is to be consistent with his earlier writings, then the aether must indeed be perceptible in principle in order to exist – though perhaps it is perceptible only to very fine instruments we do not yet have, or to spirits. See I. C. Tipton, 'The "Philosopher by Fire" in Berkeley's Alciphron', in Turbayne, op. cit. G. Dawes Hicks, by contrast, thinks that Berkeley has here abandoned his earlier immaterialism (Berkeley, Oxford, 1932, p. 213), and J. O. Urmston also believes this view to be incompatible with Berkeley's immaterialism. See his 'Berkeley's Philosophy of Science in the Siris', in History of European Ideas, no. 7 (1986). Slavoj Žižek notes a similar concern with a kind of spiritualised matter or corporeal spirit in the philosophy of Schelling. See Žižek's The Indivisible Remainder (London, 1996), p. 4.

whose very determinacy undoes them by allowing us to imagine something beyond them. What *Siris* is after is a kind of sublime materiality, one so impalpable and Byzantine that it is no longer really distinct from the realm of spirit. And though Berkeley gives the names of aether, light or elemental fire to this substance, it is not hard to see it as nothing less than writing itself, a process which confounds the distinction between material and ideal. If Nature for him is itself a language, it is not least because, like writing, it dismantles the opposition between the sensible and the spiritual. But it is also because it is not just discourse but *text*, in which juices and fluids and forces have meaning only in their complex constellations, their hydraulic interactions. It is this which renders them, like words in Berkeley's pragmatist semiotics, creatively indeterminate, definable only in their differences and effects; and *Siris,* in seeking for a final term to anchor all this, succeeds simply in showing for the most part how all material elements are intertextual, derivatives or sublimates of something else. As with the Freudian dream-text, there is a 'navel' or *omphalos* to this mundane script which finally beggars all interpretation: 'in the analysis of bodies', Berkeley writes, '[the vital principle] is always lost, escaping the skill of the artist, and passing through the closest vessels' (433).[33] Philosophy thus shares the condition of theology, which can grasp something of its sublimely ineffable object only in the aesthetic form of the world he has created, in what can be shown but not said. For the ultimate (non)-foundation on which all else rests is of course for Berkeley God himself, that abyssal (non)-grounding as assuringly solid and utterly evanescent as aether – or indeed as script.

We may consider, finally, a quite different relation between Berkeley and contemporary deconstructive thought. Nature may be God's language, and thus 'symbolic', but these signs for Berkeley are also in an important sense arbitrary.[34] In this sense, his work can be seen as dismantling the now familiar linguistic distinction between the motivated and the arbitrary sign. Sight is a kind of visual language, in the sense that, for example, the smallness or faintness of a visual image may be a signifier of the physical remoteness of an object. In this sense, language signifies relations, figures, qualities, dimensions, proportions and situations rather than discrete objects, and meaning is thus both contextual and performative. Grasping the relation of (say) faint-

33. C.f. *Tristram Shandy*: 'Madam, we live among riddles and mysteries – the most obvious things, which come in our way, have dark sides, which the quickest sight cannot penetrate into; and even the clearest and most exalted understandings amongst us find ourselves puzzled and at a loss in almost every cranny of nature's works...' (vol. 4, ch. 17).

34. AE (George Russell) thought the name 'George Moore' such an arbitrary signifier: 'I think George Moore ought to be a generic title', he writes, 'like Pharoah, King of Egypt, and when one goes, another qualified person ought to take his place and fulfil his function' (Alan Denson [ed.], *Letters of AE* [London, 1961], p. 72).

ness and remoteness becomes regulative of our actual conduct, interwoven with our social practices even if it is not itself reducible to one. But this is not a relation immediately or iconically present to us: it is a matter of rules or interpretation, learnt by custom, practice and experience, which Berkeley cherishes quite as much as Burke in the teeth of some abstract Reason. A man born blind but restored to sight would have to decipher these relations with our help.[35] He would need to learn these relations as he would learn a language. This is not to claim in conventionalist style that such relations are nothing *but* custom or consensus: on the contrary, that a distant object appears to us small and faint is a matter of physical laws. The relation is not simply 'constructed'. But faintness does not resemble remoteness; nor is there any necessary inferential relation between the two, since faintness or smallness might always signify something else. And to this extent the semiotic connection between perception and thing is neither iconic nor indexical, but arbitrary or unmotivated.[36] It works, as Berkeley comments in the Fourth Dialogue of *Alciphron*, 'by the arbitrary imposition of Providence' (section 10), a phrase which neatly combines necessity and non-necessity.

In a smiliar way, so Berkeley points out, a Chinese hearing the words *man* and *tree* for the first time would not of course call to mind their referents. We hear such sounds as words in much the same sense in which we learn to perceive shapes as men and trees. But we repress the labour of this learning, so that when we come to read, the mind passes lightly over the signs themselves 'so as to carry its attention immediately on to the things signified' (section 12). We lapse, that is to say, into what Paul de Man has called 'the phenomenalisation of language', that confounding of words and things which is for him the founding gesture of all ideology.[37] It is this naturalisation of discourse which the rhetoric of *Siris* thwarts by its poeticality, and which Berkeleyan semiotics want to oppose by inverting the phenomenalisation of language into the linguistification

35. There is perhaps a remote parallel between the rule-governed language of Nature and the rule-Utilitarianism which Berkeley espouses in his essay on 'Passive Obedience'. Berkeley rejects act-Utilitarianism both because it would lead to moral relativism, and because we simply don't have time to figure out the moral effects of each of our actions, which is why we need rules to follow. Rules are thus a sort of 'shorthand' way of getting us from our immediate situation to the universal good, just as the language of Nature automatically articulates our immediate sensible experience with other parts of the world, thus allowing us to act consistently. See 'Passive Obedience', *Works*, vol. 3, p. 112–14.
36. There is perhaps a distant relation between this case and Berkeley's argument in his discourse on 'Passive Obedience' that though social institutions like marriage and property are *contractual*, they are nevertheless *natural*, and so not to be violated.
37. See in particular Paul de Man, 'Phenomenality and Materiality in Kant', in G. Shapiro and A. Sica (eds.), *Hermeneutics: Questions and Prospects* (Amherst, Mass., 1984).

of phenomena. His argument, to be sure, involves a dubious analogy between verbal or phonic signs and pieces of visual sense-data: the latter are not signs in the sense that, normally speaking, what we actually see is a fuzzy orange patch from which we then infer the referent 'sun'. For an epistemological realist like Aquinas, what I experience when I see an elephant is an elephant, not the word or the concept or a patch of grey.[38] Even so, this semiotics consorts remarkably well with Berkeley's poetics of the world, combining difference and unity in equal measure. Just as the artefact is a blend of free play and organic integration, each reinforcing the other, so Berkeley's semiotics manages to avoid at a stroke a structuralist determinism of the sign and a post-structuralist voluntarism or randomness of it. The sign does not automatically yield me a referent, but neither am I at liberty to interpret it as I choose.

Sight, and the practical activity with which it is bound up, is a matter of the creative interpretation of signs,[39] a thesis which can be used to challenge the ideological assumption that our perceptual experience is somehow self-evident, along with the rationalist prejudice that it is merely a function of the world's given structure. It also explodes any symbolist ideology of the signifier, whose signified can never be unmediatedly present within it. Yet if this semiotic indeterminacy or free play is anti-iconic, neither is it an arbitrary affair in the post-structuralist sense. It is, after all, always possible to speak the language of Nature imperfectly. Interpretations for Berkeley can be right or wrong – the object may prove to be faint because of its remoteness, or for some quite different reason – since the connections we are deciphering here are inscribed in Nature, as the very grammar of God himself. The *langue*, so to speak, is his business, whereas the *parole* is ours. As Berkeley argues in his *New Theory of Vision*, what is arbitrary from God's viewpoint is necessary from ours: we hear words and instantly grasp their meanings, but this apparently internal relation is wholly a matter of custom, education and experience. As with Saussure, *langue* has no necessity when viewed from the outside, but necessarily binds those within it. 'It is indeed arbitrary', Berkeley writes in Saussurean vein, 'that, in general, letters of any language represent sounds at all; but, when that is once agreed, it is not arbitrary what combination of letters shall represent this or that particular sound'.[40]

Marcel Proust shared much the same viewpoint: 'we associate sounds with movements', he writes in his great novel, 'and in that way they serve the purpose of warning us of those movements, of appearing to make them natural and necessary'.[41] The language of Nature as a whole is symbolic of God, expressive of his Reason; but our putting this to human use involves a more

38.   For Aquinas on knowledge, see Brian Davies, *The Thought of Thomas Aquinas* (Oxford, 1992), ch. 7.
39.   A case argued from a quite different direction by Raymond Williams in 'The Creative Mind', in *The Long Revolution* (London, 1961).
40.   *Works*, vol. 1, p. 101.
41.   Marcel Proust, *Remembrance of Things Past* (Harmondsworth, 1983), vol. 2, p. 72.

'arbitrary' kind of semiosis, one which requires creative acts of inference rather than the coercive force of a univocal sign. And this is one implication of John Milbank's claim that Berkeley rejects at once 'a Stoic fatalism which sees the connection of signs as a determinate chain (like Spinoza or even Leibniz) [and] a fully fledged nominalism–voluntarism'.[42] If vision is the discourse of God, then in one sense his laws are directly inscribed in our experience, which tends to undermine any surface/depth model. But since the laws of vision are really laws of the relation and proportion between objects, a question of *situations* rather than of the structure of the object; and since these laws are not spontaneously given to us along with our sense-data but need to be interpreted and applied, the grammar of God allows for our own creative actions or utterances.

It is not that these utterances, *à la* Saussure, are *contingent* – that God's grammar sets the absolute bounds within which some random free play is possible, in a structuralist yoking of the systemic and the accidental. Our freedom is rather to be found in the fact that the interpretation and application of the laws of perception involves a certain *indeterminacy*, which is one implication of God's signs being arbitrary.[43] The pointing finger, as Wittgenstein argues, impels us in a particular direction only on a certain interpretation of it, which could always have been different. And this indeterminacy, like that of the work of art, is built into the nature of the world itself. The signs of this great book of the world are also indeterminate because – again like the work of art – they are overdetermined, since each element is so textually interwoven with the others that it becomes saturated with diverse significances. In this sense too, indeterminacy is an effect of structure rather than, as on a 'negative' view of freedom, some inexplicable lacuna within it. Just as Bertolt Brecht remarked that humanity is free because it is the product of too many determinations rather than too few, so Berkeley's sense of the ultimate mystery of creation, the microscopic fringes and fissures where it sublimely outruns our knowledge, is not an alternative to grasping the world as significant design, but the actual consequence of a design so intricate as to be no more ultimately totalisable than a literary text. In this sense, his conservative rage for order and his conservative insistence on the limits of human reason are resolved in the idea of a *textual system*. Creation is a stratified structure, which satisfies the requirements of order, but one so finely blended that it eludes both the reductions of mechanical materialism and the hubristic epistemology of rationalism. The problem with this theory, as we have seen in our discussion of *Siris*, is that the phrase 'textual system' borders on the oxymoronic, as the former term perpetually offers to unravel the latter.

42.   *The Word made Strange*, Milbank, p. 102.
43.   See David Kline, 'Berkeley's Divine Language Argument', in Ernest Sosa (ed.), *Essays on the Philosophy of George Berkeley* (Dordrecht, 1987), who compares Berkeley's sense of the arbitrariness of the sign to Descartes's.

The language of vision is thus grasped in *Alciphron* in just the kind of tex-
tualising terms which are used in *Siris* of the world in general:

> It is equivalent to a constant creation, betokening an immediate act of power
> and providence. It cannot be accounted for by mechanical principles, by atoms,
> attractions, or effluvia. The instantaneous production and reproduction of so
> many signs, combined, dissolved, transposed, diversified, and adapted to such
> an endless variety of purposes, ever shifting with the occasions and suited to
> them, being utterly inexplicable and unaccountable by the laws of motion, by
> chance, by fate, or the like blind principles, doth set forth and testify the imme-
> diate operation of a spirit or thinking being; and not merely of a spirit, which
> every motion or gravitation may possibly infer, but of one wise, good, and
> provident Spirit, which directs and rules and governs the world.[44]

Like the world, the language of perception is a stupendously intricate text
whose very complex plurality is testimony to a governing order and intention
inscribed within it. What the post-structuralists see as opposites, then, Berkeley views as necessarily interrelated: it is precisely because this language is so
sublimely subtle that it testifies to a design. And since this design is no externally imposed will of a divine clockmaker but is immanent in every particle
of our experience, as God 'takes care of our minutest actions and designs
throughout the whole course of our lives' (section 14), we are speaking here
of a unifying principle which, as with the aether of *Siris*, is the very well-
spring of difference and plurality, intimately at one with the smallest sensuous particular. We are therefore speaking of the language we call Nature as
inherently aesthetic; for the aesthetic, classically conceived, is precisely this
ineffable interplay of unity and difference. But the world can also be said to
be aesthetic because we take pleasure in our senses, so that Berkeley's theory
of the divine discourse brings together three features of language which in
English culture are becoming rigorously distinct. The language of Nature is
rational, informative or communicational; it is aesthetic, or sensuously
delightful; and it is rhetorical too, since by this means God persuades us of
his own presence behind his creation. The task of science, for Berkeley as for
a later German sociology of *Verstehen*, is aesthetic or hermeneutical rather
than realist, concerned not with causal laws but with 'a greater largeness of
comprehension, whereby analogies, harmonies, and agreements are discovered in the works of nature, and the particular effects explained, that is,
reduced to general rules'.[45] As in the case of art, relations of semiotic implication here replace causal ones: the fire I see, implausibly enough, is not the
cause of my burnt finger, but a mark which forewarns me of it.

To this extent, Berkeley has traded a naturalising or phenomenalising ideology for an aestheticising one. He speaks in his *Principles* of the language of

44.   *Alciphron*, Fourth Dialogue, Section 14. *Works*, vol. 2, p. 219.
45.   *Principles*, p. 210.

Nature as a tune, and refers elsewhere to the 'theatre' of the world of experience. (In the theatre, one might claim, *esse est percipi* is literally true: nothing
exists but what the audience sees, and off-stage 'events' are entirely unreal.)
Even so, this aestheticising move allows him to challenge the sovereignty of
the visual, which in English empiricist thought has always been a privileged
source of the self-evident. Vision as language is the visual as a version. And
this is one current of Berkeley's thought which will pass down to his compatriot Edmund Burke, in whose aesthetics the visual qualities of poetry are
always suggestively indeterminate. Much the same view of suggestive indeterminacy can be found in the German Alexander Baumgarten, whose *Aes-
thetica*, published in 1750 only a few years after Berkeley's *Siris*, examines like
that work a phenomenon which has something of the systematic nature of
Reason, but which displays at the same time a 'confusion' or interweaving of
sensible elements which finally defeats all rational analysis. In naming that
mode, Baumgarten bequeathed to the world the word 'aesthetic' in its modern sense. Berkeley, for his part, believes that a certain obscurity is built into
ordinary language itself, which is to this extent already aesthetic. He holds
that there is a mixture of obscurity and prejudice in human speech and reasoning, and that, this being so, the veils of prejudice and error must be
removed slowly and singly. The image recalls Burke's celebrated denunciation
of the Jacobins in *Reflections on the Revolution in France*, who rudely tear the
decent drapery of custom from the body of the state.[46] Berkeley is enough of
an Enlightenment thinker to believe in the necessity of this demystification;
but he is also enough of a conservative to desire a slow striptease.

Berkeley did not believe that objects were unreal, or that they existed only in
the human mind, or that they ceased to exist when we were not perceiving
them. 'Real' and 'material' are not in his view synonyms – a doctrine shared
as it happens by most materialists, for whom envy is real enough but not in
the sense that emeralds are. Materiality is just one language for describing
reality, and not in Berkeley's view the most illuminating one. Few philosophers have been the subject of such relentless travesty, even if some of his
views were outlandish enough.[47] What he did was to exorcise the ghostly
'material substance' which for the empiricists underlay our sense-data, since
this phantasmal being, as sublimely unknowable as Kant's *numenon*, could not

46. In one of the more regrettable literary might-have-beens, Burke was to have
contributed an essay on Berkeley to a dictionary planned by Goldsmith which
never came to fruition. See Ralph M. Wardle, *Oliver Goldsmith* (London, 1957),
p. 262.

47. For essays on Berkeley's epistemology, see John Foster and Howard Robinson
(eds.), *Essays on Berkeley* (Oxford, 1985). There is further useful discussion in
A. A. Luce, *George Berkeley: The Dialectic of Immaterialism* (London, 1963), a
case taken to task by I. C. Tipton in his *Berkeley: The Philosophy of Immaterialism* (London, 1974). See also George Pitcher, *Berkeley* (London, 1977), ch. 8.

itself be an object of experience and so ran counter to the epistemology of empiricism itself.

One can imagine the *Eureka*-like exhilaration of the young Berkeley as he stumbled upon this key to all knowledge, his Emperor's-new-clothes discovery that this shapeless, weightless, colourless 'substance' solemnly acknowledged as fundamental by his philosophical elders was in truth, just as it sounded, nothing at all. For him, it was not this nothing which sustained things in being, but something more like the nothingness of Scottus Eriugena, *néant* rather than *rien*. Substance for Berkeley was a kind of fetishism, and a belief in a realm of independently existent objects a form of idolatry surprisingly close to Marx's notion of reification. For both philosophers, men and women end up worshipping the work of their own hands. The great secret Berkeley thinks he has laid bare is that what the appearances are concealing is not some ineffable mystery, some *Ding an sich* or ultimate core of reality; they are concealing the fact that there is nothing behind them, that the veil is veiling nothing and so is not a veil at all, that this hard core of substance is as flimsy as a fantasy. The imaginary object we call substance is simply a fantasy-object filling the void of our desire, one which like all such fantasy objects we construct backwards from the 'appearances' and then posit as their cause.

If purging reality of this McGuffin of material substance was in one sense an iconoclastic gesture, it was also a conservative one. Berkeley did it partly to rid the world of scepticism, since it placed things beyond our reach as surely as the theological representationalism of a William King or Peter Browne pushed the Almighty beyond our cognition. The God of the fideists, who cannot be known in himself, is as stripped of perceptible properties as Locke's vacuous matter. Berkeley's exotic move in eradicating substance is thus, ironically enough, made in the name of the common sense he cherished. Its point is not to abolish objects but to give us direct access to them – not, in the manner of naive realism, by passing directly from our 'ideas' of things to the things themselves, but by the daring masterstroke of converting things themselves into our ideas or perceptions of them, viewing objects as no more than assemblages of sense-data. It really is the pineapple I feel and taste and smell, not just my ideas about the pineapple, since the pineapple is nothing but those ideas. The world is thus restored to us rather than dissolved. This is a conservative strategy in another sense too, since by cancelling material substance all the way through, Berkeley succeeds in leaving everything exactly as it was. *Esse est percipi* or *percipere* makes all the difference and none. Like some modern-day anti-foundationalists, he is out not to transform our behaviour but to offer us a startlingly new description of what we do anyway, which affects what we do not a whit. The Newtonian universe is left firmly in place, but a *Tractatus*-like distinction is enforced between what science can say and what it cannot, in a coupling of positivism and theism.

There is a kind of late-Wittgensteinian, 'back to the rough ground' aspect to this endorsement of our given practices.[48] In throwing over the Lockeian belief that language represents clear and distinct ideas, or indeed necessarily represents ideas at all, Berkeley acknowledges like Wittgenstein that the pragmatic or rhetorical character of language holds sway over its denotative function.[49] Meaning for both thinkers is not a 'mental process' (no image of 'man', Berkeley reminds us, inevitably flashes up in my mind when I pronounce the word),[50] but 'an apposite choice and skilful management of signs'[51] which combines them contextually in order to generate certain dispositions and catalyse certain modes of conduct. We can thus move directly from signs to practical life without having to pass through the medium of 'abstract ideas', which for Berkeley are an absurdity. One upshot of this contextual semiotics for both Berkeley and Wittgenstein is a certain irreducible obscurity or indeterminacy in our speech, an indeterminacy which can be seen as both 'aesthetic' and everyday. There is thus no special problem for Berkeley with theological discourse: if a clear image of the word 'grace' is hard to come by, so is a clear image of 'maybe' or 'tomorrow'. There is a touch of sublimity about our most commonplace utterances. Sterne's Tristram shares just the same Wittgensteinian epistemology: 'All I contend for', he writes, 'is that I am not obliged to set out with a definition of what love is, and so long as I can go on with my story intelligibly, with the help of the word itself, without any other idea of it, than what I have in common with the rest of the world, why should I differ from it a moment before the time?' (*Tristram Shandy*, Book 6, ch. 37).

By spreading theological indeterminacy into the rest of our language games, Berkeley manages to defend it by de-privileging it, suggesting just how workaday such ambiguous discourse really is. Semantic indeterminacy, interestingly enough, is here yoked to a conservative rather than radical politics, in contrast with, say, Berkeley's friend Alexander Pope, for whom a traditionalist political vision goes hand in hand with the Augustan virtues of lucidity and the iconic sign (its sound an echo to the sense). Pope, who believed we could scan man but not God, may well have learned of some of Archbishop King's ideas on the same topic from Bolingbroke, who in turn derived them from Leibniz;

48. See Antony Flew, 'Was Berkeley a Precursor of Wittgenstein?', in William B. Todd (ed.), *Hume and the Enlightenment* (Edinburgh, 1974), an essay that says remarkably little about Wittgenstein.
49. See David Berman, 'Berkeley's Semantic Revolution', *History of European Ideas*, no. 7 (1986).
50. Tristram Shandy observes that when translating a piece of Latin he understands what a certain phrase means even though he cannot conceptualise it: 'The moment I pronounced the words, I could perceive an attempt towards a vibration in the strings, about the region of the heart. – The brain made no acknowledgement. – There's often no good understanding betwixt 'em. – I felt as if I understood it. – I had no ideas' (vol. 4, ch. 1).
51. *Alciphron*, *Works*, vol. 2, p. 313.

but the translucent language of Pope's poetry, which proposes that there are limits to our secular knowledge too, denies the very cognitive indeterminacy it asserts. Samuel Johnson was later to write a whole dictionary in a confessedly forlorn attempt to banish such fuzziness from the English language.

Irish culture, by contrast, clasps a belief in semantic indeterminacy much closer to its heart, as befits a society in which theology is so dominant a discourse; and it is perhaps worth speculating whether this may not be one of the many sources of the extraordinary flourishing of modernism in twentieth-century Ireland. In any case, Berkeley's 'ordinary language' appeal against theological representationalism cannily shifts the terms of the argument, whereas his dismantling of material substance is possible only from within the very empiricist framework it prises apart. He is not out to argue directly that we really *can* know God, but to take issue with his opponents' use of the word 'know'. As *Alciphron* puts it, 'The objections made to faith are by no means an effect of knowledge, but proceed rather from an ignorance of what knowledge is'.[52] If one had a less exalted view of common knowledge, one would be less puzzled by talk about truly exalted matters. The theological representationalists have thus thrown up as much of a pseudo-problem as someone who wondered exactly where the concept of whiteness was located. Berkeley, by contrast, has an eighteenth-century Tory respect for the *sensus communis*, claiming as he does that 'our notions about faith are . . . taken from the commerce of the world, and practice of mankind, rather than from the peculiar systems of refiners. . . .'[53] Metaphysics is a political as well as theoretical danger: as soon as we entertain notions like 'abstract ideas' we risk opening the floodgates to all kinds of fantastic verbiage, and so threatening order and right reason. In this, as in his belief in custom and tradition, he is a *confrère* of Edmund Burke. Epistemological doctrines in Berkeley become political positions in his successor.

Euphranor, Berkeley's spokesman in *Alciphron*, remarks that after reading the 'minute' or materialist philosophers 'I consider myself as a man left stripped and desolate on a black beach'.[54] It is the kind of image one might encounter in Beckett, whose stark, starved figures are among other things a reaction against a 'Gaelic' gusto and robust concreteness. It might be claimed that there is something of a Gaelic, particularising cast of mind in Berkeley's disdain for abstraction, but it is just as much an Anglo-Irish dread that the metaphysical breeds religious scepticism and so distracts the plain people of Ireland from their pious duties. If Berkeley is indeed an apologist for the mob, as he arrestingly remarks of himself, it is in the self-undoing sense that he catches up something of their common sense and turns it against the sort of

52.   ibid.
53.   ibid, p. 311.
54.   ibid, p. 40.

scholastic quibbling which might lead them to forsake their duties in life.[55] It is, in short, an elitist sort of populism, as the idea of a divine language of Nature is too: God is ordinary in that his presence can be felt in our routine sense-experience, yet it takes an extraordinary thinker to disclose this truth.

It takes such a thinker because, for Berkeley as for Wittgenstein, common sense is itself a form of metaphysics to be combatted, as well as a source of anti-scholastic wisdom. In this sense too, Berkeley combines his philosophical populism with an elitism wary of *hoi polloi*. The metaphysical is not some ethereal realm to be set against the everyday, since for both Berkeley and Wittgenstein, and for Jacques Derrida too, it is the very form of our spontaneously reifying speech. Language, Berkeley observes in the *New Theory of Vision*, is accommodated to the common notions and prejudices of men, which means that the philosopher's own discourse, rather like the language of Nature, must operate as rhetoric, taking this popular *doxa* into account and circumnavigating it rather than confronting it head-on. Like Wittgenstein, his aim is to let the fly out of the fly-bottle, which means putting himself in this fly-like reader's place. His readers must not fetishise his words, 'stick[ing] in this or that phrase or manner of expression, but candidly collect my meaning from the whole sum and tenor of my discourse, and, laying aside the words as much as possible, consider the bare notions themselves. . .'[56] As with Wittgenstein, it is the contextual use of signs which de-fetishises them; if the philosopher's rhetoric sets itself against popular metaphysics, it must do so, paradoxically, by appealing to the contextual indeterminacy of common speech. In reading Berkeley, we must discard the signifiers and attend somehow to the naked signifieds – an ironic enough appeal, to be sure, since his philosophy warns us that we get into epistemological trouble by forgetting that things are just ideas in our minds, and trying instead to stare through these ideas to a sphere of supposedly independent objects. What holds at the level of the relation between signifier and signified is reversed at the level of the relation between sign and referent.

Berkeley's concern with the language of the senses suggests just what a sensuous thinker he is, despite his immaterialism. Indeed his *New Theory of Vision,* in which everything is centred on the bodily or phenomenological, can read at times like an early version of Maurice Merleau-Ponty's *The Phenomenology of Perception,* brooding as it does on the ratio between one mode of per-

55.   Berkeley's descriptions of material substance as 'brute', 'stupid', 'unthinking', and so on sound rather like a Yahoo-like version of the populace, which the ruling order can understand no more than we can grasp the nature of matter. But I leave such speculations to vulgar Marxists. For Berkeley's political authoritarianism and patrician contempt for the common people, see *A Discourse Addressed to Magistrates and Men in Authority* and *A Word to the Wise: An Exhortation to the Roman Catholic Clergy, Works,* vol. 3.

56.   *Works*, vol. 2, p. 90.

ception and another. Burke's great work on aesthetics, another thoroughly corporeal text, is also phenomenological in just this sense; indeed the word 'aesthetic' is nothing less than the eighteenth century's term for this kind of inquiry.[57] But the sensuous body at the root of Berkeley's thought is a dislocated or 'decentred' one, in which any given unity of the senses is rejected as an illusion. The elephant I see before me is not the same elephant whose hide I feel, since ideas which were shared between the senses would be general ideas, for which Berkeley has nothing but scorn. There is a kind of slippage or hiatus between the different senses here, as there is, we moderns might add, with the psychological condition of aphasia. An aphasiac may be able to say the word 'knife' when she is holding one but not when she is not, somewhat in the way that a very young infant has to learn to associate the hand it sees with the hand that is stroking it. Microscopes, rather similarly, dislocate the senses of sight and touch, as Berkeley remarks in his *New Theory of Vision*. His riposte to what eighteenth-century Ireland knew as the 'Molyneux question' is an unequivocal 'no': a blind man restored to sight would not be able spontaneously to link his new visual images of objects to his previous knowledge of them through touch.[58] In contrast to Romantic symbolism or synaesthesia, we have to figure our way from the visual appearance of the elephant to our haptic sense of it, and these different ideas or images, which bear no iconic relation to each other, may thus be said to partake of the nature of allegory rather than of symbolism. A rose might well have smelt quite differently from the way it does; there is nothing in its visual presence from which its odour can be inferred. We establish that an object really exists by associating our various ideas of it in some consistent way, which is to say by recounting a coherent narrative of it. What I am seeing is an elephant if one bit of sensuous signification generates another – if, as in the act of reading, I can set up here some sort of inferential discourse. And as with the event of reading, this process goes on wholly within the medium of signs themselves, at no point buttoning down upon some transcendental signified. Which is not to claim that we can tell just any old narrative about the world we want, since what centres and coheres what might otherwise appear as a mere modernist chaos of experience is God himself. It is he who has determined that what looks like a rose should smell like one too – though in the great scheme of things, since God is pure freedom, this connection which is necessary for me to find my way around is in a deeper sense purely contingent.

What also finds its way around for Berkeley is money, which is one of the topics of his economic-nationalist discourse *The Querist*. David Berman has

57. See Terry Eagleton, *The Ideology of the Aesthetic* (Oxford, 1990), ch. 1.
58. For this important Irish philosophical motif, see M. J. Morgan, *Molyneux's Question* (Cambridge, 1977). Morgan points out that all the participants in the debate make the dubious assumption that one born blind but restored to sight could indeed instantly 'see' in some fairly unproblematical sense of the term.

pointed to the relations between Berkeley's anti-metaphysical economics and his pragmatist semiotics: monetary signs work not by representing some deeper material substratum – gold or silver, for instance – but, like words, by their variety of practical uses in a form of life. 'As words could have meaning without ideas', so Berman succinctly puts it, 'so money could have value without gold'.[59] (A similar parallel is made by Wittgenstein, who suggests a contrast in the *Philosophical Investigations* between thinking of the value of money in terms of its use, and misconceiving its value in terms of the object you want to buy with it.) Industry, like language, is for Berkeley a matter of practical energies, of what we do, not in the first place of certain fixed resources like land or goldmines. If he does not have the word 'reification', he certainly has the concept. Money allows for a quick, vigorous circulation of force, 'quickening commerce, and . . . putting spirit into the people';[60] it is the 'life' of industry as meaning is the life of language, and a political state without this circulation is struck 'gouty and inactive'.[61] Money, in brief, is a kind of tarwater of the body politic, animating its sluggish parts and purging it of obstructions. As words regulate our moral conduct, so monetary signs stimulate our economic life; and Berkeley is stern on gambling (and by extension what we would call finance capitalism), in which, as in some symbolist poetics, signs are deployed merely for the sake of other signs. The language of money thus differs from the divine language of Nature, since that sign-system involves both use and aesthetic enjoyment together; whereas for Berkeley those who relish money in itself, rather than as a set of counters or notional marks, reify it objectionably, just as those who attend to words-in-themselves are a kind of miser. Berkeley's acid comments on the capricious 'fancy' of those who devote themselves to 'gathering counters . . . multiplying figures [and] enlarging denominations . . . without having a proper regard for the use, or end, or nature of things',[62] strikingly prefigure the language of Marx's *Economic and Philosophical Manuscripts* of 1844.

The Querist is cast in the form of rhetorical questions to the reader, questions confidently anticipating the answer 'yes'. It is, in short, a dialogical form, suitable for a man who held that we can be sure of the existence of another mind when we hear another speak to us. Yet the dialogism is strictly limited, as with the various tedious straw targets of materialist philosophy which Berkeley sets up in his Platonic dialogues in *Alciphron*. In the hands of a Swift, these questions would have made us unsettlingly uncertain of their appropriate answers. Berkeley's dramatic talent is notably scant, in contrast to the dizzying dialogism of the fouth book of *Gulliver's Travels*, *Tristram Shandy* or Flann O'Brien's *At Swim-Two-Birds*, in which one text or position jostles ver-

59.   Berman, 'Berkeley's Semantic Revolution', p. 169.
60.   *Works*, vol. 3, p. 382.
61.   ibid, p. 390.
62.   ibid, p. 381.

tiginously with another. As in *Siris*, there is a tension between textual open-endedness and philosophical authority, the deconstructible and the divine. Yeats saw Berkeley as playing God, legislating the world out of existence as God had promulgated it into being; but this not only garbles the epistemology (Berkeley did not, as Yeats wrote, prove all things a dream),[63] but misses the fact that what God creates is a mundane text so complex as to be open-ended, one which thus challenges the authority of our knowledge and which, moreover, constrains our conduct at every point. Yeats mistranslates Berkeley into his own lordly epistemological terms, as a man conjuring up objects at will in a kind of philosophical equivalent to the cavalier Ascendancy aristocrat. But Berkeley is not a voluntarist or a Romantic, and has no conception of that creative imagination by which humanity usurps the role of its Creator. On the contrary, the mind for Berkeley is the passive receptacle described by empiricism in general, and it is exactly in the fact that we don't choose our own sensations that we can detect the providential finger of the deity organising them on our behalf. For Berkeley, God and the passivity of the human mind are intimately linked; the mind has no power of its own, as it has for Romantic humanism. But it is assigned, even so, a highly privileged status; and this then opens the way to the Romantic doctrine of its transcendent capacities of which W. B. Yeats is one modern inheritor.

It is fashionable these days to see rhetoric, ambiguity and indeterminacy as radical virtues, in contrast to the authoritarianism of the transparent sign. But the judgement is absurdly unhistorical. In an Irish lineage from Berkeley and King to Browne and Burke, a suggestive obscurity of language is harnessed to a stoutly conservative politics. In early eighteenth-century Ireland, it is plain speaking and univocal meaning which are revolutionary; and the prime name for this phenomenon is the extraordinary John Toland, whose picaresque progress might have sprung straight out of the fiction of Daniel Defoe.

Toland, said by some to be the bastard offspring of a priest and a prostitute, and probably of an ancient bardic family, began life as an Irish-speaking shepherd in Inishowen, County Donegal, and ended up as a renowned European intellectual respected by Leibniz and admired by Voltaire, a vital influence on the *philosophes* of the French Enlightenment.[64] He was recommended

63.   'A Denis Johnson character voices a similar kind of voluntarism, perhaps again with garbled echoes of Berkeley, in his play *The Old Lady Says 'No!'*: 'I tell you, we can make this country – this world – whatever we want it to be by saying so. . .' (*Selected Plays of Denis Johnson*, Gerrards Cross, 1983, p. 70).

64.   For accounts of Toland, see the admirably erudite work by Robert E. Sullivan, *John Toland and the Deist Controversy* (Cambridge, Mass., 1982). See also Robert Reed Evans's excellently detailed monograph, *Pantheisticon: The Career of John Toland* (New York, 1991), and, for a briefer portrait, J. G. Simms, 'John Toland (1670–1722), a Donegal Heretic', in *Irish Historical Studies*, vol. 16, no. 63 (March, 1969).

to John Locke as 'freespirited and ingenious', though Locke seems to have kept a wary distance from his alarming religious heterodoxy.[65] He was, according to his namesake Jack Toland, fictional protagonist of a recent Irish novel, 'one of Europe's greatest minds', who disclosed the pantheistic secret that God was matter and universal space.[66] Known fondly to his Donegal neighbours as 'Owen of the Books', and rather less fondly as a sixteen-year-old renegade to Protestantism, he became a militant Presbyterian in Glasgow, a consort of free thinkers in Leiden, an intellectual bruiser in the coffee-houses of Oxford, a literary hack and *habitué* of radical circles in London, and in his final years in Dublin a protégé of Robert Molesworth, patron of the Irish intellectual left. It is also possible that he had an affair with the sister of George I. Bumptious, intemperate and pathologically indiscreet, Toland invented the terms 'pantheist', 'free thinker', and perhaps 'West Britain' and 'North Britain' to boot,[67] dabbled in occultism and probably in secret societies, mastered some nine languages, and roamed at large in a louche underworld of religious heretics, shady political operators and radical republicans. He was probably a freemason, and might have belonged to a hermetic Dutch society known as the Knights of Jubilation. Dubbed 'the father of Irish philosophy',[68] he lived it up in Berlin at the court of the Electress Sophia, may have been a spy, and along with Swift, Defoe and Matthew Prior was for a while on the payroll of the politician Robert Harley as a propagandist.

A mercurial fantasist or traditional Irish trickster who glided between doctrines and identities, Toland obscured some pieces of his personal history and fabricated others. He sometimes passed himself off as English, indeed in typical émigré fashion as more English than the natives, but he was also a considerable Celtic scholar, impressively learned in Irish letters, archaeology and ancient history, and while at Oxford developed plans for an Irish dictionary and a comparative study of Irish and Breton.[69] His Celtic studies, characteristically enough, included work on an old Armagh manuscript stolen from a Parisian library by a spoilt priest crony. He also seems to have used the Irish Catholic monastic network in Europe to get around, securing a reference from

65. See Margaret C. Jacob, *The Radical Enlightenment* (London, 1981), p. 152. Jacob doubts that Toland was in fact a Christian at all, apart from being a Protestant for political reasons.

66. See Richard Kearney, *Walking at Sea Level* (London, 1997), p. 14.

67. There is now some doubt about his coining of all of these terms. See Stephen H. Daniel, 'Toland's Semantic Pantheism', in Philip McGuinness, Alan Harrison and Richard Kearney (eds.), John Toland's *Christianity not Mysterious* (Dublin, 1997), p. 306.

68. By David Berman in his essay 'The Irish Freethinker', in P. McGuinness *et al* (eds.), Toland's *Christianity not Mysterious*, p. 224.

69. For an excellent summary of Toland's native-Irish aspects, see Alan Harrison, 'John Toland's Celtic Background', in P. McGuinness *et al.* (eds.), Toland's *Christianity not Mysterious*.

the Prague Franciscans which testifies, perhaps bogusly, to his patrician Gaelic descent. He admired Milton, Harrington, Giordano Bruno and William III, saw Moses as a republican, was a passionate Commonwealth man and a philosophical materialist, and kept one foot in the world of Whig *realpolitik* while the other remained planted in more heterodox circles. In 1701 he was entrusted to carry the Act of Succession to Hanover, thus playing a modest but historic part in securing the British throne for Protestantism. A champion of Judaism and an apologist for Islam, he was an eccentric mixture of plain-speaking and hermeticism, radical tolerationalism and virulent anti-Catholicism.[70] In a venerable Irish lineage from John Scottus Eriugena (with whom he compared himself) to James Joyce, he was exile, heretic and goliard rolled in one, a cosmopolitan vagrant or 'Irish adventurer in scholarship'[71] who nonetheless touted a brand of early Irish Christianity and praised as 'Western latitudinarians' the island's ancient monks, of whom he himself was a deviant off-spring. Richard Kearney discerns in him a typically Irish doubleness: 'at once Irish and non-Irish, Gaelic-speaking and English-speaking, Catholic by birth and deist by choice, native and cosmopolitan, devotee of ancient Celtic sects and champion of Enlightenment reason, inventor of countless pseudonyms yet never forgetful of his original Irish name'.[72] Toland *was* in fact 'forgetful' of his original Irish name, a spurious version of which he promulgated to the world; but like Joyce he kept a kind of faith with his Gaelic past, while openly urging that sectarian conflict between Catholics and Protestants be sedulously fostered in the interests of the latter's ascendancy.

It is worth pausing to reflect on the number of Irish writers who, like Toland, were caught up in English politics. Jonathan Swift became the Tories' chief propagandist and helped to write the monarch's speeches to parliament. Richard Brinsley Sheridan was the most trusted adviser to the heir to the

---

70.   For Toland's Protestant triumphalism, see his *Anglia Libera* (London, 1701), a hymn of praise to an English liberty which has now arrived at a state little short of perfection, and *The State-Anatomy of Britain* (London, 1717), ch. 4, for an assault on Roman Catholicism. On Toland's political contradictions, see Philip McGuinness's articles 'Tolerant Sectarian' in the *Times Literary Supplement* (27 September 1996) and 'John Toland and Eighteenth-Century Irish Republicanism', in *Irish Studies Review* (summer, 1997). See also, for Toland's thought, David Berman, 'The Irish Counter-Enlightenment', in R. Kearney and M. Hederman (eds.), *The Irish Mind* (Dublin, 1984), S. H. Daniel, *John Toland: His Methods, Manners and Mind* (Kingston and Montreal, 1984), and the same author's quasi-Foucaultean or postmodern reading of Toland, 'The Subversive Philosophy of John Toland', in P. Hyland and N. Sammels (eds.), *Irish Writing, Exile and Subversion* (London, 1992).

71.   The phrase is David Berman's, in P. McGuinness *et al* (eds.), Toland's *Christianity not Mysterious*, p. 229.

72.   Richard Kearney, 'John Toland: An Irish Philosopher?", in McGuinness *et al* (eds.), *Christianity not Mysterious*, p. 219.

British throne, might easily have become Prime Minister, and almost single-handedly managed the major constitutional crisis triggered by the supposed insanity of George III. Edmund Burke was the star performer of the Rockingham Whigs and England's premier spokesman for anti-French reaction. One might even, in more modest vein, include Bernard Shaw's later Fabian propagandising. All of these men were *arrivistes* in the English metropolis, down-at-heel Irish adventurers who had nothing to hawk but their command of language. The role of the political hack, broker or pamphleteer was thus an obvious way for the émigré writer to survive; but politics also provided these landless, moneyless, untitled blow-ins with one of the few available means of fulfilling their thrusting social ambitions. Sheridan was far more interested in becoming a grandee politician than a celebrated dramatist, and almost nothing that Swift wrote was 'literary'.[73] With the outsider's mixture of truculence and conformism, they could harness irony, satire and an acerbic wit to a defence of the Establishment interests with which, as colonial mimic men, they wished to identify. But their language is typically double-edged, turned as easily against the nation they still resent as surrendered into its service. Behind all this may be a memory of the politically functional role of the traditional Gaelic bard – of a pre-modern society in which 'literature' had never achieved the autonomy which it is granted in the epoch of modernity, but is pressed instead into the service of social and political power. Thomas Moore is perhaps the first Irish writer in England to win fame as an 'aesthetic' figure, as the pragmatic eighteenth century passes into its Romantic aftermath. What defines the Irish writer in the metropolitan nation is the image of Burke and Sheridan as co-prosecutors of Warren Hastings, in one of the most extraordinary spectacles the House of Commons ever witnessed: two colonial-bred rhetoricians verbally annihilating an eminent representative of British imperialism, unleashing the full force of their colonial invective and *rassentiment* on the system he symbolises, but doing so in the name of an ideal version of that system with which both outsiders wish to integrate.

Toland remarks sardonically in his *Christianity not Mysterious* on the wondrous convenience by which 'what is our highest interest perfectly to understand, should . . . both be maintain'd to be obscurity, and very industriously made so!'[74] For him as for William Blake, mystery is at root mystification, a strategem of priestcraft, and equivocation is the obscurantism by which the rulers maintain their dominion. The antithesis of Reason is Authority, which in order to validate itself appeals in a vicious hermeneutical circle to a body of texts which it has itself legislated to be divine. If there are really no Christian mysteries, then the political implications of this view are explosive: as

73.   See Oliver W. Ferguson, *Jonathan Swift and Ireland* (Urbana, 1962), and Ian Higgins, *Swift's Politics* (Cambridge, 1994).

74.   John Toland, *Christianity not Mysterious* (reprinted Stuttgart-Bad Cannstatt, 1964), p. vi.

David Berman notes, 'there could [then] be nothing to separate the rival Christian religions or sects. And then there could be no basis for the Penal Code.'[75] By undermining Protestant Ascendancy, free-thinking implicitly advances the Catholic cause, a consequence which was not at all welcome to Toland himself. Mystery is where power and epistemology meet, and the gibberish of the Divinity schools is for Toland 'the language of the Beast'.[76] Elsewhere, he castigates those who 'boast of a superior and supernatural knowledge, not subject to the rules of criticism, nor a proper object of the understanding'.[77] As one who suffered under them himself, Toland has a well-nigh Foucaultean sense of the relations between discourse and power; he is aware of how truth can become ideology, in the doctrine that 'the common people, being incapable of reflection, ought to be manag'd by guile. . .'.[78] The war of interpretations is one of his abiding themes. He has, as we shall see, no unambiguous faith in the common folk; but his interweaving of radical politics and epistemology is remarkably sophisticated, and for him the place where these converge is in the violence of language, warped out of true by sinister interests.

Given his own experience of calumny and abuse, Toland understands how discourse can maim and incarcerate, how words can starve a man by depriving him of employment, or rhetoric fashion a new religious object for sectarian wrangling. In his Enlightenment faith that 'truth is always and every where the same', that what is repugnant to clear and distinct ideas is contrary to Reason, Toland strikes a radical blow against those who would seek to manipulate texts for their own oppressive political ends. It is a case which our own postmodernists, for whom such re-readings are generally assumed to be subversive, might do well to ponder. If anything can be made to mean anything, so Toland argues, then those in authority can use writing to impose their own imperious political will. He is thus out to confound those who believe that

> . . . the words of scripture, tho never so equivocal and ambiguous without the context, may signify every where whatever they can signify: and, if this be not enough, believe that every truth is a true sense of every passage of scripture; that is, that any thing may be made of every thing . . . I promise you, there's no explication, tho never so violent, tho never so contradictory or perplex'd, but you may as easily establish as admit.[79]

75. David Berman, 'The Irish Counter-Enlightenment', in Richard Kearney (ed.), *The Irish Mind* (Dublin, 1985), p. 137.
76. ibid, p. 147.
77. John Toland, *Clidophorus*, reprinted in *Tetradymus* (London, 1720), p. 64.
78. ibid, p. 64.
79. ibid, pp. xxv–vi.

If meaning is relativised to context, then the path is thrown open to political sophistry: any obnoxious power can justify its actions by interpreting its situation as it finds convenient. A wise man, Toland comments, will judge the merits of a cause 'consider'd only in it self, without any regard to times, places or persons'.[80] There is, of course, no such form of knowledge; but in Toland's hands the politics of this rationalist doctrine are explosive. Truth must be rescued from its ideological function of ratifying the partial interests of specific times, places and persons, and restored instead to its disinterested status – which for Toland is not at all the same thing as political neutrality. Truth cannot be the private property of individuals, a prey to their whims and wiles:

> 'Religion is not to be modell'd according to our fancies, nor to be judg'd of as it relates to our private designs.'[81]

Those who see meaning as shifting in accordance with its context, and so as chronically ambiguous, must admit by their own logic that there are contexts in which plainness is preferable to ambiguity. You do not want shouts of 'Fire!' to be semantically open-ended. 'If the trumpet gives an uncertain sound', writes Toland, 'who should prepare himself to the battel? And except words easy to be understood be utter'd, how shall it be known what is spoken? . . . Syllables, though never so well put together, if they have not Idea's [sic] fix'd to them, are but words spoken in the air. . .'.[82] As a good rationalist, but also as one scornful of élites, Toland is allergic to darkness and uncertitude: God would not have been so snobbish or inconsiderate as to have made the truths necessary for our salvation hard for the humble to grasp. Religious truth, rather as for Archbishop King, is to be judged pragmatically, 'from undoubted effects, and not from words and letters'.[83] Toland is not a fundamentalist, acknowledging as he does that the language of scripture is often figurative; it is just that he cannot see how one can sincerely acquiesce in what one cannot conceive. Miracles may be unnatural, but they must be in some sense intelligible, otherwise we would not be able to say what it was that was unnatural. Toland can thus advance the bizarre proposition that the gospel 'affords the most illustrious example of close and perspicuous ratiocination conceivable',[84] as though St Mark were a close rival to Bertrand Russell. In his pamphlet *Hodegus*, for example, he argues that the pillar of fire which guided the Old Testament Israelites was an entirely natural phenomenon.

As far as mystery goes, Toland exploits the same epistemology as Berkeley to arrive at the exactly opposite conclusion. Nothing, he thinks, can be said

80.   ibid, p. xv.
81.   ibid, p. xii.
82.   ibid, p. 28.
83.   ibid, p. 32.
84.   ibid, p. 46.

to be a mystery just because we lack an adequate idea of it, or a distinct view of all of its properties at once, because then anything whatsoever could be called a mystery. We do not call water mysterious because we cannot say how many particles form a single drop of it. It is true that we cannot know the essence of God; but on good Lockeian grounds we cannot know the essence of anything else either, even though we still lay claim to an adequate idea of objects. It is quite enough to understand the practical properties of a thing, to know it as it bears some relation to ourselves. Toland, ironically enough, thus shares something of Berkeley's pragmatic anti-essentialism, holding to Locke's doctrine of 'nominal essences' as Berkeley holds to no essences at all. Yet while Berkeley defends divine mystery by pointing to the equally ambiguous nature of sublunary language, Toland turns the argument on its head by insisting that our everyday discourse is sufficiently determinate for our purposes, and so therefore is our talk about God. Indeed S. H. Daniel reads him as a kind of Austinian philosopher *avant la lettre*, holding that our ordinary language, with its common stock of self-evident notions, is the ground of all intelligibility. Our knowledge of things takes place within a rhetoric of shared communication or practical form of life; and to know the real essences of God, bodies or the soul would presuppose a meta-language whose intelligibility we would in turn need to judge in terms of some further meta-language, and so on *ad infinitum*. In fact, we need only know the 'nominal essences' of things, the way they are 'to hand' to us, in Heideggerian phrase, in the communicative context of our common life forms. We cannot hope to comprehend the very discursive matrix which opens up comprehensibility for us in the first place.[85]

Toland is much taken with questions of hermeneutics and textuality, and returns to them constantly in works supposedly devoted to quite different matters. In *Vindicius Liberius*, a defence of *Christianity not Mysterious*, he rebukes those who, like his critics, 'suspect the plainest apologies [one] can make, discover a hidden poison in [one's] words even when they are of their own prescribing'.[86] Scandalised by the spiteful, slanderous language of his opponents, he adopts for his own part what we might now call the principle of hermeneutical charity. If words admit of a double sense, 'which is hard to be always avoided in any language', we ought to place the fairest interpretation we can on their meaning. His enemies have sliced up his texts, ripping his words from their contexts, and 'ten thousand absurdities will follow . . . upon taking a few words of any author without showing their connection with the rest of his discourse. . . '.[87] Context, then, is important after all, not least when one's own arguments are under fire. In the course of his reading, so he tells us, he has collected from time to time 'such passages as relate to

85.   See Stephen H. Daniel, 'Toland's Semantic Pantheism', in P. McGuinness *et al* (eds.), *Christianity not Mysterious*, pp. 307–9.
86.   John Toland, *Vindicius Liberius* (London, 1702), p. 7.
87.   ibid, p. 89.

the expunging, castrating, suppressing, burning, or other ways of censuring books among the Heathens, Jews, Christians, and Mahometans. . .',[88] so that his concern for textual integrity lies very close to his passion for civil liberty. Because of the libels heaped upon him, he finds himself obliged 'beforehand to disclaim all explanations made of my meaning, beyond what is warranted by the express words of my books; having constantly indeavour'd not only to write intelligibly, but so as that none can possibly misunderstand me'.[89] This is of course epistemologically naive: what counts as the 'express' meaning of one's words is just as much a question of interpretation as the most outlandish significance foisted on them by others. And how can Toland believe that no one could possibly mistake his meaning, since if this were true he would not be writing his apologia in the first place? Similarly, in *Amyntor*, he defends his biography of Milton by claiming that in that work he transcribed Milton's own words to obviate any risk of misinterpretation, as though his selection of those words were not already an occasion for precisely that.

Toland wrote *Amyntor* partly to refute the charge that he had called the gospels spurious, a topic which leads him into much wrangling about how to sort genuine from inauthentic documents. In a brief history of scholarly debate over scripture, he shows just how chancy an affair the New Testament canon is: true gospels were once bound together with apocalyptic ones, and illicit versions were accepted at an early stage before the canon had really crystallised. Yet for all the pitfalls of this history, Toland believes that he himself could write an entirely dispassionate account of it, quite uncoloured by personal bias. A recognition of the snares of textuality is instantly countered by a positivist assertion. And despite the chequered history of the canon, which Toland admits allows heretics to draw 'mischievous inferences', he still feels confident in defending the authenticity of the New Testament – though it would not, to be sure, have been open to him not to do so without impunity, in an age when one could be imprisoned for questioning the doctrine of the Trinity.

What he *did* accuse of fraudulence in his life of Milton was the claim that the poet's *Icon Basilike* was the work of Charles I, and this plunges him in *Amyntor* into a good deal of literary sleuthing, the summoning of fragmentary testimony as to the text's true authorship, bibliographic researches and the like. Thus the first half of the book, devoted to biblical scholarship, sees how the whole notion of canonicity is caught up in political interest and historical accident, plagued by textual indeterminacy and tussles of judgement; while the second half of the book, concerned with *Icon Basilike*, sets out to retrieve the exact historical truth as though none of this had been mentioned. Toland includes in support of his case the narrative of a witness whose account he describes as 'exactly copied from the original'; two other witnesses, he insists,

88.   ibid, p. 25.
89.   ibid, p. 160.

attest that the narrative in question is 'exactly conformable to the original', which means that his own argument, dependent as it is on the opinions of two other people that one report of an event is in line with another, is at four or five removes from the truth. Having stated this, a suspicion of textual indeterminacy is then reinstated: the document in question is conformable to the original only 'as far as it goes': it is perhaps no more than a fragment of a longer story, which was 'accidentally hindered' from being copied down. Toland does not know why, but when he finds out he will, so he assures us, broadcast the reason to the world in an appendix to his book. It is clear to him in any case that the evidence for Charles's authorship of *Icon Basilike* is fragmentary and contradictory: the king was apparently seen writing a book, but he may well have been transcribing another's manuscript which he then passed off as his own. The manuscript we have may be in the royal handwriting, but then again only the interlinear corrections may be authentic. All of this is hypothesis, but Toland treats it as, so to speak, gospel truth.

What is extraordinary about *Amyntor* is the way in which a sense of the textual indeterminacy of truth sits undisturbedly with an insistence on its accessibility. Toland, who saw his own life as a kind of text,[90] is fascinated by the arcane and esoteric, by secret scripts and textual tangles, at the same time as he bears noisy witness to the transparency of truth and the self-identity of meaning.[91] In *Nazarenus*, he notes that we find 'all the books of the learned fill'd with complaints, that the ancient Egyptian language and letters, with the means to decipher their hieroglyphicks, are irreparably lost'.[92] The work looks to the Nazarene sect as representative of a primitive, originary Christian faith; but since these early believers also formed 'wrong conceptions of the doctrine and designs of Jesus', the snake of misinterpretation would seem to have been present at the Edenic source. This sect, so Toland holds, had an original gospel of its own, the so-called Gospel of the Hebrews, which predated the New Testament; but this document was destroyed except for a few fragments. Toland thus concludes that 'if the truth may be freely spoken, there remains very little on record, very little that's any way certain or authentic, concerning the *originals of Christianity*. . .'.[93] Given the vicissitudes of textual transmission, it becomes after a while 'almost absolutely impossible to distinguish history from fable, or truth from error'.[94]

90.   The epitaph he wrote for himself ends with the words: 'if you would know more of him Search his Writings'.
91.   Slavoj Žižek notes this contradiction in Freemasonry, which combines hermetic rituals with a belief in the clear light of Reason. See his 'Multiculturalism as the Logic of Multicultural Capitalism', *New Left Review*, no. 225 (September /October, 1997), p. 47.
92.   John Toland, *Nazarenus* (London, 1718), p. 2.
93.   ibid, p. 60.
94.   ibid, pp. 73–4.

All Christian sects vainly boast an uninterrupted tradition and succession – 'the most chimerical pretences in nature', in Toland's view, 'which not only shows how little any oral tradition whatever is to be valu'd; but that no truth of universal concern can possibly depend on so slight a foundation, as the way of bandying about an old story for numerous generations'.[95] Oral tradition Toland associates with specious fable and Roman Catholicism. A Catholic fetishism of tradition is to be countered by an appeal to the plain sense of the New Testament itself – as though that document were at all accessible to us outside its conflicting histories of interpretation. Toland wants to pit a single piece of writing against the corrupt intertextuality of tradition, but does not seem to see that this supposedly singular work is constructed out of it. He praises the gospels as models of unequivocal sense, yet remarks that it is impossible for any text to escape diverse interpretations, which presumably must include the New Testament too. The Mahometans, he thinks, are more scrupulous of the integrity of their sacred text than are Christians: since they believe every word of it to be divinely inspired, there is 'therfore [sic] no room left, one wou'd imagine, for *various readings*, or other such criticisms. The minute the learned may alter, add, or substitute, what to them shall seem most becoming the divine spirit, there's an end at once of *inspiration* (according to these gentlemen) and the book becomes thenceforth their own: meaning, that it is then the product of different times and diverse authors, till nothing of the original is left, tho the book continues as bulky as ever. . .'.[96] Hermeneutic pluralism and the historicity of truth must be denied, if biblical meaning is to remain authoritative; but Toland has no sooner emphasised the point than he observes that different readings of a work are in fact inevitable, and that even his admired monological Mahometans have been known to produce them.

For all these problems of textual transmission, Toland feels himself quite capable of portraying an ancient Irish Christianity uncorrupted by Roman Catholicism. Indeed he describes his own account of it as consisting of 'points that, without manifest prevarication, will not admit of any valid exception, of any ambiguous construction, or other sophistical evasion. Most of 'em are positive facts, deliver'd by authentic writers. . .'.[97] Such authentic writing is to be distinguished from 'the chimerical and visionary testimonies of legendary authors'.[98] though by quite what criteria one is supposed to sort the authentic from the chimerical is not made clear.[99] Toland's own account of the

95. ibid, p. 82.
96. ibid, p.10.
97. ibid, p. 39.
98. ibid, p. 41.
99. This, as James Hardiman observes in his Introduction to *Irish Minstrelsy, or the Bardic Remains of Ireland* (London, 1831), is a problem peculiar to Irish history as a whole. Given the destruction of documents and the commingling of fact and myth, so Hardiman notes, an authentic reconstruction of the country's past is particularly hard to achieve.

ancient Celtic faith is in any case closed to interpretative challenge, even though he informs us in the same book that no writing can hope to escape a variety of readings. History and fiction are almost wholly inseparable when it comes to the origins of Christianity itself, and claims to unruptured traditions completely sham; but Celtic antiquity can apparently be repossessed by the present whole and entire, and the distinction between fact and fantasy is in this case curiously watertight. The truth of the Christian gospel cannot possibly depend on so frail a foundation as 'the way of bandying about an old story for numerous generations', but in the case of early Irish Christianity such narratives are a guarantee of the genuine article rather than its betrayal.

Similar ambiguities abound in Toland's *History of the Druids*, which denounces the druids as the very prototype of a deceitful priesthood, papist clerics *avant la lettre*, yet is curiously fascinated by their esotericism. Indeed Toland, as we have seen, was quite possibly a member of various secret societies himself, and was suspected of Rosicrucian leanings in his student days in Edinburgh.[100] Druidic occultism connects to what Toland sees as an ancient tradition of secret writing in Ireland, the word *Ogham* or *Ogmius* (''tis one of the most authentic words of the language') signifying in his view both the secret of letters and the ancient Irish alphabet itself, which grows gradually unintelligible as Roman characters come to take its place. Toland likes to believe that his countrymen preserved this antique script, alongside their more modern writing, as a place where they could encrypt their secrets. Ireland, he boasts, has more ancient manuscripts than any other nation, and has been especially solicitous in preserving them; he himself, he adds in a rather cavalier gesture, will get round to cataloguing them one day. Despite this solicitude, however, some of these documents are now indecipherable though he instantly adds that in the most valuable pieces we have, it is easy enough to distinguish the authentic from the superadded. Once more, his own writing lurches between an assurance that we can possess the truth and a thoroughgoing 'textual' scepticism. The Druids themselves did not write,[101] but this, Toland implausibly assures us, is no obstacle to compiling a history of them, since there are sufficient allusions to them in the writings of others.

In a lengthy prolegomenon to this work, Toland sidetracks himself into the subject of the Celtic languages, and of language in general:

> For as every thing in the universe is the subject of writing, so an author ought to treat of every subject smoothly and correctly, as well as pertinently and perspicuously; nor ought he to be void of ornament and eloquence, where his matter peculiarly requires it. Some things want a copious style, some a concise, others to be more floridly, others to be more plainly handl'd, but all to be properly, methodically, and handsomely expressed.[102]

100. See Robert E. Sullivan, *John Toland and the Deist Controversy*, p. 3.
101. See Tom Duddy, 'Derrida and the Druids', in *Religion and Literature*, vol. 28, nos. 2–3 (Summer–Autumn, 1996).
102. John Toland, *History of the Druids* (reprinted Montrose, 1814), p. 66.

Toland, unlike Tom Paine, is not opposed to the florid or ornamental as such; there is a place for rhetoric as there is for plain speaking. But this is really a concessionary move within a stylistics which insists chiefly on pertinence and perspicuousness. Toland opposes truth to writing, elevating the unadorned truth of the gospels, which come ready-equipped with their translucent meanings, above the uncertain, open-ended, insidiously corrupting nature of oral and written tradition. He is wary of the sway of the signifier, and scornfully remarks in his *History of the Druids* that 'objects of divine worship have been coin'd out of the rhetorical flights of orators. . .'.[103] But he is clearly enthralled by textual occultism, as his pamphlet *Clidophorus* would suggest. And for one so enamoured of clarity, his own texts are remarkably ambivalent and inconsistent. Most major philosophers, he argues in *Clidophorus*, have a two-fold doctrine, the one 'exoteric' or adapted to the prejudices of the vulgar, the other 'esoteric', conformable to the nature of things and confined to the *cognoscenti*.[104] The situation becomes complicated when Toland describes how Pythagoras spoke to his esoteric audience 'in a plain, perspicuous, and copious speech', and to his exoteric one 'in a perplex'd, obscure, and enigmatical manner'[105] – the point being that you can be frank with fellow initiates but must conceal the truth from the vulgar.

The reasons for this split between science and ideology, or truth and *doxa*, are at root political. It is the tyranny of priestly censorship and persecution which has forced the philosophers into ambiguity, equivocation, coded utterances. 'Daily experience sufficiently evinces', Toland observes, 'that there is no discovery, at least no declaring of TRUTH in most places, but at the hazard of a man's reputation, imployment, or life'.[106] The priests couch their doctrine in equivocal terms lest, being clearly seen as charlatans, the mob should laugh at them; the philosophers obscure their true doctrine for fear of being denounced by both priests and mob. Textual secrecy is the child of political domination, giving rise in philosophical discourse to 'shiftings, ambiguities, equivocations, and hypocrisy in all its shapes. . .'.[107] Toland's attitude to this discursive indeterminacy is itself interestingly ambivalent. On the one hand, he stresses its necessity if truth is to survive the machinations of power; on the other hand, as the word 'hypocrisy' indicates, it is a palpable affront to his faith in lucid meaning.[108]

103. ibid, p. 88.
104. Archbishop Richard Whately's influential *Elements of Rhetoric* (Dublin, 1865), while generally urging a perspicuity of style, allows that obscurity may be employed when some truth might be rejected out of hand if expressed directly (see pp. 172–3).
105. *Clidophorus*, p. 73.
106. ibid, p. 67.
107. ibid, p. 68.
108. A rather similar interplay between definiteness and secrecy is to be found in Henry O'Brien's *The Round Towers of Ireland*, which at one point claims to have a 'true interpretation' of a word in Irish relating to round towers, but darkly refuses to say what it is (London, 1898 edition, p. 51).

But the ambivalence runs deeper. The Toland who champions clarity is the apologist for an ideal of the people; the one who sees the need for enigma is the radical élitist for whom the actual people are the 'property' of the priests. Candour and plainness of expression would be preferable in the utopian long run; but for this discursive change to come about, a political transformation would first be necessary, establishing 'full and impartial liberty'. Meanwhile, as long as there is an unholy alliance between scheming clerics and red-necked mob, the subtext of secrecy which Toland claims to have uncovered throughout the history of philosophy is positive and necessary, as the one place in a politically deceitful world where truth may be preserved. The mode of philosophical communication must necessarily be sibylline and oblique, and thus at odds with the lucidity of the content. Power splits form and content down the middle.

There is another way of viewing this running battle in Toland between exoteric and esoteric. According to some commentators, Toland was a pantheistic materialist for whom the world was God's body, and who saw this doctrine as the concealed core of an ancient hermetic lineage passed from the Greek and Asiatic sages to the Druids and Giordano Bruno. In *Pantheisticon*, he sees the whole of creation as animated by ethereal fire, a kind of super-subtle matter much like the elusive ether of *Siris*, though Berkeley himself is of course neither pantheist nor materialist. All of this belongs to the esoteric side of Toland's thought; but this vision of a universe of eternal recurrence, in which infinite variations of motion play themselves out within an immutable whole, is also highly 'exoteric' – nothing less, in fact, than a kind of cosmic Enlightenment materialism, which oddly prefigures the secular materialist world-view of James Joyce as well as the cyclical Nature of W. B. Yeats. Indeed one thing which Toland believed would eternally recur, self-identical yet ceaselessly different, was John Toland, who as the epitaph he wrote for himself states 'is frequently to rise himself, yet never to be the same Toland again'. This, in fact, is not a bad description of Toland's actual life, however it might apply to his risen self. The point, however, is that, as often in Irish thought, the ancient and the avant-garde form strange bedfellows. Modern science is just antique mystery recycled, reconfirming the Nature religion of the Druids; but the masses are not yet ready for the disclosure of this truth, so that the most 'exoteric' of perceptions – a materialist theory of the universe which has banished all transcendence – must ironically remain the property of an esoteric élite. Just as for Freud the veil hides the fact that it is concealing nothing, so the greatest secret of all, as Toland writes in his *Letters to Serena*, is that Nature is all there is.

There is, even so, a distinction between this politically essential reticence, and a purely ideological attitude towards truth which fosters superstition so as 'to keep the common people in good order'.[109] Toland accepts that the scriptures need to use symbol and metaphor to illustrate the divine essence

109.   *Clidophorus*, p. 81.

and its properties; but he also has a Platonic suspicion of fiction and fable in general, and holds that they have no place in religious discourse. Once you allow that fact may be exemplified by fable, the whole vital dichotomy threatens to crumble to nothing in your hands: 'who can accurately distinguish, whether the point in question be a real matter of fact, or a fable invented at pleasure? when we see the learned and unlearned, whole communities and nations, divided on the subject. What is a history to CAIUS, is a fable to PUBLIUS.'[110] A fictional supplement to the truth will end up supplanting it altogether, ruining the distinction between history and fable on which Christian faith relies. Toland, as we have seen, in fact discerns just such an 'undecidability' of history and fable in the early origins of Christianity; but when it comes to the sacred texts themselves, magically extricated from their problematical history, no such deconstruction can be tolerated. This literalism is in the cause of political dissent: the common people are not to be duped with fairy-tales dreamed up by their rulers in order to keep them docile. The more élitist side of Toland, however, aware of how firmly in the grip of false consciousness the people actually are, feels the allures of esotericism. If he is enough of a radical *Aufklärer* not to wish the people deceived, he is also well aware of their ideological bigotry, and so of the need for strategic deception. And in this, ironically, he is close to Berkeley.

Toland's scholarly forays into textual history, however critical in intent, threaten to deconstruct his own faith in a truth quarantined from the ravages of time and interpretation. If he is loath to admit that truth bears the mark of the material signifier in the case of the gospels, he finds himself unable to avoid this conclusion when inspecting other kinds of writing. He contrasts the self-evident simplicity of the New Testament with priestly obscurantism; yet he also acknowledges that our grasp of the gospel has been 'miserably deform'd and almost ruin'd by those unintelligible and extravagant terms. . .'.[111] In claiming that truth is immutable, he ends up by confessing that all writing breeds multiple readings; in drawing upon notions of authentic textual transmission, he also puts them unavoidably into question. His own words must be taken in context, so he complains, but appeals to context are in other contexts dangerously relativist. In *Christianity not Mysterious* he rejects the scriptural commentary of the ancient Fathers as 'so multifarious, and inconsistent with it self, as to make it impossible for any body to believe so many contradictions at once';[112] yet the New Testament itself is mysteriously dispensed from any such textual slipperiness. In the same work, Toland asserts that reason is always clear in itself, but notes that the *word* 'is become as equivocal and ambiguous as any other'.[113] The signifier is plagued and

110. ibid, pp. 85–6.
111. *Christianity not Mysterious*, p. 148.
112. ibid, p. 2.
113. ibid, p. 8.

tainted, but what it signifies remains serenely self-identical. There is, he believes, a pure rational faculty in every individual; it is just that the actual use of this faculty is often exceedingly corrupt. This is rather like arguing that everyone's eyesight is in principle perfect; it is just the state of their vision which leaves something to be desired.

Other such inconsistencies litter Toland's writings. Evidence, he informs us, is the infallible rule by which propositions are to be judged: 'It is impossible for us to err as long as we take *evidence* as our guide. . .'.[114] But the idea that the evidence itself may be obscure and contentious seems not to strike him. Moreover, if the evidence compels us to assent to certain utterances, why is it that some individuals deny them? Because, Toland ripostes, what is perspicuous to me may be obscure to you. But to argue, as he does, that perspicuity is a relative matter is to account for why some people refuse the self-evident only at the risk of undermining his own rationalism. It leaves his own perspicuity open to being defined as obscurantism; indeed one of his more dim-witted or dishonest critics claimed to find *Christianity not Mysterious* itself 'mysterious, abstruse and intricate'.[115] To believe in scripture 'reasonably' is to believe it 'not upon its own bare assertion, but from a real testimony consisting in the evidence of the things contain'd therein; from undoubted effects, and not from words and letters. . .'.[116] Once again, capricious signifier and rock-solid signified must be judiciously separated.

Toland sees faith as founded on reason and evidence, but this then makes it hard to distinguish from certain knowledge. For Christian orthodoxy, faith is indeed a matter of certainty rather than probability, but not because its object is rationally self-evident. If it were, then no one could help believing, and faith would be no sort of merit. Like Bishop Berkeley and Archbishop King, Toland is a kind of pragmatist about knowledge, holding as he does that the only understanding which matters is one which concerns our own needs and uses. Truth in the end means truth for us, and both Toland and Berkeley – deadly enemies in so many respects – share a scepticism of metaphysical essences. We do not need to know things in themselves to know them truly, only as they relate to us. This move, as we have seen, then allows Toland to counter the case that to know something for sure would mean grasping it in all of its labyrinthine complexity. He sees well enough that this is just a mistake about the word 'know', of the kind made by, say, those modern-day ultra-deconstructionists for whom, since we cannot totalise the potentially infinite textuality of any given element, we cannot be said to have a certain grasp of it all. But the price for Toland of rebuffing this particular objection to rationality is to let in the thin edge of relativism, as a pragmatist notion of knowledge enters into conflict with a high-rationalist conception of it.

114.   ibid, p. 19.
115.   See Oliver Hill, *A Rod for the Back of a Fool* (London, 1702), p. 14.
116.   ibid, p. 32.

Toland's defence of plain style, like Tom Paine's, involves a politics of literary form. In good populist fashion, he wants to oppose the intelligible to
the obscurantist, convinced that indeterminacy is merely the priest's way of
not having to justify his privileges. Yet the more he delves into the business
of writing, the more this distinction between the plain and the pluralistic is
cast into doubt. The militant populist in Toland is at war with the scholar who
appreciates complexity and is beguiled by the occult. We find a similar tension in Swift's *A Tale of a Tub*, which declares itself written 'for the universal
improvement of mankind', yet which is ridden with occultism and inscribes
on its title page a piece of meaningless Hebrew which was a snatch of jargon
repeated by heretics in initiation rites.[117] We have noted a rather similar combination in the case of Berkeley, who also believes that the esoteric philosopher must take account of prejudice when speaking exoterically to the
common people. For Berkeley, moreover, the everyday and the esoteric are
not wholly at odds with each other. Since common sense for Berkeley is itself
shot through with ambiguity, there is, at one level at least, no real break
between the discourse of divinity and our routine understandings. Toland, as
we have seen, argues for a similar continuity, but in a way which dispenses
with mystery altogether. In the end, the difference between the two men is
that Berkeley appeals in populist vein to everyday indeterminacy, the rough
ground of our common life,[118] but does so as a way of reinforcing a theological authority which keeps the common people in their place. Toland, for his
part, wishes to demystify that authority in order to set them free – but not yet.
Demystification must be deferred; and this leaves the radical who nourishes
the plain truth in prudent secrecy looking uncomfortably like the priest who
keeps it hidden in order to strengthen his sway over others.

The man who reported Toland's *Christianity not Mysterious* to the public magistrate, which led to the book being condemned by ideologues who had not
read a word of it and burnt no less than twice by the public hangman, was
Peter Browne, Fellow and later Provost of Trinity College.[119] When Browne
was later promoted to the bishopric of Cork, Toland drolly claimed the credit.
    The political conflict between Toland and the Anglican divines is over the
question of authority. If Toland is right about the scope of reason, then the

---

117. See J. A. Downie, *Jonathan Swift: Political Writer* (London, 1984), ch. 6. See also
      for the estoericism of the *Tale* Miriam Starkman, *Swift's Satire on Learning in 'A
      Tale of a Tub'* (Princeton, 1950), and Ronald Paulson, *Theme and Structure in
      Swift's 'Tale of a Tub'* (New Haven, 1960).
118. For an excellent treatment of Wittgenstein's 'rough ground' concept in terms of
      the contrast between *techne* and *phronesis*, see Joseph Dunne, *Back to the Rough
      Ground* (Notre Dame, 1993).
119. For a lucid account of Browne's career, see Arthur Robert Winnett, *Peter Browne*
      (London, 1974).

clergy are out of a job. The theological wrangles between them, on the other hand, are really over the semiotics of sublimity. They are hermeneutical in the etymological sense of the term, concerned with secrets and enigmas. Toland himself distinguishes between mysteries which spring from some inherently plain truth being camouflaged by, say, clerics, and propositions which are innately inconceivable however clearly they may be expressed. One might express this distinction semiotically as one between a cryptic signifier linked to a luminous signified, and a lucid signifier coupled with an opaque signified. The Christian gospel, Toland claims, contains only mysteries of the former kind; the whole point of it is that truths which were previously concealed have now been disclosed in Christ, whose own language in scripture is scarcely recondite. There can be no theological truth against or beyond reason, since it is senseless to speak of assenting to the unintelligible.

The idea of an obscure truth, however, needs more explaining than Toland grants it. Words like 'clear' and 'obscure' pertain to language rather than to the world. There can be no states of affairs which are obscure in themselves, as there can be states of affairs which are dangerous or farcical in themselves. Situations can be *complex*, but complex situations can be clearly described, just as simple ones can be obscurely depicted. God seems the nearest we can come to a truth obscure in itself, since nobody could possibly comprehend him, but even he is presumably not a mystery to himself. Things like square circles or married bachelors are inconceivable in the sense of being illogical, but the words 'square circle' and 'married bachelor' are perfectly intelligible in themselves. One understands the meaning of the *words*, if not the *meaning* of the words. This, then, would be an instance of a plain signifier yoked to an impenetrable signified.

Peter Browne agrees with Toland that one cannot believe what one understands nothing of. The Ascendancy theologian Edward Synge, in his *A Supplement to a Gentleman's Religion*, is likewise quite at one with Toland that divine truths must not be esoteric but available to all.[120] But this for Browne is beside the point. Toland is pitching the notion of comprehension too high: there are plenty of options between clear and distinct ideas on the one hand, and utter unfathomability on the other. Browne sees in his *Letter in Answer to a Book Entitled 'Christianity not Mysterious'* that there are various modes and degrees of intelligibility, and various transactions between them: we have some clear and distinct ideas which lead us to believe in other ideas of which we have only a confused and imperfect understanding. Indeed we assent to all kinds of things of which we have less than exact understanding. This, in effect, is how theological language works: we know what a father is, and so transfer this analogously to God even though, since he presumably has no testicles, we can really have no idea of what we mean in affirming this. All we know is that God is as *truly* a 'father' as a natural father is, even though what

120.   Edward Synge, *A Supplement to a Gentleman's Religion* (Dublin, 1733), pp. 70–1.

it means for him to be this is entirely incomprehensible. We have no proper idea at all of God's real nature; but we have some useful improper ideas of it, by analogy with our own. Edmund Burke will inherit this doctrine in his aesthetic treatise, which speaks of the unintelligibility of God.

Browne, then, proposes a two-tier semiotic system, in which a language in which signifier and signified are wholly at one becomes in turn the signifier of truths which cannot be properly signified. Theological discourse thus has the structure of allegory. The first system is wholly lucid: to say that the Father begot the Son is in one sense just as intelligible as to say that I begot a son, even if in another sense we have no clue as to what this could mean. Browne is drawing here on something like Frege's distinction between *Sinn* and *Bedeutung* – between knowing a meaning in the sense of knowing how to use a word, and knowing a meaning in the sense of grasping the context within which a specific use of a word makes sense. Browne himself would express this in his own philosophical jargon as the difference between the meaning and the substance of a term. Theological talk involves the ambiguous, polyvalent and unrepresentable, extrapolating from one code to another rather than, as in some more logocentric notion of language, seeing a transcendent meaning as incarnating itself directly in a material sign. Browne's theory of the *logos* is not a theory of the *Logos*. For him, one determinate meaning can signify another indeterminate one, in a way which slides a division between signifier and signified.[121] Toland, by contrast, holds to the sign as realist or representational – as a seamless unity of word and concept which banishes interpretative ambiguity. For Toland, theological language is 'proper'; for Browne it is just one catachresis after another.

In his major philosophical treatise, *The Procedure, Extent, and Limits of Human Understanding*, Browne's theology leads him to deconstruct the opposition between literal and figurative discourse. God is not literally Jesus's father, but to claim that he is is not just a figure of speech either. The analogical occupies some third space between the two; though it is worth adding that if Browne had a less 'literalist' conception of the figurative, he might not have needed this extra category in the first place. 'Mere metaphor' is just the flipside of 'hard fact'. And Browne's critics pressed him more than once on how there can be an analogy betwen the finite and the infinite, two utterly incommensurable realms. As usual, however, there is a politics to this semiotics. Christian doctrine must be determinate enough for there to be something to be believed – here Browne is at one with his rationalist arch-opponent – but it must also finally elude this determinacy if the transcendent authority of God, and so the authority of his commissars on earth, is to be safeguarded from rationalist reduction. We have seen a rather similar problem in the case of Berkeley,

---

121.   The starkest example in Irish writing of this interplay of the determinate and indeterminate is surely Samuel Beckett, whose writing, as we shall see in chapter 9, is at once exact and elusive, weaving imponderables with pedantic precision.

caught as he is in *Siris* between the need to ground the world but not thereby to reduce its mystery. 'Aether' or its analogues, in the eighteenth century, was always a convenient verbal resolution of this dilemma. Like Berkeley, Browne confronts the problem of how to preserve mystery without emptying the world to the ineffable, and so like the mystics or symbolist poets cancelling out his own discourse. Berkeley himself certainly thought Browne and his colleagues in dire danger of offering us a God who was entirely unknowable, and thus no sort of God at all. On the other hand, if reality is made too determinate, one risks selling the pass to the politically dissident rationalists. It is not for nothing that Browne's major theological treatise ends with a political assault on Toland. Theology is on the defensive in an empiricist age which equates knowledge with clear, distinct ideas, a clarity with which God-talk is distressingly ill-supplied. Like literature, then, such talk needs to insist that it means something, but not in accordance with the dominant canons of meaning. Like any other language, theology cannot get along without a metaphysical jargon of substance and process, essence and appearance; it is just that it is aware at the same time of how violently this betrays the reality of a God who is nothing whatsoever.

Browne sees shrewdly that one way out of this embarrassment is to challenge the dominant model of knowledge. There are, so he maintains in Lockeian style, simple ideas which are 'an *immediate* and direct representation of the object, [which] is perceived without the mediation or *intervention* of any other object or idea whatsoever'.[122] Our representations of material things would seem to him, curiously enough, non-differential and non-relational. But there are, he insists, more mediated forms of understanding too, which extrapolate from these more direct acts of cognition or use them as analogies. He thus endorses and refuses empiricism at the same time, underwriting its theory of sense-perception while insisting that there is more to knowledge than this. (In fact, he should have turned the argument on its head, pointing out that our knowledge of concrete objects is itself mediated, and that we can sometimes grasp an abstract truth just as 'directly' as we can sometimes recognise a coathanger. True to his empiricist roots, Browne regards general truths as complex and indistinct, and particular ones as clear and direct; for Karl Marx, by contrast, it was the concrete which was complex and the abstract which was simple.) The relation between heavenly truths and our own representations of them is in Browne's view rather like that between things and their reflections in a mirror. It both is and is not accurate to say that we 'see a man' in the glass: the image we actually see has no more of the substance or essence of a man than has his shadow, but we speak even so of 'seeing' a human form. Browne here contributes his widow's mite to an Irish preoccupation with mirrors which runs from Maria Edgeworth to James Joyce; indeed just as for him we

122.   Peter Browne, *The Procedure, Extent, and Limits of Human Understanding* (London, 1728), p. 103.

do and don't see something real in the mirror, so Oscar Wilde's middle-class Caliban rages both when he does and does not glimpse his own unlovely lineaments in the glass.

Much of Browne's anti-representational argument was anticipated by William King, Archbishop of Dublin and doughty apologist of Ascendancy.[123] King argues in his *Divine Predestination and Foreknowledge* that our language about God bears something like the oblique relation to God himself that a map does to the terrain it depicts, and that we can no more have a true notion of him than a blind man can have of colour. King sees that some of the difficulties which arise in theology spring from taking figurative language literally, or as Wittgenstein will later put it, illicitly conflating one language-game with another. Similarly, in his major theological work *On the Origin of Evil*, King claims eirenically that different moral views are just alternative ways of discursively framing the same objects.[124] For him as for Browne, theological language is analogical speech, and the example he chooses to illustrate this is nothing less than language itself. If, he points out, 'we were to describe to an ignorant *American* what we mean by *writing*, and told him, that it is a way of making words *visible* and *permanent*, so that persons, at any distance of time and place, may be able to see and understand them', this would no doubt seem curious to the American, who 'might object, that the thing must be impossible, for *words* are not to be *seen*, but *heard*, they pass in their speaking, and it is impossible that they should affect the absent, much less those that live in distant ages'.[125] The oral is to the written as common experience is to divine truth; spoken words are to written ones as 'three persons' is to 'Trinity'. The figure is interestingly perverse: against its own intentions, it offers writing as an image of the living *Logos*, and the invisibility of oral language as a type of the everyday rather than of that which transcends it. It would surely be more logical to equate the evanescence of speech with the mystery of God, and writing with the sublunary stuff which imperfectly translates it into material terms. What deflects this logic may be the priorities of an oral culture, in which, for the Archbishop of Dublin as much as for *Tristram Shandy*, it is speech which is normative and script which is a roundabout, mysterious mode of it.

123. See for King's latter role his *The State of the Protestants in Ireland* (London, 1691), and his *Of the Bogs and Loughs of Ireland* (Dublin, 1685), which offers the bogs of Ireland as testimony of Irish indolence. For a scholarly account of King and his works, see David Greenwood, *William King: Tory and Jacobite* (Oxford, 1969).

124. William King, *An Essay on the Origin of Evil* (London, 1731), p. xii. The original Latin text of this work, *De Origine Mali*, was published in Dublin in 1702.

125. William King, *Divine Predestination and Foreknowledge* (Dublin, 1709), p. 16. One takes it that by 'ignorant American' King is referring to native Americans, unless the process known today as 'dumbing down' set in rather earlier than is generally considered.

If the divine is unknowable, what is the point of revelation? King's answer is a pragmatic one. Theological language, like literary discourse, is really performative utterance masquerading as constative speech. Its point is not to describe an object (one recalls Lenin's gibe that theology is a subject without an object), but to breed certain effects in the listener, and so, in the terms of modern linguistics, to be conative rather than referential. What looks like the indicative is really the imperative. Just as for Berkeley Nature itself is a kind of rhetoric, so for his fellow Anglicans God is a sort of rhetoric too, a language which gets something done, a truth known only in its consequences.[126] God is a way of doing things. We cannot know what God is in himself, only in his transformative effect on our practice. To claim that God is good is rather like saying that there is colour in the rainbow or light in the sun, rather than seeing light as just an effect of the sun in us. Ordinary theological discourse is reificatory, as much of our commonplace speech is for the later Wittgenstein. It turns into a graven image that which is the condition of all representation. It was Nietzsche who prophesised that God would not be abolished until we had transformed our grammar.

For King and Browne, by contrast, theological utterances are just ways of moving us to appropriate states of conduct or mind, such as awe, admiration, obedience, dependency, gratitude and the like. These utterances are, in Althusserian terms, 'ideological' rather than 'theoretical', but have fallen victim to a naive epistemological realism which imagines that, say, God is omniscient in the sense that he knows everything whereas I know just a few things, that he has foreknowledge in much the same way that I might get a glimpse of what is going to happen next Tuesday, or that he created the world rather like a cook rustles up an omelette but with rather fewer raw materials at his disposal. This just ignores the fact that God does not know or foresee or create in anything even remotely like the sense that we do. The point of divine discourse is not cognitive but political: it is 'to teach and oblige us to live reasonably, to perform our duty to God, our neighbours and our selves, to conquer and mortify our passions and lusts, to make us beneficent and charitable to men, and to oblige us to love, obey and depend upon God'.[127] You do not need ever to have seen your prince, King remarks, in order to honour him; 'it is not necessary that we should personally know our Governor to oblige us to perform our duty to him. . .'.[128] Indeed one might add that the less one knows one's lord, the more numinous and authoritative he becomes. There is a link here between the theology of King at the opening of the eighteenth century and the politics of Burke at its close.

There is a link also between the conservative Anglican theologians and what, later in the eighteenth century, will come to be known as sentiment or

126.   There are perhaps remote resonances here of Spinoza's doctrine of a structure or substance known only in its effects.
127.   King, *Divine Predestination*, p. 19.
128.   ibid, p. 21.

sensibility. The politics of these two currents, like much else about them, may well diverge; but they have something epistemologically in common, in their common rejection of rationalism for the language of the affections, their concern less with the object than with our relation to it, their shared preference for the emotive utterance. This was a preference of Berkeley's too, though he disagreed with the view that God's attributes were unknowable in themselves. If, as we shall see in the next chapter, there was a major Irish contribution to the cult of sensibility, and if the official dominant discourse of the society – theology – was cast in non-cognitive mode, then this is partly because, with a few stalwart exceptions like John Toland, rationalism never took root in this intensely religious, custom-bound society. There is no Irish tradition equivalent to that of Descartes, Leibniz, Spinoza; and the effects of this absence on Irish culture's view of the relations between body and mind, not to speak of a whole host of kindred subjects, is still to be properly explored.

THE GOOD-NATURED GAEL

Consider a clutch of names associated with the mid-eighteenth century English movement of sensibility and sentimentalism: Steele, Hume, Ferguson, Burns, Goldsmith, Adam Smith, Mackenzie, Hugh Blair, Frances Sheridan, Sterne, Charlotte Brooke, Henry Brooke, Hutcheson, Macpherson, Burke, Macklin, Hugh Kelly, David Fordyce. All of these authors are either Irish or Scottish; and when the London-born poet Thomas Gray wished for an emotional pattern more plangent and intense than the suavely modulated feeling of his 'Elegy Written in a Country Churchyard', it was to the figure of a Welsh bard that he turned. What is the significance of this extraordinary predominance of Gaels in the culture of 'English' sensibility? Why is it, as Brian Coleborne claims, that 'some of the late eighteenth-century Anglo-Irish poets . . . tend to be more sentimental than their English counterparts'?[1] Can it be that Gaels are more affectionate, more genial and intuitive, than the emotionally inhibited English?

Such a suggestion is bound to offend the liberal or radical conscience, and for excellent reasons. To view the Gael as genetically warm-hearted would itself be an egregious example of sentimentalism. The Irish Irelander D. P. Moran writes of his compatriots that 'good nature we have always with us', but those who felt the lash of Moran's satirical tongue may well have demurred.[2] Yet though ethnic stereotyping has wreaked untold damage in human affairs, it is perhaps time, after all the postmodern clamour against such 'essentialising', to put in a good word for it. For a materialist thinker, it would be remarkable if men and women who had for a lengthy period shared roughly the same conditions of material life revealed no psychological traits in common. Within such shared life-forms, to be sure, there are enormous divergences of class, gender, region, occupation, ethnic provenance and the like; but many features will nonetheless be common to a people who inhabit more or less the same history, and one would expect on materialist grounds that these would show up to some degree in their habits of mind, patterns of behaviour and emotional dispositions. Stereotypes are not to be confused with reality, and many of them are simply baseless; but they may occasionally provide clues to specific social conditions. The image of the immigrant Irish labourer as powerful but feckless, careless of tomorrow and much given to festivity, has some basis in the fact that small-farming in Ireland did indeed demand sustained bouts of muscular work, but in a sporadic, non-industrial

1. Introduction to 'Anglo-Irish Verse, 1675–1825', in Seamus Deane (ed.), *The Field Day Anthology of Irish Writing* (Derry, 1991), vol.1, p. 395.
2. D. P. Moran, *The Philosophy of Irish Ireland* (Dublin, 1905), p. 7.

rhythm which allowed for a fair degree of leisure time. On a rented small-holding, moreover, working harder might not be especially profitable to the tenant himself (what mattered was the size of your farm, not your productivity), and might even prove the reverse if the landlord confiscated your improvements by raising the rent. The emotional anaesthesia of the English upper classes has more to do with the public school system and the demands of running an empire than with some genetic deficiency of Englishness. The English, stereotypically speaking, are not an unemotional people, simply hamstrung in expressing the stuff; and this is no doubt one reason why they have sometimes taken a guarded delight in the supposedly more extrovert Gael, as one warms to those in polite company who have the nerve to blurt out what everyone else is impolitely thinking. If the English left you to bleed to death in the gutter, it would not be because of hard-heartedness, but because they were anxious not to interfere with your privacy.

There is nothing necessarily essentialist in claiming that the English upper classes have typically exhibited a certain emotional reserve, in contrast, say, to the characteristic emotional disposition of working-class Greeks or Italians. Nor does one refute the stereotype by pointing to the swollen ranks of convivial English and ungregarious Greeks, a response which involves a simple misunderstanding of the term 'stereotype'. There is no need to imagine, as many a postmodern theorist seems to, that to attribute a set of characteristics to a people is falsely to ascribe to them some timeless racial essence. One hears that Bill Gates's employees tend to display remarkably similar psychological traits – a fact which is no doubt a condition of their remaining his employees – but it would be curious to assume that this was because of some spiritual essence in which they all mystically participate, rather than because they have all been thoroughly brainwashed into a particular character pattern. It is striking how a supposedly 'materialist' criticism today has overlooked this partial truth of stereotypes, lapsing as it does into the liberal-humanist piety that stereotyping is nothing more than a racist or sexist ploy on the part of our rulers. For such critics, 'cultural specificities' is an acceptable category, whereas 'national characteristics' is mysteriously not. The materialism of the eighteenth century, lamentably mechanistic though it could be, understood the complex relations between region, climate, economy, social institutions, cultural life and 'national character' far better than some more sophisticated materialist thought of our own epoch.

Indeed not only did modern materialist thought begin with the Enlightenment rather than with Marx; it began with that now most scorned of 'idealist' creeds, cultural nationalism. It was an eighteenth-century 'national' preoccupation with the relations between culture, place, people, language, history and social conditions, which first laid the groundwork for what was later to become an historical–materialist concern with the relation of spiritual phenomena to their material surroundings. Cultural materialism has its roots in 'national' sociology; and this, in what were then the British isles, was much more a matter of the Gaelic peripheries than of the metropolitan centre, from where we derive the quite different cultural ideology of timeless, universal values spun out by solitary geniuses. For broadly political reasons, the peripheries were more likely to relate their culture to their historical circumstances.

It is not, needless to say, that Gaels are necessarily more genial than the English, a proposition which many an eighteenth-century landlord would have taken leave to doubt. It is rather that they have been on the whole more *congenial*. They have been, as the etymological root of that term suggests, more of the *gens* or clan,[3] members of societies in which the ideology of possessive individualism arrived rather later than in England, and which, when it emerged, found itself at odds with some still-powerful residues of clannish custom and tradition. Gladys Bryson remarks in her study of the eighteenth-century Scottish Enlightenment that some of its theorists anticipated the German sociologist Tönnies's distinction between *Gemeinschaft* and *Gesellschaft* – between a social order founded on kinship and custom, and one based upon more impersonal or contractual relations. While these thinkers accepted, by and large, the inevitable transition from the one to the other, it is a feature of their thought, so Bryson argues, that 'much of the sentiment and loyalty of the older *Gemeinschaft* carries over into the *Gesellschaft* . . . we find in all their writings great attention to communication, sympathy, imitation, habit and convention. . .'.[4] John Dwyer agrees that the Scottish drive to a refined, advanced economy incorporated a concern for the preservation of national integrity and a traditionalist moral suspicion of unbridled commercialism. 'Sociability, not individualism', he writes, ' was the critical ingredient in the Scottish definition of sensibility';[5] the need to cherish moral community in an increasingly self-interested social order. And Alasdair MacIntyre claims that the Scottish Enlightenment's rationalist belief in a stock of self-evident first principles has one of its sources in the common fund of taken-for-granted beliefs of a pre-modern society.[6]

3.   The term 'clan' is not to be taken too literally. Eoin Mac Neill among others casts doubt on the idea of some fully-fledged Irish 'clan system' (*Phases of Irish History*, Dublin, 1919, ch. 10).

4.   Gladys Bryson, *Man and Society: The Scottish Inquiry of the Eighteenth Century* (Princeton, 1945), pp. 172, 146–7. See also, for an excellent account of eighteenth-century Scotland, Peter Womack, *Improvement and Romance* (London, 1989).

5.   John Dwyer, *Virtuous Discourse: Sensibility and Community in late Eighteenth-Century Scotland* (Edinburgh, 1987), p. 39. The germ of this book can be found in Dwyer's essay ' "A Peculiar Blessing": Social Converse in Scotland from Hutcheson to Burns', in *Eighteenth-Century Life*, vol. 15, nos. 1 and 2 (February and May, 1991). See also I. Hont and M. Ignatieff (eds.), *Wealth and Virtue: The Shaping of Political Economy in the Scottish Enlightenment* (Cambridge, 1982).

6.   Alasdair MacIntyre, *Whose Justice? Which Rationality?* (London, 1988), p. 223. The book contains a valuable chapter on Francis Hutcheson.

In the 'stagist' evolutionary theories of these writers, history is a matter of progress; but in Hegelian style each historical stage subsumes rather than cancels the preceding one, so that modernity is supposed to preserve some of the distinctive features of the more communitarian order it outstrips. In his *Essay on the History of Civil Society*, Adam Ferguson gloomily contrasts the solidarity of a closely knit tribal culture with the 'detached and solitary' individuals of modern commercial society, in which 'the bands of affection are broken'. Despite the prevalence of malice, envy, competition, Ferguson is still able to believe that 'love and compassion are the most powerful principles in the human breast'.[7] His colleague Adam Smith, despite his enthusiasm for the market place, thought commerce was spiritually debilitating, a judgement which his present-day disciples have triumphantly vindicated. Most of these thinkers, Bryson observes, espoused an 'ethics of feeling';[8] and the virulently anti-Gaelic Samuel Johnson found them all too complicit with nationalist mythologies. It was such progressive intellectuals who funded James Macpherson's antiquarian pursuits, just as eighteenth-century Irish champions of 'modern' civil liberties were also often enough custodians of traditional culture. Indeed the author of the *Ossian* poems became a kind of middleman between the Edinburgh literati, anxious to construct for themselves a suitably venerable cultural heritage, and the verse-reciting folk of the Isles and Highlands, who supplied Macpherson with some of the fragments necessary for his project. Travelling to far-flung outposts of cultural production, Macpherson would relieve them of their oral booty and bear it back, suitably edited and refined, to the Scottish capital.[9] He was himself a transitional figure between *Gemeinschaft* and *Gesellschaft*, between the clan society into which he was born and the world of polite letters to which he aspired.[10] Katie Trumpener writes of his *Ossian* that it 'announces the end of an heroic age and the beginning of a sentimental one',[11] while Fiona Stafford sees Macpherson as introducing into his translations 'a vein of sentimentality and wistful lyricism that is not to be found in the original Gaelic'.[12]

7.   Adam Ferguson, *An Essay on the History of Civil Society* (reprinted Dublin, 1767), p. 53. There is a useful account of Ferguson's attitudes to social progress in Peter Stein, 'Law and Society in Scottish Thought', in N. T. Phillipson and Rosalind Mitchinson (eds.), *Scotland in the Age of Improvement* (Edinburgh, 1970).

8.   ibid, p. 27.

9.   See Fiona Stafford, *The Sublime Savage* (Edinburgh, 1988).

10.   There may here be an indirect relation between two Gaels, Macpherson and Richard Steele. Fiona Stafford writes of how Macpherson turned to the periodicals to refine his literary taste, and it seems to have been Steele's *Tatler* and the *Spectator* which first created a market for these in Scotland. See Stafford, pp. 41–2.

11.   Katie Trumpener, *Bardic Nationalism* (Princeton, New Jersey, 1997), p. 76.

12.   Stafford, *The Sublime Savage*, p. 127.

The Scottish *Aufklärer* were men for whom, *contra* Hobbes, human society was natural to individuals, an extension of domestic kinship, the gregarious medium in which individuals came to self-consciousness. Indeed to view the faculty of benevolence as natural, in the manner of Francis Hutcheson and David Hume, is just another way of claiming that sociality is of the essence of humanity. And it would surely be perverse not to relate this philosophical creed, however obliquely, to the fact that, good modern *bourgeois* though these intellectuals were, they sprang from Gaelic fringes which as colonial enclaves had been slower to modernise than the metropolitan English centre, a centre which housed the oldest capitalist class in the world. It is hardly surprising that a culture of sensibility, one which hymned the virtues of benevolence, fellow-feeling and human solidarity, should have crept into that metropolitan society from Gaelic margins which were still in some ways premodern – far-flung peripheries in which the grip of custom, the authority of kinship and tradition, the social importance of personal affiliations, were fighting a rearguard action against the sway of political contractualism and economic individualism, as well as with the sovereignty of law over sentiment. Charles Kingsley writes in his 1859 preface to the Irishman Henry Brooke's *The Fool of Quality*, a novel which runs to five volumes of swooning and snivelling, that 'The characters [in the novel] are gifted with a passionate and tearful sensibility, which is rather French or Irish than English, and which will irritate, if not disgust, many whose Teutonic temperament leads them to pride themselves rather on the repression than the expression of emotion. . .'.

It may well be, then, that these Scottish thinkers had something in common with the German idealists who were to follow them. Just as Karl Marx saw that idealism as a kind of modernity of the mind which compensated for backward political conditions, a nurturing in the realm of spirit of a progress which was still not possible in historical reality, so the eighteenth-century Gaelic intelligentsia draw some of their most precious insights from a social history which lags behind the nation of Hobbes, Locke and Mandeville. Precisely because of their backwardness, certain forms of collective cultural consciousness, later to be associated with 'progressive' currents of thought, were able to spring up in these impoverished spots far earlier than they did in England itself. It was a time-warp which was to be repeated earlier in our own century, with the flourishing of a distinctively Irish modernism. It may also be significant in this respect that the grandfather of all such 'sentimentalism', the English neo-Platonic philosopher Shaftesbury, was the intellectual offspring of a pre-modern, aristocratic English polity at war with the bourgeois mean-spiritedness of Hobbesian man. Ideologically speaking, Shaftesbury was an internal émigré within English middle-class society, a residue of nobility, serenity and blitheness of spirit in an increasingly utilitarian milieu. It is intriguing, then, how English patrician and Gaelic outsider, laird and gamekeeper, join hands in a common front against the ideologues of unfeeling Reason.

It is not, then, a question of the convivial yet melancholic Celt with a song on his lips and a tear in his eye, one hand wrapped around the ale-jug and the other thrust out in affable welcome to the stranger. It is a question of the way in which, in family-based agrarian communities, personal and social relationships are less easily separable than they are in the market-places or political institutions of modernity. It is no easy task to distinguish blood-ties from social relations on the family farm; and if one wanted a suitably inglorious material base for the finer flights of 'Gaelic sentiment', one might do worse than discover it here. If the 'sentiments' have a central place in such traditionalist orders, it is not because such communities are not often brutally utilitarian in their dealings, and certainly not a matter of the spontaneous impulses of the heart. The Gaelic peasantry was every bit as anti-Romantic as Jane Austen, if for rather different reasons. It is rather that social conduct in these regions is more thoroughly governed by questions of custom, lineage and kinship which cannot themselves be wholly reduced to a 'rational' calculus, as the British colonialists in Ireland were to discover to their cost. Even so, these a-rational sanctions and pieties are quite as systematic and authoritative as any more modern brand of instrumental reason, quite at variance with that sudden upsurge of benevolence or affective whim by which English sentimentalism will raise the whole issue of social relations to the condition of the aesthetic. Matters of property, marriage, inheritance, moral authority, social welfare, emigration, social obligation and the like are still partly interwoven with custom and kinship. A paternalist landlord system, of the kind which flourished in eighteenth-century Ireland, then reinforces this dovetailing of the public and domestic, as the social functions of employer, magistrate, moral guardian and political representative are condensed into the single, knowable personage of the local squire. The official bastions of political and juridical authority may well be experienced as alien and oppressive; but what replaces them in the allegiance of the people is not, as in the ideologies of modernity, certain 'free' areas of the private, sexual or domestic beyond the pale of the public sphere, but a public counter-culture of power, law, resistance, social relationship and 'moral economy' which is intricately bound up with families and communities. Whereas modernity drives a wedge between public and private, society and sentiment, pre-modern communities tend to breach this frontier in their routine conduct.

The baleful effects of this transgression are familiar enough. Those who idealise such set-ups forget that the personalising of power can mean the whim of the patriarch, the coerciveness of kinship, the claustrophobia of bickering, begrudging communities, the arbitrary sway of custom and tradition. 'The personal is political' is by no means an inherently progressive slogan, whatever some today may consider. When an independent political state finally emerges from the communitarian set-up of previously colonised societies, it tends to bear that history within it in the form of a potentially corrupt clientelism. We shall see something of these constrictions later, in our survey of the Irish novel. It is these forms of authority which modernity seeks to overturn, severing personal from social relations, the affective from the economic, so that men and women may be released into an impersonal public arena in which they have, in theory at least, rights to equality and autonomy quite independent of tribe or pedigree. The locus of that enlightenment is the political state; but since a colonised society has no state to call its own, it is left with the *Gemeinschaft* of the clan or the nation. It is thus incapable of entering fully upon that universal realm which would rip individual lives from their parochial roots and reconstitute them as citizens of the world.

This, need one say, is at once triumph and catastrophe. The political state may be, in Marx's eyes at least, a form of alienation; but Marx was alert to the positive side of all such estrangements, and even put in a good word for commodity exchange and market relations. The august anonymity of the liberal state may be something of a deception; but it is also the enemy of all local despotism and tribal tyranny, ruling out of its remit all those sexual, artistic, domestic or doctrinal matters which are best left to the desires of the free individual. This enlightened humanism then brings in its wake a withering of local bonds, a contempt for tradition, the dwindling of a sense of place, the sidelining of the sentiments. It dismisses as so much rural idiocy or benighted traditionalism a world in which some form of everyday fellowship really did flourish, whatever its stifling conformisms; in which labour, however backbreaking and unprofitable, had not as yet been wholly alienated to an impersonal industrial process; and in which men and women could celebrate their neighbourliness and love the places they lived in, however much they might also find them oppressive and monotonous.[13] The modernist dismisses such values as so much romantic nostalgia, while the traditionalist believes that such an organic society actually flourished. Both are surely mistaken: it is rather that when social orders begin to reckon the pains as well as the profits of modernisation, they delve back into their past, select certain real but partial features of it, and project these in idealised form as the complete truth of their ancestry. So it is that when the Romantics strive to recall society to these threatened values, they will find themselves scorned by the custodians of calculative reason as so many idle utopianists.

Eighteenth-century sentimentalism, however, had been there before them, not least on those colonised edges where the absence of a native political state meant that human relationships were rather less rationalised, bureaucratised and anonymously administered than they were at the imperial centre. Such regions were indeed in a sense more simple than the metropolitan nation, though not at all in the sense that enthused some of the

13.   I might register here my view that one of the enduring strengths of Marxism, for all its grievous problems, is that it offers the only truly *dialectical* evaluation of the pains and pleasures of modernity of our time, rejecting both organicist nostalgia and technological triumphalism.

English Romantics. The Gaelic labourers and small farmers were no doubt every bit as canny, devious and self-interested as William Pitt;[14] but the places they inhabited lacked their own unwieldy apparatuses of foreign diplomacy, military power, social engineering and court intrigue. It is chastening to speculate how much more fatiguing the study of Irish history would be if the country had had a foreign policy of its own. When the clan was reinvented by Irish nationalism as the political nation, it was, for both good and ill, in *gemeinschaftlich* terms, as an extended family whose blood-ties had now been sublimed to the level of 'culture'. Nationalism is of course a product of political modernity; but it is also a 'pre-political' current which elevates sentiment over the state, historic bonds over the effective management of the economy, the instinctive over the institutional. None of this proved particularly welcome to the metropolitan establishment; but in the form of 'Gaelic sentiment' it could furnish a precious resource for an England increasingly conscious of the emotional anaemia attendant on modernity. If it is grotesque to imagine the political state as a family, it is far easier to figure the nation in those terms; and this, as the Westminster rhetoric of the Irishman Edmund Burke testifies, was an image of which a progressively individualist England had urgent ideological need. If the economic unit of the small Gaelic farm was literally a domestic community, the political society of Great Britain could be metaphorically recast as one, not least by those who brought the good news of Gaelic *Gemeinschaft* from the exotic edges to the overbred centre.

Nationalism depends upon solidarity, which is another reason why congeniality was a feature of the Gaelic outbacks. Thomas Bartlett notes that 'one notable feature of Irish rural life from the 1770s onwards had been the emergence of the phenomenon of sociability, the growing pressure to associate for various purposes'.[15] Militant dissenters harnessed some of the traditional forms of social gathering – pub, shebeen, wake, pattern, fair, market – to political uses, dovetailing two forms of communality. In this sense too, fellow-feeling was more than a whimsical affair: it imposed itself as a material necessity rather than spontaneous impulse.

To cleave the personal from the political, as is the way of modernity, is among other things to privatise the affections, as domesticity and sexuality come to figure as little more than quaint personal idiosyncrasies, with less and less resonance in the public realm. Yet this is only one aspect of the narrative of modernity. As the bearer of universal rights, the middle classes in their militant phase must dismiss these matters as so many distractions or false consolations, contemptuous as they are of a cult of kinship and genealogy which

---

14. Indeed W. Bence Jones, in his poignantly entitled *The Life's Work in Ireland of a Landlord who Tried to Do his Duty* (London, 1880), presses the point to racist limits when he remarks that 'Jews cannot live in Ireland. They have no chance' (p. vi). He means because of the craftiness of the natives.

15. Thomas Bartlett, *The Fall and Rise of the Irish Nation* (Dublin, 1992), p. 311.

would seem the preserve of the detested nobility.[16] Once securely in power, however, the mercantile or commercial bourgeoisie finds itself sorely in need of just that realm of interpersonal sentiment which it has been busily reducing to something of a sideshow. In a familiar post-structuralist logic, the supplement proves itself utterly indispensable after all. It is not, need one say, that the business of statecraft or commercial enterprise can afford to be blown off course by domestic claims or the vagaries of feeling, obstructed by the play of fancy, instinct or sentimental benevolence. But a commercial society needs to construct a frame of human solidarity within which its competitive individualism may enjoy free rein; and this fellow-feeling is now considerably more difficult to establish at the political or philosophical levels, given that the state has been reduced to a mere contract of utility, and individuals stripped to solitary, self-determining atoms. If the human bonds which will oil the wheels of commerce are to be reinvented, they must now be located elsewhere, in those elusive regions of subjecthood and sensibility which can no longer be rationally justified, but whose presence is as immediate and incontrovertible as the taste of peaches or the odour of a rose. In the kingdom of possessive individualism, benevolence and affection are forced to migrate from the domestic hearth to become a metaphor of broader political significance. Sentiment – the quick, perhaps wordless exchange of gestures or intuitions – now appears the only form of sociality left in a world of bleakly isolated individuals, as *Tristram Shandy* uproariously exemplifies. But commerce and sentiment can still go hand in hand, allowing Henry Brooke to write in *The Fool of Quality* of how the merchant 'brings the remotest regions to neighbourhood and converse . . . and thus knits into one family, and weaves into one web, the affinity and brotherhood of all mankind' (vol. 1, p. 41). Brooke himself, despite this rhapsody, was a rapaciously mercenary character who despite his anti-Catholic views wrote pro-Catholic pamphlets for profit.[17]

So it is that the proliferating of commercial relations between men will bring in its wake a deepening of their mutual sympathies, which will in turn render the conduits of commerce all the more frictionless and efficient.[18] An extreme sentimentalism separates the feelings from their social contexts and reifies them to things in themselves; it is a kind of false currency unsupported by real emotional resources. The new 'commercial humanism', by contrast, is

16.   See, for this connection between the domestic and the aristocratic, Luke Gibbons, '"A Shadowy Narrator?": History, Art and Romantic Nationalism in Ireland 1750–1850', in Ciaran Brady (ed.), *Ideology and the Historians* (Dublin, 1991), p. 104.

17.   See Bartlett, *The Fall and Rise of the Irish Nation*, p. 54.

18.   See, for this 'commercial humanist' ideology in the eighteenth century, G. A. Pocock, *Virtue, Commerce, and History* (Cambridge, 1985). See also Terry Eagleton, 'Deconstruction and Human Rights', in Barbara Johnson (ed.), *Freedom and Interpretation* (London, 1993).

a way of reuniting the sentiments with social relations, as the extension of trade and the spread of sympathy become mutually enriching. The basis of prosperity is peace; and the barbarous values of militarism, honour and male *hauteur*, all badges of a predatory aristocracy, must yield to the virtues of uxoriousness, sensibility, civility and *tendresse*.[19] In the cult of sensibility, the bourgeoisie discovers a complex code all of its own, to pit against the rituals of its social superiors.[20] In an emotionally repressed society, sentimentalism allows you to be both fashionable and respectable precisely by being fervent or enraptured, lively or lachrymose. Social conduct must be aestheticised as 'manners', and the republic of letters must instruct an uncouth bourgeoisie in new structures of feeling, tempering their hard-headedness with an infusion of the domestic affections. Virtue, so to speak, is now a matter of phenomenology; and the novel and periodical, literary forms which deal in this realm of mannered conduct, accordingly become central 'theoretical' genres. The advertisement to the 1780 edition of Laurence Sterne's complete works announces that reading them will foster benevolence in society.

Pity, pathos and the pacific, of which woman is seen as the primary custodian, must now be translated from the domestic to the social arena. This 'turn to the subject' was anyway implicit in bourgeois individualism, for which the self is the measure of reality; but for this ethic to become truly hegemonic in social life, it must go hand-in-hand with an enriching of spiritual subjectivity too, which conveniently discovers a venerable Protestant tradition of the cultivation of inwardness to draw upon. Sentimentalism and sensibility are, so to speak, the eighteenth century's phenomenological turn, rehearsing in the realm of the passions and affections a ritual of subjecthood which is already well-established in the fields of economic and political life. Exchange can be spiritually as well as commercially profitable, in that act of putting ourselves in another's place which for Adam Smith is the compassionate imagination. Smith's views of political economy and his theories of imaginative projection are by no means ill-assorted. We have a capacity to exchange ourselves, as well as our commodities, with others; and the Man of Feeling is the one in whom this responsiveness to another's need or distress has evolved into a well-nigh pathological sensitivity. It is only later, in the Romantic epoch, that these two acts of exchange – commercial and imaginative – will enter into outright conflict, though the seeds of this quarrel are already ripening in eighteenth-century sentimentalism. Sociability, like sex, is a necessity for human existence, but the Almighty has so cunningly contrived

19. See R. F. Brissenden, *Virtue in Distress* (London, 1974), Jean Hagstrum, *Sex and Sensibility* (Chicago and London, 1980), David Marshall, *The Surprising Effects of Sympathy* (Chicago and London, 1988), and Terry Eagleton, *The Ideology of the Aesthetic* (Oxford, 1990), chs. 1 and 2.
20. See Paul Langford, *A Polite and Commercial People: England 1727–1783* (Oxford and New York, 1989), pp. 461–518.

human affairs as to make them both a potent source of pleasure. For David Hume, sympathy and benevolence are at the very nub of human society, which is held together in the end by nothing more rationally demonstrable, yet nothing less spiritually coercive, than habits of feeling.

Philosophically speaking, this turn to the subject takes the form of an empiricism for which immediate experience is the groundwork of all our more elaborate speculations. For David Hume, what distinguishes a real from an imaginary object is just a different intensity of feeling, and in his *Treatise of Human Nature* sentiment lies at the source of all moral judgement. But experience is a capacious affair, never rawly factual: as the ambiguous term 'sensation' suggests, it always comes to us coloured by some feeling-tone, dipped in the affections or aversions, so that empiricism and sensibility are in fact closely linked terms. It is only an age like our own, which so often confuses the empiricist with the positivist, which could find this at all surprising. To start, *pace* the rationalists and Platonists, with whatever is radically given in humanity is unavoidably to engage with the passions and sentiments. It is, after all, somewhat easier to see ideas rather than feelings as socially acquired; the concept of jealousy seems less of a raw datum than the thing itself. So it is that the 'benevolists' of the Scottish school are also devout empiricists; indeed it is significant that these Scots were known both as the 'Common Sense' and the 'Sentimentalist' school, yoking together the empirical and the affective. As anti-Cartesian Lockeians chary of the metaphysical, they shared a kind of capacious humanism and rough, common-sense empiricism which was closer in tone to the common people than any vein of high rationalism. And W. B. Yeats was right, for all his fantasy of a seamless eighteenth-century Anglo-Irish 'tradition', to find a common link in this respect between Swift, Berkeley, Goldsmith and Burke. While not all philosophical empiricists, all these men shared a profound contempt for non-practical reason, disdainful of fancy speculations which had severed themselves from the stuff of common experience. Indeed one can appreciate why such scorn for scholasticism should thrive on the underdeveloped Gaelic margins, despite the powerful metaphysical heritages of Catholic Ireland and Calvinistic Scotland. A sceptical stance to rationalist philosophical systems, of the sort Tristram Shandy displays in abundance, is likely to be all the more pronounced in societies where want and dispossession, the sheer dinginess of everyday life, make such lucubrations seem rather more scandalous a luxury than they might appear in more prosperous conditions. Sir Henry Craig describes the social background of the Scottish Enlightenment as a 'mingling of pride with poverty, of high notions of aristocratic dignity with an almost ludicrous simplicity and quaintness of social habit . . .'.[21] These, surely, are just the conditions for satire, sentimentalism and an anti-metaphysical animus, the latter two of which at least the Scottish philosophers evinced in full.

21.   quoted by Bryson, *Man and Society*, p. 7.

This, then, may be another reason for the astonishingly fertile Gaelic contribution to the English eighteenth-century cult of sensibility. I have described that cult elsewhere as the 'feminisation' of English social life;[22] but 'Celticisation' might be just as appropriate a term, and the two conditions have of course been habitually linked by the English. It is time that we looked again, a little more critically, at the now rather stale opposition between the barbarous Celt and the civilised English. This, to be sure, has been a recurrent ideological distinction;[23] but it obscures the ways in which the Celt in English eyes has meant sociability as well as savagery, the clubbable rather than the Calibanesque. At various stages of its evolution, the dominant culture of England has, so to speak, called upon its Gaelic peripheries to help it out. It was Irish dramatists, well placed to exploit the humorous tension between insider and outsider, who furnished England with much of its stage comedy, so that from Farquhar to Behan, as a prophylactic against its puritan gloom, English culture has swallowed regular doses of a stage-Irish rumbustious vitality. In the late eighteenth century, so Katie Trumpener has argued in her bold redrawing of literary cartography, Irish and Scottish 'national' tales and antiquarian research nourished the roots of the Gothic and historical novel.[24] Earlier this century, it was Ireland which provided the only site for a home-grown literary modernism in what was then the United Kingdom; and we shall see in chapter five how a certain kind of eclectic Irish intellectual admirably fulfilled the requirements of London's Grub Street at the turn of the eighteenth century. In a similar way, just at the point where the eighteenth-century English middle class needed for their own purposes to cultivate congeniality and fine feeling, they turned to a small army of Gaelic immigrants into England, who were not slow to exploit this career opportunity.[25] The pivotal figure between the nations in this respect was the Dubliner and English knight Richard Steele.

Yet it is not simply that these Gaels obediently supplied an English need, in a kind of spiritual equivalent of their agricultural exports. If the cults of benevolence and sentimentalism fitted well enough in some ways with the emergent sensibility of bourgeois England, there were plenty of other senses in which they offered to undermine it. Sensibility, like the figure of the woman with whom it is associated, is an eminently contradictory phenomenon, at once part of the dominant structure of feeling and its discarded victim. If feeling could oil the wheels of commerce, it also threatened to derail the whole

22.   See Terry Eagleton, *The Rape of Clarissa* (Oxford, 1982), Introduction.
23.   See, for example, Seamus Deane, *Civilians and Barbarians* (Derry, 1983).
24.   Katie Trumpener, *Bardic Nationalism*, Part 1.
25.   The underrated essayist Arthur Clery writes with a touch of patriotic hyperbole that 'At a period when English prose had reached its highest level . . . every great prose writer, save Addison alone, was Irish' (*Dublin Essays*, Dublin, 1919, p. 88). Clery is excluding fiction from his judgement.

project in the name of some less crassly egoistic vision of human society. If Richard Steele represents the more conservative face of sentimentalism, deploying his drama and journalism to unfurl a whole agenda of polite manners and agreeable sentiments for a hitherto uncivil middle class, Oliver Goldsmith's critique of economic exploitation in the name of custom and compassion was a rather less dewy-eyed affair. Indeed the realities of exploitation lay near the root of the whole Gaelic sentimentalist current. Pathos, elegy, melancholy, nostalgia: it is hardly surprising that these modes of feeling flow from countries whose traditional ways of life are under the axe. The Scottish *Aufklärer* are writing in the wake of the Scottish Highland clearances after the failed Jacobite insurgency of 1745, when whole regions of the nation are undergoing forcible anglicisation, militarisation, depopulation. After 1746, Highlanders were forbidden to bear arms, play the bagpipes or wear their distinctive dress, and the estates of some of the most prominent rebel chiefs were forfeited to the crown. It is just at this historical point of the collapse of clan society that what can no longer survive in reality is forced, as so often, to take refuge in art. Something similar happened in Ireland after the Flight of the Earls. The human sympathies which this art celebrate are already a kind of memory, as the Scottish Highlands become idealised by the English the more the threat of political insurrection fades after 1745.[26] Something similar will happen in the years after the Anglo-Irish Union, when disagreeable English memories of 1798 will fade gradually into a Celtophilic mist. But when the Scottish philosophers are writing, this memory is extremely recent. What the colonial powers are destroying, it is up to culture to salvage; and the chief name for that project in eighteenth-century Scotland was the poems of James Macpherson.

'Sentiment', then, for all its luxurious repleteness, is already secretly hollowed out by a sense of loss. Pity, as William Blake reminds us, thrives on the very misery it finds so unendurable, its mere presence a sign that the unspeakable has already happened. Pathos and pity in eighteenth-century England are impulses as tender as they are impotent, more substitutes for action than spurs to it. The just society would display no pity, since there would be no need for it. 'Weeping tear on infant's tear', as Blake's image slyly puts it, is a matter of redoubling the marks of woe rather than erasing them. The bourgeois world is fixed and given, and freedom now resides only in one's sympathetic response to it – a response which for authors like Sterne or Francis Hutcheson is really an involuntary affair, and in that sense no more free than its object. Just as German idealism performs in the mind what cannot yet be accomplished in reality, so the cult of sensibility is among other things a form of displacement or sublimation, fostering a change of heart just because a change of institutions is inconceivable. And such a change would in any case inconveniently remove the objects of one's pleasurable responses.

26.   See Stafford, *The Sublime Savage*, p. 61.

This whole ethic assumes that charity is first and foremost a matter of feeling, as though a charitable action unaccompanied by a warm inner glow ceased on those grounds to be virtuous, or a callous one could be converted into virtue by being coupled with some affable inner emotion. As long as you torture with love in your heart, so 'sensibility' suggests at an extreme, you are free of the mark of immorality.

Etymologically speaking, the word 'benevolence' locates goodness in the will which motivates an action, rather than in the nature of the action itself. As the eighteenth-century writer Elizabeth Carter tartly observed of this doctrine: 'Merely to be struck by a sudden impulse of compassion at the view of an object in distress is no more benevolence than is a fit of gout.'[27] In seeking to make compassion natural and universal, as much a built-in human response as sneezing over a pepper pot, one is at risk of robbing it of the very moral worth one seeks to ascribe to it. One is also in danger of subjectivising morality away altogether, as Sir John Hawkins sardonically accused the sentimentalist school of doing: 'Their generous notions supersede all obligation: they are a law to themselves, and having *good hearts* and abounding in the *milk of human kindness* are above those considerations that bind men to that rule of conduct which is founded in a sense of duty.'[28] There is something anarchic about sensibility, and compassionate about obligation: if you succour others only as the spirit moves you, then it is logical to rebuff their demands when one happens to be feeling morally indolent. A rule-bound ethics, which sentimentalism luridly paints as cold-hearted, just means that you should behave humanely towards others whether you happen to feel like it or not. The ethic of neighbourliness is an impersonal 'law' precisely to the extent that it does not state that one should help only those neighbours whom one finds agreeable. It is the cult of the heart, not the Kantian *Sollen*, which is exclusionary and egoistic. One might add too that sentimentality is just the kind of bogus or theatrical feeling which appeals most to those hard-headed types unskilled in any of the more subtle affective modes. It was Marx who observed that the Romantic and the Utilitarian were bedfellows. The weeping politician is just the flipside of the war-mongering one, rather as Joyce once remarked that the idea of the artist as bohemian immoralist is the burgher's notion of him, the suburban fantasy of all that one is not oneself.

Politically speaking, the cult of sensibility is strikingly ambivalent. Eighteenth-century imaginative sympathy may be a way of forging factitious bonds between gentlemen who are commercially at each others' throats; but in the hands of a Goldsmith or Macpherson it is also an act of solidarity with those casually abandoned by the march of modernity. Something similar, as we shall

27. Quoted by Arthur Hill Cash, *Sterne's Comedy of Moral Sentiments* (Pittsburgh, 1966), p. 55.
28. Quoted by Ann Jessie Van Sant, *Eighteenth-Century Sensibility and the Novel* (Cambridge, 1993), p. 6.

see, might even be claimed of that tender-hearted *habitué* of genteel English drawing-rooms, the Irish émigré Laurence Sterne. 'Gaelic sentiment' can be read on the one hand as a refinement of turbulent feeling for polite English consumption; in other literary forms of the day – Gothic, ballad, 'national' historical novel – those disturbed emotions will erupt in rawer, bleaker, more surreal and dishevelled forms. At its finest, this kind of writing about the pains of dispossession confirms that even nostalgia, as Walter Benjamin reminds us, can be a revolutionary mode. If the English and Irish found it hard to agree, it was partly because an appeal to the past was conservative for the former party and radical for the latter. But what is rugged, paranoid or farouche in the fiction of a Morgan or Maturin can always be distilled into a milder brew suitable for metropolitan consumption. The exemplary Irish case of this is Thomas Moore, whose songs sublimate historical trauma into a plangent sweetness, feeding back to the English the sentiments provoked by their dominion in Ireland, but tactfully shorn of the events which generated them. Feeling, as in all sentimentalism, is severed from its material context, and history returns home as the aesthetic. Laurence Sterne's Uncle Toby, a paragon of sentimentalism, is forever whistling 'Lillabullero', a song which his author must have known is actually a mocking Williamite satire of Gaelic Jacobite hopes.[29] But that turbulent history has now been refined to a wordless sweetness. Adam Smith is much concerned with how to harness the disruptively anti-social 'passions' to the cause of civility, and in a kind of Freudian displacement sees economic self-interest as substituting itself for the lust, power-hunger and military ambition of the *ancien régime*. Francis Hutcheson distinguishes a 'calm' desire for wealth from the passion of avarice; the Earl of Shaftesbury speaks with remarkable blandness of the possession of wealth as 'that passion which is esteemed peculiarly *interesting*';[30] and Montesquieu, whose *Esprit des lois* is the source of much of this philosophy of *le doux commerce*, had a touching faith in the civilising power of bills of exchange. The cultural point of commerce was that it feminised you, rendered you more docile and gregarious; the political point, however, was that it provided a mighty counterweight to the insolence of autocratic power. Commercial wealth, being diffusive and mercurial, is less easy for that power to confront or confiscate; and it allows you the independence necessary to be critical of the state. The Scottish philosopher John Millar even ropes the proletariat into this project: when labourers are massed together by the same employment and the 'same intercourse', so he asserts, they 'are enabled, with great rapid-

29. The song, properly entitled 'Lilli Burlero', is now thought to be the composition of Thomas Wharton, Lord Lieutenant of Ireland from 1708 to 1710. Its verses crudely parody the accents of a triumphalistic 'Teague' or common Irishman. See Seamus Deane (ed.), *The Field Day Anthology*, vol. 1, pp. 475–6.
30. Quoted in Albert O. Hirschman, *The Passions and the Interests* (Princeton, 1977), p. 37.

ity, to communicate all their senses and passions'[31] and the basis for plebeian solidarity is thus laid. Capitalism, in short, introduces the working class as well to sensibility, forging them into a single sensorium or community of sentiment; and Millar, far from regretting this potential oiling of the wheels of dissenting discourse, positively welcomes it as providing more power to the middle class's political elbow in the state.

But sensibility also has its utopian dimension, as the best by way of a critique of Enlightenment rationality of which pre-Romantic English culture proved capable. The man of feeling, as Janet Todd comments, 'does not enter the economic order he condemns; he refuses to work to better himself or society . . . From the outset [sensibility] opposed the individualistic and thrusting values that were transforming Britain into an industrial and imperial power'.[32] There is a touch of hyperbole here, as the actual interweaving of commerce and sensibility would suggest; Oliver Goldsmith hardly neglected self-improvement, and there is scant evidence that the sentimental Irish dramatist Hugh Kelly espoused a collectivist politics. It would be truer to say that sentimentalism replaces the individualist with the subjectivist, which challenges it at one level while confirming it at another. The emotional consequences of possessive individualism may be held against that doctrine by the newly self-conscious subjects it has helped bring into being. What you possess and consume is now your feelings rather than your property, even if to do this effectively you need a fair amount of property in the first place. All the same, there is something of the Benjaminian *flâneur* about the Man of Feeling, which cuts against the grain of a crassly utilitarian order. In one sense, as we have seen, sentiment and commerce are twinned at birth; in another sense, the sheer lavishness and excess of sensibility, its smug or generous-hearted refusal to calculate, its emotional spendthriftness, its carelessness of due proportion, its giving for the sheer sake of it, all represent a kind of implicit assault on exchange value. Samuel Taylor Coleridge, apologist for church and state, was certainly badly rattled by the movement, remarking in his *Aids to Reflection* that the mischief perpetrated by Sterne and his sentimentalist acolytes outweighed all the evil done by Hobbes and the materialist school. If Sterne was felt to be subversive, it was by no means in the first place because of his supposed indecency; and Denis Donoghue perceives something in him 'alien to the English spirit'.[33] What eighteenth-century England found rebarbative about Sterne, one suspects, is rather what contemporary conservative criticism finds scandalous about deconstruction: its perverse refusal of the conceptual highways, its myopic fascination with the marginal, its digressive

---

31.   Quoted ibid, p. 90.
32.   Janet Todd, *Sensibility: An Introduction* (London and New York, 1986), pp. 97, 129.
33.   Denis Donoghue, 'Sterne our Contemporary', in Arthur H. Cash and John M. Stedmond (eds.), *The Winged Skull* (London, 1971), p. 55.

disproportioning, its 'morbid' self-involutions. In the case of both the Irish Sterne and the Algerian Derrida, these are among other things features of the work of colonial émigrés askew to a metropolitan society.

The cult of feeling in the eighteenth century was certainly to issue in one dissident movement in the subsequent century, that of nationalism. Nationalism is of course a complex, contradictory social phenomenon, by no means reducible to the verities of the heart; but it is the kind of politics for which, as with feminism, feeling bulks remarkably large. Thomas Kettle speaks in *The Day's Burden* of nationalism as the elevation of sentiment from private experience to political principle, and offers the novel-form as an analogue of this public rehabilitation of feeling.[34] But nationalism has a more particular point of contact with sentimentalism, in that both of them involve a certain 'relative autonomy' of the affections in respect of their material contexts.[35] We shall see in a moment how this is true of sentimentalism; as for nationalism, Sir Horace Plunkett (no friend of Irish Home Rule) writes that the British in Ireland blundered by 'under-estimating the force of sentiment' there.[36] In one sense, this is no more than a political platitude; in another sense, it grasps the important truth that nationalism is not in the end a matter of facts. It has, to be sure, more of a grounding in them than the self-consuming emotionalism of some eighteenth-century specialists of the heart; but it is not reducible to political and economic terms, and it is this which many a well-intentioned colonialist (or, as we shall see in our final chapter, revisionist) fails to recognise. A people are unlikely to be diverted from their demand for political independence simply because they are relatively prosperous and culturally self-assured, since such independence – like, say, the demand for women's emancipation – is in the end a matter of moral principle rather than the reflex of an intolerable situation. And this, as we shall see in chapter ten, is one reason why showing that colonial situations were not always as grisly as they have been painted makes no difference whatsoever to the axiom of national self-government.

It is possible, if somewhat perilous, to draw a distinction in eighteenth-century England between benevolence and sentimentalism. Janet Todd chronologises the difference, distinguishing between an early novel of sentiment of the 1740s to 1750s which praises benevolence and generosity, and a later novel of 'sensibility', from about 1760 onwards, which luxuriates in refined feeling.[37] John Mullan argues that benevolence in the sentimental novel is generally a *de haut en bas* affair, a question of relieving the deserving poor

34.   Thomas Kettle, *The Day's Burden* (Dublin, 1910, reprinted 1937), p. 10.
35.   Robert Mahony traces the process by which Swift, after becoming acceptable in English eyes as a great Irish patriot by Walter Scott's edition of his works, blended into the Celticising English sentimentalism of the post-Union period. Goldsmith's Irishness, by contrast, was not thought relevant to his cult of feeling. (See his *Swift: The Irish Identity*, New Haven and London, 1995, p. 73.)
36.   Horace Plunkett, *Ireland in the New Century* (London, 1904), p. 15.
37.   ibid, p. 8.

rather than a universal ethical principle. Such philanthropy actually goes to confirm class distinctions – indeed some considered that these distinctions were ordained precisely as a heaven-sent opportunity to exercise one's charity. If benevolence is a quality of some saintly simpletons in sentimental novels, so Mullan claims, 'sensibility' is more a trait of their self-regarding readers. *Tristram Shandy* is a case in point: wherever was spontaneous feeling observed with such intense self-consciousness? 'The intensity of a special experience of feeling', Mullan remarks astutely, 'was a substitute for common and prevailing sympathies.'[38] The cult of feeling as a privileged, sporadic sensation emerges from the ruins of some real or imagined experience of human community, both preserving and displacing it.

Roughly speaking, benevolence is a question of laughter, while sentimentalism is a matter of weeping; but this is a finer distinction than one might suspect, since the weeping in question is a peculiarly self-satisfied tearfulness, and so curiously close to the geniality which expresses a newly confident middle class's sense of cosmic well-being. Sentimentalism is the feel-good factor of the eighteenth century. Both benevolence and sentimentalism imply self-assurance: the sentimentalist is complacently pleased with his fine feelings and flaunts them as so many affective commodities; the philanthropist has a strong enough core of self to decentre himself into others without fear of undermining his identity. This gives us a clue to the more useful distinction between the two modes, which is surely that benevolence is a centrifugal virtue, which bears you out of yourself in compassion for another, while sentimentalism is centripetal, a self-regarding condition whose true object is less what evokes one's sympathy than the sensation of sympathy itself. The distinction is by no means clear-cut: Sterne, in his sermon 'The Temporal Advantages of Religion', recommends benevolence on self-interested grounds, as the best way to amass riches, health, credit and reputation. Virtue is a sort of tonic or purgative, cleansing the system and making you both cheerful and prosperous.[39] For the most part, however, this self-regard lies on the side of sentimentalism. In this delicate form of egoism, an object is valuable only for the emotions to which it gives rise, of which it is the mere arbitrary occasion; and to this extent sentimentalism can be seen as a kind of commodification of the affections, exchanging its various objects in blithe indifference to their use-value. Indeed the Yorick of Sterne's *A Sentimental Journey* makes this connection explicitly, reflecting on the sentimental balance-of-payments deficit which inevitably befalls a foreign tourist: 'It will always follow . . . that the balance of sentimental commerce is always against the expatriated adventurer: he must buy what he has little occasion for, at their own price; his conversation will seldom be

---

38. John Mullan, *Sentiment and Sociability: The Language of Feeling in the Eighteenth Century* (Oxford, 1988), pp. 144–6.
39. James P. Browne (ed.), *The Works of Laurence Sterne* (London, 1873), vol. 3, p. 311.

taken in exchange for theirs without a large discount. . .' ('In the Desobligeant', Preface). Since any object whatsoever can provoke this exquisite sympathy, inherent values are struck from the world just as they are in the act of commodity exchange.

Sentimentalism thus involves a comic or alarming disproportioning of classical hierarchies, as Yorick refuses charity to a mendicant friar but effuses over a caged sparrow. It is a self-consuming affair, in which the material world becomes so much gratuitous raw material to fuel one's desire to feel. Just as, for psychoanalytic theory, one's true desire is just to keep on desiring, so for sensibility what one feels most intensely is the need to feel. Yorick, in Byron's scathing phrase about Keats, frigs his imagination, dreaming up images of distress in order to relish the orgasmic pleasures of pity. Just as the subject of empiricist philosophy experiences not the world but its own sense-impressions of it, so the Man of Feeling is a moral pelican who feeds off his own emotions, which are no longer in the phenomenological sense 'intentional'. Sensibility is really sympathy with one's own act of sympathising, and so sympathy to the second power. The subject retains quite as much lordship over the object as in the most rigorous Cartesianism, and its experience is just as self-evident; it is simply that this subject is now an affective rather than rational entity, whose egoism has become so tenderly aestheticised that it is well-nigh indistinguishable from its opposite.

Laurence Sterne, who purveyed sentimentalism in plenty, seems to have it obliquely in mind in a sermon which denounces pride. The proud man, he observes, acts as if every other mortal were void of sense and feeling, 'yet is possessed with so nice and exquisite a [sensibility] himself, that the slights, the little neglects and instances of disesteem, which would be scarce felt by another man, are perpetually wounding him. . .'.[40] Sensibility, in short, is a kind of pathology, the mark of the neurasthenically overcivilised.[41] When it is a question of consuming one's own feelings of pity for the distress of another, sentimentalism becomes a kind of second-hand sado-masochism, in which one savours not the other's misfortune but one's own 'melting' affinity with it. It is pleasant to identify with wretchedness because of the gratifying coincidence it involves between spectator and object, which suggests that sympathy, rather like the Kantian aesthetic unity of mind and object, is a purely formalistic affair. The sheer fact of the coinciding of subject and object moves you at least as much as the discomfort of the object. The Scottish moralist David Fordyce writes of the benevolent man as finding 'a sort of pleasing anguish' in human misery, which culminates in 'self-approving joy'. Markman Ellis sees this as a kind of non-transcendent version of the sublime, which involves an equally masochistic delight in the disagreeable.[42] Even when such a philanthropist cannot set the suffering in question to rights, so Fordyce

40.   ibid, p. 264.
41.   See Mullan, *Sentiment and Sociability*, ch. 5.
42.   See Markman Ellis, *The Politics of Sensibility* (Cambridge, 1996), p. 6.

observes, 'he is still conscious of good affections, and that consciousness is an enjoyment of a more delightful savour than the greatest triumphs of successful vice'. Another moralist speaks of 'a very delicious relish in doing good'.[43]

There is no simple distinction here between outgoing benevolence and inward-looking sentimentalism; but of the various Irish contributors to the cult, it is significant that, with the possible exception of Sterne, who can be seen as an intriguingly ambiguous case, benevolence predominates over sentimentalism. The greatest Irish dramatist of the eighteenth-century stage, Richard Brinsley Sheridan, stands largely apart from the sentimentalist current: when he took over the Drury Lane theatre at the age of twenty-five, his first act was defiantly to stage a series of Congreve comedies, an instance of the hard-boiled worldliness which the cult of sensibility abhorred.[44] One might also add the later name of that brisk anti-sentimentalist Maria Edgeworth, whose social values were in many ways close to those of Oliver Goldsmith. Edgeworth was much influenced by Rousseau in her educational theory, but her political views are eminently rationalist, and in her moral tale *Angelina* she satirises a foolish young woman seduced into excessive sensibility by too much novel-reading.

There would seem some obvious reasons for this Irish penchant for benevolence as against sentimentalism. The latter, after all, involves the kind of mannered, aestheticised milieu which was hardly much in evidence on the small farms or in the big houses. 'Mannerly' is the last epithet one would use of the rumbustious eighteenth-century Anglo-Irish gentry. If sentiment consorted with commerce, then there was not a great deal of the latter in eighteenth-century Ireland, and certainly little trace of an ethic of commerce along the lines of English civic humanism. The self-conscious cultivation of tender feeling belongs in England to a tradition of bourgeois interiority not so marked in the less individualist culture of Ireland, where a Catholic concern with codes of conduct, rather than a complex Protestant inwardness, was for most of the populace the order of the day. English sentimentalism was an ideology as alien to Goldsmith, who deeply disliked it, as the sentimental Victorian novel was to Yeats. In its consumption of private feeling, it draws upon a domestic scene sharply separate from the spheres of work and politics, which was not, as we have seen, the typical experience of family- or clan-based societies. Benevolence belongs with workaday social relations; sentimentalism springs from a divorce between emotion and actuality, a subjectivising of the world in which, as with Husserlian phenomenology rather later, one's experience becomes the object of one's experiencing.

43.   Quoted by R. S. Crane, 'Suggestions toward a Genealogy of the "Man of Feeling"', in *The Idea of the Humanities* (Chicago and London, 1967), p. 211. Crane finds the provenance of the eighteenth-century cult of sensibility in the anti-Hobbesian Latitudinarian divines of the late seventeenth century.

44.   See Fintan O'Toole, *A Traitor's Kiss* (London, 1997), p. 124.

In its resort to gesture and expression as more trustworthy media of feeling than language, the cult of sensibility betrays a scepticism of speech which sits a little uneasily with an oral culture; indeed Sterne was to guy this privileging of wordless gesture in *Tristram Shandy*, where even typography is wrenched ironically into its service. Sentimentalism, as we have seen, has a close relation to empiricism, a philosophy far less entrenched in Ireland than in England – though one should add that since the fashion was sometimes seen in England as typically French, this could be enough to damn it in the eyes of a people whose Francophobia was a prime constituent of their nationhood. The current owed something too to a Methodist cult of fervent emotionalism which was similarly less in evidence in Ireland. Whereas benevolence can be a form of 'practical' reason appropriate to working communities, sentimentalism is a more theoreticist affair, a kind of spiritual consumerism more native to the middle-class metropolis. The cherishing of dainty feelings demands a material infrastructure which was hardly much available in the colony, just as the bourgeois belief in human goodness which it reflects had rather fewer grounds for thriving there. A swooning, melting self-involvement was scarcely an emotional register native to Irish culture; and whereas the doctrine of benevolence can plausibly be seen as having some basis in Gaelic agricultural communities, the typical gesture of sentimentalism is to idealise this experience as the 'rural'.

On the other hand, as Janet Todd points out, sentiment is the sworn foe of linear middle-class narrative, as the tedious maunderings of Henry Brooke's *The Fool of Quality* would strongly intimate. In the typically sentimentalist text, feeling has the edge over action, fragmenting the narrative into so many episodic digressions, and sentiments are reified to so many beauties detachable from the flow of the text. This broken-backed structure, which Sterne will press to farcical proportions in his great novel, fits rather more obviously with a culture where teleology was never the most persuasive way of interpreting history. Goldsmith's novel *The Vicar of Wakefield* starts out with the best of linear intentions, but shifts in its second half into a frenzied parody of realist action, one in which catastrophes come so thick and fast that they cannot help but remind us, in the very act of rubbing our noses in the real, that we are in the presence of nothing more alarming than fiction. And since sentimentalism tends to subvert conventional hierarchies of value, playing havoc with the distinction between what is central and what trifling, so this perverse, digressive, myopic mode of writing lends itself peculiarly well to the experience of societies beyond the historical mainstream, where, as we shall see in the following chapter, a certain textual waywardness or eccentricity reflects a deviation from metropolitan norms. Moreover, since feelings are more easily accessible than complex ideas, the novel of sentiment has a certain democratic air to it, however hierarchical the society it portrays.

It is worth noting too that sentimentalism, though socially idealist, is somatically materialist. In a striking paradox, this high-minded cultivation of feeling in divorce from its social surroundings is also, physiologically speaking, a kind of primitive, mechanistic form of materialist thought. Sensibility in the eighteenth century is a discourse of nerves and fibres, pulses and vibrations, excitations and irritations. If it has relations to the novel, it also has affinities with neurology. '"Feelings"', remarks Vicesimus Knox, 'is a fashionable word substituted for mental processes, and savouring much of materialism.'[45] The very word 'feeling', which can mean both physical sensation and emotional impulse, the act of touching and the act of experiencing, provides the eighteenth century with an anti-Cartesian nexus between body and soul, the excitation of the nervous fibres and the subtle motions of the spirit. Despite all its vaunted delicacy and spirituality, the language of sentimentalism has its roots in the gross business of vapours and fluids, the electrical effects of physical stimuli on an exquisitely vulnerable nervous system; indeed Laurence Sterne will reap comic or bathetic capital from this philosophical monism in *A Sentimental Journey*. You can thus congratulate yourself on your emotional refinement while affecting to be reporting on the state of your nerves: Lady Morgan bemoans in her *Memoirs* her 'unhappy physical organisation, this nervous susceptibility to every impression which circulated through my frame and rendered the whole system acute',[46] but she is really just saying how compassionate she is. Her husband Sir Charles Morgan wrote a treatise on physiology, perhaps influenced by observing his wife. In this neuro-physiological sense of the word, insects and vegetables can be said to display sensibility quite as much as the creatures of the *beau monde*. Newton's *Principia*, not unlike Berkeley's *Siris*, regards ether as a subtle spirit pervading the whole of creation, creating sensations by exciting vibrations along the nerves. If 'sensibility' is a normative term, it is also an empirically descriptive, quasi-medical or scientific one. It can refer neutrally to the sheer business of sense data, or more qualitatively to the fineness of one's sensations. Ann Jessie Van Sant sees 'sensibility' as associated with the body and 'sentiment' with the mind, but 'sensibility' can also mark the spot where both spheres intermingle. Delicacy of feeling is a kind of super-subtle bodily reflex; it is now the nervous system, rather than the soul, which mediates between the physical and immaterial realms.[47] Sensibility is a kind of rhetoric of the body, a semiotics of blushing, palpitating, weeping, fainting and the like. It is the eighteenth century's riposte to philosophical dualism, in which a theory of twitching and tingling offers a solution of sorts to the neo-Platonic mystery of how anything as sublime as the mind could have truck with anything as sordid as the body. It is, quite literally, a solution felt on the pulses.

Oliver Goldsmith, as we shall see a little later, was aware that virtue could easily appear ludicrous rather than fashionable. The name for the eighteenth-century project of rendering goodness agreeable rather than absurd is the

45.   Quoted by G. J. Barker-Benfield, *The Culture of Sensibility* (Chicago and London, 1992), p. 2.
46.   *Lady Morgan's Memoirs* (London, 1862), vol. 1, p. 431.
47.   See Van Sant, *Eighteenth-Century Sensibility and the Novel*, ch. 1.

Tatler and the *Spectator*. The Dubliner Richard Steele, who launched the former periodical and co-edited the latter, was a devout Christian moralist, but he was also said to display the stereotypically Irish qualities of liveliness, good humour and congenial companionship. He was both high-minded moralist and a living paradigm of the good-natured family man, a blending of grace and *gravitas*, and this was a combination of which an English middle class still struggling to shed its puritan heritage were sorely in need. Steele described himself as 'an English gentleman born in the city of Dublin',[48] though the critic John Dennis claimed maliciously that he came of an old Tipperary family, and that his native country was stamped on his face, his writings, his actions and above all on his vanity. In fact, as one who had passed from Charterhouse to Christ Church to the Coldstream Guards, Steele was hard to write off as a Paddy. He was the grandson of a colonialist merchant-adventurer, which may account for some of his Whiggish zeal for the trading interest, and he represented the third generation of his family in Ireland; his mother was of Gaelic extraction, just possibly from Antrim.[49]

As one who was a soldier and later a politician, killed a colleague in a duel, knew the inside of a debtor's prison, married a widow for her money and was later arraigned for sedition before the House of Commons, Steele was both intellectual and man of the world, and his enormously influential writing moves constantly at this conjuncture. He stood at the centre of a number of overlapping circles: soldiers, churchmen, tavern wits, philosophers (he was a friend of Berkeley), grandee Whig politicians and the like. He was neither philosopher, theologian nor major literary author himself, and this was precisely the point: his role was to achieve something distinctive and unique in the history of English letters, as an 'organic' intellectual of the English bourgeoisie who drew up on their behalf nothing less than a whole ideological programme which his journalism was to disseminate throughout the land. Steele speaks of the 'commerce of discourse', and clearly viewed his own efforts in the cultural sphere as a kind of civilising exchange parallel to that of the merchants he so much admired.

Along with his colleague Joseph Addison,[50] Steele was the architect of a new form of cultural consensus, one which he partly constructed and partly articulated. Between them, the two men broadcast a style and set a social agenda, providing a talking-point for the coffee houses and cultural institu-

---

48.   Quoted in George A. Aitken, *The Life of Richard Steele* (London, 1889), vol. 1, p. 8. Isaac Bickerstaff, Steele's persona in the *Tatler*, complains that the critics deride his ancient family as low-bred. See George A. Aitken (ed.), *The Tatler* (London, 1899), vol. 3, p. 266.

49.   See Calhoun Winton, *Captain Steele: The Early Career of Richard Steele* (Baltimore, 1964), ch. 1.

50.   A writer who deeply influenced the enlightened Scottish literati. See Dwyer, *Virtuous Discourse*, p. 39.

tions of the English gentry. For Steele, the theatre was quite as vital an instrument in this campaign as periodical journalism: 'There is', he writes in the *Tatler*, 'no human invention so aptly calculated for forming a free-born people as that of a theatre.'[51] In seeking to refine the middle classes, he and Addison also strove to domesticate the aristocracy, reflecting at the level of culture that ambiguous unity between the two interests (later to be re-cemented in the public schools) which was to make the English governing bloc so resilient in the face of its political antagonists. Their brief ran all the way from educational reform to polite manners, the reform of dress to keeping Italian opera off the English stage, homilies against duelling to eulogies of commerce. The *Tatler* and *Spectator* deal in Cits, Snuff-Takers, Rakes, Freethinkers, Pretty Fellows and Very Pretty Fellows. Their authors were the founders of a whole new cultural politics, the lynchpins of the emergent public sphere of early eighteenth-century England, and it is indeed partly from their work that Jurgen Habermas originally derived that now-fashionable theoretical concept.[52] The literary artist has been recycled as moral legislator and social semiotician, reinventing a public role for himself which perhaps carries with it a remote echo of the socially privileged Gaelic bard.

T. S. Eliot once observed that sensibility is only altered by a man of genius, and Steele, though hardly that, helped to crystallise a whole new structure of feeling for early middle-class England. The role of this Irish émigré in both drama and journalism was to construct an English national character appropriate to changed social conditions, schooling a whole society in ethics and aesthetics, retrieving moral philosophy from the clerics and schoolmen and adapting it instead to the salon, theatre and coffee house. His role was to revise it in light of the needs, manners and institutions of a newly confident social class, one which was leaving a more querulous, sectarian age thankfully behind it and settling down to the steady business of making money and defining its spiritual identity. Satire, with its coarse belligerence, was a cultural residue of that more abrasive world, and was now to be tempered by an eirenicism and good humour which sprang from the middle and upper classes' inexhaustible belief in their own beneficence. These men and women are now to be seduced rather than scourged into virtue, upbraided and cajoled by men who share their styles and sensibilities rather than by some disgruntled outsider. Mr Spectator may be one of life's observers, as his name suggests, but he is also an intimate part of the scene he surveys.

Whereas Swift and Pope find moral deviations ontologically threatening, Steele and Addison see them as social foibles to be amusedly corrected. The critic, Steele writes in *Tatler* no. 29, must be companion rather than censor:

51. George A. Aitken (ed.), *The Tatler*, vol. 3, p. 280.
52. See Jurgen Habermas, *Strukturwandel der Offentlichkeit* (Neuwied, 1962). I have discussed some of these matters already in *The Function of Criticism* (London, 1984).

'A thorough critick is a sort of puritan in the polite world . . .'. The *beau monde* loved to read about itself, and the *Tatler* and *Spectator*, along with Steele's other journals, cannily exploit this narcissism for their own ends. Geniality of spirit and urbanity of tone, raillery and beguilement, were now to sugar the pill of moral correction for an audience which would not take kindly to satire or polemic. The typical tone of this journalism was 'lightly learned, good-humoured, confident, a bit patronising, sometimes pedantic'.[53] Vanity and affectation, the constant targets of Steele's affably amused journalism, are not after all the most heinous of crimes, so that criticism can be blended with complacency. A new kind of Christian manliness is in the making, hostile to false wit and aristocratic libertinism, tender and fervent in its idealisation of women, wedded to the virtues of truth, meekness, simplicity, decency, good sense, non-violence, generosity of spirit, honour, chivalry and connubial affection. 'I have long entertained an ambition to make the word Wife the most agreeable and delightful name in nature', Steele writes in *Spectator* no. 40, and with grotesquely misplaced good intentions he chose the title 'Tatler' in honour of what he calls the fair sex. The journal carried vignettes of family life while rooting itself in the broader bourgeois world. One of Steele's political pamphlets, which likens an economic policy for the nation to making provision for one's children, is entitled 'A Nation a Family',[54] and we shall see later how this remodelling of social on domestic affections was to be developed by Edmund Burke. John Toland, too, viewed sexuality more as an extension of conviviality than as a matter of passion.[55]

The point of this moral campaign is to make virtue lively, easy and fashionable, to aestheticise values previously in the grip of an unlovely puritanism. The enterprise was to prove extraordinarily successful: 'It is incredible', writes the dramatist John Gay, 'to conceive the effect [Steele's] writings have had on the town; how many thousand follies they have either banished, or given a very great check to; how much countenance they have added to virtue and religion . . .'.[56] It is hard to see how anyone could actually know this, and Steele, who drank too much, was hardly a cynosure of virtue himself. But it was agreeable to his readership to hear the Sermon on the Mount described in terms of drawing-room discourse ('He gives us his divine precepts in so easy and familiar a manner'),[57] and to regard divine grace as akin to a kind of elegant deportment of the soul. The barbarous old patrician values of military

53.   Aitken (ed.), *The Tatler*, vol. 3, p. 105.
54.   See Rae Blanchard (ed.), *Tracts and Pamphlets by Richard Steele* (Baltimore, 1944).
55.   See Robert E. Sullivan, *John Toland and the Deist Controversy* (Cambridge, Mass., 1982), p. 189.
56.   Quoted in Aitken (ed.), *The Tatler*, vol. 3, p. 154.
57.   Rae Blanchard (ed.), Richard Steele, *The Christian Hero* (Oxford, 1932), p. 44. Steele is said to have written this tract while on guard duty at the Tower of London.

heroism were to be replaced by a meekness redefined as 'sublime and heroick', and Christianity was recommended in stoical style as 'the way to ease and composure of the mind in unhappy circumstances',[58] a kind of *sang froid* of the spirit.

Steele, like most of his fellow Irish expatriates, is a devotee of benevolence, a term which conveniently reconciles the moral and the mannerly, the New Testament and the Whitehall club. God, he argues in *The Christian Hero*, has impressed upon us a common nature which 'presses us by natural society to a closer union with each other . . . and by a secret charm we lament with the unfortunate, and rejoice with the glad; for it is not possible for a human heart to be averse to any thing that is human: but by the very mien and gesture of the joyful and distress'd we rise and fall into their condition; and since joy is communicative, 'tis reasonable that grief should be contagious, both which are seen and felt at a look, for one man's eyes are spectacles to another to read his heart. . .'[59]. Here, *in parvo*, is the philosophy of Francis Hutcheson. It is interesting that ethics are now to be based on one's response to the sufferings of others rather than, as in a more evangelical vein of Christianity, to one's own moral condition, since the *beau monde* is unlikely to be plunged into an excessive degree of distress itself. Morality is to be both aestheticised and eroticised: Steele speaks in Shaftesburyian terms of the 'bliss' of human reconciliation, and compares the compassionate man who dissolves into pity for another with the amorous one who is melted by beauty. Jean Hagstrum writes of these moments, with conscious oxymoron, as a kind of 'complacent ecstasy'.[60]

Steele's letters to his wife are full of such impeccably polite swoonings. She is his 'Dear Creature', 'Dear Ruler', 'Dearest Being on Earth', and he signs himself at one point 'Yr Affectionate Tender Oblig'd Husband & Lover'. These hasty notes of a few lines each are peppered with allusions to God, Truth and Love, and sometimes arrive along with the gift of some tea or the odd guinea. In fact, the point of most of these missives is to tell his wife that he is dining with some bigwig and cannot come home; but he keeps private and public worlds in scrupulous equipoise, writing in one note in Richardson-like 'to the moment' style that 'I am just drinking a pint of wine and will come home forthwith', and in another that 'I dine with Lord Halifax and shall be at home half hour after six'. On a new line he adds: 'I dye for Thee I languish'.[61] The social and the domestic are divided by a blank, but inhabit the same textual space. It is now *de rigueur* for the energetic man of affairs to be uxurious; it is mannerly to be unmanned. Steele and Addison blur the boundaries between private and public realms, and the family, along with 'manners', provides the middle

58.   ibid, p. 75.
59.   ibid, p. 77.
60.   Jean H. Hagstrum, *Sex and Sensibility* (Chicago and London, 1980), p. 163.
61.   For Steele's letters to his wife, see Rae Blanchard (ed.), *The Correspondence of Richard Steele* (Oxford, 1941), pp. 208–79.

ground between the two: the domestic sphere, as Michael Ketcham points out, 'is seen as a source of social interaction'.[62] The new 'companionate' family, as Lawrence Stone calls it, can now be the model for other forms of social cohesion, the original unit of human benevolence, a kind of commonwealth or economy in itself.[63] Besides, the whole point of Steele's kind of journalism lies in making the mind's inward dispositions instantly visible and communicable, which is an epistemological way of crossing the frontier between subjectivity and society. Lionel Grossman speaks of this as 'the modern "bourgeois" dream of intimate and inward communication';[64] though by the time of *Tristram Shandy* it is mute feeling and gesture, no longer the buoyant script of a Steele, which will come to provide the medium of such contact.

Even so, one should not exaggerate Steele's sentimentalism. If his effusions can be embarrassing, he was also much derided for speaking up for the simple virtues, a plea in which one can perhaps detect a touch of his native country. His prose is less purple than emulsive, more whimsical than flatulent. He can gently send up romantic passion, and despite his condescension to women he believed that the female mind was different from the male variety rather than inferior to it. His play *The Conscious Lovers* was the very model of sensibility, but his rather more convincing dramatic effort *The Tender Husband* uses less solemnly elevated language. As for the *Tatler*, its language can be both mawkish and rational. Steele and Addison are in search of a form of rhetoric which will befriend rather than simply edify their readers, so that the very form of their journalism, reformulating the relations between authors, readers and texts and concocting a kind of literary *Gemeinschaft* from them, reflects the benevolism of its content. Laurence Sterne, equally eager to convert readers into bosom pals, will press this project to his usual parodic extreme. Indeed Michael Ketcham reads *Tristram Shandy* as a kind of crazed extension of *The Spectator*, whose amiable digressiveness has now escalated into a wholesale collapse of system.[65] Family, letters, social bonds and economic intercourse in the early eighteenth-century periodicals are now merging together, so that Addison, an enthusiast for commercial humanism, can write in the *Spectator* of trade as enlarging and enriching human friendships, as though the Bristol docks were a kind of dating agency.

It was left to the Ulsterman Francis Hutcheson to raise benevolence to the dignity of a full-blown philosophy.[66] Perhaps we are too little struck by the

62.   Michael G. Ketcham, *Transparent Designs: Reading, Performance and Form in the 'Spectator' Papers* (Athens, Georgia, 1985), p. 9.
63.   See Lawrence Stone, *The Family, Sex and Marriage in England 1500–1800* (Harmondsworth, 1979), ch. 5.
64.   Quoted ibid, p. 10.
65.   Ketcham, *Transparent Designs*, p. 173.
66.   I have discussed Hutcheson's moral philosophy in *Heathcliff and the Great Hunger* (London, 1995), ch. 3.

oddness of this, as we would no doubt be astonished if someone had spun a philosophy out of envy or irascibility. But Hutcheson sees that, with the collapse of certain rationalist or Platonic models of human nature under the assaults of empiricism, the social sympathies need a firmer ontological grounding than the impulses of the individual heart; and he discovers this in the celebrated 'moral sense' by which, taking a leaf from empiricism's book, he sees men and women as ineluctably stirred to joy by another's act of benevolence as they are inevitably nauseated by a foul stench or enraptured by a sublime prospect. The point of the passivity of the moral sense, which lies no more within the scope of the will than do taste or hearing, is to make the existence of virtue rather more plausible than it might otherwise be were it left to our conscious resolution. But if we can help compassionating and commiserating no more than we can fail to remark an elephant in our field of vision, this fellow-feeling is naturalised only at the cost of being diminished in merit. The more virtue becomes a well-nigh bodily reflex, as thoroughly built into our constitution as the instinct to snatch our finger from a flame, the more assuredly it can be founded; but the less, by the same token, we can congratulate ourselves on it. For Sterne's Uncle Toby, sympathy comes as naturally as sneezing, and so might be seen as a foible no more to his moral credit than his military crankishness.

Commentators continue to wrangle over just what kind of moralist Hutcheson is. William Frankena and William T. Blackstone read him as a forerunner of modern emotivism, holding that moral judgements are just coded ways of expressing our approval or condemnation of an action. Blackstone believes that such judgements for Hutcheson are non-cognitive, even though facts and reasons are relevant to them. We need to know whether an action really was benevolently motivated, or really will lead to the greatest happiness of the greatest number, but what makes it good or bad is the aversion or approbation it provokes in us. As with Steele, this is essentially a spectator's morality. The moral question for Hutcheson is less 'What am I to do?' than 'How do I feel about what you do?'. But Blackstone does not see Hutcheson as an ethical relativist or subjectivist: actions are not virtuous just because they please *me*. Instead, he pitches Hutcheson's writings somewhere between rationalism and subjectivism: one must strive to rationally justify one's moral judgements, but this is not what makes them moral.[67] T. D. Campbell likewise sees Hutcheson as occupying some terrain between naïve

67.   See William T. Blackstone, *Francis Hutcheson and Contemporary Ethical Theory* (Athens, Georgia, 1965). See also, for a somewhat similar interpretation, W. B. Frankena, 'Hutcheson's Moral Sense Theory', *Journal of the History of Ideas*, vol. 16, no. 3, June 1955. For the 'aesthetic' quality of 'moral sense', see David Paxman, 'Aesthetics as Epistemology, or Knowledge without Certainty', *Eighteenth-Century Studies*, vol. 26, no. 2 (Winter, 1992/3). The fullest account of Hutcheson's aesthetics is to be had in Peter Kivy, *The Seventh Sense* (New York, 1976).

realism on the one hand and non-cognitivism on the other.[68] V. M. Hope, by contrast, regards Hutcheson as a kind of intersubjectivist, for whom virtue is relative not to the individual but to the consensual agreement of the species as a whole.[69] David Fate Norton goes further and boldly claims him as a moral realist.[70]

Hutcheson's philosophical texts are both ambiguous and inconsistent enough to lend support to all of these contending interpretations. But it seems clear that his benevolism was not a sentimentalism, a bias which aligns him with the general trend of Irish contributors to eighteenth-century 'sensibility'. It is doubtful that he was a full-blooded ethical subjectivist, arguing as he does in *A System of Moral Philosophy* that '. . .we do not say that [an object] is beautiful because we reap some little pleasure from viewing it, but we are pleased in viewing it because it is antecedently beautiful'.[71] Much the same would seem for him true of moral objects. He is not claiming that nothing is good or bad but feeling makes it so. But Hutcheson's positions slide bemusingly around, and there are other places where he sounds much less of a realist.[72] In his *Inquiry Concerning the Original of our Ideas of Virtue or Moral Good*, he speaks of moral goodness as 'some quality apprehended in actions, which procures approbation, and love toward the actor, from those who receive no advantage by the action. . .'.[73] 'We do not love', he argues, 'because it is pleasant to love; we do not chuse this state, because it is an advantageous, or pleasant state: this passion necessarily arises from feeling its proper object, a morally good character.'[74] The hedonism of 'sensibility' is thus firmly rejected, along with its voluntarism: it is not a question of arbitrarily indulging an emotion, but of a response which 'necessarily' arises from a specific situation. Benevolism looks to a 'proper object', holding to an internal relation between sentiment and its occasion, whereas that relation with sentimentalism is rather more gratuitous. Like Goldsmith and Burke, for example, but unlike some sentimental universalism, Hutcheson holds that it is natural for us to love those closest to us more than those at a distance.[75] Empiricism and domesticity, what immediately strikes the senses and the priorities of kinship,

68. See his essay on Hutcheson in R. H. Campbell and Andrew S. Skinner (eds.), *The Origin and Nature of the Scottish Enlightenment* (Edinburgh, 1982).

69. See V. M. Hope, *Virtue by Consensus* (Oxford, 1989).

70. See his *David Hume: Common-Sense Moralist, Sceptical Metaphysician* (Princeton, N. J., 1982), ch. 2. A contrary line is taken by Kenneth P. Winkler, 'Hutcheson's Alleged Realism', *Journal of the History of Philosophy*, no. 23 (July 1985).

71. Francis Hutcheson, *A System of Moral Philosophy* (London, 1755), vol. 1, p. 54.

72. See R. S. Downie (ed.), *Francis Hutcheson: Philosophical Writings*, Introduction, p. xxxi.

73. London, 1726, p. 111.

74. ibid, p. 154.

75. Though he also wanted to foster fellow-feeling for cultures remote from our own, 'look[ing] for traces of affection, decency and moral sense among natives

are thus yoked together. At times, to be sure, Hutcheson writes as though the world is really just a convenient springboard for the exercise of our sensibility, as when he remarks of such conditions as labour, hunger, thirst, poverty, pain and danger that 'the virtues which [they] give us occasions of displaying, are so amiable and excellent, that scarce ever is any imaginary hero in romance or epic, brought to his highest pitch of happiness, without going thro them *all*'.[76] But he also notes, perhaps with the cult of sentimentalism in mind, that ''tis some appearance of friendship, of love, of communicating pleasure to others, which preserves the pleasures of the luxurious from being nauseous and insipid'.[77] Like Goldsmith, he prefers social bonds to subjectivist self-indulgence.

What Hutcheson is out to refute is the rationalist case that moral values are as much objective properties of the world as the condition of being poisonous or oblong, and that moral action springs simply from one's cognition of these qualities. For how would we ever leap from this mere fact to the business of value? For Hutcheson, the moral sense does not simply identify goodness in the world but responsively enacts it, and so is both constative and performative together. It is an expression of the very fellow-feeling it approves, and is thus (at least on one reading of his work) cognitive and normative at the same time. This bridges fact and value, knowledge and feeling, in just the way that the sentimentalists cannot, since for them feelings have become autonomous of the objects they are supposed to intend. Moral sense, by contrast, struggles to hold the subjective and objective together: it situates the ethical realm neither purely within the subject nor wholly in the world, but in a human response evoked by what is the nature of the case. It is not that this response itself determines the goodness or otherwise of an action, but neither is it purely incidental to it. An action which did not in principle invite our approbation would not be virtuous, but it is not virtuous just on account of that approbation. Goodness cannot be defined outside our response to it, but it is not reducible to it either. Edmund Burke grasps the point well when discussing the importance of what he calls 'moral taste' in his *Letter to a Member of the National Assembly*: 'A moral taste', he writes, 'is not of force to turn vice into virtue; but it recommends virtue with something like the blandishments of pleasure.'[78] The moral sense is a matter of discerning qualities, but these qualities are not just its own projections. This faculty is as

... previously identified as savages' (Daniel Carey, 'Travel Literature and the Problem of Human Nature in Locke, Shaftesbury, and Hutcheson', unpublished DPhil thesis, Oxford University, 1994, p. 200. (This excellent thesis illuminates Hutcheson's markedly liberal views on race and cultural difference.)

76.   ibid, pp. 245–6.
77.   ibid, p. 249.
78.   Edmund Burke, *A Letter to a Member of the National Assembly* (reprinted Oxford and New York, 1990), p. 38.

much a fact about us as touch or taste, but its whole being is a perpetual valuing. We are still a long way here from the Romantic doctrine of the dynamic
interaction of mind and world; but in this notion of the moral sense as a
mutual mirroring of how things are and how we feel about them, we have
advanced some way beyond that schism between subject and object which in
different ways characterises both rationalism and sentimentalism.

Hutcheson is scandalised by the vulgar Hobbesian view that self-interest
lies at the source of human actions, and speaks up instead for a less bloodless
conception of human behaviour. As he observes in his *Inquiry Concerning the
Original of our Ideas of Virtue or Moral Good*, 'As soon as any action is represented to us as flowing from love, humanity, gratitude, compassion, a study
of the good of others, and a delight in their happiness, altho it were in the
most distant part of the world, or in some past age, we feel joy within us,
admire the lovely action, and praise its author.'[79] The point of the spatial or
temporal distance is to emphasise disinterestedness, which for Hutcheson
means a pleasurable decentring of the self into the loving action of another,
not the Olympian neutrality to which some radical thought today has briskly
reduced it. Goldsmith's Dr Primrose in *The Vicar of Wakefield* takes just such
a Hutchesonian delight in the charitable acts of others. 'Men', Hutcheson
writes in his *Short Introduction to Moral Philosophy*, 'approve deeply that beneficence which they deem gratuitous and disinterested';[80] and 'gratutitous' here
is a smack at the logic of the marketplace. Hutcheson does in fact believe that
benevolence is in our interests, being by far the best recipe for mundane happiness, and in this he is at one with Laurence Sterne. But he also seems to
think that to be virtuous for the *sake* of self-interest would be like drinking
whiskey in order to get drunk rather than to enjoy the liquor itself. To drink
for drinking's sake would be to subordinate the use-value of the whiskey to
its exchange-value, since any other form of alcohol would do just as well for
the purpose. Sentimentalism, similarly, gives in abundance for the sake of the
sensation the act induces, rather than for the sake of others. For Hutcheson
there is no *point* to virtue, any more than we can ask why it is that the moral
sense should relish such goodness so deeply. It is just part of our nature or
species-being that we should be built in this way, and to adduce reasons in
support of the moral sense would be to draw on the very moral intuitions one
was trying to ground. Our sense of pleasure in another's beneficence, Hutcheson observes, 'is antecedent to advantage or interest, and is the foundation
of it'.[81] Possessive individualism can never account for 'the principle actions
of human life such as the offices of friendship, gratitude, natural affection,
generosity, public spirit, compassion'.[82] With Hobbes, in short, we have a

79.   Reprinted in L. A. Selby-Bigge, *British Moralists* (London, 1897), p. 75.
80.   Francis Hutcheson, *A Short Introduction to Moral Philosophy* (Glasgow, 1747), p.
      18.
81.   ibid, p. 70.
82.   See Bernard Peach (ed.), *Illustrations of the Moral Sense* (Cambridge, Mass.,
      1971), p. 106.

supposedly comprehensive moral discourse which can make nothing of most of what men and women hold to be precious, other than perversely claiming that these virtues are mere rationalisations of self-advantage.

Lurking beneath Hutcheson's benevolism is a remarkably sanguine view of human nature which sits uneasily with his Presbyterianism. Even such a liberal, 'New Light' Presbyterian as he was sails perilously close to Pelagianism in claiming that our minds show a strong bias 'toward a universal goodness, tenderness, humanity, generosity, and contempt of private goods. . .'.[83] (Eoin Mac Neill, incidentally, reports that St Jerome called Pelagius Irish, but that this was probably a put-down; he also calls him a porridge-eater.)[84] Hutcheson cannot bring himself to acknowledge that men and women are capable of what he calls 'malicious disinterested hatred' – that just as the finest virtues are autotelic, so there is a human viciousness which destroys just for the hell of it. Evil is 'aesthetic' too. But such grim metaphysical considerations would merely ruffle the lightness of his moral tone. As with Steele and Shaftesbury, altruism for Hutcheson is aestheticised in the form of social manners: virtue goes hand-in-glove with a love of poetry, music and natural beauty, with neat dress and 'humane deportment', a 'delight in and emulation of every thing which is gallant, generous and friendly'.[85] Both art and compassion hinge on the empathetic imagination. Goodness is now in every sense a matter of grace, a socialised commodity as cultivated yet instinctive as a taste for port. In the blithe Hellenism of this newly self-satisfied middle class, charity and clubbability, the benevolist and the *bon viveur*, are becoming hard to tell apart. Though Hutcheson is not a hedonist, goodness and sensuous enjoyment are subtly interwoven: benevolence is a kind of robust bodily pleasure, a *jouissance* which savours the moral delectability of others as one might smack one's lips over a dish of prawns. Virtue, for Hutcheson as for Sterne, is *comedy*, the foe of all puritan self-repression, an antidote to grim-lipped Protestant earnestness. It includes 'an inclination to cheerfulness, a delight to raise mirth in others, which procures a secret approbation and gratitude towards the person who puts us in such an agreeable, innocent, good-natur'd, and easy state of mind, as we are conscious of while we enjoy pleasant conversation, enliven'd by moderate laughter'.[86] The harbinger of the kingdom of God is now less the church than the dining club.

So it is that Hutcheson attacks Hobbes's vision of humanity by challenging his deeply uncomic theory of laughter. Whereas Hobbes sees laughter as a sign of superiority, Hutcheson reverses the judgement: laughter springs not from superiority but from its collapse, from the puncturing of false grandeur

83. *Inquiry Concerning the Original of our Ideas of Beauty and Virtue* (London, 1726), p. 257.
84. Eoin Mac Neill, *Phases of Irish History* (Dublin, 1919), p. 247.
85. ibid, p. 257.
86. ibid, pp. 257–8.

in a carnivalesque lurching from high to low. For Hutcheson as for many Irish writers, the comic sense lies close to the ludicrous or bathetic. The comic is a kind of politics, deflating our tendency to venerate whatever seems greater than ourselves; it is thus the very opposite of Burke's sublimity, which fosters precisely such numinous feelings. Hutcheson has great fun in demolishing Hobbes's unpleasant notion that we laugh at those inferior to ourselves: 'It is a great pity', he remarks, 'that we had not an infirmary or lazar-house to retire to in the cloudy weather, to get an afternoon of laughter at these inferior objects. . .'.[87] Given the Hobbesians' case, he adds with *faux* bemusement, it is odd that they do not assiduously collect inferior creatures like owls, snails and oysters 'to be merry upon'. Like Goldsmith, Hutcheson espouses a traditional conception of comedy as satiric ridicule, and his account of its purpose could be Richard Steele's: 'men have been laughed out of faults which a sermon could not reform'.[88] As with Steele, comedy is double-edged, at once a foretaste of a more convivial world to come, and a reformist instrument for attaining it. This is why, for Steele, Hutcheson and Goldsmith, humour must temper its satire with good-nature, blend benevolence with critique. Hutcheson regards laughter as 'none of the smallest bonds of common friendship';[89] if society is about communication, then nothing is more instantly communicable than a good joke, which thus comes to figure as a metonym of social intercourse in general. Humour forges pleasurable social bonds, and so is a kind of sublunary echo of divine *caritas*. The world, Sterne reminds us, is big with jest – though if he and Goldsmith are purveyors of the sudden glory of mirth, Steele prefers a steady state of serenity.

It is easy to see, so Hutcheson thinks, how the desire for wealth and power can come to be mistaken à la Hobbes as among the primary motivations of human life. They are misconstrued as this because they are so universal; but they are universal because they represent the *sine qua non* of most other human aspirations, not because they are themselves the most fundamental human appetites. This is a shrewd point, which Marx too will enforce in his own way. Marx does not argue that the economic is what men and women consider most central to their lives, or even that, whatever they might consider, it *is* what is most important. People have all kinds of desires beyond wealth and power; it is just that wealth and power provide the material conditions essential to fulfilling most of them. They are, as Hutcheson puts it, 'the means of gratifying all other desires'.[90] One cannot sustain a decent personal relationship if one is starving. The struggle for resources and entitlements, which is to

87.   Francis Hutcheson, *Thoughts on Laughter, and Observations on the Fable of the Bees* (Glasgow, 1758), p. 12. One might say that Hutcheson responds to Hobbes as a modern-day humanist might to Freud.

88.   ibid, p. 51.

89.   ibid, p. 37.

90.   *An Essay on the Nature and Conduct of the Passions and Affections* (London, 1728), p. 6.

say economic and political life, is more important than composing some splendid symphony in the sense that it is a necessary condition of it; but it is not more important in the sense of being more valuable than it. One could imagine a visitor to our world trying to select amongst a whole range of goods – foreign travel, fresh air, becoming a trapeze artist, studying philosophy, eating tofu eight times a day – before gradually becoming aware that this choice was unnecessary, since there existed on our planet a single good which allowed you to enjoy all of these other pursuits together. It was, so to speak, a kind of magical distillation of all other goods, a meta-good or alchemical elixir which allowed you to shunt with the minimum of effort from one form of gratification to another, or to permutate one with the other, and its name was money. Would this alien then be surprised to find that human beings invested so much of their energy in attaining this precious stuff, even if it meant nothing in itself, and even if many humans are themselves both surprised and scandalised by the Marxist doctrine of economic determination?

A materialist theory of history of this sort is more likely to consort with benevolence than with sentimentalism. It recognises, as sentimentalism does not, that a material foundation must be in place simply for us to yearn or hanker; that the emotions are not autonomous of their origins or occasions; that desire depends upon power, even if power is itself a modality of it. It is this world-view which we can now turn to in the work of Oliver Goldsmith.

We have seen already that posterity has not been especially mindful of William Dunkin; but he certainly came to the attention of Oliver Goldsmith, who reviewed his *Epistle to the Earl of Chesterfield* in the pages of the *Critical Review*. Confronted with a fellow Irishman ill-starred enough not to have emigrated, Goldsmith assumes the superiorly condescending tones of the English metropolis. 'The man who is bred at a distance from the centre of learning and politeness', he proclaims, 'must have a great degree of modesty or understanding, who does not give a loose to some vanities which are apt to render him ridiculous every where but at home. Bred among men of talents inferior to himself, he is too apt to assume the lead, as well from the press as in conversation, and to over-rate his own abilities.'[91] This is pretty rich, coming from one bred far from the centre of learning and politeness in County Westmeath, who became a penniless vagrant in Europe and an impoverished hack in London.[92] The supposedly parochial Dunkin was actually granted a doctorate of divinity at Trinity the year before Goldsmith himself graduated from the same academy with a somewhat more modest degree. And 'ridiculous', from all accounts, is a term more appropriate to the clownish Goldsmith himself than to anything we know of his Dublin colleague. Provincialism, from

91.   Arthur Friedman (ed.), *Collected Works of Oliver Goldsmith* (Oxford, 1966), vol. 1, p. 231.

92.   For a meticulous study of Goldsmith the journalist, see Richard C. Taylor, *Goldsmith as Journalist* (London and Toronto, 1993).

Goldsmith's adopted English neo-classical standpoint, is a kind of disproportioning, just like sentimentalism: living without peers in an intellectual backwater, you get a distorted estimate of yourself, so that the small appears great and everyone becomes his own measure.

It is just this situation which Dunkin's patron Swift dramatised through the persona of Lemuel Gulliver, who is pitched from one falsifying perspective to another and can never know how tall he really is, never get a grip from the outside on his true condition. One way to do this is by that study in comparative culture we know as travel, by which, as in Goldsmith's own poem *The Traveller*, one vantage-point may be checked off against another in order to arrive at some judicious estimation of the whole. But Gulliver never seems to learn from his travels, born anew as he seems with each expedition, a gullible *tabula rasa* at the start of each voyage. Like the sentimentalist, Swift's anti-hero is either too complacently cocooned within his own experience to take the measure of otherness, or like some credulous postmodernist goes instantly overboard for otherness and loses all hold on his own judgemental criteria. The result of this cultural relativism is madness and despair, which is hardly the typical condition of the Man of Feeling. An excess of sensibility, one might claim, is more neurotic than psychotic; yet it involves a similar incapacity to sort the central from the peripheral, since 'feeling' will yield one no epistemological clue to such distinctions. As a stout Tory, Goldsmith rejects a condition in which every individual is the measure of himself, whether economically or affectively. For him as for Swift, there is something sinisterly anti-social about such eccentricity, which is not at all the endearing 'humour' or amiable idiosyncrasy it is for his compatriot Laurence Sterne.

Goldsmith writes as an Englishman, though the adjectives commonly used of his literary style – smooth, genial, easy, limpid, tender, elegant, charming, simple, graceful, good-humoured – suggest an intriguing blend of stereotypically Irish and English traits.[93] It is an Anglo-Irish mode of writing in every sense of the term, with the oxymoronic quality of an easy elegance or polished spontaneity. If his foreign visitor to England in *The Citizen of the World* is Chinese rather than Irish, it is partly because, as one critic bluntly remarks, 'in 1760 an Irishman's reaction to English life would have interested no one'.[94] Goldsmith himself acidly remarked that England was a country where being born an Irishman was enough to keep one unemployed, and the fact that he adopted the rather hackneyed alien-observer form in the first place has its own significance. If you are a second-class subject in Britain, you can always compensate by becoming a citizen of the world, which is a grand way of being a citizen of nowhere. Seamus Deane points out that 'of all the Irish writers of the eighteenth century, [Goldsmith] is perhaps the least

93.   For a survey of Goldsmith criticism, see G. S. Rousseau (ed.), *Goldsmith: The Critical Heritage* (London and Boston, 1974).
94.   Ralph M. Wardle, *Oliver Goldsmith* (London, 1957), p. 111.

affected by any national sentiment'; his Ireland is a fond prelapsarian memory viewed almost with the eyes of a foreigner, not the actual country of penal laws and agrarian disturbances.[95] Some early letters from Edinburgh reveal him as homesick, which is not the same thing as feeling patriotic, and astutely aware of how the British stereotype him: 'I have spent more than a fortnight every second day at the Duke of Hamilton's, but it seems they like me more as a *jester* than as a companion . . . I shew'd my talent and acquir'd the name of the facetious Irishman. . .'.[96] He has, he remarks, an unaccountable fondness for his native country, but instantly undercuts the compliment by claiming that he is entirely at a loss to say why. The Irish are neither fine, witty, learned or good company; their productions in learning amount to 'a few tracts in laborious divinity' and their productions in wit 'to just nothing at all'.[97]

A review by Goldsmith in the *Weekly Magazine* takes just this lordly attitude to his fellow countrymen. If Irish Protestants are 'affable, foolish, prodigal, hospitable, and often not to be depended upon', the 'original Irish' are too frequently 'fawning, insincere, and fond of pleasure, prodigality makes them poor, and poverty makes them vicious. . .'.[98] To cap it all, Irish women's legs are too thick. It is property, Goldsmith considers, which draws individuals into communities and forms them into a people, and the Irish have too little of this to count as a *bona fide* nation. They have no important national concerns to make them anxious, whereas the melancholic English are heavy with the gloom of imperial responsibility, and when transported to their Irish colony grow gayer and 'less addicted to reasoning'. There can be no Irish philosophy, so Goldsmith implies, since philosophy flourishes only in conditions of national freedom, political burdens and seriousness of mind. Here, then, in the fact that Ireland lacks an empire, is a novel explanation both for the Gaelic contribution to the cult of benevolence, and for the Irish incapacity for reasoning. Had Ireland owned England rather than *vice versa*, the nation would no doubt have produced some glum, heavy-duty theoreticians. Goldsmith wrote a notable essay on the Irish bard O'Carolan, liked to knock around with fellow Irishmen in London, and speaks in a review about Ireland of 'the manifest error, in politics, of a government which endeavours to enrich one part of its dominions by impoverishing another, and of chusing to have but one flourishing kingdom when it might be possessed of two';[99] but elsewhere he strongly intimates that Ireland's wretchedness is largely the upshot of its defective national character.[100] Stephen Gwynn judges from a linguistic blunder

95. Seamus Deane (ed.), *Field Day Anthology*, vol. 1, p. 660.
96. Katherine C. Balderston (ed.), *The Collected Letters of Oliver Goldsmith* (Cambridge, 1928), pp. 17, 18.
97. ibid, pp. 28–9.
98. Friedman, *Collected Works of Oliver Goldsmith*, vol. 3, p. 25.
99. Friedman, *Collected Works of Oliver Goldsmith*, vol. 1, pp. 91–2.
100. For an admirably thorough exposition of Goldsmith's attitudes to Ireland, see Wolfgang Zach, 'Oliver Goldsmith on Ireland and the Irish', in Heinz Kosok

Goldsmith makes in his journal *The Bee* that he spoke no Irish, even though he must have heard a good deal spoken around him as a youth.[101] In a catalogue of national deficiencies in *The Citizen of the World*, Ireland is characterised by the term 'absurdity', which is pretty well what Goldsmith's cronies thought of him. The Dubliner Richard Steele uses much the same language about Ireland in the *Spectator*.[102] Though *The Traveller* is dedicated to an Irishman, the country itself is clearly too eccentric to the European cultural mainstream to warrant treatment in the poem itself.

In an essay now thought to be authentic, Goldsmith writes of the 'enthusiasm [with which] I again revisit the happy island where I drew my first breath, and received the early pleasures and institutions of life'.[103] On the following page, true to his self-masking habits, he names this happy island as Britain, and dutifully celebrates it as the home of liberty. No sooner has he done so, however, than he puts in a word for cosmopolitanism: his ambition is to 'make the man who now boasts his patriotism, a citizen of the world', to 'level those distinctions which separate mankind', and to 'improve our native customs by whatever appears praise-worthy among foreigners'.[104] This, clearly, is the distinctly unJohnsonian voice of the cultural migrant, though the tension between Goldsmith's cultural liberalism and his Enlightenment universalism is severe enough. If he praises the Eskimos in one essay as blissfully content in their pre-civilised state, his liberal sympathies do not quite extend to the natives of New Holland, who 'scarce seem possessed of the intellects even of a monkey'.[105] Goldsmith is a kind of cultural Darwinist who recognises that traits labelled as barbaric by the developed nations may well be perfectly adapted to different social conditions. The Tartars speak a barren and defective language, but since they have few ideas to express in the first place, this is no great loss. They also live mid-way between 'savage wretchedness' and 'excruciating refinement', which perhaps makes Goldsmith himself a sort of honorary Tartar. As for the Irish, they are 'remarkable for the gaiety and levity of their dispositions',[106] content with pleasure and indolence; but since they have no important national concerns to be damaged by these defects, they can be blandly exculpated.

> (ed.), *Studies in Anglo-Irish Literature* (Bonn, 1982). For a slighter sketch, see Robert W. Seitz, 'The Irish Background of Goldsmith's Thought', *PMLA*, vol. 52 (1937), which views Goldsmith's adoption of English middle-class values as a reaction to his Irish roots.

101.   Stephen Gwynn, *Oliver Goldsmith* (London, 1935), p. 59. Goldsmith receives only one passing reference in Gwynn's popular potboiler *Irish Literature and Drama in English* (London, 1936).
102.   See D. Bond (ed.), *The Spectator* (Oxford, 1965), vol. 1, p. 87.
103.   Ronald S. Crane (ed.), *New Essays by Oliver Goldsmith* (Chicago, 1927), p. 14.
104.   ibid, p. 17.
105.   ibid, p. 25.
106.   ibid, p. 51.

Goldsmith's *History of England* praises William of Orange's campaign in Ireland, notes Catholic but not Protestant atrocities, and produces what must be one of the most emollient accounts of the flight of the Wild Geese and the penal era on historical record: 'Roman catholics, by this capitulation [i.e. the defeat at Limerick], were restored to the enjoyment of such liberties in the exercises of their religion as they had possessed in the reign of Charles II – about fourteen thousand of those who had fought in favour of king James had permission to go over to France, and transports were provided for their reception.'[107] It is gratifying to learn that the Wild Geese did not have to slog it on foot to Paris. Goldsmith was no Ascendancy *parvenu*: he sprang from an Anglo-Irish family which had settled in the country in the sixteenth century, and which claimed some kinship with Cromwell; and though his writings strive occasionally to counter anti-Irish prejudice, it is scarcely surprising that his view of *merus Hibernicus* should be so drearily formulaic. It is no more surprising that Goldsmith, an Irishman, should find the mass of the Irish shiftless and fawning than it is that an English Victorian banker should find Lancashire mill-workers idle and contumacious. In this respect at least, class is a good deal thicker than ethnicity.

If Goldsmith was keen to put some daylight between himself and his native soil, however, others were less eager to co-operate. His Victorian biographer John Forster draws a direct connection between his celebrated good humour and his Irish roots: 'His generous warmth of heart, his transparent simplicity of spirit, his quick transitions from broadest humour to gentlest pathos, and that delightful buoyancy of nature which survived in every depth of misery, – who shall undertake to separate these from the Irish soil in which they grew, where impulse predominates still over reflection and conscience, where unthinking benevolence yet passes for considerate goodness, and the gravest duties of life can be overborne by social pleasure, or sunk in mad excitement?'[108] It is interesting to note how the compliment grows steadily sourer as it unfolds, until what begins as commendation ends up as accusation. Here, with a vengeance, is the Gael with the tear in his eye and the smile on his lips, though with one hand wrapped a little too tightly around the ale-jug. Forster will later write of the Scottish Boswell in much the same stereotyping terms, as 'a goodnatured jolly fellow. Everybody admits that the frost of our English nature melted at his first approach. . . .'.[109] 'Melted' is a key sentimentalist term; and Goldsmith himself writes of the 'luxuriance of his [own] nature', meaning his genial love of good company.[110]

107. *A History of England*, in J. W. M. Gibbs (ed.), *The Works of Oliver Goldsmith* (London, 1886), vol. 5, p. 338.

108. John Forster, *The Life and Times of Oliver Goldsmith* (London, 1854), vol. 2, p. 84. The Cork artist Daniel Maclise, a topic of chapter 5, contributed some of the illustrations for this volume.

109. ibid, pp. 368–9.

110. Balderston, *The Collected Letters of Oliver Goldsmith*, p. 46.

Goldsmith himself did not help matters by conforming in real life to the stereotype of the colonial blow-in far too eager to please. Desperate to be loved, he regularly made a fool of himself in company with all the pathetic insecurity of the outsider. That he was also bald, remarkably ugly, scarred by smallpox, furnished with a thick brogue and with the mien of a 'low mechanic' no doubt contributed to this anxiety; but it is hard even so not to discern something of the expatriate cringer in his conduct. (As far as the brogue goes, we know that he did not regard 'key' and 'be' as a rhyme.) According to Sir Joshua Reynolds, '(h)e would therefore, to draw the attention of the company upon [himself], sing, stand upon his head, [or] dance about the room'.[111] Forster describes him dressing up in smart clothes, and provides an onlooker's account of the grotesque effect: 'with what a ludicrous assumption of dignity he would show off his cloak and his cane, as he strutted with his queer little figure, stuck through as with a huge pin by his wandering sword . . .'.[112] There is a touch of Wilde about this flamboyant self-exhibiting, though the elegant Dubliner carried it off with a good deal more aplomb than the scrawny Midlander. 'All his adult life', observes his biographer Ralph Wardle, 'he indulged in extravagant flourishes designed to dazzle'.[113] Like Wilde too, Goldsmith preserved a secret pact with poverty and failure: even in his more affluent years, he looked back with fond nostalgia on the low dives he had haunted as a recent immigrant to London. What he wrote of David Garrick – that he was natural, simple and affecting on stage, and acted only when he was off it – was surely a self-comment too. In real life, Goldsmith tried too hard for the limelight and cut an absurd figure; it was only in the artifice of writing that he could be himself.

Ralph Wardle speculates intelligently that Goldsmith's apparent foolishness might have been to some extent a matter of cultural crossed wires. What he probably uttered in jest was taken as clumsy portentousness by the Johnson circle, who did not share his impish, fantastical vein of humour.[114] 'Goldy' was the butt of the group, and when Johnson was once asked whether Goldsmith had not been greatly helped by the partiality of his friends, he replied: 'No, sir, the prejudice of his friends was always against him.'[115] To

---

111. Rousseau, *Goldsmith: The Critical Heritage*, p. 174.
112. Forster, *The Life and Times of Oliver Goldsmith*, vol. 1, p. 395.
113. Wardle, *Oliver Goldsmith*, p. 11.
114. There seem to have been several Irish members of the Johnson circle apart from Goldsmith himself: Edmund Burke, the dramatist Hugh Kelly (who was born near Killarney but then moved to Dublin), the Roscommon actor and playwright Arthur Murphy, an Irishman named Glover who was a protégé of David Garrick, and perhaps the Donegal-born playwright Charles Macklin, who inadvertently killed a fellow actor in Drury Lane as George Farquhar had injured one on stage in Dublin. Two such incidents would appear more careless than tragic. Taken together with the Scot, Boswell, this makes for a remarkably high proportion of Gaels in the entourage of a man who despised them.
115. Quoted by Gwynn, *Oliver Goldsmith*, p. 13.

complete his stage-Irish properties, he was recklessly generous, the easiest touch in the world for some spare change.[116] Extravagantly improvident, he represented in his own life everything against which his soberly neo-classical writing protests, and was thus 'Anglo-Irish' in a schizoid as well as ethnic sense, fissured down the middle between an English petty-bourgeois prudence and a stereotypical Hibernian good nature. Much of his work can be read as an auto-critique or strategic resolution of this contradiction, seeking some acceptable balance between benevolence and frugality, dependence and autonomy, *sancta simplicitas* and a necessary vigilance to evil. Style is one aspect of this resolution, since simplicity is a near neighbour of polished lucidity, and thus a Gaelic entry-ticket to the literary metropolis. Wit, similarly, is both the *arriviste's* way of impressing the insiders, and a technique for venting one's genuinely subversive impulses in socially acceptable form. In Goldsmith, as much as in Shaw and Wilde, it is critical and conformist together, not least since wit is traditionally both the property of the Irish populace and of the English upper classes.

But the real-life conflict in Goldsmith nonetheless persisted: 'I have passed my days', he writes from England to his brother Henry in Ireland, 'among a number of cool designing beings and have contracted all their suspicious manner, in my own behaviour. I should actually be as unfit for the society of my friends at home as I detest that which I am obliged to partake of here. I can now neither partake of the pleasure of a revel nor contribute to raising its jollity. I can neither laugh nor drink, have contracted a hesitating disagreeable manner of speaking, and a visage that looks illnature itself, in short I have thought myself into settled melancholy and an utter disgust of all that life brings with it.'[117] Melancholia was ranked among the prototypical English diseases, and it may well be that the image of the Gael as more light-hearted than the Anglo-Saxon had to do with the absence of a puritan inheritance in most of the colonial island. However that may be, Goldsmith finds himself marooned between two worlds, in exile both at home and abroad. Indeed he was in all kinds of ways a divided self: a shy, brash man who praised originality and consistently plagiarised others, polished as a writer and buffoonish in real life, a spendthrift who spoke up for frugality, a hard-pressed hack who denounced the professionalisation of letters, a man who delighted in simplicity but revelled in masquerades, a scribe with a feckless streak who nevertheless churned out in a period of a few years a play, two biographies, a clutch of poems, a two-volume history of Rome, a four-volume history of England and the best part of an eight-volume *History of the Earth and Animated Nature.* He was one of the busiest loungers in the business, and many, if not all, of his

116. For an account of Goldsmith's spendthrift character, see Edward L. McAdam, Jr, 'Goldsmith, the Good-Natured Man', in F. W. Hilles (ed.), *The Age of Johnson* (New Haven and London, 1949).
117. Balderston, *The Collected Letters of Oliver Goldsmith*, p. 58.

contradictions can be related to his expatriatism. If he regretted what he saw as the more congenial atmosphere of Ireland, he nevertheless preserved a strain of it in his criticism, which is always marked by a most unAugustan affability. 'While we censure as critics', he notes in *The Critical Review*, 'we feel as men.'[118] Charity, in short, begins at home – which is where, for Burke, lack of charity begins in revolutionary France.

Goldsmith was well-known as an enemy of sentimentalism in the theatre, fearing as he did that humour in stage comedy was being swamped by tears and tender feeling.[119] Of Richard Steele's play *The Conscious Lovers*, the very paradigm of such effusions, one eighteenth-century critic observed with remarkable understatement that 'for risibility here is no food'.[120] Goldsmith himself damned his compatriot Steele with faint praise, characterising his comedies as 'perfectly polite, chaste, and genteel'.[121] Of the three epithets, one suspects that only 'chaste' would win Goldsmith's unqualified approval. As a traditional satirist, he rebukes sentimental comedy for indulging rather than chiding the folly of extravagant feeling and excessive generosity, for its bland ideology of goodness of heart, its lack of ridicule and criticism. His own drama took its cue not from his countryman Steele but from his compatriot George Farquhar,[122] who stood to Steele somewhat as Goldsmith himself stood to his theatrical rival Hugh Kelly, sentimentalist son of a Dublin tavern keeper. He wrote consciously against 'genteel' comedy, all tremulous pathos, high-toned moralism and heavy sententiousness, so that his reversion to a more venerable comic tradition became a radical smack at the 'progressives'. In this anti-sentimentalist project on the English stage, his closest affinity was with one of his compatriots, Richard Sheridan. Both of his major plays were a good deal too 'low' for English taste. Goldsmith begins his *Enquiry into the Present State of Polite Learning in Europe* by confessing that the theme of the work – the decline of learning in contemporary society – is something of a cliché, so that he is 'adopting the sentiments of the multitude in a performance that at best can only please the Few'.[123] This recalls Berkeley's rather similar blend of populism and élitism. In Goldsmith's drama *The Good-Natur'd Man*, as Thomas Kilroy points out, the two theatrical styles of popular comedy and high sentiment mix but do not blend, as the main characters speak the language of refined feeling while the minor figures display a collo-

118. Friedman, *Collected Works of Oliver Goldsmith*, vol. 1, p. 160.
119. See 'An Essay on Theatre', ibid, vol. 3.
120. Quoted by Shirley Strum Kenny (ed.), Richard Steele, *The Conscious Lovers* (London, 1967), p. xvi.
121. *A History of England*, in J. W. M. Gibbs (ed.), *The Works of Oliver Goldsmith* (London, 1886), vol. 5, p. 345.
122. Christopher Murray describes Farquhar as helping to 'alter the style and tone of English comedy by abandoning the usual city setting for (in his best plays) a rural setting where a more uninhibited study of human nature could be undertaken' (*Field Day Anthology*, vol. 1, p. 503).
123. Friedman, *Collected Works of Oliver Goldsmith*, vol. 1, p. 258.

quial naturalness and vigour.[124] 'The natural man', Kilroy writes, '(i.e. the one beyond the pale of civility), untutored in the ways of the world is a figure representing, alternatively, alien, crude values or values that offer restorative powers to a jaded civilisation.'[125] It is a neat way to summarise the Gaelic input into eighteenth-century English culture.

In *She Stoops to Conquer*, as Kilroy notes, the low, commonsensical, rural style is allowed to triumph over metropolitan sophistication. The play turns on a transposition of public and private spaces, as its English gentlemen mistake a domestic setting for an inn. But the opposition is complicated: an inn in any case occupies some indeterminate zone between private and public, both for its customers and for those who run it. If the Hardcastles' home is taken for a tavern, it remains a home even so for the family who live there, rather as the Irish small farm is both a working space and a domestic arena. Confusing the private and the public in this way, which is what Edmund Burke thought the French Jacobins did, is a kind of reversal of Burke's own political values, which convert civil society into a family just as Goldsmith's mystified protagonists transmute a family into a public sphere. It is, so to speak, an anti-sentimentalist blunder on the part of Marlow and Hastings, who project public anonymity onto a realm of intimacy rather than *vice versa*.

The comedy has fun with the fact that the same material space or discourse mutates according to one's way of contextualising it: conventional frameworks alter physical reality, as a piece of behaviour comes to signify quite differently depending on whether one takes it to be happening in an alehouse or a private house. What is acceptable in the one case becomes rank arrogance in the other. The Irish writers were peculiarly well-placed to storm the heights of English comic theatre because as outsiders on the inside they could appreciate that simultaneous givenness and arbitrariness of social convention on which comic drama thrives. Goldsmith, not least in his poem *The Traveller*, wandered some way down the path of cultural relativism. His work stands at a point where Enlightenment universalism is now being modified by a 'culturalism' thrown up by an interest in 'national' history and sociology; and when he writes in *An Enquiry into the Present State of Polite Learning in Europe* that the rules of criticism 'should be taken from among the inhabitants, and adapted to the genius and temper of the country it attempts to refine',[126] we hear a kind of literary equivalent of Edmund Burke's insistence that colonial nations must be governed according to their own customs. Enlightenment universalism no doubt figured for Goldsmith as a welcome escape from Irish parochialism; but at the same time the émigré is likely to be more responsive to cultural difference than metropolitan intellectuals like Samuel Johnson, who for the most part despised it.

---

124.   Thomas Kilroy, 'Anglo-Irish Playwrights and the Comic Tradition', in M. P. Hederman and R. Kearney (eds.), *The Crane Bag Book of Irish Studies* (Dublin, 1982).
125.   ibid, p. 440.
126.   Friedman, *Collected Works of Oliver Goldsmith*, vol. 1, p. 295.

The émigré needs and envies social conventions because he is insecure, but also mocks and sees through them as alien to the very self they shore up. If Wilde was unconventional, it was partly by parodying English conventions with such (mock) fidelity that they became unreal. Marlow is brash in a public setting but bashful in a private one, just as Goldsmith himself was a curious blending of coyness and exhibitionism. For the expatriate, the two go logically together – not only because boisterousness can be a familiar mask for shyness, but because the outsider is both intimidated by the social establishment and spurred into frenetic self-display in order to court its favour. Goldsmith was a convivial creature who sang, gambled and played the flute, blurted out his feelings in polite company and wore his heart ostentatiously on his sleeve; but he seems to have had no sexual life to speak of, and to have lived much of the time in solitude. But this private/public contradiction in the émigré is just what allows him a shrewd insight into the character of the upper-class insiders. If Marlow is typically English, it is because he is, as it were, naturally unnatural, stammering, socially inhibited, constrained by convention and unspontaneous by nature, and can only be more truly himself when the artifice of anonymous public convention intervenes between him and his interlocutors. He can flirt with a woman whom he takes to be a barmaid, but is gauche and tongue-tied in the presence of a lady. The English, so the play intimates, need their class-structure in order to be themselves, depend on the conventional for the authentic. One is reminded of the old adage that the great advantage of being born a gentleman is that one never needs to behave like one. For a young blood like Marlow, taking liberties with a lower-class woman is itself partly a matter of role-playing and convention, but the protective distance of class here allows him to feel free while making free, as, paradoxically, the intimacy of talking to a female of his own rank does not. There is no simple antithesis between nature and convention: the latter does not just stifle true feeling but can help to nurture it, rather as for the sentimentalists there is nothing more socially prestigious than the display of 'natural' emotion. Class is a mediator as well as a barrier, since it provides surer signals and a more instantly intelligible code than the vagaries of the heart.

Marlow, like his creator, is in some respects a kind of internal émigré, one of life's onlookers who confesses to his crony that he has lived in the world but in a private, solitary fashion. What he needs to feel at ease with himself is a social inferior to dominate, and it is this with which Mr Hardcastle unwittingly supplies him. The piece is very acute in grasping the internal relations in English society between private reserve and public arrogance, as opposed to the benevolistic ethic of treating strangers as friends and social inferiors as companions. Marlowe should treat Hardcastle the innkeeper more like he treats Hardcastle the gentleman. He is too much the gentleman to be spontaneous, but too uncivil when he feels at home, and so too little the gentleman in a moral rather than social sense of the term. He is either too free or too unfree, whereas true friendship involves an equipoise of intimacy and respect. Since an inn is both a place for conviviality between equals and a social hierarchy, it models two conflicting kinds of society, one which may remind Goldsmith of the contrast between Ireland and England. (The error on which the play revolves was one made by Goldsmith himself in County Longford, so that to this extent the plot has an Irish root.)[127]

Urban overcivility breeds its own form of undercivility, as Marlow issues his imperious orders to a man he takes to be an innkeeper, a brusqueness which is only not rude because it is socially conventional. In this, he becomes a kind of inverted mirror-image of the loutish Toby Lumpkin, whose churlishness is tolerable only because it is natural. There is, so the implication runs, no natural or absolute rudeness; what counts as insolence is contextually defined, and if this is extended to the whole gamut of human feeling, then the sentimentalist's assumption that emotions are as natural as cabbages is satirically undermined. Sentiment and convention are complexly interwoven as well as at odds with each other; and this is an insight more accessible to the émigré than to the insider, who tends to regard feelings as natural because he is too much on the inside of the codes which govern them. At the same time, the play exploits the clash between passion and social code in the venerable English comic question of what constitutes an appropriate marriage. What is comic about desire is that it is absolutely no respector of social distinctions, which is also what is most alarming about it.

The meeting-place of social codes and structures of feeling is known as national character, which provides the motif of Goldsmith's *The Traveller*. The traveller is another insider/outsider, distanced enough from a place to scrutinise its manners closely, but also detached enough to move on. This formal ambivalence in the traveller figure, who is in one sense independent of his environment yet is also, as a vagrant, parasitic upon it, then reflects in the poem's structure part of what it observes, which is different kinds of national imbalance between stout autonomy and social bonding. Goldsmith habitually sees excessive or sentimentalist benevolence as a kind of 'colonial' oppressiveness: he who insists on putting others in his debt by his prodigal generosity is in fact a slave to those he favours, since it is insecurity of selfhood, a too-eager desire for others' applause, which motivates his lavishness in the first place. Young Honeywood, the protagonist of *The Good-Natur'd Man*, is absurdly munificent, and so 'too much every man's man'. As one who 'calls his extravagance, generosity', he needs to be brought to his senses by a fictional device, whereupon he resolves to stop being 'the voluntary slave of all'. At the close of the play, he comes to a kind of independence or separatism of spirit, a 'self-dependent power' as *The Deserted Village* puts it. Goldsmith thus mends in art what he apparently could not rectify in life, whereas Wilde invested in his life much of what never found expression in his art.

127.   See Forster, *The Life and Times of Oliver Goldsmith*, vol. 1, p. 20.

To please everyone means debasing the currency of your kindness and so giving away much less than you imagined. Shakespeare's *Timon of Athens* turns on this paradox. The man who bestows himself promiscuously simply to shore up a weak ego has little of himself to give in the first place, and depletes himself the more with each act of apparent liberality. This cult of self-expenditure, as Goldsmith perceives, is in fact a devious form of egoism, which is one reason for his hostility to sentimentalism: it is a kind of *trompe l'oeil* by which what you appear to proffer is secretly conferred on yourself. Bountifulness pressed to a parodic extreme collapses back into selfishness. The Sterne of *A Sentimental Journey* will reap devastating comic capital from this ambiguous co-existence of the altruistic and the self-regarding, which in that proto-Freudian novel takes the form of the closeness and discrepancy between the ego and the unconscious. Those who seek too hard to please, like the more conformist and obsequious of the Irish, need to have their identity recurrently reconfirmed in the eyes of those they feel to be their superiors, aggressively reversing that power-relation by their flamboyant good nature.

A kindness which fails to reckon the cost is just a symptom of self-brooding anxiety, and in cavalierly overriding the intrinsic values of things it is secretly indifferent to the very objects it purports to cherish. Generosity, Goldsmith considers, is a mortifying, detestable virtue which degrades its recipient by making him cravenly obliged; but he is clearly thinking here of whimsical acts of great-hearted largesse, and explicitly contrasts this with a rule-bound, customary generosity which involves reciprocal obligations. It is, one suspects, a contrast between the self-indulgent tenderness of the English upper classes, and a social order like Ireland in which human sympathies are seen as bound up with a traditional way of life. A native benevolence, once it becomes caught up in unequal exchange with others, corrupts into sentimentalism, and in alienating those whose approval one courts, it shifts from a form of self-giving to a mode of self-estrangement. Goldsmith himself seems to have felt that he existed only episodically, in the patronising good-will of his English friends, returning in the intervals to a kind of solitary non-being. In this sense too, then, emotions are intricately bound up with power, subjugation, convention, and the sentimentalist's view of them as natural, the pre-social root from which sociality itself stems, is once more covertly demystified. That sentimentalism involves a kind of inequality is evident in the fact that its favoured objects are very often children and animals.

In *The Traveller*, it is the French, sentimentalists *par excellence*, who gain the unenviable title of Europe's prime grovellers, by-passing the 'solid worth of self-applause' in their scrambling for the praise of others. Goldsmith shares with Maria Edgeworth the characteristically English feeling that the French talk about feelings rather than experience them, cerebralise the whole business of the affections in a rhetoric as icy in form as it is passionate in content. France is the home of the phantasmalisation of feeling, and Edmund Burke will later aim just this accusation at its revolutionaries, whose doctrine of universal benevolence is in his eyes entirely bogus, a kind of spectral parody of authentic affection rather than the warm-hearted thing itself. What Burke dismisses as benevolence from the standpoint of genuine feeling, Goldsmith spurns as sentimentalism from what we might call the viewpoint of benevolence. The terms are different but the attitudes more or less identical. The English in *The Traveller*, on the other hand, veer too far the other way in their possessive individualism: these 'self-dependent lordlings' overvalue an independence which 'Keeps man from man, and breaks the social tie'.[128] They are sectarian, contentious and uncongenial, replacing the bonds of nature with the 'fictitious' ties of 'wealth and law', so that 'All claims that bind and sweeten life' are unknown to them. It is worth recalling that a respect for the binding power of customs and traditions which had become second nature to them is part of what distinguished the Irish from an English trust in the juridical contract. In an essay in his journal *The Bee*, Goldsmith elevates custom over law in just this Irish style: since custom 'partakes of the nature of parental injunction . . . it is kept by the people themselves, and observed with a willing obedience'. As with Burke rather later, custom is a familial ('parental') sort of law, a fusion of public and domestic spheres which is thus all the more willingly internalised, and so all the more hegemonic.[129]

There is a faint hint of oxymoron about that most common of figures, the 'Irish exile', since the noun marks a lonely individualism which the adjective stereotypically undercuts. The problem, it would seem, is how to foster communitarianism without conformity or servile dependency, and how to achieve self-reliance without courting social anomie. The expatriate bears a kind of answer to this problem within himself, since like the traveller he is inside and outside others at the same time, so that his material situation can itself become the figure of an equipoise between being too dissociated and being too dependent. The traveller is in one sense more dependent than the natives because he is far from home and needs their help, but in another sense he is less so, since he can always move on. It is just that in reality, as Goldsmith found in his own life, this balancing-act is bafflingly hard to pull off. Sentimentalism, by contrast, which turns subjectivism itself into a medium of social intercourse, is a false as well as ironic resolution to this dilemma. It is a kind of homeopathy of the spirit, seeking to cure an isolating individualism with a dose of the very subjectivism which is its mirror-image in the realm of culture. Like the sentimentalists, Goldsmith wants to root civil society in social sympathies; but like his compatriot Francis Hutcheson he also wants to

128.   A Goldsmith verse characterising the writer Richard Cumberland ends with the line 'He grew lazy at last and drew from himself'. For a discussion of this anti-egoism and a defence of Goldsmith as neo-classical conservative, see Robert H. Hopkins, *The True Genius of Oliver Goldsmith* (Baltimore, 1969).

129.   See Friedman, *Collected Works of Oliver Goldsmith*, vol. 1, 'Custom and Law Compared'. For Burke and hegemony, see Terry Eagleton, *Heathcliff and the Great Hunger* (London, 1995), ch. 2.

define those sympathies as being as given and objective as political society itself. When Roger Lonsdale writes of Goldsmith's 'blending of traditional form, content and style with a new sensibility and rhetoric',[130] or of the way that the 'objective' account of *The Traveller* is framed within a subjective standpoint, he points to the formal equivalents of this resolution.

Sentiment in *The Deserted Village* is controlled by being focused on the observed details of the actual place, which provides it with an objective correlative and restrains it from lapsing into mere self-indulgent nostalgia. One might contrast this with Gray's *Elegy*, in which the churchyard itself, its details suitably dimmed down by dusk, is little more than a peg on which to hang a melancholy which turns out in the end to be self-regarding. Mortality in the poem is finally more a problem for poets than for peasants. The spare, lucid realism of Goldsmith's poem, however emblematically edited, is played off against a feeling which is also held in place by the tight, pointed couplet form. It is worth noting how finely adapted that form is, with its neat structure of antitheses and chiasmic inversions, to the capturing of social contradictions: 'The robe that wraps his limbs in silken sloth, / Has robbed the neighbouring fields of half their growth'. The very compression of elements required by the economical couplet form shockingly heightens the sense of dialectical oppositions.

But the poem's shapely form, while gaining an edge over its unheroic materials, does not break faith with them either. If it stands off from them enough to frame an affectionately ironic commentary of which the villagers themselves might not be capable, its simplicity has a root in their lives. Goldsmith knows more than these people, but that superior knowledge is part of what inclines him to look at the world from their own standpoint. When he writes that the village poor are 'To me more dear, congenial to my heart, / One native charm, than all the gloss of art', the unguarded directness of the comment performatively enacts what it announces. This ironic balance of simplicity and complexity – a 'pastoral' affair, in Empson's terms – then reflects itself in the poem's language, which in neo-classical style is at once plain and overcoded, as the couplets pack a plethora of information into their slim space and force every element to work overtime. In this poetic form, nothing can be allowed to idle: every verb or epithet must add its small freight of modifying significance to a whole which absorbs them without losing grip on its steady march of sense. Gray's *Elegy*, by contrast, makes no attempt to bridge the gap between its own elaborately self-consciously literary language and the 'swains' it contemplates. Poet and peasant are linked only by a common mortality, in what Raymond Williams might have called a 'negative identification',[131] and the abyss between them is part of the point, underlining a

130. Roger Lonsdale (ed.), *The Poems of Gray, Collins and Goldsmith* (London, 1969), p. 672.
131. Williams actually uses this term of *The Deserted Village* itself, a poem which he curiously takes to be 'self-regarding', and which he describes as 'baffling'

solitude on the poet's part which the villagers share objectively with him because they are dead, but which for just the same reason they cannot share with him subjectively.

Goldsmith's piece gradually fans out from the village itself to a more global indictment of a whole social order. But though the poem evolves from small beginnings into a comprehensive critique, its Empsonian-pastoral technique of putting the complex within the simple means, once more, that it does not break faith with the people whom this critique is supposed to serve, and who return at the end, suitably allegorised, in person as it were. The synoptic view of the poet, one also evident in *The Traveller*, enhances rather than diminishes the status of the local tragedy in a deft interweaving of concrete and abstract, sometimes within single phrases. The poem's register is neither detailed personal experience nor generalising sententiousness, but some negotiated territory between the two. These humble individuals are important on humanistic grounds, since all people matter, but also because the forces which are afflicting them are of global range and import. This is one reason why it matters so little whether the village in question is the author's Irish Lissoy or some English counterpart, for both of which there is some persuasive evidence. It does not matter not because locality does not matter, but because, as John Clare also recognised in gazing on his newly enclosed village, it is now part of the inner meaning of locality for it to be decentred outside itself. If Auburn is indeed a composite of Irish and English, then Goldsmith has here achieved what eludes him elsewhere, an equitable interaction of cultures; but this comes about not through some 'Anglo-Irish' literary synthesis, rather through the ironically negative fact that what links these different spots is the same exploitative economic system. Native and colonial depredations are aspects of the same political reality, and it is this, not some spiritual hands-across-the-sea, which is the most significant connection between the two islands.

Towards the end of *The Deserted Village*, Goldsmith compares a countryside ravaged by 'luxury' to a woman who, having lost her natural beauty, tarts herself up to attract lovers:

> But when those charms are past, for charms are frail,
> When time advances, and when lovers fail,
> She then shines forth sollicitous to bless,
> In all the glaring impotence of dress.
> Thus fares the land, by luxury betrayed,
> In nature's simplest charms at first arrayed,
> But verging to decline, its splendours rise,
> Its vistas strike, its palaces surprize...

---

without really explaining why. See *The Country and the City* (London, 1973), pp. 74–9.

The image is interestingly awry: the pomp of an 'improving' rural order is not intended to *seduce* anybody, and certainly not those labourers who are trooping from the land rather as the woman's lovers are casting her off. Read too literally, the image absurdly suggests that improving or enclosing landlords raise their piles and throw up their palaces in a desperate attempt to woo the countryfolk into remaining on the land. But the lines which follow then undercut this unintended implication:

> While scourged by famine from the smiling land,
> The mournful peasant leads his humble band . . .

The land is 'smiling' not to charm the mournful peasant into staying, but, as Donald Davie remarks, in a kind of heartless indifference to the peasants' plight.[132] Goldsmith is always at his least secure when he is pondering images of insecurity, since they remind him too much of his own condition. A rural landscape which by the poem's argumentative logic ought to be shown as haughtily estranging its inhabitants is actually portrayed as the excessively benevolent individual who, rather like the poet himself, whores after others' attentions without a shred of self-respect. This is no doubt because Goldsmith associates luxury in the economic sense with that more ethereal form of voluptuousness which is sentimentalism, and the wires between the two meanings have become momentarily crossed. For him, frugality is in the sphere of economics what anti-sentimentalism is in the realm of feeling. Sentimentality is emotion which is disproportionate to the object which motivates it, just as the fruits of an economic surplus detach themselves from the history which created them. W. J. Galloway points out that Goldsmith is inconsistent in his attitudes to luxury, sometimes assailing and sometimes justifying it: 'prudence and generosity [are] alternately exalted'.[133]

As for sentimentalism, *The Citizen of the World* pointedly refuses to exoticise Chinese culture, and ridicules the Orientalist vogue of the sentimentalists from an Enlightenment-universalist viewpoint. Moreover, whereas for the sentimentalist virtue is usually triumphant in worldly terms, Goldsmith is akin to Henry Fielding in holding that few individuals are in fact virtuous, and that worldly happiness more typically results from prudence rather than from nobility of character. As with Fielding, this is as much an implied criticism of the kind of society in which the virtuous find themselves as a metaphysical doctrine. Fielding remarks in *Tom Jones* that the belief that the good will reap their reward in this world has only one drawback, namely that it is not true.

132.   Donald Davie, *Purity of Diction in English Verse* (London, 1967), pp. 50–1. For something of the classical background to the poem, see Gail Bayliss, 'Goldsmith's "The Deserted Village": Images of the Dispossessed', in Joseph McMinn (ed.), *The Internationalism of Irish Literature and Drama* (Gerrards Cross, 1992)
133.   W. J. Galloway, Jr, 'The Sentimentalism of Goldsmith', *PMLA*, vol. 48, no. 4 (1933), p. 1167.

Goldsmith comments in *The Bee* that happiness depends in great measure upon 'constitution', meaning that the fortunately constituted can find something to provoke their good humour even in calamity. Sterne shares this brand of stoicism, the implication of which is that society itself is too harsh to lend itself to human felicity, a condition which must be achieved despite it. The puzzle for both Fielding and Goldsmith is how it can be that virtue is in one sense natural and in another sense in notably short supply, given that they both reject some progressive environmentalist explanation for this deficiency. Tom Jones's malign educators influence him not at all. Also, as far as 'sensibility' goes, the countryside of *The Vicar of Wakefield* is prosperously bourgeois rather than, in sentimental vein, rural-primitivist; and this one might see as among other things an Irish feature, since – for harshly obvious reasons – there is notably little aestheticisation of landscape in Irish literary culture.[134] Finally, Goldsmith's love of the thrifty and provident is also closer to his petty-bourgeois Irish provenance than it is to English upper-class consumerism. Indeed his politics can be seen as lying at the conjuncture between the stoutly self-reliant values of the lower middle class from which he sprang, and the English Tory distaste for commercialist extravagance which he adopted. Both positions have a robustly populist vein, and to be lower-middle-class is to be inside and outside polite society in much the same way as the émigré.

In *The Citizen of the World*, Goldsmith defends luxury in historical terms, outlining a sketch of human evolution with remarkable affinities to historical materialism. For science to flourish, a country must first become populous, developing its productive forces by what Marx will later dub a division of labour: 'the inhabitant', Goldsmith writes, 'must go through the different stages of hunter, shepherd, and husbandman, then when property becomes valuable, and consequently gives cause for injustice; then when laws are appointed to repress injury, and secure possession, when men by the sanction of those laws, become possessed of superfluity, when luxury is thus introduced and demands its continual supply, then it is that the sciences become necessary and useful; the state then cannot subsist without them. . .'.[135] Pastoral or nomadic society, an ensuing division of labour through the growth of private property, the consequent flourishing of a legal superstructure to regulate property rights, the development through these means of an economic surplus ('luxury') which lays the material basis for organised knowledge: the Anglo-Irish traditionalist is here strikingly at one, in historical if not in political doctrine, with the German revolutionist. For Goldsmith, this historical process recapitulates itself in the career of individual writers, who should strive for an economic surplus to emancipate themselves from dependence on the booksellers, and so be free to write what they want. His theory of the legendary English liberties is a thoroughly materialist one, not least because

134. See Terry Eagleton, *Heathcliff and the Great Hunger*, ch. 1.
135. Friedman, *Collected Works of Oliver Goldsmith*, vol. 2, p. 338.

he himself had bitter experience of how cultural autonomy and individual conscience were reliant on economic sufficiency. This is the voice of a hard-pressed émigré hack struggling to make good, not of an English cultural idealism oblivious of its own material conditions.

Once knowledge has established its autonomy on the back of a material surplus, however, it should, so to speak, curve back upon itself and justify its privileges by practical usefulness. Like Swift, Berkeley and Burke, Goldsmith disdains mere speculative reasoning, a prejudice which can be read both as a feature of commonsensical English Toryism and, as we have seen, of a colonial society in which such cerebrations seem an idle extravagance. The Scottish Enlightenment was similarly sceptical about metaphysical notions, viewing the intellect as a practical force to be harnessed to a developing economy. As far as the uses of knowledge go, all four Irish writers, along with Francis Hutcheson, are poised at the transition from a classical humanism to a modern utilitarianism. It is especially ironic in this respect that Goldsmith, apologist for a humane learning which predates the division of intellectual labour, should have been condemned to earn his living precisely by that odious professionalism, reviewing works with titles like 'An Essay on the Nature, Causes, and Cure of the Contagious Distemper among the Horned Cattle in these Kingdoms'. The fact that he did so at all, however, was testimony to the very ecumenism of vision which the volumes under review could be read as denying. When it comes to the historical growth of knowledge, Goldsmith sees like Marx that this depends on superfluity, on a certain structural dislocation between consciousness and circumstance; yet the irony, as with Marx, is that this privileged fissure between mind and world is itself materially determined. To this extent, Goldsmith conjures a politico-historical theory of the rise of systematic knowledge from a very English empiricism, which is alive to the way that understanding is anchored in need and desire. As far as the actual application of knowledge goes, he is opposed to what one might call the luxury or surplus of metaphysical conjecture, viewing knowledge in Baconian or Nietzschean style as entirely motivated by interest and desire. Wisdom has its lowly roots in pleasure and the drive for happiness: 'we . . . only are curious after knowledge when we find it connected with sensual happiness',[136] for 'the senses ever point out the way, and reflection comments on the discovery'.[137] Sterne, rather similarly, observes in *Tristram Shandy* that sense makes up half of reason.

Epistemological idealism is thus decentred, and philosophical empiricism extended to a sociological account of the relations between knowledge, interest and desire. Indeed Sterne himself will press this materialism to a typically travestying extreme, as the mind becomes helplessly dependent on the vagaries of the body. 'We consider', writes Goldsmith, 'few objects with ardent

136. ibid, p. 51.
137. ibid.

attention but those which have some connection with our wishes, our plea-sures, or our necessities.'[138] This, as we shall see, is an important move too in the quarrel between benevolence and sentimentalism, the former espousing a kind of practical affectivity which elevates the close-to-hand – which means, in effect, the family, clan or nation – over the abstractly political, the latter promoting an ethic of universal feeling remote from the specificity of its objects. When Goldsmith admonishes us not to separate 'sensual and senti-mental enjoyment',[139] he is pressing a benevolistic case for the unity of feel-ing and its material object, as against a sentimentalist abstraction of the affections from such workaday circumstances. The Yorick of A Sentimental Journey regards his sentiments as finely autonomous of the sensual, while betraying at every step their guilty complicity with it.

Just as the mind must be cognitively bent to its object, so for Goldsmith emotion must be appropriately adapted to its occasion. Thornhill in The Vicar of Wakefield was excessively benevolent as a young man, and makes the con-dition sound like an illness: it involved 'a sickly sensibility of the miseries of others', like one whose whole body is so exquisitely tender that the slightest touch gives pain. Such a cult is especially distasteful to Goldsmith because it presses to a sort of pathological extreme the kind of communal sympathies he himself cherishes. In an essay in The Bee on 'Justice and Generosity', he insists that true generosity is a duty with all the sternness of a law, a rule imposed upon us by reason 'which should be the sovereign law of a rational being'.[140] The Kantian language, so to speak, is revealing: Goldsmith wants to decon-struct the opposition between law and generous feeling by converting the lat-ter into an obligation; and in this he is true to the Christian gospel, for which charity is a question of law rather than a matter of personal whim. The notion that the Jews of the so-called Old Testament adhered to law rather than love is a piece of Christian anti-Semitism, since for a pious Jew the law in question was precisely the law of love. Only a Protestant subjectivism or naïve liber-tarianism would regard law and love as opposites. But Goldsmith's case is also in line with his Irish background, in which, as we have noted, the law of the imperial judiciary was often enough set aside for the equally binding edicts of custom, kinship and tradition. Because authentic generosity is 'lawful', it has nothing to do in Goldsmith's view with some sentimentalist yielding to the impulse of the moment. He desires instead a rational charity, and even goes so far as to praise avarice as socially useful, no doubt in a somewhat extrava-gant reaction to his own real-life profligacy.

A rational charity is not one in which warm-heartedness is judiciously repressed by the dictates of abstract reason, but one in which prudence, as it were, spaces charity out, organising and distributing it so that you don't give

138.   ibid, p. 335.
139.   ibid, p. 37.
140.   ibid, vol. 1, p. 406.

away all you have to the first beggar and leave yourself empty-handed when encountering the next. (As a student, Goldsmith gave away all his blankets to a destitute family and burrowed into his mattress to keep warm, from whence he had to be extricated by his friends.) Rationality is in the service of human benevolence, not (as in some Romantic or postmodern thought) its imperious opposite. Indeed Goldsmith seems to grasp the theological point that charity is not just one virtue to be ranked among others (prudence, fortitude, meekness and the like), but is rather the supreme virtue of which all others are no more than expressive modes. Patience, chastity, long-suffering and the like are unintelligible outside the context of charity. This differs from the view of the sentimentalists, for whom charity would seem a quirk of individual disposition, one optional life-style among several. It is as though there are those Christians who specialise in charity as a kind of private hobbyhorse, while others prefer to cultivate their personalities in terms of mysticism or self-flagellation. Sir Joshua Reynolds remarked that Goldsmith felt 'with exactness'; and though he was thinking of how he wrote his poems, the comment captures his sense that feeling itself must be shaped and structured like a sort of reason. Indeed the 'aesthetic' was the eighteenth century's name for this condition, in which love and law, the whims of the heart and unfeeling abstraction, could be deconstructed by an artefact whose affective pattern had all the rigorous necessity of an impersonal prescription. Burke understood this too, so that it is ironic that Goldsmith, in his generally favourable review of Burke's treatise on the sublime and the beautiful, should accuse the author of 'proceeding on principles not sufficiently established . . . He rejects all former systems, and founds his philosophy on his own particular feelings'.[141] This is to upbraid Burke for advocating just the kind of French philosophical method he was later to abhor.

Goldsmith's aversion to speculative reason goes hand-in-hand with his distaste for sentimentalism. 'A man', he writes in *The Bee*, 'who has taken his ideas of mankind from study alone, generally comes into the world with a heart melting at every fictitious distress.'[142] Heroic passions and big-hearted gestures are the stock-in-trade of theoreticians, whereas benevolence champions the ordinary, unglamorous, petty-bourgeois virtues of sobriety and frugality, however 'low' these may be considered by the spendthrifts of sensibility. Reckless improvidence is just as much a way of being out of touch with reality as academicist theory, though its softheartedness tends to conceal the fact. In populist spirit, Goldsmith trusts to the necessary rather than the superfluous, even though he is aware of how unfashionable this self-conscious meagreness must sound in the ears of some of the English upper classes. Necessity, roughly speaking, is Tory, a matter of hard-earned, home-grown production, whereas superfluity is Whig, a question of foreign importations which debilitate the native economy. England should not ruin its

141. ibid, p. 28.
142. ibid, p. 408.

emotional economy by importing sentimentalist goods from the likes of the French. Like his friend Samuel Johnson, Goldsmith is the best kind of Tory, one who believes that only such paternalism will protect the poor from the depredations of the free market. If he is a monarchist, it is because he holds in the manner of Burke that the throne is an essential counterweight to the invidious power of self-appointed oligarchies. He also entertains the rather odd belief that in a democracy those who transgress the law must be all the more severely punished just because they are also the people who prescribe it, whereas in a monarchical order such laws may occasionally be relaxed without danger to the constitution. Monarchism, in short, allows for a certain 'ductility' of law, an opinion which perhaps carries a resonance of an Irish rather than English attitude to legality. However that may be, there is no doubt that Goldsmith supports the monarchy because he sees in it a source of freedom for the common people.

The immigrant who enters a sophisticated metropolitan society from some more communitarian margin is clearly at risk of being taken for a ride. His innocence is a dangerous commodity, not least because it is likely to be the cause of vice in others. Tory novelists like Henry Fielding, as we have seen, believe that virtue is in some sense natural, yet that despite this there is mysteriously little of it around. 'Natural' here is certainly not 'average'. This broaches a dilemma, since if most people are morally indifferent then the good will need to look sharp for themselves and start calculating, in which case their virtue will no longer be spontaneous and so no longer be truly virtue. The more you are forced to defend your good nature, the less of it you have. Those who need to concentrate on their moral condition all the time are vulgar petty-bourgeois evangelicals, more Richardsonian than Goldsmithian. A gentleman does not need to work at his spiritual state any more than he needs to work at his accent. The problem for the Tory writer is that he combines a genteel belief in the non-laborious nature of virtue with a conservative estimate of its availability; and this means that good nature is likely to come under siege from the corruption encircling it without being equipped with the sort of devious resources necessary for repelling these assaults.

One way of resolving his difficulty is to split the self down the middle, adopting the mask of a satiric misanthropist while harbouring a benevolent heart behind it. This is the strategy of the Man in Black of *The Citizen of the World*, who, rather like Sterne's Yorick, is satirist and sentimentalist in the one body. Indeed Goldsmith thinks this a typically English condition: the English in his view are outwardly ill-natured, but 'with hearts sympathising with every distress'.[143] If they are hypocrites, then, they are hypocrites the right way round. Richard Steele thought similarly that the average English citizen 'conceals under a rough air and distant behaviour a bleeding compassion and womanish tenderness',[144] and Dickens reaps an almost erotic *frisson* from the

143. ibid, vol. 3, p. 85.
144. Quoted by Ketcham, *Transparent Designs*, p. 169.

paternalist figure who is outwardly gruff but inwardly melting. Many of Goldsmith's figures, as Seamus Deane points out, are dangerously impulsive philanthropists, from Honeywood and the Man in Black to Beau Nash and Dr Primrose.[145] His *Life of Richard Nash*, while less of a potboiler than his perfunctory biographies of Berkeley or Parnell, is a puzzling work just because the motivation for writing about so supremely trivial a character seems perversely obscure. The work makes sense only as covert autobiography, as Goldsmith confronts a man who, like himself, mixed ostentatiousness with a simple-minded trust of others and suffered from a disastrous excess of good nature. Other of Goldsmith's characters, like the protagonist of *The Chinese Letters*, Lien Chi Altangi, are at once ironists themselves, and gently satirised by their author for a naïve sententiousness.[146] It is a familiar double-focusing in eighteenth-century fiction: Swift uses Gulliver as a device to satirise some of the outlandish societies he encounters, but both they and Swift objectify him in turn. The Fielding of *Joseph Andrews* exploits the ingenuousness of Parson Adams to expose the worldly vice around him, but at the same time deploys that degeneracy to send up Adams's ludicrous naïvety.

Similarly, Primrose in *The Vicar of Wakefield* is both an ironist and an object of irony, a man who has seen through the snobbisms of his family but who also yields to them and to some degree shares them.[147] Like his expatriate author, he is a contradictory mix of participant and detached observer – in one sense an embodiment of the practical virtue Goldsmith approves, in another sense a moral theoretician comically remote from reality. Primrose is much given to sententious moralising, but he is also to some extent vigilant to worldly evil, and so neither saintly idiot nor hardboiled cynic. The geniality of the novel's irony similarly combines a humorous acceptance of the world with some astute satire of it. There is now something faintly ridiculous about virtue, which in bourgeois society has become bland and earnest in contrast to the dynamism it could display in an earlier, more heroic age. Virtue is amusing because of its gullibility, impotence, passivity, vulnerability and purely theoretic status; it has the preposterousness of an idea which is fine in theory but could not possibly be realised, so that the benevolent character comes to resemble a kind of mad inventor. It also has the tedium of a stock notion with which everyone is all too familar, but to which one can do absolutely nothing but formally assent, so that the virtuous personality is also a kind of bore. Like the speculative knowledge which Goldsmith despises, it

---

145. Seamus Deane, 'Goldsmith's *The Citizen of the World*', in Andrew Swarbuck (ed.), *The Art of Oliver Goldsmith* (London, 1984).

146. See Ronald Paulson, *Satire and the Novel in Eighteenth-Century England* (New Haven and London, 1967), pp. 217–18.

147. For a resolutely anti-sentimentalist reading of the novel, see Ricardo Quintana, '*The Vicar of Wakefield*: The Problem of Critical Approach', in *Modern Philology*, vol. 71 (August, 1973).

is true but pointless. In a social order where virtue signifies for the most part abstinence, constraint, negativity, the devil is bound to have all the best tunes.

Goldsmith, like Fielding and Austen, sees all this, but sees too, in an ironic double-take, that the world is predatory enough to render such ridiculousness quite unavoidable. Virtue is more praiseworthy if you have a low Tory estimate of the moral worth of most people, rather than, like the purveyors of sensibility, if you see it as a symptom of some supposed universal good nature. Its rarity is part of its value, but also of course poses a serious problem. The point of ironising Primrose's high-mindedness while taking it seriously – his politics, for example, are pretty much Goldsmith's own – is to capture this dialectical condition. If being good renders you derisible, then this is finally the fault of those who exploit you rather than of virtue itself, and those who find your virtue funny are at once right and morally dangerous. This is not a problem which can be resolved in practice; but it can be overcome by a literary form in which satire and romance are so blended that, as Seamus Deane remarks of the *Vicar*, 'irony subverts sentimentality, [and] sentimentality softens irony'.[148] The two are in any case likely to be blended in the Irish immigrant writer from Goldsmith to Shaw, who finds something eminently satirisable in the moral earnestness and high Arnoldian sentiment of the English, but who also finds his own more congenial or communitarian values being challenged by just the same set-up. If English society conjoins sensibility and social exploitation, the former as in some measure the acceptable face of the latter, then it is hardly surprising that it should provoke its critical observers into a mixture of satiric wit and benevolent feeling. The struggle between Primrose, a petty-bourgeois rural parson like Goldsmith's own father, and an oppressive landowning society can thus be seen to reflect a conflict between the two nations or value-systems which Goldsmith straddled, as well as one between the hardy virtues of the English yeomanry and a profligate aristocracy.

Goldsmith thought sentimentalist novels cheap and flashy, and with *Tristram Shandy* well in mind writes scornfully in *The Citizen of the World* of how 'readers must be treated with the most perfect familiarity; in one page the author is to make them a low bow, and in the next to pull them by the nose. . .'.[149] All this seems to him a vulgar self-indulgence, a grotesque parody of the kind of fellow-feeling which he himself speaks up for. Benevolence has degenerated into an arch manipulation of the reader, and social sympathy into an ill-bred knowingness. But he also disliked this literary mode because it struck him as a kind of prurient prying into the recesses of subjectivity, and the language he uses to decry it is thoroughly Burkeian. With tongue well in cheek, he praises such writers for the way they strip the veils of decency from human life: 'The veneration we have for many things, entirely proceeds from

148.   Deane, 'Goldsmith's *The Citizen of the World*', p. 48.
149.   Friedman, *Collected Works of Oliver Goldsmith*, vol. 2, p. 224.

their being carefully concealed . . . with what a noble spirit of freedom therefore must that writer be possessed, who bravely paints things as they are, who
lifts the veil of modesty, who displays the most hidden recesses of the temple,
and shows the erring people that the object of their vows is either perhaps a
mouse, or a monkey.[150] The sentimentalists do for Goldsmith just what the
Jacobins do for Burke, abolishing emotional and epistemological distance in
what looks like a new fraternity but is in fact a new form of domination.
Pressed too far, subjectivism converts others into objects. What appears like
compassion, a new ethic of feeling to counteract Enlightenment abstraction, is
in reality just a brutal desire to know, though now in the realm of the heart
rather than the sphere of the mind. The sympathetic imagination, when it runs
to excess, plunders others of their emotional booty to feed one's own voracious
sensibility.

Whether Laurence Sterne was practising sentimentalism or sending it up is a
contentious issue among his critics. The participants in a conference on his
work some years ago were unable to agree: one of them points to the way in
which Sterne satirically debunks his own sentimentalism, whereas another,
perhaps a shade too subtly, finds 'a kind of self-exhibiting through the puncturing of one's own sentiment which becomes a kind of playing with oneself'.[151] Perhaps the truth is that Sterne is indeed a sentimentalist, but that he
presses this to a point where it veers into satire, raises it to the second power
until it becomes simultaneously a kind of mordant wit.

   Satire and sentimentalism are usually seen as opposites; but both, one
might claim, are appropriate modes for the Irish expatriate. The venomous
spleen of a Swift is that of the disaffected outsider caught between two equally
rebarbative nations, the one a spiritual home which casts you out, the other
a native territory sunk in barbarism. Passed over by one nation and sidelined
by another, Swift has the ferociously compounded aggression of the dual outcast, clinging to an imaginary ideal which is everywhere flouted; and his satire
germinates in the tension between the ideal and the sordidly actual, obsessed
with the grotesque and misshapen, defending civility with all the rhetorical
savagery which that civility is supposed to sublime. Émigrés like Steele or
Goldsmith, by contrast, display the benevolent charm which will smooth
their path to metropolitan advancement, giving voice to their insecurity in a
rather too plausible drive to integrate rather than, as with Swift, in a pathological drive to deface. Steele and Goldsmith draw upon the 'congenial' elements of a tightly knit social order to satirise the affectation or emotional
anaemia of the metropolis; but they also find this cult of sympathy an eminently exchangeable commodity in making their own way into that sphere. In
its suspicion of possessive individualism, this colonial congeniality fits well

150.   ibid, p. 223.
151.   See Cash and Stedmond (eds.), *The Winged Skull* p. 90.

enough for Goldsmith with a traditional English Toryism. It is then possible
to see Sterne's writing as some undecidable blending of the two modes, full of
the dewy-eyed sensibility which made its author such a lapdog of literary
London, but shot through with a satiric debunkery which is very far from that
milieu.[152] His sentimentalism is also qualified by his bawdiness. Like Wilde
later, Sterne is both serious in his adoption of a fashionable social tone, and
pushes it to the point of unsettling parody. If he delighted his fondly doting
readership, he also rattled the guardians of literary taste by his excess and perversity, mischievously crossing some hair-thin line between an engaging play-
fulness and an alarming eccentricity. There is something disturbingly
monomaniacal about his laid-back ludic spirit; indeed as John Mullan points
out, the cult of sympathy which Sterne supposedly offers us as a safeguard
against hobbyhorsical tunnel vision is something of an obsession in itself.[153]

If Goldsmith's irony is at once genial and critical, Sterne characteristically
presses this ambivalence to an extreme. His writing is brimful of melting sentiment, tender-hearted to a fault; yet in thus flattering the dainty sensibility of
his readers, he overloads his narrative with risible or weepable stuff and so
explodes the conventions of English realism, leaving his audience bereft of all
coordinates in the very act of appearing to pander to them. *Tristram Shandy's*
ostentatious attempts to be reader-friendly, its ambling, button-holing style,
throws up a thick web of pauses, asides, digressions, self-qualifications,
mock-elaborate apologies, which leaves the reader as nonplussed and disori-
entated as most of the characters, drawn seductively into the text only to suspect that she is being covertly satirised by it. Sterne's apparently affectionate
invitation to the reader to imagine his or her own Widow Wadman, for all the
world as though he had been reading Wolfgang Iser on filling in textual
blanks, may in fact be a mixture of laziness and insolent indifference. The narrator must not edit his tale, since this would be to pull rank on the reader:
textual selectivity would be uncompanionable and inequitable, a kind of
autocratic manipulation on the author's part. Yorick remarks that 'the very
essence of gravity [is] design, and consequently deceit' (vol. 1, ch. 11), meaning among other things that to narrate is to be immoral. All plots are plots
against the reader.

152. Sterne's mother Agnes was born in Flanders but was of the Nuttall family of
 Clonmel. Her father seems to have been a Captain Christopher Nuttall who
 owned property in Dublin, and Agnes had lived in Clonmel off and on as a
 child. Sterne himself is said to have learnt to write as a child in a Dublin bar-
 racks where his English officer father was stationed, and left for England at the
 age of ten. See Arthur H. Cash, *Laurence Sterne: The Early and Middle Years* (London, 1975), ch. 1.
153. Mullan, *Sentiment and Sociability*, p. 163. George Eliot refers in *Middlemarch* to a
 'fanaticism of sympathy', deftly deconstructing the opposition between egoism
 and altruism.

But the matiness, as often with Sterne, may well be phoney, since not to edit is to plunge the hapless reader into a vast ocean of textuality in which she threatens to sink without trace. There is a sort of smiling sadism about all this: Sterne is well aware that writing is a form of power, and observes to the reader at one point that ''tis enough to have thee in my power' (vol. 7, ch. 6). Being gentle with the reader is not a relinquishing of such authority, simply a clement exercise of it, which cannot help reminding us that the text could always get tough with us if it chose. Sterne's writing is not just about benevolence but a living example of it, a performative utterance which enacts what it describes. The reader must not simply be palmed off with the finished literary product but rather, in a phenomenological turn, let in on the process of textual production as an intimate accomplice, allowed to grasp the experience in its very moment of formation so as to be robbed and cheated of nothing. Indeed in *Tristram Shandy* the finished product is identical with its process of production. Print is anonymous, non-benevolent, the language of *Gesellschaft*; Tristram is all voice and wheedling presence, the residue of an oral culture still bemused by how uniform marks on a page can capture the blurriness of meaning. Writing philanthropically 'to the moment', disarmingly holding nothing back, Tristram yearns (or so he may feign) for a face-to-face intimacy with his reader that would dissolve the alienating materiality of his text into pure co-presence, wrenching typography itself into expressive gesture and converting the unwieldy apparatus of the book itself into a medium of spontaneous communication. Text and book would then be as closely united as body and soul, jerkin and lining, law and desire; and each reader would secretly recognise, in Tristram's unavoidably impersonal appeal to 'the reader', an interpellation of himself alone.

This is a temporal affair too: Tristram tells us that he intends to develop a friendship with the reader as his narrative evolves, a textual sociability which can be seen in part as a substitute, in the solipsistic society of the novel, for the real thing. Text must be instantly soluble into the psyche of both author and reader, writing recuperated by voice, if nothing is to impede the love-affair between Tristram and his public.[154] But if subjectivity is as delicate and lubricious as these fictions persuade us, it resists even the most tortuous act of narration and threatens to slip through the net of language. The richer the sensibility to be communicated, the less of it can be expressed. And if the writing subject can share his intricate depths with the reader only through a suitably convoluted literary form, that form will diffuse the authorial self in the very act of seeking to convey it whole and entire. One can then read this either as the pathos of ineffable feeling, or as a satirical gibe at it. The novel's

154. Edith Birkhead describes Sterne's sentimentalism as a 'pleasant philandering with emotion' in her 'Sentiment and Sensibility in the Eighteenth-Century Novel', *Essays and Studies*, vol. 11 (Oxford, 1925). For a bibliographical essay on the sentimentalist literature influenced by Sterne, see J. C. T. Oates, *Shandyism and Sentiment, 1760–1800* (Cambridge, 1968).

tender solicitude for its audience, patiently unravellling every nuance of sense, arresting one time-stream so that they will not inconveniently miss out on another, may also be read as an act of sadistic aggression which continually frustrates and bamboozles the reader in the very gesture of sedulously smoothing his progress. Sentimentalism subverts hierarchies of value, since the death-pangs of a worm may be just as much an occasion for authentic emotion as the fall of princes; but if everything has equal value in this market-place of the emotions, then nothing is inherently more significant than anything else, and benevolence, now hard to distinguish from bland indifference, may not be quite as benevolent as it looks. In the mighty textual web of the world, trivial events can breed momentous ones, and so are hardly trivial at all; but neither, by the same logic, are weighty occurrences – the death of a child, for example – intrinsically more important than scratching one's nose. If only the feeling subject can confer value, in a world now drained of inherent meaning, then objects themselves become levelled, inert and exchangeable. A 'progressive' dismantling of oppositions between the marginal and the central thus hovers on the edge of a cynicism which is always the concealed underside of sentimentalist doctrine. And how considerate is it to the reader to force her to trudge through a vast welter of anarchic detail in the name of the apparently benign belief that nothing is beneath one's attention?

Just as the body in *Tristram Shandy* obtrudes its bulk to foil all fancy schemes, as that 'outside' of us we can never quite reduce to transparency, so narrative and the material world prove to be an unmasterable exteriority forever outrunning Tristram's efforts to centre them in his own subjecthood. As he struggles to be the source of a story which unmasks him at every step as no more than its effect, the endless digression of his life threatens to disappear beneath the act of enunciating, as the signified is subdued to the signifier quite as rigorously as the hapless autobiographer himself is crushed – literally so, indeed – by the sway of the Law of the Father. The body in this novel is a damaged contraption, and Tristram's own body is multilated by signification, as a false or untimely word mars in turn his conception, birth and genital organs. The rationalist Walter Shandy believes that the concept or signifier constructs and determines the material world; his empiricist son is all too aware of the world's recalcitrance, its habit of kicking back to subvert the best-laid schemes. If mind races ahead of matter in the act of writing, matter outstrips mind in the world you are writing about. The very act of autobiography splits Tristram down the middle between being subject and object of his utterance, so that he can never achieve self-identity, never catch up with his own existence. The more he strives for an imaginary unity of these two selves, trusting like all autobiography that human beings can finally coincide with themselves, the more text he generates, and so the more writing intervenes between past and present Tristrams to detotalise his selfhood. His past self is either blankly irrecoverable, or a mere textual projection of the present.

It is indeed, as Viktor Shlovsky remarked, the most typical novel of world literature, since in all this it simply writes large the condition of the writing or living subject in general. Since Tristram goes on living during his writing, he would need to put his existence on ice in order to deliver a coherent tale of it, in which case he would be able to write nothing at all. He would need, moreover, to calculate the act of writing his life-history into his account of that history, and then reckon that act too into the equation. Since the subject emerges into existence only through the Other – through the existence of anterior subjects who put him inexorably in place, utter him more than he expresses himself – Tristram must describe these others in order to get round to himself, which is why he never quite does. His history is thus 'digressive, and it is progressive too – and at the very same time' (vol. 1, ch. 22), describing the kind of gyre or cycle familiar in Irish culture all the way from the intricate spirallings of its medieval art (Sterne's novel of humours is a thoroughly medieval affair) to Joyce's Viconian roundabouts. As with Beckett, Tristram must go on even though he can't, improvising arbitrary narratives on the hoof, living forwards but writing backwards, dragged into the past like the subject of Freud's *Beyond the Pleasure Principle* in the very gesture of striving for a future; or like Walter Benjamin's *Angelus Novus*, blown backwards into that future with his eyes fixed on the mounting pile of rubble which is his catastrophic life-story. Just as Ireland is a digression or after-thought of England, so this ruin of triumphalist teleology which is *Tristram Shandy*, resolutely anti-Enlightenment in its deviant temporality, is set in a stagnant rural enclave bypassed by the march of progress, full of crippled, washed-up characters whose history has petrified into one enormous synchrony. And just as Irish nationalism will later hunt for the mythic source of that collective injury, so Tristram tries to reconstruct the origins of his wounded subjecthood in a writing which will forever disperse and displace them. Like much in Irish culture, *Tristram Shandy* is at once atavistic and avant-garde, astonishingly 'modernist' in its experimentations just because the novel-form as such is still at a probationary stage in which its conventions, not least in the eyes of a cultural outsider, are fluid, provisional and unnaturalised.

The act of writing is Tristram's sole edge over a dismally determining history whose injurious traces he bears on his body, the fantasy by which he can compensate for his victimhood by wreaking that form of vengeance upon time's ravages which is satirical wit. There are those philosophers who seek to change the world, but the point is to laugh at its absurdity, punish it for its importunity in that act of vainglorious self-assertion which is script. That writing unravels itself at every step, as its referent is pressed to vanishing-point by the very torrent of discourse sent out in pursuit of it. You cannot use language to track down that which lies at its origin, the lack or desire from which discourse itself wells up, the absence which keeps it going. It would be like inquiring at what exact moment time began, or trying to become one's own progenitor. But at least the potential infinity of this textual process, which springs from the fact that it can never quite coincide with what it means and so must always begin afresh, represents a kind of protest against material limit, just as with some other Irish authors (Synge, Joyce, O'Casey) it is a prodigal richness of language which strives to make amends for a starved reality.

This infinitude of script is in fact an illusion, since Tristram's writing determines its own future at every point; but as a knowledge of necessity, in Engels's grim phrase, it is the nearest one can come to freedom in a brutally determinist world. Liberty has now dwindled to whimsicality, and would be valueless in any case because there is nothing inherently precious in the world on which to exercise it. Writing is simply a matter of trying to fill in some gaping abyss glimpsed in the silence between one's disjointed signifiers, an abyss which is nothing less than human subjectivity itself. For the novel sees that the subject must articulate itself in signs whose meaning lies only in other signs, and so will slip down the cracks between them, losing itself in the act of trying to fix its identity as surely as Tristram's autobiographical writing unhinges him from his life in the act of trying to button him down upon it. Subjectivity, to put it another way, emerges into being only under the sign of castration, in Tristram's case almost literally so. What shelters you from this void, plugs it like a fetish, is that pathological armature known as the hobby-horse – in Tristram's case the writing of the novel itself, which is also a way of sounding that chasm from behind one's protective defences. 'I Shandy it more than ever', Sterne remarks in a letter, 'and verily do believe, that by mere Shandeism sublimated by a laughter-loving people, I fence as much against infirmities, as I do by the benefit of air and climate.'[155] Just as Goldsmith can reap stoical humour from dire conditions, and Francis Hutcheson sees comedy as a kind of utopian fraternity, so Tristram Shandy hopes to construct 'a kingdom of hearty laughing subjects' (vol. 4, ch. 22) who can transform their common victimage into collective derision.[156] What Yeats will later call 'tragic joy', that haughty Nietzschean self-delight which dances defiantly on the brink of ruin, is prefigured here, rather more humanely, as the business of extracting jest from a tragic world pregnant with comedy. The two dimensions merge in Tristram Shandy in the figure of Yorick, whose name recalls both the jester and the skull.

Language, however, is self-defeating in another sense too, since for Tristram Shandy as much as for Wittgenstein's Tractatus, what is important in the end is what can be shown but not said. You cannot capture the uniqueness of the self except in discourse; but you cannot capture it there either, since all utterance is plagiarised, déjà lu, a tissue of stale quotations, just as in the novel's Oedipal drama human beings are so many plagiarisms or recyclings of

155. Percy Lewis Curtis (ed.), Letters of Laurence Sterne (Oxford, 1935), p. 163.
156. For the Rabelaisian humour of Sterne, see Henri Fluchère, Laurence Sterne: From Tristram to Yorick (London, 1965), p. 445.

their parents. The medium of our self-expression is always itself estranged, which is one reason why subjectivity is self-alienation. Like Berkeley, Sterne mocks general ideas because they give rise to clashing particular connotations, and so to miscommunication. But since there is no language without general notions, the specific is always refracted out of shape by the only medium in which it can come into being. Subjecthood is what slips through the net of speech, leaving only a pale trace of itself behind; and the ambiguity of all signs is redoubled (not least in *A Sentimental Journey*) by the slippery subtext of the unconscious, stuffed with all those tangled signifiers on which one's own speech depends for its sense, but which must be necessarily absent from what one says if one is to speak coherently at all. One receives back one's own utterance refracted through this great cacophony of other voices – which is to say that Tristram's identity will be constructed for him by the letter of his father's treatise on his upbringing, that crazed rationalist tract against which his own mad modernist text is a kind of mischievous Oedipal strike. His desire is no longer the desire of the Other in the sense that he will be determined by his father's wishes, but the desire of the Other in the sense that he wants to usurp that very symbolic location.

Like all human beings, but more literally than most, Tristram is 'written' before he speaks; and what he speaks – the novel itself – is warped out of true by that anterior script. Since the denotative functions of words are treacherous, you can cling instead to their emotional connotations – a move which bears some affinity to the semantic emotivism of Berkeley and the conservative Irish divines. But since, in a Lockeian universe, there are as many connotations as there are speaking and listening subjects, one is forced back finally on to the body, on to physical gesture and *frissons* of fellow-feeling, as the only dependable medium of communication. This itself, of course, is an enormous irony, since bodily motion becomes expressive gesture only by virtue of being interpreted, and so only from within language. One does not escape the mark of the verbal signifier by scribbling a wavy line or inserting a marbled page. The one thing in the world which resists mechanistic reduction is the motions of the heart – though *why* the sentiments should be thought to evade the impress of the signifier is mysterious enough. There is no common sense in this society, only common sentiment. Benevolence, then, is no longer the mark of a supremely self-assured social group for whom all is cosmically harmonious, but all that remains in the face of a near-collapse of rationality itself. All that can now leap the gap between isolated, pathologically eccentric individuals is feeling, which for some reason is presumed to be immune to misprision. But if feeling is as sporadic and elusive as it appears, then it can no longer provide the social cement which will bind men and women together. Benevolence has now shrunk to the odd wordless epiphany, an impulse as wayward as it is irrefutable.

Compassion, in any case, now seems to have been reduced in the case of Uncle Toby to just one more hobbyhorse, more a mild idiosyncrasy than a social doctrine. There is perhaps less virtue than the novel thinks in not taking offence when you are, like Toby, too ingenuous to recognise offensiveness with any certainty. Toby is the very model of the Man of Feeling, but also something of a saintly simpleton, who plays with physical models of his past just as his nephew sports with textual ones. If for Steele, Hutcheson and Goldsmith the ideal comic tone mingles satire and sentiment, ridicule and good humour, these in Sterne's novel have come badly unstuck, as Toby's bleeding heart confronts Tristram's cerebral wit. They are united only in the figure of Yorick, a compassionate ironist who manages to combine affection with acuity. In him alone, an early eighteenth-century 'Augustan' satirical impulse has survived its tempering at the hands of mid-century sensibility.

We are invited to weep with Uncle Toby, but also to laugh at him; and this ambivalent response to the cult of sensibility is reflected elsewhere in Sterne's writing. He remarks in a letter of a tragedy he is reading that 'it has too much sentiment in it, (at least for me)',[157] but his *Journal to Eliza* is notoriously cloying stuff. Few of us, on the other hand, might escape the charge of sentimentalism were our private love letters to be scrutinised; and it has been claimed that Sterne was no more sentimental in his letters and journal than was fashionable at the time.[158] On the other hand, in a sermon on the parable of the Good Samaritan entitled 'Philanthropy Recommended', he converts the fable into a example of sensibility, attending to those 'emotions of pity and deep concern' in the tale about which the New Testament itself actually says nothing. For the gospel writer, the emotions lie in the Samaritan's action of neighbourliness itself, not in some putative warm glow which inspires it. The New Testament has no interest in 'interiorising' Jesus, or even in telling us what he looks like; whereas Sterne in his sermon actually puts into the Samaritan's mouth a kind of interior monologue straight out of sentimental comedy: 'Good God! what a spectacle of misery do I behold . . .'[159] Unlike Goldsmith, Sterne recommends philanthropy as in our best worldly interests, while like Hutcheson he sees a benevolent temper as a kind of tonic, contributing to our physical health. Goodness for both men is a kind of gusto, indissoluably physical and spiritual. Unlike Goldsmith too, Sterne has the sentimentalist's largely sanguine view of human nature, declaring that there is no passion more natural to humanity than love. As with Hutcheson, his benign latitudinarianism revolts against doctrines which leave out of account the natural goodness of humanity – what he calls in a sermon on the 'Vindication of Human Nature' 'the inward promptings of benevolence'.

On the other hand, there is evidence in the sermons that Sterne subscribed no more than Hutcheson to some brand of ethical emotivism. He

157. Curtis, *Letters of Lawrence Sterne*, p. 162.
158. See Rufus S. Putney, 'Laurence Sterne: Apostle of Laughter', in J. L. Clifford (ed.), *Eighteenth-Century English Literature* (London, 1959).
159. James P. Browne (ed.), *The Works of Laurence Sterne* (London, 1873), vol. 3, p. 30.

announces his belief in absolute laws of right and wrong, and holds that we should make our moral judgements according to Nature and reason rather than passion or impulse. It is Christian authority, not affections, which should lie at the source of virtue. Sterne's view of human nature may be excessively optimistic, but his opinion of the circumstances in which it finds itself is certainly not. He has a Johnsonian sense of human existence as an endless tangle of petty vexations, as well as of a Nature which is no longer ordered and translucent but an obscure Humean muddle. As a chain of capricious occurrences which nevertheless sets up an inexorable determinism, this process combines the worst of both modern and ancient worlds. A Sentimental Journey actually starts with a refusal of benevolence, as Yorick turns away a mendicant Franciscan friar, even if he instantly feels bad about doing so. This second Yorick figure looks satirically on his own sentimentalism,[160] a split which has now become one between the tenderly altruistic ego and the erotically self-interested id. There is a fissure running through the mind itself, not just one between mind and body. Tristram is engaged in the feat of trying to dredge to consciousness the forces which have gone into his making – an impossible enterprise, to be sure, since consciousness itself springs into being only through a repression of what went into its constitution. But if Tristram, despite his endlessly resourceful intelligence, can thus never be quite transparent to himself, the Yorick who stands at the centre of the Journey is comically self-opaque, apparently blind to the libidinal subtext of his own compassion. It is remarkable how easily he is moved to generosity by a pretty face. If philanthropy really is self-advantage, and this is the source of the subtlest comedy, then the Hutchesonians will need to think again. But the comedy is precisely the point: the suspicion that our altruism may be secretly self-interested itself inspires us to a wry, self-ironising awareness of our frailties which can become the basis of mutual tolerance and good humour. In this way, sentimentalism is able to make capital out of the very accusations directed against it.

Tristram Shandy is a thoroughly defeatist work, hilariously hopeless, which like many an Irish text from Swift to Beckett plays off the humiliated body against the hubris of the mind. The conflict between Walter Shandy's pedantic scholasticism and the sorry mess of his son's life prefigures something of the tension between the mythological and naturalistic texts which go to make up Joyce's Ulysses. In both cases, the rigorous orderings of the former are at loggerheads with the commonplace contingencies of the latter. Ulysses was written by a scholastic who claimed to have the mind of a grocer, and a similar

160. Ian Jack, in his edition of A Sentimental Journey, thinks Sterne's sentimentalism is ambivalent though not wholly bogus (A Sentimental Journey, Journal to Eliza and Political Romance, London 1968, Introduction), while Gardner D. Stout Jr thinks the work both satirical and sentimental (A Sentimental Journey, Berkeley and Los Angeles, 1967, Introduction). John M. Stedmond develops much the same viewpoint in The Comic Art of Laurence Sterne (Toronto, 1967), ch. 6.

combination of the metaphysical and the humdrum was necesary to produce Sterne's great fiction. Both are carnivalesque modes of consciousness, and both works are out to undermine the institution of Literature itself. No sooner has the realist novel made its historic appearance in English letters than an outsider to that milieu, perhaps rather more alert to the arbitrariness of convention than those more intimate with it, perceives the Emperor's-new-clothes truth that the novel is a literary genre quite without rules and that literary representation is in any strict sense impossible. There is a complex relation in such writing between an anti-realist experiment in form and a support for the underdog in content. *Tristram Shandy*, quite as much as any Beckett fiction, is a tale of the battered and blighted, of impotence and disfigurement, of lives of quiet desperation conducted far from the centres of power and prestige. Its unravelling of literary form is an oblique assault on the cultural dimension of that power, just as Beckett's scrupulously meagre forms and parsimonious language represent a kind of anti-Literature. Moreover, none of these Irish authors is in the least interested in lending support to that most central of English literary myths, the family.[161] There is indeed a family at the focus of *Tristram Shandy*, as there is at the centre of *Finnegans Wake*; but the latter is less a private grouping than a microcosm of human history, and the former is about as dysfunctional as you can get outside the covers of some Freudian case history. The family of Shandy Hall, an isolated bunch of freaks, madmen and emotional cripples, is indeed a benign refuge from the comfortless world which lies beyond it. But in a devastating thrust at that whole sentimentalist ideology, it is as disabled as it is because it is also a mediation of that wider sphere, not simply a defence against it. Walter's deranged metaphysics, Toby's doomed military monomania, Tristram's attempts at literary authorship: all of these, along with the social practices of obstetrics, law, theology, domestic service and the like, are eminently public matters which mould and warp the family from within. For a benevolist like Burke, society must become a family; for Sterne, the family is already a society, the private already public, in all the bleakest ways, and it is this which laces his domestic sensibility with a dash of acerbic satire.

Like Berkeley, Goldsmith and Sterne, Edmund Burke distrusts metaphysical ideas – not least, in his case, the belief that politics should be guided by theoretical doctrine, universal principle and appeals to abstract rights. All of this Burke counters with his very English insistence on custom and received practice, *phronesis* rather than *techne*, the untheorisable shape and texture of a form of life. It is just such historical pragmatism which has endeared Burke to those English conservatives for whom theories and ideas can be left to pretentious foreigners and shaggy-haired intellectuals. There is something rather

---

161. For a discussion of this aspect of Joyce's *Ulysses*, see Seamus Deane, *Celtic Revivals* (London, 1985), ch. 6.

ironic, not to say grotesque, about praising one of England's greatest political thinkers as a man without an idea in his head.

In fact, Burke's insistence on the need to adapt to circumstance was very different from the unprincipled opportunism of some of those who have laid claim to his inheritance. Burke was quite ready to alienate his Bristol constituents for the sake of his beliefs. He was not a rather more eloquent version of some philistine Tory county councillor, believing that what matters is what works in practice. The East India Company worked well enough in practice, but this did not stop Burke from clamouring for its abolition. If he had an extraordinary veneration for the *status quo*, it did not extend to quite a few of its component parts, such as the corrupt cabal which surrounded the monarchy. If he denounced one revolution, he supported another: the British 'right' to tax the Americans seemed to him an empty abstraction, so that to reject a metaphysical wisdom for a pragmatic one turned out in this case to have revolutionary implications. If Burke thought little of such abstract rights, so did Karl Marx. An appeal to local circumstance is not necessarily on the side of political reaction, though Burke could also practise a radical universalism when the occasion demanded. Far from dismissing universal absolutes as so much unpragmatic mythology, he insisted that Warren Hastings's shabby behaviour in India should be judged by just the same moral principles which governed men and women's conduct at home. In this, he turned on those apologists for Hastings, including the man himself, who sought to excuse his crimes by appealing sophistically to the different cultural circumstances of the country he governed. Burke certainly held that the British must rule their colonies with due respect for local custom and tradition; but he was not prepared to extend this cultural relativism to a moral relativism as well, unlike some supposedly radical postmodernists of our own time.

If a concern with cultural circumstance is not necessarily conservative, neither is an appeal to history. Burke's doctrine of prescription – the idea that we validate our rights and titles by recounting a certain narrative of them, the lengthier the better – is indeed a rationale for what we do in terms of what we have done already. But in the hands of some of Burke's compatriots, this doctrine was to become politically subversive. The Irish tenantry also believed in time-honoured custom, such as their right to the land which the English had taken from them, an antique memory which the traditionalist English would have preferred to bury. In England, an appeal to tradition is usually on the side of the *status quo*, whereas in Ireland the opposite has generally been the case. Some English smallholders were also to stand by their traditional rights in the face of enclosing landlords, a stance which was not especially welcome to their traditionally-minded superiors. It is remarkable how eager conservatives can be to discard tradition when it is a question of other people's heritages at odds with their own.

The writings of Burke, an Irish émigré, stand at the fountainhead of the quintessentially English 'Culture and Society' tradition, which was to develop his concern with 'organic' relations between human beings, and his scorn for a mean-spirited utilitarianism, into a resourceful critique of industrial capitalism.[162] This is not, need one say, to claim this eighteenth-century Whig as a closet Marxist. But few things could be more of an affront to his values than the neo-liberalism of our own day, in which an abstract, universal drive for profit threatens much of what he held dear: the cultural needs of particular communities, the importance of human affections and customary bonds, the sense of history as a living process, the rootedness of men and women in particular places, the preciousness of that which cannot be bought or sold. Modern-day market forces, with their uprooting of whole communities, their severing of traditional bonds, their bogus universalism, their contractual view of society and eradication of history represent, in Burkean terms, a virulent new strain of Jacobinism, even if the abstract dogmas in question are now those of Brussels bankers rather than French *philosophes*. The terms in which Burke censures the French revolutionaries of his time apply with striking specificity to the apologists for the global market-place today.

Burke's hostility to the French revolution was not entirely reactionary. He opposed it not only because he detested its political doctrines, though he certainly did, but because he thought that those doctrines spelled the death of political society as such. For him, the revolution was an assault on the very conditions of possibility of political culture – a kind of transcendental error, so to speak. In Burke's eyes, one result of destroying the institutions of civil society was to do away with the medium by which political power is tempered and made tolerable to its subjects. He believed in conservative style that authority must be shrouded in mystery; but this was partly because he feared the consequences for the common people of being exposed to its intimidatory glare. Power for him must be rooted in love – which is to say that no political authority can be secure unless it intertwines itself with the affections of its subjects. And here a piece of good old-fashioned English Whiggery comes together with what might be seen as an Irish concern for clannish bonds. The discourse of domestic ties and sentiments is accordingly transferred to the realm of political government: there must be 'a community of interests, and a sympathy in feelings and desires between those who act in the name of any description of the people, and the people in whose name they act'.[163] What sweetens the pill of inequality is the mutual sympathy between governors and governed, without which all political authority is in Burke's view doomed to collapse. Power must accordingly be aestheticised: 'To make us love our country', Burke declares, 'our country ought to be lovely'.[164] 'Men', he announces in the *First*

162. See Raymond Williams, *Culture and Society 1780–1950* (London, 1958).
163. R. B. McDowell (ed.), *The Writings and Speeches of Edmund Burke*, vol. 9 (Oxford, 1991), p. 247.
164. L. G. Mitchell (ed.), *The Writings and Speeches of Edmund Burke*, vol. 8 (Oxford, 1989), p. 129.

Letter on a Regicide Peace, 'are not tied to one another by paper and seals. They are led to associate by resemblances, by conformities, by sympathies. Nothing is so strong a tie of amity between nation and nation as correspondence in laws, customs, manners, and habits of life. They have more than the force of treaties in themselves. They are obligations written in the heart.'[165]

As a devout culturalist, Burke understands that culture is stronger than politics – that this is where real power is sedimented, and thus the place where authority will need to entrench itself. A subsequent lineage of Irish nationalism was to take this doctrine of local affections to heart, as this passage from Canon Sheehan suggests:

> Great philosophers may argue on cosmopolitan lines, and say: 'We are all one race, and we have all a common heritage. Why limit our interests to one little span of earth . . .? Our sympathies are universal, and embrace every race, even the flattened heads and yellow faces, that make for the progress of mankind'. It won't do. Back we come from philosophy to affection; and purple mountain, brown bog, and granite shore loom up through the mist of tears to awaken recollection . . .[166]

Sheehan vulgarises the Burkeian heritage to a racist chauvinism, opposing purple mountain to yellow face. Yet Burke himself seemed to find no contradiction between his 'national' affections and his passion for international justice, and neither did the most creative currents of Irish nationalism, which often looked outward to other subject nations. We shall be looking at one such example later, in the writings of Frederick Ryan. The primacy of place and the affections had also long been noted by a succession of colonial governments in Ireland, which recognised that their primary political antagonist was culture. The more astute among them did not make the mistake of believing, in the words of Isaac Butt, 'that grievances which may be called "sentimental" are therefore no grievances at all'.[167] And just as culture is anterior to politics, so the family is prior to the state – a priority exemplified above all by the royal family, at once the source of the state yet transcendent of its analytic brand of reason. There is something peculiarly pre-modern in Burke's insistence on sympathy rather than contract, custom and manners rather than script and seal. 'Obligations written in the heart' is not a bad way of characterising that crossing of the border between public and private which we have observed in Gaelic culture, in which customary bonds take on something of the implacable force reserved by fully modern societies for the law.

Burke displayed an excessive reverence for the political forms of his adopted nation; but this may easily blind us to the fact that for him it was not in the end politics which really mattered. It was not, finally, a question of

165. McDowell, *The Writings and Speeches of Edmund Burke*, p. 247.
166. Canon Sheehan, *Early Essays and Lectures* (London, 1906), p. 284.
167. Isaac Butt, *The Irish People and the Irish Land* (Dublin, 1867), p. 24.

power, but of how far such political forms nurtured the interests and well-being of the people as a whole. On this point, Burke and political radicals are entirely at one; it is just that they disagree over whether the institutions which Burke so zealously defended were indeed the most capable of promoting this end. His appeal to the historical rather than metaphysical nature of these political arrangements was intended to underline their validity: what had been so long in the evolving could not be lightly set aside. History was a form of rationality of its own, incomparably more intricate than any political calculus. But this historicism can equally be seen to emphasise the humanly created nature of political forms, which since they have been fashioned can always be changed. 'History' is in the end too shifting, heterogeneous a foundation for conservative principles.

Burke is a benevolist who believes that love is the basis of authority and affection the cement of the state. Society must model itself on a family; indeed Seamus Deane points out how when Burke wants to portray an impious offensive on the French *ancien régime*, he chooses, metonymically, a (royal) family under brutal assault.[168] His *Letter to a Member of the National Assembly* is largely an onslaught on sentimentalism, a current which, as epitomised by the odious Rousseau, he considers the very opposite of genuine fellow feeling.[169] Genuine human sympathies are bound up with specific places and affinities; 'benevolence', which is Burke's rather confusing word for what we have been describing in this chapter as 'sentimentalism', is a mere spectre or phantasm of authentic affection, a bogus, cerebralised brand of feeling which betrays its true indifferentism in claiming that one should love kinsfolk and strangers equally. (Swift's Gulliver went one further than this ordinance, despising his relatives and adoring alien quadrupeds.) Like Francis Hutcheson, Burke thinks it natural to love those nearest to us, and rejects this abstract, universalist sympathy as unreal. In his *Tracts on the Popery Laws*, he turns his wrath on the hypocrisy of those Irish Protestants whose hearts are stirred by the distress of their persecuted co-religionists abroad while they themselves oppress Roman Catholics at home. Such men 'transfer humanity from its natural basis – our legitimate and homebred connections . . . and meretriciously hunt abroad after foreign affections, [in] such a disarrangement of the whole system of our duties, that I do not know whether benevolence so displaced is not almost the same thing as destroyed. . .'.[170] Rousseau

168. See Seamus Deane, *Strange Country* (Oxford, 1997), ch. 1.
169. For a discussion of Burke and Rousseau, see Tom Furniss, *Edmund Burke's Aesthetic Ideology* (Cambridge, 1993), ch. 10. Burke, with Rousseau in mind, accuses the age of 'a certain intemperance of intellect', an accurate description of much of his own ridiculous hyperbole in this essay and his other writings on France. When he generously admires Rousseau's literary style as 'glowing, animated, enthusiastic' (p. 41), he perhaps reads a little of himself into him. Burke was always rather too impassioned, theatrical and excessive for English taste.
170. Edmund Burke, *Letters, Speeches and Tracts on Irish Affairs* (London, 1881), p. 35.

advocates universal benevolence without 'one spark of common paternal affection. Benevolence to the whole species, and want of feeling for every individual with whom these professors come in contact, form the character of the new philosophy.'[171] The Swiss philosopher is a kind of Houyhnhnm, 'a lover of his kind, but a hater of his kindred', smiling serenely upon humanity while casting off his own bastard children. For the French, lack of charity begins at home.[172] Thousands admire the sentimental writer; the affectionate father is hardly known in his parish.'[173] 'Vanity' is Burke's name for this 'omnivorous' cult of sensibility, which is entirely promiscuous in its choice of object and intent only on exhibiting itself. He sees it more or less as John Toland describes florid language or the cult of the signifier in his *History of the Druids*: 'a mercenary prostitute, wholly acting by vanity, artifice, or interest, and never speaking but in ambiguous or unintelligible terms.'[174]

France has become in Burke's eyes pretty much what English sentimental comedy was in Goldsmith's. It is a theatre full of hollow posturing and counterfeit emotion, and Burke makes the aesthetic analogy himself: 'Statesmen [in France], like your present rulers, exist by every thing which is spurious, fictitious, and false; by every thing which takes the man from his house, and sets him on a stage, which makes him up an artificial creature, with painted theatric sentiment, fit to be seen by the glare of candle-light, and formed to be contemplated at a due distance'.[175] The domestic has yielded to the theatrical, the private to the public, intimacy to estrangement, substance to fiction, sympathy to spectacle, the connubial to the counterfeit. Burke understands well enough that what is in train in France is what we might nowadays call a cultural revolution – a transformation of forms of subjectivity as well as of social institutions, in which radical ideologues are seeking to re-mould the former to the fresh requirements of the latter. And the main stake to be played for here is the family. What has happened is that the idea of love has been ripped from its domestic setting and transfigured into a philosophy, a mixture of coarse sensuality and metaphysical speculation which has been abstracted from social mores, and so is no longer capable of acting as a social force. In Burke's view, 'the modes and principles on which [love] engages the sympathy, and strikes the imagination, become of the utmost importance to the morals and manners of every society'.[176] Rousseau and his ilk, by etherealising and sentimentalising human affection, have divorced it from that natural alliance with social con-

171.   Edmund Burke, *A Letter to a Member of the National Assembly* (reprinted Oxford and New York, 1990), p. 35.
172.   ibid. This is evidently a misinterpretation of Rousseau, who satirised the theory of universal benevolence himself.
173.   ibid, p. 35.
174.   John Toland, *History of the Druids* (reprinted Montrose, 1814), p. 89.
175.   *Letter to a Member of the National Assembly*, p. 36.
176.   ibid, p. 42.

duct that it forges in the bosom of the family. The family is the vital mediation between feelings and social forms, affection and authority, the hinge or pivot between private and public worlds. As 'that tribunal of conscience which exists independently of edicts and decrees',[177] it provides us with a living model of hegemonic rather than coercive power, naturalises authority, and presents the political state with subjects who, having undergone the discipline of 'manners', are now ready to receive the impress of its sublime law. Like pre-modern society, the family is an anti-contractual system which runs not upon laws and edicts, but upon customary obligations and the responsibilities of kinship. It is thus the ideal image of a political power or subservience which is actually pleasurable, a community in which bondage is freedom, obedience is inspired by affection, and hierarchy seems entirely natural. In France, however, sentimentalism is 'subvert[ing] those principles of domestic truth and fideltity, which form the discipline of social life'.[178] The family is no longer microcosmic of the good society but a 'socialised' affair: if you oppose the revolutionary regime, your children may be punished too. The private realm has thus been publicised; but one can also see the public sphere as having been privatised, governed now (if Rousseau is to have his way) by the vagaries of sentiment.

The opposite of the sentimental philosophy Burke castigates, writes Seamus Deane, is 'actual feeling'.[179] This was true also for Goldsmith and Hutcheson; but in the age of Burke, as the revolutionary temperature rises, the stakes have become correspondingly higher. The distinction we have been tracing between benevolence and sentimentalism has become with Burke one between conservative and revolutionary, tradition and experiment, liberty and anarchy, England and France. What began life as a conflict of literary modes is now a world-historical political struggle.

177.   ibid, p. 44.
178.   ibid, p. 43.
179.   Deane, *Strange Country*, p. 15.

THE MASOCHISM OF
THOMAS MOORE

Thomas Moore remarked that he was more confident of the sound of his *Irish Melodies* than of their sense, a fitting view for a proto-symbolist poet. For a full-blooded *symboliste* like Mallarmé, poetry has become a kind of music, as the signified effaces itself beneath the signifier; for Moore, writing at an earlier stage of this aesthetic, poetry is not yet music but is intimately wedded to it, and music, so he insists, is the dominant partner of the marriage. If language for Pater or Verlaine is music, music for Moore is already a kind of discourse; the point of his *Irish Melodies*, he writes, is to interpret 'the touching language of his country's music'. The *Melodies* are not so much a matter of adding words to airs as of coaxing the enigmatic tongue of music into verbal articulation, an articulation which remains low-breathing enough to preserve its musical character. Moore is translating music into words rather than, as with the *symbolistes*, metamorphosing words into music; but these words are somehow already inherent in the music itself, the sort of thing it would say were it able to speak. There is, as it were, an iconic rather than unmotivated relation between musical and verbal signs, as though only this particular poetic phrasing could unpack the covert sense of the tune. In putting words to an air, you transfer to them something of the emotional logic of the music itself, thus imbuing them with an aura of inevitability.

'Music, oh how faint, how weak, / Language fades before thy speech!', Moore sighs in his song 'On Music', downgrading language not by contrast with the non-linguistic, as in the usual *symboliste* cliché, but with a superior form of speech. Music is a kind of discourse beyond signification, and so both a symbol of freedom – it has shaken off the shackles of meaning, as Ireland may one day break the chains of political oppression – and an instance of the ambivalent or contradictory, which as we shall see figures centrally in Moore's verse. The medium is thus as equivocal as the message. And just as Moore's verses conjure words out of music, so, reciprocally, the airs coax out the more musical aspects of his own language, foregrounding tone, cadence, rhythm and assonance, while downplaying discursive sense. When he remarks in the *Irish Melodies* that music and politics converge in Ireland in tone, meaning that the melancholia of his pieces is historically motivated, he gestures to a politics of the signifier. Archbishop John MacHale of Tuam then completes the circuit by translating Moore's *Melodies* into Irish, transforming them, as it were, into what they had essentially been all along.

There is a political dimension to this aesthetic. If Moore's verse is to distil the pure essence of national feeling, then it must dim down its referents by loosening up the relations between signifier and signified. It must do this because the spirit of the nation is by definition indeterminate, a desire which transcends all particular programmes or formulations, a yearning which can be made manifest in the texture of one's verse but not uttered outright. This spirit is as plangent and tremulous as it is precisely because of the bitterly specific historical 'referents' or situations which helped to breed it; but it can only be fully evoked, attended to in its own right, if these concrete contexts are discreetly shaded out. As Seamus Deane writes, Moore's Irish past is 'so deeply buried that it was not recoverable except as sentiment'.[1] His poetry thus makes a kind of phenomenological turn, bracketing its real-life objects so as to explore all the more single-mindedly the spirit which animates them. In doing so, it highlights and intensifies that feeling, thus lending its support to Irish nationalism, at the same time as it veils the rebarbative history to which it belongs, thus soothing nationalism's English opponents.

There are other political reasons why Moore's poetry has something of the semiotic indeterminacy of music. The nationalist desire is indeterminate because what it demands in the end is not this or that particular reform, but a recognition of the nation's autonomous being, of its right to demand in the first place. It is for this reason that the Irish seemed to the English always to be changing the question, since no specific question could exhaust the significance of their claim. But because any such absolute recognition can only manifest itself in this or that determinate act, the nationalist demand is always liable to feel short-changed, and thus to be deflected into the empty, excessive hankering of desire, which is just what we find happening in Moore's lugubrious lyrics. Demand has an object, whereas desire does not; and though Moore's disconsolateness would seem to have an obvious enough referent – the tragic condition of Ireland – it is easy at times to suspect that the country figures for him as what Jacques Lacan would call the *objet petit a*, that contingent scrap of reality in which the subject's desire for something altogether nameless and inexpressible has momentarily been invested.

A poem like 'The Origin of the Harp' suggests that the mingling of sombreness and joy which Moore elsewhere sees in terms of Irish history is in fact primordial, that sorrow was present at the origin itself. A lot of Moore's dolefulness is more *Weltschmertz* than patriotic distress. Desire is indeterminate, then, because it is so implacable; but it is also because a demand for freedom, at least as the Romantics understood it, must elude definition, since any such conceptual constraint would negate what it tried to identify. In any case, the nationalist demand is for something which has yet to emerge into material existence, and so is bound to remain somewhat opaque to itself. If Moore's sentiments are bodiless, it is partly because the nation is. All nationalism, then, approaches the condition of music, and so is fit subject-matter for poetry. One of Moore's most treasured terms, 'Erin', is poetically evocative but

1. Seamus Deane, *Celtic Revivals* (London, 1986), p. 14.

means little enough as the name of a country, being simply the genitive form of 'Eire'.

But if the indeterminacy of Moore's verse springs from a certain absoluteness, it also serves to camouflage it. The sway of the signifier is also the dominance of an agreeable sweetness over an occasionally subversive content. Poetry as veering towards pure signification intensifies 'national' feeling, but by the same token defuses it. The French critic Thérèse Tessier finds it little short of a miracle that Moore was not arrested for slander or sedition, given that the composers of Irish political ballads could be imprisoned for much less offensive stuff.[2] But though he was vilified as a treacherous firebrand by the Tory press, the low semantic profile of his drawing-room pieces, with their elegantly treasonable sentiments, no doubt helped to keep the political state from the door. An example of this aestheticising of the disreputable crops up in 'Let Erin remember the days of old', where the English act of appropriating Ireland is portrayed as 'the emerald gem of the western world . . . set in the crown of the stranger', an image which unwittingly dignifies what it deplores. And there were, of course, reasons other than poetic charm why Moore was not clapped in chains. The Irish Melodies, so he unctuously explains to his political critics, are beamed not at the ignorant multitude, but at those more patrician souls who can 'afford to have their national zeal a little stimulated'. They are, so to speak, more harmless foreplay than rough trade.

Moore's verses are indeterminate not only in the sense that their sonorous mood-music resists close verbal analysis,[3] but in the sense of being hybrid, composite, emotionally oxymoronic. Their imagery is liminal, crepuscular, caught between opposite categories. His lyrics are full of muffled lights, tearful ecstasy, mist-wrapped sunbeams, sweet bleedings, ruined splendours. They are loud with sighings and breathings, noises which hover indecisively between sound and silence. Sometimes one indeterminacy is compounded with another, as the poet sighs over ruins or weeps joyfully at a bright place wreathed in mist. All this is meant to represent a stereotypically Irish blending of joy and melancholy, though it would be more accurate to see it as

2.   See Thérèse Tessier, *The Bard of Erin: A Study of Thomas Moore's Irish Melodies (1808–1834)* (Salzburg, 1981), p. 88. For the nationalism of the *Irish Melodies*, see also Joep Leerssen, *Remembrance and Imagination* (Cork, 1997), pp. 79–83. For Moore's own nationalist prose, see his *Letter to the Roman Catholics of Dublin* (London, 1810); *Memoirs of Captain Rock* (London, 1824); and his *Life and Death of Lord Edward Fitzgerald* (London, 1831). Useful biographies of Moore are L. A. G. Strong, *The Minstrel Boy* (New York, 1967), Terence de Vere White, *Tom Moore, the Irish Poet* (London, 1977), and H. H. Jordan, *Bolt Upright: The Life of Thomas Moore*, 2 vols. (Salzburg, 1975).

3.   In his 'Letter on Music' appended to the third number of the *Irish Melodies*, Moore himself writes rather wistfully that the 'humble nature of my contributions to this work may exempt them from the rigours of literary criticism'. One is sorry to have to disappoint him.

reflecting the ambivalent sensibility of nationalism. Nationalism hopes and laments in more or less equal measure, turning its face to a joyful future precisely by recollecting a sorrowful past. If too much nostalgia paralyses political action, too rapt a focus on the world to come represses the suffering which makes that future necessary. Moore's *Memoirs of Captain Rock* pokes fun at the cynical insurrectionary view that Grattan's parliament was just an illusion, while confessing that this view turned out to be justified. Fatalism must be qualified by hope, and hope tempered by realism.

There are other political reasons why each mode of feeling must modify the other. Moore's emotional compositeness is a matter of strategy as well as sensibility. Put bluntly, too much unnuanced nationalist hope would risk alienating his metropolitan audience, just as too much unalleviated sorrow would risk appearing morbid or rancorous. The poems need to hope without triumphalism, and mourn without sullenness. The mourning must have no embarrassingly specific object, and so approaches the condition of melancholia, which Freud described as mourning without an object. This imbalance of feeling and object then highlights the mourner rather than the material situation, which is another way of containing the poetry's disruptiveness. It invites us to savour a subjective feeling, rather than to inquire how historically justified that state of mind might be.

Sadness evokes the reader's pity, but since part of Moore's pathos is a sense of impotence, it also provokes a certain relief. The tragic point about Irish history is that you can apparently do nothing *but* bewail it, which is also what is reassuring about it, at least for the more conservative-minded of Moore's audiences. His lyrics are self-consciously *post factum*, acts of grieving or commemorating which are possible only because the catastrophe has already happened. If what his art says risks giving political offence, its very existence testifies to the absoluteness of the historical defeat which brought it to birth, and so to its own political ineffectualness. The point is not to change the world but to lament it. The most that the *Irish Melodies* can do by way of political intervention is to redouble the pathos, provoke one tear with another, by ensuring that 'The stranger shall hear [Ireland's] lament on his plains', and presumably join in the wailing. But since this subserviently implies that political agency in Ireland is up to the colonialists, its air of bold intrusiveness, buttonholing the English and rubbing their respectable noses in Ireland's woes, is somewhat qualified. It is worth pointing out that this lachrymose helplessness in the face of an oppressive world is what Moore's English contemporary William Blake saw as the last word in false consciousness.

This composite sensibility of Moore's is interestingly at odds with his Whiggish-nationalist teleology. Politically speaking, sunshine and sorrow can indeed be clearly distinguished along a chronological axis. First there was the joyous light of a free Erin, a beacon which has now been sadly extinguished, but which will shine forth once more in an emancipated political future. If this is what Moore thinks, however, it is not at all how he feels. In fact his imagery suggests how this linear scheme must be undercut simply to be sustained. If freedom is to flourish in the future, then its traces must already be somehow inscribed in the present, inherited from the liberated past. So what secures this political teleology is also in danger of reducing history to one enormous synchrony, in which the past is immanent in the present in the shape of the future. Compositeness in Moore is really a substitute for development, as well as for emotional complexity. The poems move in a set of achieved cameos from one blend of antithetical feelings to another, but the emotions in question are incapable of evolution, just like the imagery in which they are crystallised. Moore has an extraordinarily exiguous supply of images at his disposal, forever shuffling the same emblematic items into different permutations in a way which reflects at the level of poetic form something of the static or cyclical quality of his vision of history.[4]

The major contradiction of the *Irish Melodies*, however, is that Moore's political hankering for the pure white light of future liberty is at odds with his aesthetic delight in the dappled, ambiguous nature of things. Politically speaking, the current epoch of emotional cross-breeding, in which tears vie with smiles and hopes with griefs, is merely a transitional stage between two positive, determinate conditions, one past (Ireland's ancient glory) and the other still to come (its future emancipation). Morally speaking, however, the poems' claims run contrary to this historicism. They urge, as universal rather than transitional truths, that grief tempers a too boisterous joy, that the most tender love springs from suffering, that the rarity of happiness increases its value, that absence intensifies presence, that time the destroyer of beauty is also the enhancer of love and virtue. What appear as negative and positive values in Moore's historical scheme show up in his moral vision as opposites in dialectical need of each other. The pure white light of liberty would dispel the shadedness he relishes. If pain intensifies pleasure, how could one enjoy the future liberated Ireland as keenly as the bitter-sweet process of struggling to create it?

A typical gesture of Moore's lyrics is thus to defer the transcendental signified of political freedom, or at least to take advantage of the fact that it is for the moment unavailable. This deferment then intensifies the desire for that ideal moment, at the same time as it may show it up as something of a self-deception. 'The Song of Fionnuala' formally regrets the fact that 'Still doth the pure light its dawning delay', yet since this dawn would also signal death for Fionnuala herself, this light is also a kind of darkness. Robert Emmet's celebrated speech from the dock, in which he postpones the writing of his epitaph to the moment of Ireland's emancipation, might have been specially staged for the benefit of his old Trinity comrade, and Moore was not slow to capitalise upon it in 'Oh breathe not his name'. If Emmet postpones writing

4.   Robert Welch notes the 'static non-progressive grace' of the *Irish Melodies* in *Irish Poetry from Moore to Yeats* (Gerrards Cross, 1980), p. 26.

to the future, Moore's own art hangs precariously in the twilight zone between past conquest and future victory, and is thus indeterminate, suspended in its full significance, by virtue of its very historical conditions. His poetry listlessly fills in an historical void, but because its truth must finally be referred to a future which may never arrive, it cannot be fully in possession of itself. It is, as it were, undermined retrospectively by the possiblity of that future not emerging, reduced by that possible non-event to velleities, frail hopes, enervated sentiments, blurred meanings and mechanically recycled images.

Robert Emmet, by contrast, will wait upon the fullness of a future history to authenticate his text, which is what the Minstrel Boy does too. Whereas Moore usually sees music or poetry as the continuation of war by other means, a strain or gleam of the heroic past still fretfully alive in the present, the Minstrel Boy, once vanquished, destroys his harp to avoid the contamination of having to play it in conditions of political oppression. For him as for Emmet, a free art depends on a free society. He thus throws down an ultra-leftist gauntlet to his more politically compromised author, who has no intention whatsoever of shutting up his lucrative piano. But this, to do Moore justice, is partly because he would like to believe that art can be politically functional even now – not in the Romantic sense of transfiguring reality, but in the Benjaminian sense of furnishing a culture with those rituals of remembrance without which, in the *carpe diem* of the eternal present, it would even forget that it had been offended. A similar abandonment of the harp takes place in 'Dear Harp of my Country', though why Moore should lay down his instrument here is not entirely clear. He tells us that it is because some less unworthy hand may come along to pluck it; but if, as he instantly goes on to claim, the harp's music is somehow immanent in it, and the harpist a mere occasion for the release of its 'wild sweetness', exactly who is plucking it wouldn't seem to matter that much.

Something of Moore's ambiguities can be found in the following slight piece:

> Erin, the tear and the smile in thine eyes,
> Blend like the rainbow that hangs in thy skies!
>   Shining through sorrow's stream,
>   Saddening through pleasure's beam,
>   Thy suns with doubtful gleam,
>   Weep while they rise.

> Erin, thy silent tear never shall cease,
> Erin, thy languid smile ne'er shall increase,
>   Till, like the rainbow's light,
>   Thy various tints unite,
>   And form in heaven's sight
>   One arch of peace!

The logic of this seems coherent enough: just as the tear and the smile blend in the stereotypical Irish sensibility, so its various political 'tints' (green and orange, no doubt) must unite too. But this symmetry is in fact spurious. For when the political 'tints' of Ireland unite, the effect will be to undermine its emotional unity of tears and smiles, since there will then be no need for the former. The smiling will simply put paid to the weeping. The poem draws on an ambiguity in words like 'blend' and 'unite', which can mean either compounding different elements until they become a single substance, or cohering them while preserving their difference. It is as though the song, anxious at the prospect of a unitary emotional state in which joy will no longer be creatively abated by sorrow, displaces this hybridity to the political future, which – so the 'rainbow alliance' image suggests – will unite contending Irish interests without damage to their particular colouring. Political emancipation will thus deprive the poet of the pleasures of affliction, but only to reinstate this unity of opposites at a different level.

Moore's 'official' teleology can be found in a set piece like 'Erin, oh Erin', where the bright spirit of Irish freedom shines on 'unfading and warm' through the 'long night of bondage', and the 'full noon of freedom' is about to pierce through 'slavery's cloud'. The danger with this metaphorical mode is that in recovering the continuity of the national spirit, it risks underplaying the reality of the bondage it has endured. If the spirit of the nation really is unfading and warm, a lily unchilled by the rain or a heart frowned on in vain by sorrow, can its political tribulations have been as grievous as all that? The more indomitable the Irishry, the less reprehensible the English, at least on one view of the matter. One might feel equally sceptical of the continuity asserted in 'Believe me, if all those endearing young charms', which protests that the poet will still love his partner even when she has become, as the piece rather indecorously puts it, a 'dear ruin'. This is chivalrous of him of course, but it is hard to avoid the suspicion that this constancy is bought at the price of an indifference to the woman's material identity.

Moore's verses quite often dematerialise women in this apparently commendatory way, suggesting that their appearance is as nothing to their impalpable spiritual essence, and so robbing them of their bodies in the name of disowning a frivolous eroticism. Much the same may be said of his attitude to Ireland. Sometimes a double dematerialising takes place, as the physical reality of a place or person is disowned for the spirit, and that spirit dissolved in turn to a ray of heavenly truth. In any case, the point about lyrics like 'Believe me, if all those endearing young charms' is that constancy in love seems the acceptable face of a rather less appealing act of abstraction. 'I but know that I love thee, whatever thou art', he declares to his beloved in 'Come, rest in this bosom', a notably back-handed compliment. In 'Take back the virgin page', the woman is compared to a blank text, so virginally uninscribed as to be a semiotic nothing.

But the historicist bent of a poem like 'Erin, oh Erin' is at odds with the stance of a lyric like 'Remember me', which argues in 'decadent' vein that it is exactly Ireland's sufferings which the poet finds most enthralling. If the country were 'great, glorious, and free', so Moore candidly confesses, he would probably love it less. It is Erin's running blood and rankling chains which make it 'painfully dear' to its sons, so that his political desires are at odds with his sado-masochistic fantasies. Pure ecstasy is less pleasurable than when it is lent an admixture of pain, so that the *Irish Melodies* yearn for an historical future against which their emotions rebel. Leaving the blessed island of Innisfallen, Moore is glad that it is raining:

> Far better in thy weeping hours
>   To part from thee, as I do now,
> When mist is o'er thy blooming bowers,
>   Like sorrow's veil on beauty's brow.
>
> For, though unrivall'd still thy grace,
>   Thou doest not look, as then, *too* blest,
> But thus in shadow, seem'st a place
>   Where erring man might hope to rest. . .
>   ('Sweet Innisfallen')

Gloom, or a misty indistinctness, humanises what might otherwise loom up as too untinted, harshly singular an ideal. The island is 'all the lovelier for thy tears'. The piece goes on to compare Innisfallen's despondency to that of the trees of Eden weeping when humanity fell – a subtle move, since it affirms a unity between Nature and humanity at the very point of registering their disjunction. *Lalla Rookh* admires a kind of light

> . . .through summer foliage stealing,
> Shedding a glow of such mild hue,
> So warm, and yet so shadowy too,
> As makes the very darkness there
> More beautiful than light elsewhere!

Moore's oxymoronic fantasy is a completely dark light, a glowing shadow, an absence which is also pure presence. Politically speaking, this means an heroic activism which is somehow compatible with sensuous pleasure. Sexually speaking, it means a woman who is both utterly ethereal and warm-bloodedly human. Another of the *Melodies*, 'While gazing on the moon's light', unfavourably compares the 'lone and distant glory' of the stars to the milder, more humanised moon. Moore's verses admire purity, but they are allergic to it too. The conflict emerges in 'Oh, call it by some better name', which in *symboliste* fashion strains beyond language to a sexual relationship unsullied by such shop-soiled words as 'love', 'friendship' and 'passion', yet a relationship which, though 'something purer far' than these, is nonetheless just as human as they are.

The *Melodies* thus prefer the dimly lit gloaming to the untempered glare of noon, just as they prefer, masochistically, to reap their delights from suffering. 'Fly not yet' speaks fondly of the midnight flower which 'scorns the eye of vulgar light', and informs us with physiological assurance that women's hearts are cold at noon but kindle towards nightfall. 'Gleam' is one of Moore's most habitual images, since it dims down the light without actually quenching it, gives an oblique foretaste or memory of freedom without actually incarnating it. Gleams or rays are a kind of visual echo, hovering as they do between life and death, the material and immaterial. They are the frail filaments which bind the Irish past to the Irish present, allowing you to stress either the darkening of the ancient glory or the fact that it still lives on in spectral yet indestrucible form – indestructible *because* spectral, perhaps.

The song 'In the morning of life' similarly elevates 'the cloud and mist of our own Isle of showers' over 'climes full of sunshine'. The full bright light of political idealism, which Moore entirely believed in, is betrayed by the poem's imagery as inferior to an equivocal condition of sweetness and tears, of damp mists which nonetheless evoke a sumptuous fragrancy. The stress of the piece is masochistic: it is from suffering, not 'mid splendour, prosperity, mirth', that love's essence is distilled. Yet splendour, prosperity and mirth are doubtless what the reformist Moore wishes for his country. The love which inspires nationalism is thus at odds with its political outcome. There is a touch of the Irish begrudger or cult of failure in the fabulously successful Moore's sniffiness about achievement: 'Forget not the Field' prefers a patriot's grave or prison to all the trophies of worldly triumph. The spoils in question are admittedly those of the conqueror: 'Accursed is the march of that glory / Which treads o'er the hearts of the brave'. But the problem is that the steady march of history would seem, for Moore as much as for Walter Benjamin, to be the conqueror's inalienable property, which then makes it hard to see how those dispossessed by it can construct a history for themselves. Moore's verses accordingly swerve between weaponry and wine, between a rather callow nationalist version of this ruling historicism, and a retreat from history itself, now seen as irredeemably ruined and tainted, into the standard Romantic alternatives of the inebriating, the erotic, the aesthetic and the grave. The nationalist project of aestheticising history constantly splinters into an opposition between history and the aesthetic.

'In the morning of life', like several of Moore's songs, regards the ravages of time as creative rather than destructive, since it is our consciousness of mortality which fosters tender feeling. In a familiar Romantic paradox, death lends an exquisitely keen edge to pleasure: by living backwards from it, so to speak, we increase the value of our fleeting experience at the same time as we risk subverting it entirely. The rosebud-gatherer is the one prepared to take this risk, trading a sharpened sense of mortality against a constant replenishing of the cup of sensation. The poem, as usual with its author, privileges twilight over morning, holding that affection is truest when hopes fade away; but this inverted temporality runs against the grain of Moore's politics. For Moore the nationalist, love of country and hope for its freedom are inseparable rather than at odds. Politically speaking, ruins are meant to be an occasion for heartache, not welcome signs of the flowering of boisterous youth into tender-hearted maturity. 'Love's young dream' sees such youthful energy as the sweetest thing in life, but also as entirely illusory, so that at our most robustly vital we live a fiction. Despite this, the piece 'I Saw from the beach' irritably rejects the supposed comforts of old age and wants that 'wild freshness' of youth back again. 'Whene'er I see those smiling eyes' is likewise a straight piece of nostalgia for the unblemished purity of youth.

Other of Moore's lyrics, however, are more Wordsworthian in their sacrifice of such animal impulses to the more intricate pleasures of experience. His poetry, in short, does not know whether to read historical evolution as a lapse away from some primordial wholeness, or as moving from some too-unqualified vision to a more congenially chequered form of experience. To call the heart 'a vase in which roses have once been distill'd' may sound like an expression of regret, but the point is that the roses' fragrance, once it has impregnated the vessel, will last longer than they did themselves, just as gleams outlive the drowned sun and song survives the military disasters which give birth to it. As Moore writes with typical triteness in 'Farewell! – but whenever you welcome the hour', 'You may break, you may shatter, the vase, if you will, / But the scent of the roses will hang round it still'. The intangible odour is more indestructible than the material object, just as the spirit of the nation is less perishable than its population.

There are really two time schemes in Moore, which correspond roughly to the distinction between pleasure and gloom. There is the thoughtless immediacy of enjoyment, but also that depth of ancestral *Erfahrung*, at once dire and nourishing, which is the *longue durée* of the suffering nation. These time schemes interpenetrate just as past and present do, or happiness and grief: when Moore discerns 'death beneath our smile' in 'Sail on, sail on', he is really glimpsing the bleak grand narrative of history through the crevices of its surface joys. These banal lines from 'Fly not yet' bring together a whole range of his antitheses: beam/dark, smile/ruin, warm/cold, the caught moment versus the on-rush of time:

> As a beam o'er the face of the water may glow,
> Where the tide runs in darkness and coldness below,
> So the cheek may be ting'd with a warm sunny smile,
> Though the cold heart to ruin runs darkly the while.

The relation between joy and sorrow is 'vertical' rather than serial, synchronic rather than diachronic. It is certainly not a matter of historical development. Here gladness is of the surface and sadness of the depth, but Moore sometimes reverses these priorities: common-or-garden griefs may bring fond memories bursting to the surface of consciousness, which is another reason for masochistically treasuring despondency. It is as though gloom churns up the otherwise too-smooth surface of experience so as to throw up precious relics from the past. Memory is itself a compound of pleasure and pain, presence and absence, since what you remember is gratifying, whereas the fact that you have to remember it is not. Moore sometimes consoles himself with the bleak thought that at least they can't rob you of your memories, which are in some ways more real than the present. The absent past hollows the present to a mere spectre of itself, and thus grows more vividly present the more it dematerialises one's current perceptions. Thus Fate, in 'Farewell! – but whenever you welcome the hour', can do its worst, but cannot destroy certain 'relics of joy'. These relics are, in Benjamin's sense, auratic – traces of a sacred past which are sedimented in the mind, and which can survive the fragmentations of mere *Erlebnis* or daily experience.

But the *Irish Melodies*, like Benjamin himself, are deeply ambivalent about how resistant to history's depredations these spots of time really are. In their more crassly triumphalistic mood, they suggest that the heroic past can never die, that its rays, gleams or echoes will reverberate to infinity. Moore's own poetry is one instance of this immortality. A lot of the *Melodies* are simply ways of cheering himself up, resolving at the level of factitious imagery what stubbornly refuses resolution in fact:

> The gem may be broke
> By many a stroke,
> But nothing can cloud its native ray.
> Each fragment will cast
> A light, to the last, —
> And thus, Erin, my country tho' broken thou art,
> There's a lustre within thee, that ne'er will decay.
>   ('The Prince's Day')

The wobbly metre of this, along with that too-delayed final rhyme, hint at the 'lip-deep' nature of the sentiments, to use Hazlitt's epithet about Moore. The lustre within is the unchanging essence which Moore's own songs strive to distil, discarding the material body of Ireland as an empty husk. The same alchemical process had to be performed on the traditional airs which he uses: the tunes, he remarks in his 'Letter on Music', were often poorly performed and transcribed, yet 'in most of them . . . the pure gold of the melody shines through the ungraceful foliage which surrounds it'. His own poetry thus involves a double extraction, freeing the pure melodic gold of its dross so as to draw from it in turn the intangible spirit of the nation. Ireland, anyway, is shattered but not dimmed, or broken but not bent, or dead but ripe for resurrection, or (in ''Tis gone, and for ever'), vanished forever but alive in memory. In this song, unusually, the gleams which the quenched light of liberty has released are actually regretted: they 'but deepen the long night of bondage and mourning'. If misery masochistically acts as a foil to joy, the reverse may also be true.

'The harp that once through Tara's halls' can find only a negative continuity between past and present: freedom now lives on only in the sigh of indignation at its disappearance. In 'Weep on, weep', things are even blacker: the song contradicts some of Moore's other poetic statements by baldly asserting that freedom's flame, once snuffed out, is gone forever. Ireland's future has been scuppered, sunk on the rocks of sectarianism. In his *Memoirs of Captain Rock*, Moore satirises what is really a caricatured version of one of his own beliefs in the *Melodies*: Rock's rebel father clings nostalgically to 'the *real* Irish, who, by a blessed miracle, though exterminated under every succeeding Lord Lieutenant, are still as good as new, and ready to be exterminated again'.[5] If this is just an exaggerated way of saying that the Irish rebel spirit never dies, then Moore himself, much of the time at least, believes precisely this, whatever his revisionist scorn for this disaffected old die-hard. His uncertainty over the question of what, if anything, survives the past is one version of a familiar nationalist conundrum: if ancient Ireland lives on, then there is perhaps no need after all to throw off the colonial power; if it does not, then there is no possibility of doing so. The past must be present enough to ensure a future, but absent enough to make that future necessary in the first place.[6]

'Oh! blame not the bard' ingeniously interweaves Moore's two time schemes – immediate experience and an encompassing History – by blaming history for the way the poet hedonistically abandons it. If he flees to the bowers of bliss, it is because historical progress has stalled, leaving him with no more responsible role. It is history's fault, not Moore's, that the Irish poet has been deprived of his traditional bardic centrality, and left only with his celebrity. The withering of the shamrock, so to speak, gives way to the plucking of the rosebuds. If the artist is now bereft of a politically interventionist role, this fact itself can be politically accounted for. For the poet, power has now yielded to desire, as his warrior's bow gives way to a lip 'which now breathes but the song of desire'. The poet's frivolous *dégagement* is thus historically rationalised, as he turns to the sensual moment because of the deadlock of the *longue durée*. This is a novel variant on the synchrony of joy and sorrow, as dismal historical necessity itself drives one into *carpe diem*

5. *Memoirs of Captain Rock* (London, 1824), p. 243.
6. There are countless examples in later Irish nationalist writing of this mixture of hope and gloom. A typical instance occcurs in AE's *The National Being* (Dublin and London, 1916): 'The gods departed, the half-gods also, hero and saint after that, and we have dwindled down to a petty peasant mentality, rural and urban life alike mean in their externals. Yet . . . there is still some incorruptible spiritual atom in our people' (p. 14).

escapism. Writing on Moore's poem *Lalla Rookh* (or 'Larry O'Rourke', as one English gentlewoman misheard it), Robert Welch detects an emptiness at its core, filled by 'erotic languishing'.[7] Carnality and historical collapse are sides of the same coin.

In 'One bumper at parting', by contrast, Moore conflates his two time-streams by suggesting that time is nothing *but* a succession of fleeting moments. The opposition between present pleasure and a grimly relentless history is deconstructed, since 'never doth Time fly faster, Than when his way lies among flowers'. Life is a delayed orgasm, a pleasurable sweetness 'so slow to come forth' that it has expired before we appreciate its value. Alternatively, it is a succession of *petits morts*, of moments 'born on the bosom of Pleasure' which instantly 'die 'midst the tears of the cup'. In his drinking songs – a faintly unconvincing genre for Moore, incidentally, since gusto is hardly his *forte* – the fleetingness of pleasure is manfully reckoned into the savouring of it, like the burst grape of Keats's *Ode to Melancholy*. The fullest moment is also the most ephemeral, and maturity consists in cold-eyedly embracing this paradox: 'Be ours the light Sorrow, half-sister to Joy'. Or, as he writes in *Lalla Rookh*:

> How exquisite one single drop
> Of bliss, thus sparkling to the top
> Of misery's cup – how keenly quaff'd,
> Though death must follow on the draught!

This is a kind of minor-key version of Yeats's tragic joy, though what in Yeats is an heroic swagger comes through in Moore as a glibly unconvincing devil-may-careness. For both poets, the worse history gets, the more defiantly exuberant you become. As 'The Irish Peasant to his Mistress' puts it, 'The darker our fortunes, the brighter our pure love burn'd'.

Since it is literally true that light shines more brightly in the dark, this is a classic instance of Moore's persistent naturalising of human conditions, casting history in terms of Nature and passing off as a moral truth some piece of logic which really works only at the level of natural imagery. His writing constantly displaces the one into the other. A striking instance of this use of imagery to drive home a specious argument is 'I'd mourn the hopes', a bitterly pessimistic piece which tries wanly to convince itself that the fading of historical hopes is nothing since the poet's beloved is still faithful to him. The two of them, Moore asserts, will journey onwards even more safely without the ray of hope to guide them, since the light of his mind and her smile will illuminate them all the better. Since it is obvious that smiles and minds don't shed as much light as rays, the sophistry of the argument is betrayed by the rigged imagery.

7.   Robert Welch, *Changing States* (London and New York, 1993), p. 22.

The point, anyway, is that Moore's *carpe diem* pieces, like the openly libertine ''Tis Sweet to Think', view the existential moment as valuable precisely because of history's futility; but this then risks undermining that moment in the very act of intensifying it. The *carpe diem* life-style for Moore is a kind of proto-existentialism which affirms value in the face of the void, living a self-conscious fiction of sensuous fullness even when you know it to be hollowed at its core by personal mortality and historical paralysis.[8] There is a touch of the existential *acte gratuit* about his tankard-wagging and rosebud-gathering, just as there is about the harpist of 'My gentle harp', who strums his instrument not to redeem the times but simply to show a world of desolation how sweet its music is. Bereft of a social function, the artist can rationalise this superfluousness by an aestheticist appeal to the sheerly gratuitous nature of singing in the jaws of defeat. The ultimate undecidability of the distinction between smiling and weeping – 'The laugh is awake ere the tear can be dried' – is less to do with some 'unaccountable mixture of gloom and levity' in the Irish temperament, as Moore himself maintains, than with the fact that loss or absence is the very condition of material presence, as Moore recognises in his own Romantic way. The *carpe diem* strategy is an attempt to circumvent this dilemma by living so fast that the next pleasure has arrived just as the last one is expiring. But absence can be celebrated as well as suppressed: if Irish exiles tend to be especially enthusiastic for their native land, Moore remarks in his 'Letter on Music', it is largely because distance softens or obliterates the country's more rebarbative features. And spiritual intimacy may overleap physical distance, as with Sarah Curran and Robert Emmet in 'She is far from the land'.

The *Irish Melodies* anticipate an unfolding presence – the unshackling of Erin – and yet can only really function in terms of absences. The idea of a bumper at parting itself involves an oxymoronic blending of presence and absence, since a bumper means a glass filled to the brim, but in this case so as to have a last toast before leaving. Memory is one such frail frontier between fullness and loss, as the dead are reanimated in ways which make them more vigorous than the living. Like the spirit of love or of the nation, memory both heightens and dematerialises, as much a form of living death as Ireland itself. In 'Go where thy glory waits thee', memory is a way of tempering the present with the past, rather as happiness, to be authentic, must be alloyed with grief. The poem urges the exile to carry his origins with him on his travels, just as Moore's own art bears the past of Ireland into his readers' present.

8.   Indeed there is a sense in which much of the *Irish Melodies* may represent the self-conscious living of a fiction. In the Appendix to his satirical poems *Corruption and Intolerance*, Moore speculates that the ideal of a glorious ancient Ireland may be an invention, but even if it is, 'who would not fly to such flattering fictions from the sad degrading truths which the history of later times presents to us?' (*Corruption and Intolerance*, London 1808, p. 61).

The past thus becomes a depth within the present – literally so in 'Let Erin remember the days of old', where it appears in the form of round towers submerged in Lough Neagh. Looking back becomes looking down, as chronology is once more folded into synchrony. In 'How dear to me the hour', twilight is valued not for itself – in fact Moore rarely values Nature for itself – but because it dissolves the actual and allows the alternative scenario of the past to flood it. Time is stacked within the present, awaiting that epiphanic fault-line or seismic emotional tremor which will thrust it once more to the surface of consciousness. Past and present are no more consecutive than pain and pleasure. But this co-dependence, which grasps the past as a creative ferment within the present, is at loggerheads with the Whiggish politics for which the past is what you struggle out from under. Doctrinally speaking, Moore himself was in this respect a thorough modernist, dismissing early Irish music as irregular and barbaric. 'It is certain that our finest and most popular airs are modern', he writes self-satisfiedly in his 'Letter on Music', and goes on to satirise the hyperbolic claims of Irish antiquarianism. In fact Moore's attitudes to such antiquarian myth-making would delight the heart of a modern-day revisionist. In his *History of Ireland*, he is dryly sceptical of the 'fondly imagined epoch of those old Milesian days', and sternly recalls his compatriots from mythical illusions to historical truth.[9] Captain Rock's mutinous father is said to suffer from such fantasies, which is more than enough to discredit them. The elegist of the poetry is the demystifier of the prose.

Moore sings of heroic themes with a distinctly non-heroic sensibility, and as such can be seen as a casualty of historical change. He writes at a point where the formal role of the public bard can still be assumed, but where a history of defeat has increasingly privatised what you can do with it. Like Tennyson after him, he either splits the sensuous from the social, consigning each to a different species of poem, or mixes a still-public form of address with subjectivist contents. At his worst, he lurches from stagey public rhetoric to coy personal sentiment. In the Appendix to his twin poetic satires *Corruption and Intolerance*, he seems to recognise that history itself, so to speak, has robbed his writing of any positive historical content. History, 'which ought to be the richest garden of the Muses, yields nothing to her [in Ireland] but weeds and cypress'. The poet in search of a positive history in Ireland would need to overleap the colonial epoch and return to the earliest period, 'before the impolitic craft of our conquerors had divided, weakened, and disgraced us'.[10] The point would seem to confirm Georg Lukács's thesis that genuine historical writing springs from a refreshed sense of history in the making, rather than from a sense of it as sheer monotonous *donnée*.[11] Moore cannot write

9.   Thomas Moore, *A History of Ireland*, vol. 1 (London, 1835), p. 88.
10.   ibid, p. 60.
11.   See Georg Lukács, *The Historical Novel* (1947; reprinted London, 1962).

authentic historical poetry, he implies, because his nation lacks a sense of historical agency. To unearth images of that agency, one needs to return to the well-nigh pre-historic – to heroic myths whose bearing on the present and recent past is then questionable. What is exemplary is too remote, while what is historically near to hand is imaginatively uninspiring.

This is surely one major reason why Moore's energies turn inwards, and in doing so risk growing morbid. A piece like 'Avenging and bright', which sees revenge on a tyrant as 'sweetest of all', is a rare instance of extraversion, unwontedly linking pleasure ('sweet' is a key Moore term) to political action. His more usual way of coupling these things is in the masochistic, self-immolatory death, turning one's destructive impulses fulfillingly upon oneself. It is thus that one can achieve action and *jouissance* simultaneously, realities which otherwise belong to quite different time schemes. The celebrated ''Tis the last rose of summer' is a Gothic exercise in sado-masochism, as the poet deliberately destroys the rose so as to save it from solitude. This benign act of euthanasia in fact turns out to be a kind of self-violence, as the song's last stanza suggests: the poet does to the rose what he would wish done to himself if he were left solitary too.

Moore's ferocious death wish – what Terence Brown sees in *Lalla Rookh* as 'a compulsive note of necrophilia'[12] – sometimes breaks out in his *Melodies* in virulently Schopenhauerian form. In 'I wish I were by that dim lake', he seems to claim *à la* Schopenhauer that delusory hopes exist just to keep you alive, and so to keep you suffering. In 'Sing, sweet harp', only the dead can be free, while 'Before the Battle' appears to be as much allured by the warrior's chance of 'sleep' (i.e. death) as by his valour. The companion piece 'After the Battle' morbidly images the sun rising just to give the injured warriors light by which to die, while death itself becomes the 'bright opening' of another world. But the death urge can also be semi-rationalised as an appeal for peace, political or personal, as in 'The meeting of the waters'. Sacrificial death is a dramatic version of what Moore's poetry does all the time, which is to conjure value from negativity. A song like 'And doth not a meeting like this' self-laceratingly suggests that we should rejoice in the rareness of our pleasures, since this can only augment their value. Death, the final absence, is also in martyrdom the fullest form of presence, and thus the ultimate expression of Moore's antithetical vision. But turning your aggression inwards also sublimates it and renders it more acceptable, so that this final act of refusal of imperial power is also, ironically, palatable enough to Moore's upper-class English audiences. In the martyr's death, a formidable power is snatched from powerlessness, rather as Moore's own sugared songs hope to beguile the mighty into tearful repentance for their anti-Irish crimes. In this way, passively lamenting Erin's fate might bring about an active transformation of its woes.

12.   Terence Brown, *Ireland's Literature* (Mullingar, 1988), p. 26.

It is hard to believe that the author of a superb political satire like *Captain Rock* was also responsible for the following lines of verse:

> Yes, my Nora Creina, dear,
> My simple, graceful Nora Creina,
>   Nature's dress
>   Is loveliness—
> The dress *you* wear, my Nora Creina.
>
> ('Lesbia hath a beaming eye')

How are we to reconcile the kitschy, cloying, maudlin Moore with the fine political polemicist? Why is it that one whiff of the sardonic irony which animates *Captain Rock* would be fatal to the sublimated sensuality of the *Irish Melodies*? Part of the answer lies surely in the determining power of genre. Moore wrote at the point where the distinction between prose and verse was being redrawn in ways which would have come as something of a surprise to John Milton or Alexander Pope. Poetry is now increasingly the preserve of private sentiment, while what might ordinarily be called thinking, along with public affairs, is becoming the prerogative of prose. Eighteenth-century sentimentalism, as we have seen, had already laid the ground for this fetishism of feeling, and some strains of Romanticism were to consummate it.

But nationalism, precisely because it is at once an historical narrative and a question of subjective identity, was bound to be deeply implicated in this division of linguistic labour. The notorious gap in Irish nationalism between rhetoric and reality has now, as it were, been generically underwritten, as 'The Minstrel Boy' takes care of the former and the *Life of Edward Fitzgerald* busies itself with the latter. The rift between the two is there also in the conflict between Moore's mild, well-bred, anti-O'Connellite brand of nationalism, and the macho militancy of some of his verse.[13] He had a fine middle-class disdain for the forty-shilling freeholders, and held like Burke that it was England's obtuse failure to placate and integrate the Irish which was driving them headlong into a fearful revolutionism. The satirical stance of *Captain Rock* is perfectly adapted to this twin rejection of colonial oppression and anti-colonial insurrection. Since it is imperial misrule which has bred rebels like Rock, the work can lampoon the English as savagely as it likes, since the consequence of their heeding its criticisms would be the restoration of Irish loyalty. This is an ingenious way of unleashing one's anti-colonialist aggression while being not a whit seditious. Indeed the more you

13.   O'Connell described Moore's *Life of Edward Fitzgerald* as containing 'treasonous truth', a phrase which Moore himself proudly quotes against the Liberator to rebut his accusation that Moore's own nationalism is lukewarm. See Wilfred S. Dowden (ed.), *The Letters of Thomas Moore* (Oxford, 1964), vol. 2, p. 786. It is worth noting that in the two bulky volumes of Moore's correspondence, there is hardly a literary insight of any significance.

expose the English as dolts and knaves, the greater the service you render to their cause in Ireland.

Moore is at root a private, deeply disenchanted poet forced by history and personal ambition[14] into a public posture, and many of his creations simply crumble under the strain. Since there is no way of integrating the sensuous and the historical, the former disintegrates into rococo prettiness and the latter stiffens into vacuous rhetoric. Moore has the melodrama of nationalism without the committee meetings. He is not so much Ireland's national bard, as testimony to the impossibility of that role. His poetry is deft but automated, like a skilful actor performing in too long a theatrical run. What he can do brilliantly is not particularly valuable, and what is really valuable he does not even attempt. But though the praise lavished on his writing by Goethe, Byron, Stendhal and Victor Hugo now strikes us as bizarre, it remains true that, however mawkishly, he placed Ireland almost single-handedly on the cultural agenda of his day, quick as he was to perceive that the country, in a certain reading of it, lent itself marvellously well to the emergent structure of feeling of post-Enlightenment Europe. Though his writing flows a good deal too easily, and his emblems are threadbare even at first sight, he furnished his successors with a new set of poetic coordinates, and alerted them to the broader significance of their own cultural experience. For later Irish writers like Joyce and Heaney, Moore loomed up less as an individual than as a collective sensibility or repository of archetypes, which could be discarded or negotiated but not ignored.[15] In his own time, he enjoyed the fame of a modern rock star rather than a writer. For posterity, he is less a person than an institution, which is at once a tribute to his extraordinarily popular achievement, and a wry comment on the blandly impersonal nature of what is offered as a uniquely subjective vision.

14. Yeats described Moore as 'merely an incarnate social ambition'. See Allan Wade (ed.), *The Letters of W. B. Yeats* (London, 1954), p. 447.
15. Joyce's work is littered with allusions to Moore. As for Heaney, see the comments on Moore in his Introduction to David Hammond (ed.), *A Centenary Selection of Moore's Melodies* (Skerries, Co. Dublin, 1979).

CORK AND THE CARNIVALESQUE

In his deservedly neglected study *The Geographical Distribution of Irish Ability*, David J. O'Donoghue claims that 'Irishmen are the cleverest people, proportionately, in the world'.[1] Men of genius, he notes, have a tendency to stammer, and Ireland can boast of many celebrated stammerers from John Wilson Croker to William Maginn.[2] Geniuses also tend to be tall (though the dwarfish Thomas Moore, Lady Morgan and Thomas Crofton Croker are, O'Donoghue confesses, unaccountable Irish exceptions to this rule), and are quite often the progeny of grocers or tavern keepers. There is no doubt, however, that 'the first among Irish counties in intellectual development and output' is not Dublin but Cork.[3]

Havelock Ellis, in the chapter on Ireland in his *Study of British Genius*, claims that of his 1,030 examples of native genius, a sizeable proportion are Irish-English or Irish-Scottish hybrids, and he too finds county Cork particularly prodigal of talent, with ten 'notables' as opposed to fifteen for Dublin and none at all for counties Sligo, Leitrim, Roscommon, Monaghan, Fermanagh, Meath and a few other dim-witted regions.[4] Ellis's glowing opinion of Cork, though rejected by the Victorian novelist Mrs Oliphant ('a place more associated with pigs and salted provisions than with literature'),[5] was anticipated by Mr and Mrs S. C. Hall, who wrote of its premier city in the early 1840s that the place 'has been celebrated more than any other city of Ireland for the production and fosterage of genius',[6] though they add that the most interesting institution is the lunatic asylum. Sir Walter Scott was also famously struck by

1. David J. O'Donoghue, *The Geographical Distribution of Irish Ability* (Dublin, 1906), pp. 5 and 22.
2. Oliver Goldsmith remarks in an essay in *The Weekly Magazine* that the great Irish scientist Robert Boyle learned to stammer as a boy by imitating others, a coupling of genius and imitation relevant to the theme of this essay. See Arthur Friedman (ed.), *Collected Works of Oliver Goldsmith* (Oxford, 1966), vol. 3, pp. 41–2. Goldsmith himself, who liberally helped himself to other authors' texts, was also said to be a chronic imitator of the manner of others, adopting with an outsider's insecurity the personae of Samuel Johnson and others of his circle. Sterne was a tireless plagiariser of his own work.
3. O'Donoghue, *Geographical Distribution of Irish Ability*, p. 22.
4. Havelock Ellis, *A Study of British Genius* (London, 1904), pp. 25–6. On the subject of Irish skin pigmentation, Ellis remarks illuminatingly that 'as measured by the index of nigrescence, Ulster anthropologically approaches Connaught' (p. 65).
5. Mrs Oliphant, *Annals of a Publishing House* (Edinburgh and London, 1897), vol. 1, p. 362.
6. Mr and Mrs S. C. Hall, *Ireland: Its Scenery, Character, Etc* (London, 1841–3), p. 20.

the 'bookishness' of the Cork people, and Thackeray, who modelled his early style on the Cork satirist William Maginn, refers glowingly to the city's literary scene in his *Irish Sketch Book*. The Corkonian Sean O'Faolain, rather less dewy-eyed, dubbed his fellow citizens 'a talented but acidulous and envious subrace'.[7] 'Cork men generally possess a greater amount of talent, and are more metropolitan in their ideas than the natives of other parts of Ireland', declared an anonymous Irish reviewer in 1852,[8] while in 1828 *Bolster's Quarterly Magazine*, a Cork periodical not wholly disinterested in these matters, announced that 'Cork can challenge even the metropolis itself [for artists], in point of worth, and almost in numbers'.[9] The claim is perhaps not entirely self-vaunting: Cork was probably a much stronger literary centre than Belfast in the late eighteenth and early nineteenth centuries, and seems to have been slightly more active than Dublin in the publication of fiction.[10]

By the time *Bolster's* judgement was delivered, the city was already passing its cultural peak, having lost most of its artists to death or emigration. Indeed the journal goes on instantly to complain that the patronage of art by the city is scandalously neglected: '. . . how ill we deserve any reputation for taste in the Arts, who neither cherish in life or in death those whose merit has lent a partial renown to our city'.[11] By the 1820s, Cork was languishing in economic recession, after its spectacular eighteenth-century expansion. The city's population had perhaps quadrupled between 1700 and 1821, and its golden age spanned the decades around the turn of the nineteenth century, with a flourishing industry in provisions, brewing and flour-milling.[12] Never much of a manufacturing centre, but furnished with a fertile agricultural hinterland and a fine natural harbour, the port, one of the busiest in the world, could gaze inwards and outwards with equal satisfaction. One particularly

7. Sean O'Faolain, *Vive Moi!* (London, 1965), p. 119. The book sketches a coldly demystified portrait of the socially devastated Cork of the early twentieth century.
8. *Irish Quarterly Review,* vol. v, no. 11 (September, 1852), p. 631. The anonymous author sours his compliment a little by adding that Cork men are also characterised by 'overweening conceit' (p. 632). The review is of the official catalogue of the Cork National Exhibition of Arts, which was held in the same year.
9. 'Irish Art and Artists', *Bolster's Quarterly Magazine*, vol. 2 (Dublin, 1828), p. 55. The magazine was published by the Corkmen John Bolster and Richard Milliken, author of 'The Groves of Blarney'.
10. I am grateful for this information to Mr Rolf Loeber of Pittsburgh.
11. *Bolster's Quarterly Magazine*, vol. 2, p. 55.
12. See William J. Smyth, 'Social, Economic and Landscape Transformations in County Cork from the Mid-Eighteenth to the Mid-Nineteenth Century', in Patrick O'Flanagan and Cornelius G. Buttimer (eds.), *Cork: History and Society* (Dublin, 1993), pp. 673–4. See also David Dickson, 'An Economic History of the Cork Region in the Eighteenth Century', unpublished PhD thesis, University of Dublin, 1977, which is especially perceptive on the vertical organisation of the pilchard trade (vol. 1, pp. 37–8). L. M. Cullen has some brief remarks on the city's economy in *An Economic History of Ireland since 1600* (London, 1972; reprinted 1987), pp. 55–6.

self-satisfied historian notes that 'practically every country in Europe received Cork beef, butter or pork', and with a touch of Corkonian hyperbole characterises the organisation of the city's butter market as 'one of the most remarkable that has ever existed'.[13] It is clear that he means human organisations in general, not just butter markets. Cork became the most significant centre for butter production in the Atlantic world.[14] In the final quarter of the eighteenth century, the city reaped the benefits of a global trade in textiles, as well as enjoying the status of Ireland's chief centre for military provisions.[15] Its international trade was to be matched, in the writings of Francis Mahony and William Maginn, by an equally cosmopolitan commerce in idioms and ideas.

The city's social dynamism gave birth to an imposing cultural superstructure.[16] There was an active Literary and Philosophical Society, which heard papers on everything from the materiality of heat to a description of the anteater, the influence of the female sex on society to the clearing of river beds. One could learn about the immorality of Sheridan's drama on one evening, and the sonorous properties of lead on the next.[17] 1803 saw the establishment of the Cork Institution for the Diffusion of Knowledge, which was to gain its royal charter four years later, and which laid on lectures for the general public.[18] Founded by the Presbyterian cleric Thomas Hincks, a disciple of Joseph Priestley, it included the socialist-feminist William Thompson among its founding members,[19] contained an excellent library

13.   William O'Sullivan, *The Economic History of Cork City* (Cork, 1937), pp. 231, 256. A more sober assessment of the eighteenth-century Cork butter market is provided by David Dickson, 'An Economic History of the Cork Region', vol. 2, pp. 428–41.
14.   See Kevin Whelan, 'The Modern Landscape: From Plantation to Present', in F. H. A. Aalen, Kevin Whelan and Matthew Stout (eds.), *Atlas of the Irish Rural Landscape* (Cork, 1997), p. 71.
15.   See John B. O'Brien, 'Population, Politics and Society in Cork, 1780–1900', in O'Flanagan and Buttimer, *Cork: History and Society*.
16.   For a general account of early nineteenth-century Cork artists, see Davis and Mary Coakley, *Wit and Wine* (Peterhead, 1975).
17.   See Day Collection U140, Section A, Cork City Archives Institute.
18.   See Thomas Dix Hincks, *Syllabus of a Course of Lectures Delivered in the Year 1803* (Cork, 1803). The syllabus encompasses poetry, natural history, language, physics, astronomy and religion, among other subjects. There is a useful account of the Institution by Margaret MacSweeney and Joseph Reilly, 'The Royal Cork Institution: Part 1: 1803–26', in the *Journal of the Cork Historical and Archaeological Society*, vol. 62, no. 195 (January–June, 1957). *The Annual Report of the Managers and Auditors of the Cork Institution* (Cork, 1816) maintains that the scientific lectures in particular were very well attended.
19.   Thompson, whose father had been lord mayor of Cork and high sheriff of the county, was also closely involved in the Cork Philosophical and Literary Society. In his pamphlet *Practical Education in the South of Ireland*, he lambasts the Cork Institution for mismanagement and waste of funds, and demands a more civic and utilitarian syllabus. The most definitive work on Thompson to date is

and also housed a museum, about which the Dubliner Thomas Moore was suitably condescending. Visiting it in 1823, he remarked in his journal that it was 'a poor display of science: among the curiosities is the jack-boot of a French postilion!'[20]

The Institution, with a canny eye to the good burghers of Cork, sought to harness knowledge to manufacture. A somewhat desperate attempt to promote this project was launched by one W. Clear, who in an address in 1820 argued that learning gave employment to printers, papermakers and the like, and portrayed the Cork Philosophical and Literary Society which he was addressing as a kind of intellectual joint-stock enterprise in which each could enrich his mental capital by uniting it with that of others.[21] We shall encounter this analogy between commerce and cerebration again, in the work of Francis Mahony. Whatever Clear's special pleading, the Cork Institution's record was an impressive one, launching the first farmer's journal in the country, pioneering adult education in the city and paving the way to the later Queen's Colleges.

In 1843 Cork hosted its first ever international conference, organised by the British Association for the Advancement of Science and attended by Dickens, Thomas Davis, Thomas Wyse, William Smith O'Brien, Charles Bianconi, a clutch of local worthies and a raft of peers and prelates. Bolster's bookshop in St Patrick's Street, visited by Sir Walter Scott and an artistic bolthole for the painter Daniel Maclise, became the Corkonian equivalent of the *Café Flore*, and Thomas Crofton Croker, at a safe distance from his native city, reported that 'several literary and scientific societies have recently [i.e. 1823–4] sprung up in Cork, which have been spiritedly supported by young men whose abilities promise to excite a revolution favourable to the advancement of literature'.[22] It is one of the few occasions on which Croker can be found supporting a revolution.

Dolores Dooley, *Equality in Community* (Cork, 1996), which claims that the city of Cork had seen throughout its history at least 1,770 groups or societies for the dissemination of literary, artistic, scientific and philosophical knowledge (p. 15). See also, for a brief account of this astonishingly original pioneer of socialist and feminist thought, Richard K. P. Pankhurst, *William Thompson* (London, 1954), and Desmond Fennell, 'Irish Socialist Thought', in Richard Kearney (ed.), *The Irish Mind* (Dublin, 1985).

20. Wilfred S. Dowson (ed.), *The Journals of Thomas Moore* (Newark, 1984), vol. 2, p. 660.
21. W. Clear, *Address to the Cork Philosophical and Literary Society* (Cork, 1820), p. 63. In a bold inversion, the Philosophical and Literary Society replaced the earlier Literary and Philosophical Society.
22. Thomas Crofton Croker, *Researches in the South of Ireland* (London, 1823–4), p. 206.

There was also a robust tradition of Irish-language manuscripts in the Cork countryside, with a school for Irish poets only seven miles from the city, and a scholarly awareness of the need to preserve such materials in the face of rapid modernisation.[23] What we shall see later as the embalming instincts of Mahony and Maginn, wrapping perishable poems in more durable linguistic stuff, is perhaps relevant to this context. The Apollo Dramatic Society flourished in the city,[24] and a Cork Society for Promoting the Fine Arts was founded in 1815 by the local poet, lawyer and layabout Richard Milliken, charged with laying on annual exhibitions. Seven years later, the city came by a lucky chance into the possession of some casts of Vatican sculptures, executed by the Italian artist Canova, donated by the Pope to the Prince Regent but diverted to Cork by the good offices of Lord Listowel. Furnished with this cultural windfall, the Fine Arts Society was to become the nursery of artists like John Hogan, Daniel Maclise and the short-lived Samuel Forde. A *Dublin University Magazine* obituary notice of Forde claims breathlessly that on the appearance of the Canova casts in Cork, 'The jarring discords in taste, politics, and religion were suspended. All ranks and parties united themselves in one common cause.'[25] If the casts serve for this euphoric obituarist as a utopian resolution, they function for others as a myth of origins – as the moment when Cork was galvanised into artistic life and shot to cultural prominence. It is appropriate, in the light of what we shall see later of Cork literary plagiarism and mimicry, that this 'originary' moment is in fact a derivative one – a translation, so to speak, from the Italian.

The interlocking of commerce and cerebration took other forms too. In accounts of the cultural life of early nineteenth-century Cork, a cluster of names of distinguished patrons regularly crop up: the antiquarian Richard Sainthill, Devon-born wine merchant and numismatist, who funded Maclise and others;[26] Sir Thomas Deane, Cork's most pre-eminent architect;[27] John Windele, local historian and antiquarian, who was enthused by Ogham

23.   Garret FitzGerald comments on the high incidence of Irish speakers in Cork city well into the second quarter of the nineteenth century. See his 'The Decline of the Irish Language', in Mary Daly and David Dickson (eds.), *The Origins of Popular Literacy in Ireland* (Dublin, 1990), p. 69.

24.   The Apollo Society is the subject of a satirical account in vol. 2, ch. 4 of a picaresque novel entitled *Peace Campaigns of a Cornet*, published in London in 1829 by one N. Beamish, a member of the Cork brewing family, and later suppressed by the publisher. This reasonably well-written work traces the fortunes and misfortunes of Pierce Butler, who moves from a Cork mercantile career to the dragoon guards.

25.   'Memoir of Samuel Forde – a Cork Artist' (anon.), *Dublin University Magazine*, vol. 25, no. 147 (March, 1845).

26.   See his ponderous two-volume numismatic study with the quaint title of *An Olla Podrida, or Scraps, Numismatic, Antiquarian, and Literary* (London, 1853).

27.   See Frederick O'Dwyer, *The Architecture of Deane and Woodward* (Cork, 1997).

stones, lent his support to Irish-language scribes around the city and was taken to task by George Petrie for his eccentric theory of Irish round towers;[28] the humanitarian Thomas Hincks, who had plans for improving the condition of the poor;[29] Richard Dowden, minor Cork wit, botanist and Dissenter, a patron of Fr Mathew; Abraham Abell, the Quaker banker and antiquarian. There was also William Carey, who came to Cork from Dublin, discovered John Hogan, and placed letters in the *Cork Advertiser* entreating 'the nobility, gentry, and opulent merchants' of the port for subscriptions with which to despatch the precocious Hogan to Rome.[30] A rather more flamboyant figure was James Roche, born in Limerick in 1771, who as a businessman and Girondist fellow-traveller in France was arrested, imprisoned in Paris and narrowly escaped the guillotine. Released on the death of Robespierre, he became a banker in Cork, went under in the monetary crisis of 1819, and was a familiar figure in the city's cultural circles.[31]

But the paronage was hardly adequate. John Windele comments that although polite literature in Cork is 'very generally extended and cultivated', the competition of English periodicals is enough to prevent 'any work of native growth, no matter what its merits, to [sic] enjoy more than a short and sickly existence – that, consequently, literary talent has never in Cork found reward or encouragement'.[32] There had been a venerable tradition of neglecting artists in the city: according to some legends, its leading eighteenth-century painter Nathaniel Grogan lived in dire poverty, as did his two artistic sons. The Fenian John O'Leary was later to complain of the absence of effective artistic patronage in the country as a whole, and advanced a nationalist solution: 'Make Ireland free, and your Foleys and Maclises may probably return, and your future Foleys and Maclises will certainly never leave'.[33]

Daniel Maclise himself commented that 'The talent which I produced appeared, from some inscrutable cause, to droop and decay, until it was trans-

28. See George Petrie, *Inquiry into the Origins and Use of the Round Towers of Ireland* (Dublin, 1845), Part 1, section 3. Windele thought the towers were used for fire worship. For a meticulous account of this fascinating controversy, see Joep Leerssen, *Remembrance and Imagination* (Cork, 1996), pp. 108–26.
29. See Thomas Hincks, *An Address to the Inhabitants of the City of Cork* (Cork, 1799).
30. See George Petrie, 'The Monument to the Memory of Dr Doyle, by Hogan', *Irish Penny Journal*, vol. 1, no. 25 (19 December 1840).
31. See his *Critical and Miscellaneous Essays by an Octogenarian* (2 vols, Cork 1850–1), which display an erudite, cosmopolitan interest in politics and letters.
32. John Windele, *Historical and Descriptive Notices of the City of Cork* (Cork, 1839; reprinted 1910), p. 3. At the very end of his book, Windele intriguingly mentions a Cork author named Miss Chetwode, daughter of the Rev William Chetwode of Glanmire and author of the novels *Blue Stocking Hall* and *Snugsborough*, who apparently lived in Moscow with one Princess Dashkoff, a woman who supposedly had a hand in the assassination of Tsar Peter II and his replacement with Catherine III. I have been unable to trace this writer.
33. John O'Leary, *Recollections of Fenians and Fenianism* (London, 1896), vol. 2, p. 74.

planted and became, as it were, an exotic in the land that gave it life.'[34] Even his romantic obituarist in the *Dublin University Magazine* is forced to confess that, though the Canova sculptures united the whole city in a common artistic project, some of the business patrons soon lost interest and fled to their villas. Indeed the irony is that Cork hit its cultural stride just as it was economically declining. 1815, the date of the founding of the Fine Arts Society, also marks the ending of the Napoleonic wars and the subsequent slump. The city probably gained its title of the Athens of the South around the time it was on a downward slope. 'Vacant stores and untenanted houses', writes Crofton Croker, 'are melancholy proofs of the declension of its prosperity; and to those who remember what the city was prior to 1815, its present appearance is extremely cheerless. . .'[35] Many of Cork's artists and writers of the early nineteenth century grew up in its golden age and reached early manhood just as the snake was sidling into the garden. It was not the only time that a civilisation had briefly, brilliantly flowered on the very threshold of its decline.

By the early nineteenth century, the city's vigour had been drastically undermined by the ending of the Napoleonic wars and the consequent collapse of British demand for Cork provisions.[36] By 1824, when the commercial clauses of the Act of Union came belatedly into play, the Cork textile industry was all but decimated, just as the Cork Capuchin Fr Mathew's temperance campaign was later to severely damage the city's vital drinks industry. In the early nineteenth century, prices rose perilously, overseas markets contracted and many of the Cork working class were plunged into destitution. John Windele, who knew the city more intimately than most, records in his private journal that 'In 1822 the committee for the relief of the poor found that the city contained over 20,000 unemployed and starving persons.'[37] Maureen Murphy reports that in 1832 over six thousand men and women in the city were utterly destitute.[38] As a traditionally conservative centre with a

34.   Quoted in W. Justin O'Driscoll, *Daniel Maclise, R.A.* (London, 1871), p. 7.

35.   Crofton Croker, *Researches in the South of Ireland* (London, 1824), pp. 203–4.

36.   Though Cormac Ó Gráda argues that the provisions trade was in decline before this somewhat magical watershed, and that some of the economic difficulties Ireland experienced in this period would probably have happened anyway (*A New Economic History of Ireland 1780–1939* [Oxford, 1994], p. 161. A similar point is made by John George McCarthy, *The History of Cork* (Cork, 1879), who offers evidence for economic decline in the city before the end of the Napoleonic wars (p. 121). Liam Kennedy and David S. Johnson argue that in Ireland in general the post-1815 recession was overlaid by the specific subsistence crises of 1816–17 and 1819, and that the more deep-seated nature of these economic problems did not fully appear until the later 1820s ('The Union of Ireland and Britain', in D. George Boyce and Alan O'Day [eds.], *The Making of Modern Irish History* [London, 1996], p. 36).

37.   Cork Papers, 12 1 4, p. 766, Windele MSS, Royal Irish Academy, Dublin.

38.   Maureen Murphy, 'The Working Classes of Nineteenth Century Cork', in O'Flanagan and Buttimer, *Cork: History and Society*, p. 28.

small-business milieu and scant traditions of labour militancy, the city's poor were ill-equipped to withstand these assaults on their livelihood. Even so, food riots and mass demonstrations broke out in the Blackpool area of the city in 1826. A sharp polarising of wealth and indigence was made more palpable by the close-packed nature of the population, with deprived and affluent areas embarrassingly cheek-by-jowl. 'Luxury and want [in Cork] exhibit a melancholy and mortifying contrast', as one contemporary observer noted.[39] Meanwhile, the Cork countryside witnessed traumatic agricultural depressions in the 1820s and 1840s, draconian belt-tightening by some landlords, the progressive elimination of middlemen and a displacement of the tenantry into the towns, where they swelled the dramatically burgeoning ranks of the pauperised. From 1815 onwards, so James S. Donnelly comments, the Cork countryside witnessed 'serious underemployment, abysmally low wages, and high conacre rents'.[40]

It is surely no accident that this was just the time when the artists and writers began to jump ship. Maginn left for London in 1823, only a year after the donation of the Canova casts, and the same year in which John Hogan departed for Rome. Around this time, Francis Mahony was completing his clerical education in Europe, and was to return to Ireland in 1830 only to leave again under an alcoholic cloud two years later. He and Maginn were to end up as professional hacks on a range of London periodicals, notably the rabidly Tory *Fraser's Magazine,* which under Maginn's editorship assembled together a bibulous group of Cork luminaries, including Daniel Maclise and Thomas Crofton Croker, and a pantheon of English literati which encompassed Thackeray, Carlyle, Southey, Ainsworth and Lockhart. As John Eglinton observes, 'just as the "Wild Geese" of the seventeenth century had taken service in Continental armies, so now (in the early nineteenth-century) the young men of talent of provincialised Ireland, the "Wild Geese" of the Protestant Ascendancy, took service more and more in the ranks of London journalism or in far-off British Colonies'.[41]

The poet Callanan left Cork for a teaching job in Lisbon in the late 1820s, to die there in 1829. James Sheridan Knowles moved to Dublin as an actor in 1808, living subsequently in Belfast, London, Glasgow and Edinburgh. His one theatrical visit to Ireland in 1834 was a failure. Crofton Croker threw up the short-lived Cork journal the *Literary Examiner* to arrive in London in 1818. Samuel Carter Hall abandoned Cork for the English metropolis in 1821, and was later unable to raise subscriptions for a memorial to his father in the town.

39.   Horatio Townsend, *Statistical Survey of the County of Cork* (Dublin, 1810), p. 696. On a more cheerful note, Townsend remarks that the people of Cork, 'though sometimes bare-legged from choice, are seldom so from necessity' (p. 99).

40.   James S. Donnelly, Jr, *The Land and the People of Nineteenth-Century Cork* (London, 1975), p. 23.

41.   John Eglinton, *Anglo-Irish Essays* (Dublin, 1917), p. 84.

John Augustus Shea sailed for the United States in 1826, and Samuel Forde died in Cork two years later. Richard Milliken had expired with an exquisite sense of timing in 1815, the date customarily selected as the turning-point in Cork's and Ireland's economic misfortunes. The painter Daniel Maclise left for London's Royal Academy in 1827. And all this despite Corney Crone's puzzled exclamation: 'I don't see why anyone ever leaves Cork . . . Isn't it lovely?'[42]

The city's material upheavals were underpinned by some fierce political contentions. In eighteenth-century Cork, a tight clique of Protestant families had disposed of most of the weighty public offices, and no Catholic merchant, however eminent, could hope to participate in municipal government.[43] But by the early nineteenth century an aspiring Catholic plutocracy had dug itself firmly in, dominating the butter, tanning and distilling trades and not far behind in banking. As this audacious new mercantile bourgeoisie laid claim to greater swathes of the city's commercial life, benefiting educationally from the relaxation of the penal laws, it found itself opposed by a rearguard action of the city's traditional Tory Protestant élite.[44] Two fairly evenly-balanced forces, locked in ferocious sectarian combat, warred for the prize of the city's economy, as new commercial interests confronted age-old political allegiances.

The conflict was complicated by a clash between urban and landed Protestant élites in the city, as a class struggle between rural and town-based ascendancies cut across religio-economic strife. Ironically, Cork urban Protestants needed the support of the Catholic middle class against a pro-Emancipation wing of their aristocratic co-religionists. The campaign for Catholic Emancipation had taken off just at the point when a nose-diving economy, land agitation and memories of the French and United Irish revolutions had made the Protestant junta most jittery. In 1820s Cork, the Catholic-born political *parvenu* Gerard Callaghan strove to fuse Catholic and Protestant middle classes against the local landed aristocracy, a project ripped asunder on the rocks of religious sectarianism. In its place emerged a stridently Protestant politics, which embraced the born-again, now trenchantly anti-papist Callaghan.[45] By 1835 the city was home to at least seven Orange lodges; but the ultra-Protestant interest suffered a crushing defeat in the municipal election of 1830, and was finally seen off by a triumphant commercial Catholicism in the election of 1841.

Two of Cork's most distinguished writers of the day reflected this religious polarity. Francis Sylvester Mahony ('Father Prout') was the son of a prosper-

42.   See Sean O'Faolain, *Bird Alone* (London, 1936), ch. 4.
43.   See John B. O'Brien, *The Catholic Middle Classes in Pre-Famine Cork* (Cork, 1979), p. 6.
44.   See Ian d'Alton, *Protestant Society and Politics in Cork, 1812–1844* (Cork, 1980), p. 123.
45.   For an account of the Cork political scene at this period, see D. Owen Madden, *Revelations of Ireland of the Past Generation* (Dublin, 1848).

ous Blarney woollen mill owner, who is said to have sheltered Edward Fitzgerald when he was on the run in Cork.[46] His son, as we shall see, was to grow up rather less well-disposed to radical politics, but with some subdued nationalist sympathies. His fellow Corkonian Samuel Hall suggests that, as the child of a Catholic manufacturer, Mahony couldn't make his way in Cork Society and had instead to be educated abroad.[47] Historically speaking, then, the eccentric Fr Prout was remarkably stereotypical, as a scion of the emergent Catholic bourgeoisie which in his childhood was busy transforming his city and his nation.[48]

William Maginn, by contrast, was the child of a well-respected Protestant schoolmaster in Cork, and harboured virulently anti-Catholic sentiments, politically if not personally. To this extent, the liaison between the ultramontane ex-Jesuit Mahony and the lusty Orange apologist Maginn is typical of how John B. O'Brien views the contradictory relations between Cork Catholics and Protestants in general at this time, mixing religious strife and political antagonism with a fair degree of cultural and commercial co-operation.[49] It was sectarian bitterness, even so, which was to help drive William Maginn out of Cork. In a letter to his publisher William Blackwood in 1823, on the eve of abandoning the city for ever, Maginn protests that 'our clergy are reviled and personally abused; our very private parties spied; our toasts controlled by authority, our churches polluted; the priests domineering, swaggering, and libelling our faith, our conduct, and our principles . . . Is the Protestant religion to be tolerated in Ireland?'[50] Maginn's flight from the Mardyke to Mayfair may have been inspired by personal self-advancement, but it was just as much an historical affair, as the bellicose response of a politically washed-up Protestantism to encroaching Catholic power.

It was a power which also made itself felt in the career of the sculptor John Hogan, offspring of an upper-class Protestant mother and a lower-middle-class Catholic father who worked as a builder for the mighty Cork architect and cultural commissar Sir Thomas Deane. Patronised in his early years by

46. See *Journal of the Cork Historical and Archaeological Society,* vol. 3, no. 35 (November, 1894). There is no allusion to this episode in Thomas Moore's *Life of Lord Edward Fitzgerald.*

47. Samuel Carter Hall, *Memories of Great Men and Women of the Age* (London, 1877), p. 238.

48. Two representative Cork intellectuals in this respect were John O'Driscol, whose *Views of Ireland* (2 vols, London, 1823) argues for manufactures, free trade and Catholic Emancipation, and Rev Thomas England, whose *Life of the Rev Arthur O'Leary* (London, 1822) celebrates an eighteenth-century Cork champion of Catholic rights. Jeremy Bentham was interested in O'Driscol's book, and obtained his address in Cork from his fellow Utilitarian William Thompson. See Pankhurst, *William Thompson,* p. 19.

49. O'Brien, *The Catholic Middle Classes in Pre-Famine Cork,* p. 15.

50. Quoted by Mrs Oliphant, *Annals of a Publishing House,* pp. 389n, 390.

Bishop John Murphy, of the Cork brewing family, and by William Crawford, son of the co-founder of Crawford's brewery, he too was to become a cultural avatar of Catholic nationalism, as his alcohol-resourced art came to play a key role in the Catholic revival. He was to reward another of his stout-making patrons, William Beamish, with a lavish memorial in which the angel of resurrection blows his trumpet over the nude cadaverous body of the brewer rising radiantly from his tomb. A friend of Cardinal Paul Cullen, and one of the first Irish visual artists to deploy national themes, Hogan adapted neo-classical forms to an ecclesiastical context, trusted that an Irish artistic renaissance would follow on the heels of Catholic emancipation, and finally abandoned his niche in Rome in ultramontanist retreat from an insurgent, anti-clerical Italian nationalism. His nationalist sympathies were in this sense strictly selective. Returning to Ireland in 1840 to witness the founding of the Repeal Association, he visited his homeland again three years later to crown O'Connell with his Repeal cap at the monster meeting of Mullaghmast.[51]

The Cork poets Jeremiah Callanan, Edward Walsh and John Augustus Shea were also fervent nationalists, children of the emergent Catholic middle class. Callanan studied briefly at the Maynooth seminary before becoming a schoolteacher and amateur antiquarian, and produced poetry shot through with a ragged patriotic religiosity.[52] Walsh, the hedge-school educated son of a small farmer from County Cork, was dismissed from his post as a schoolmaster for publishing an abrasive nationalist ballad in the *Nation*, and strove in his verse collections to reclaim a native cultural heritage. The gloomy introduction to his *Irish Popular Songs* laments the passing of the Irish language among the peasantry and blames the hedge-school masters *inter alia* for its decline.[53] John Augustus Shea, who emigrated from Cork to the USA, wrote febrile nationalist poetry and warned his adopted compatriots against the 'literary refuse' commended by 'reviewers of the British metropolis'.[54] The play-

51.　See John Turpin, *John Hogan* (Dublin, 1982). See also the anonymous appreciation, in fact penned by Jane Elgee (later Lady Wilde), in the *Dublin University Magazine,* vol. 35, no. 205 (January, 1850), which remarks that 'his physical exterior reflects no discredit on the sod' (p. 72). There is a brief appreciation of Hogan in Sarah Atkinson, *St Fursey's Life and Visions and Other Essays* (Dublin, 1907). Hogan's main pieces in Dublin are located as follows: statues of Davis, Drummond and O'Connell in the City Hall; *Pietà* in St Nicholas's church, Francis Street; *The Dead Christ* in St Teresa's church, Clarendon Street; *Hibernia, with bust of Lord Cloncurry* in the National Gallery.

52.　See *The Poems of J. J. Callanan* (Cork, 1861).

53.　Edward Walsh, *Irish Popular Songs* (Dublin, 1847), Introduction. See also his *Reliques of Jacobite Poetry* (Dublin, 1844). Walsh was actually born in Derry ('by accident', as D. J. O'Donoghue remarks, *The Geographical Distribution of Irish Ability*, p. 27), but was reared in Millstreet in Co. Cork and worked for a while in Cork city.

54.　John Augustus Shea, *Adolphe* (New York, 1831), p. vii. Adolphe, the protagonist of this remarkably tedious poem, is a persona of the author himself, nos-

wright James Sheridan Knowles, by contrast, born in 1784 into a liberal, pro-Emancipation Protestant middle-class milieu in Cork, abandoned the stage in his later years to became a Baptist minister and fulminated against papism and the Newmanites, as well as against the theatrical profession which had provided him with an (admittedly exiguous) living.[55] In this sense, his religious career paralleled the general trajectory of Cork Protestantism, shifting increasingly to sectarian extremes. Samuel Carter Hall and Thomas Crofton Croker were paid-up members of the Cork Protestant bourgeoisie, the former (born in Waterford) the child of a Devonshire army officer and mining speculator, the latter, also the offspring of an army officer, an apprentice to a Cork mercantile establishment who finished up in the Admiralty. But not all Cork Protestant careers were so auspicious: there was a sizeable Protestant working class in the city, and Daniel Maclise, Ireland's finest nineteenth-century painter, sprang from a struggling Cork family of Scots Presbyterian stock. As the proprietor of a tan-yard and supplier of provisions to the military, his father was especially vulnerable to the post-war slump,[56] even if Maclise junior managed to scramble into the middle class with the aid of a few well-heeled patrons.

It seems plain enough, then, that the extraordinary flourishing of the arts in early nineteenth-century Cork reflected not only the exuberant social and economic life of the city, but also something of its intricate pattern of religious and political affiliations. The vehement ultra-Protestant zeal of Maginn or the later Sheridan Knowles offsets the Jesuitical absolutism of Mahony and the alienated nationalist rhetoric of Walsh and Shea, while the more liberal Protestantism of a Hall, Croker or Maclise sounds the note of the city's more ecumenical middle-class forces, anxious to forge alliances with a Catholic plutocracy in the ascendent. If John Hogan was helped on his road to Rome by

talgic for Glanmire while about to depart for the USA. Shea, who views the USA as an ideal of freedom in contrast to the tyranny of Europe and Britain, comments in his Introduction that 'I am not, and hope never to be, considered a professional poet' (p. vii), a fortunate sentiment.

55.   See Leslie Howard Meeks, *Sheridan Knowles and the Theater of his Time* (Bloomington, Indiana, 1933). The author comments that he 'believes that he has the honour, perhaps unenviable, of being the only living student of the drama who has an intimate knowledge of all the published plays of Sheridan Knowles' (p. vii), an achievement which only those who have tried to read Knowles can adequately appreciate. Knowles's father was almost run out of Cork for his support for the Catholic cause; his mother was a Le Fanu.

56.   See John Turpin, 'Daniel Maclise and Cork Society', *Journal of the Cork Historical and Archaeological Society,* vol. 85, no. 241 (January/December, 1980). There is a florid memoir of Maclise by the minor Cork writer Edward Kenealy in the *Dublin University Magazine*, vol. 29, no. 173 (May, 1847). See also, for a modern commentary, Anne Crookshank and the Knight of Glin, *The Painters of Ireland 1660–1920* (London, 1978), pp. 235–40.

the patronage of Catholic bishops and brewers, he also received aid from the Evangelical banker and landowner William Newenham, along with a range of commissions from the Anglo-Irish gentry. For all their power struggles, the two religio-political groupings shared a social and cultural world in common, just as many of their émigré writers were to sink their differences in a tankard of ale in the back office of *Fraser's Magazine*.

Toryism, in fact, was to prove as powerful a bond between them as the tankard. These raffish carousals also helped to mark the Fraserians' contemptuous distance from a Cork now firmly in the grip of Theobald Mathew's temperance campaign. A dreary bourgeois sobriety had settled on the libidinous literary city of their youth, so that growing legless in London could be seen as a political strike at the Utilitarian middle class which was depriving these cavalier ruffians of their Tory Protestant birthright. The Cork Cooperator William Thompson, a friend of Jeremy Bentham and a devotee of industrial self-discipline, represents the petty-bourgeois values which the frolicking Fraserians found most contemptible. Mathew himself was closely connected with the rising Catholic middle class of the city (though he was on good terms with the Protestants too); indeed his brothers were associated with the Cork brewing industry, and he himself had been thrown out of Maynooth after a drunken party, rather as Francis Mahony was expelled from Clongowes for the same offence.[57] The minor Cork Fraserian Edward Kenealy, later to become a crazed, Casaubon-like searcher for the key to all mythologies, regrets the departure of learning and whiskey from the city, and defines Cork as 'something which interferes between me and tipple'.[58] Charles Gavan Duffy, with Mathew's campaign well in mind, asserts that Cork was the source of the most sustained, successful attempt in nineteenth-century Ireland to inculcate industrial middle-class values into the people – though he overreaches himself a little in claiming that these reforms 'have enabled a whole nation to become water-drinkers'.[59] It is just that what he as a decent bougeois nationalist approved, the rapscallion Fraserians deplored.

The Cork artists of this epoch can be roughly distributed into three camps. There are 'Micks on the make'[60] like Maclise, Crofton Croker and the Halls, who enjoy the esteem of the London establishment; those stranded at home

57.   See Elizabeth Malcolm, *Ireland Sober, Ireland Free: Drink and Temperance in Nineteenth-Century Ireland* (Dublin, 1986), ch. 3. It is of interest that the *Dublin Evening Post* expressed the hope that temperance would eradicate 'that curse to the mechanic – combination' (quoted p. 111).
58.   Edward Kenealy, *Brallaghan, or the Deipnosophists* (London, 1845), p. 79.
59.   Charles Gavan Duffy, *A Short Life of Thomas Davis* (London, 1896). It is worth recalling here that Davis was a Cork writer, though from the county rather than the city.
60.   See R. F. Foster, *Paddy and Mr Punch* (London, 1993), ch. 14: 'Marginal Men and Micks on the Make'.

like Walsh, Forde and Callanan, doomed to careers of penury and purpose-lessness; and an intermediate group (Mahony, Maginn, Hogan, Shea, Sheridan Knowles) who either achieve some precarious success abroad, or constitute a kind of internal colony within the imperial metropolis, deliberately self-mar-ginalising figures marooned somewhere between Shandon and Chelsea, polite society and bohemian rump.

Of the first category, the most fabular success story is that of Daniel Maclise, Royal Academician, crony of Dickens and friend of Queen Victoria and Prince Albert.[61] One biographer suggests that, in accordance with this elevated status, he altered his name from 'McClise' to 'Maclise',[62] though his accent evidently remained unchanged: Thomas Carlyle alludes to him as 'a quiet shy man with much brogue'.[63] Gavan Duffy mentions his membership of a London Irish Club, of a 'national' rather than 'political kind'.[64] As Fintan Cullen has argued, Maclise, rather like his compatriot Moore, catered in his paintings to 'a growing English interest in the exotica of Irish life'. A fellow Irishman, P. W. Banks, insisted that Maclise, who happened to be his brother-in-law, 'has never dabbled the least in politics, and has nothing of political feeling, excepting perhaps that instinctive disposition to free and gentle Tory-ism, which is proper in high-minded gentlemen'.[65] Maclise's soaring trajec-tory from Cork tan-yard to Cheyne Walk is outclassed only by that of one James Cavanagh Murphy, who, so Thomas Crofton Croker informs us, leapt from Cork bricklayer to architect and diplomat in Portugal.[66]

61.   'He is in great favour with the Queen', writes Dickens, 'and paints secret pic-tures for her to put upon her husband's table on the morning of his birthday – and the like' (Madeline House and Graham Storey [eds.], *The Letters of Charles Dickens, vol. 3, 1820–1839* [Oxford, 1974], pp. 549–50. See also Dickens's mov-ing tribute to his friend 'Mac' after his death, the novelist's last public words, recorded in John Forster, *The Life of Charles Dickens* (London, 1872–4; reprinted 1928), p. 849. For Maclise caught *in flagrante delicto* on Park Lane, see Robert Blake, *Disraeli* (London, 1966), p. 141. A valuable collection of some of his sketches in *Fraser's Magazine* can be found in William Bate, *The Maclise Por-trait Gallery of Illustrious Literary Characters* (London, 1883).

62.   W. Justin O'Driscoll, *Daniel Maclise, R.A.* (London, 1871), p. 58. Maclise's low-ish reputation in our own age is signalled by the brevity of the note on his work in Jeremy Maas, *Victorian Painters* (London, 1969), pp. 24–5. For Ruskin's crit-icism of the lack of indistinctness in his work, see his *Academy Notes* in E. T. Cook and Alexander Wedderburn (eds.), *The Works of John Ruskin* (London, 1904), vol. 14, pp. 95–7.

63.   Quoted by W. Justin O'Driscoll, *Daniel Maclise, R.A.*, p. 203.

64.   Charles Gavan Duffy, *Short Life of Thomas Davis*, p. 121.

65.   Fintan Cullen, *Visual Politics: The Representation of Ireland, 1750–1930* (Cork, 1996), p. 45.

66.   Thomas Crofton Croker, *Fairy Legends and Traditions in the South of Ireland* (Lon-don, 1825), p. 204n.

Croker himself landed an Admiralty post by the grace of John Wilson Croker[67] – a non-nepotistic move, for once, since the two men were not related. In his Fulham home he gathered around him a distinguished literary circle which included Fr Prout, and thrived by producing anthropological studies of his homeland which adroitly blended native inwardness with stylistic distance. His stoutly Unionist *Researches in the South of Ireland* peddles stereotypes of the Irish as indolent and improvident ('Poor, proud and sensitive, the Irish character is one to excite our pity. . .'),[68] and discloses just how little he approves of the folk who helped to make his fortune. Though a review of his *Popular Songs of Ireland* in the *Dublin University Magazine* describes him as a 'pleasant bit of a leprechaun', it would seem his diminutive size rather than his cultural allegiances which the author has in mind.[69] Douglas Hyde comments that Croker annotated folk lore texts, but adds that 'the word "text" conveys the idea of an original to be annotated upon, and Crofton Croker is, alas, too often his own original'.[70] We shall see later the relevance of this remark to the theme of Corkonian 'anti-plagiarism'.

The careers of Samuel and Anna Hall followed much the same track. Samuel, born in Waterford of a Devonshire father who opened thirteen copper mines in Ireland, grew up mostly in Cork, where he and William Maginn ran mutually hostile literary societies. The rivalry was to mark their later London careers too, with Hall frostily describing his dipsomaniac compatriot as 'one of the shames as well as one of the glories of Literature'.[71] The Pecksniffian tone was not lost on Dickens, who is said to have modelled his exemplary hypocrite on the Corkman, as Thackeray may have modelled his Captain Shandon on Maginn.[72] David O'Donoghue, politically biased through a shrewd observer, describes Hall as a 'conceited humbug'.[73] In London, Hall lodged briefly with the exiled Irish novelist John Banim in St John's Wood, assiduously edited journals, became a lawyer and parliamentary reporter, and

67.   See John Wilson Croker's *A Sketch of the State of Ireland* (Dublin, 1808) for a liberal Ascendancy view of the country, scornful of the peasantry but critical of the landlords and in favour of Catholic Emancipation.
68.   Crofton Croker, *Researches in the South of Ireland* (London, 1824), p. 225.
69.   *Dublin University Magazine*, vol. 14, no. 79 (July, 1839). Croker was known because of his stature as the Honourable Member for Fairyland. Yeats, who included some of Croker's stories in his *Irish Fairy and Folk Tales* (London, 1888), speaks of them in his Preface as 'having the dash as well as the shallowness of an ascendant and idle class' (p. xv).
70.   Douglas Hyde, *Language, Lore and Lyrics* (Dublin, 1986), p. 123.
71.   Samuel Carter Hall, *Retrospect of a Long Life* (London, 1883), vol. 1, p. 120.
72.   As one of Brinsley McNamara's characters comments: 'Was there ever such a name for a low-down hypocrite as 'Pecksniff'; but sure there's millions of him in Ireland' (*The Various Lives of Marcus Igoe*, London, 1929, reprinted Dublin, 1996, p. 231).
73.   David J. O'Donoghue, *Life of William Carleton* (London, 1896), vol. 2, p. 135.

ended up knowing almost everyone in the literary and political establishment. Indeed he is described as an Englishman in a review in the *Dublin University Magazine*.[74]

Hall and his wife open their major work on Ireland by emphasising its disinterestedness: they have exercised their judgement, they remark, 'only with a view to determine whether [a matter] is beneficial, or prejudicial, to the United Kingdom'.[75] Their writing glows with the smugly progressivist conviction that Ireland, once ill-used, is now tranquil and content, and this in the 1840s. Just as their more rumbustious Cork colleagues mix literary genres with debonair abandon, so the Halls in their own more anal-retentive way are unable to resist breaking through their sober reportage into narrative, fable and fictional dialogue. Despite their own high-minded strictures on the shiftiness of the Irish, the frontiers between truth and fantasy in their own publications are constantly transgressed. Anna Maria Hall, born in Dublin of Huguenot descent, wrote no less than two hundred and fifty or so works on Ireland in order to elevate the character of its people in English eyes while candidly dissecting their numerous flaws. Unsurprisingly, her husband reports in his memoirs that her books were never popular back home. She does, even so, display considerable skill as a portraitist of Irish life, in a condescending post-Carletonian vein,[76] and deserves greater recognition as a literary artist than she has received. Her celebrated philanthropy put the finishing touches to an eminently respectable, lethally moralistic Victorian *ménage*.[77]

The story of those who stayed behind is very different. The writer Edward Walsh had little talent for English-language poetry but a genius for losing jobs. After a spell of imprisonment for his part in the anti-tithe campaign, he lost his post as a national schoolmaster and was reduced to teaching convicts on Spike island, a dismal chore from which he was dismissed for speaking to the prisoner John Mitchel. Mitchel records the encounter in his *Jail Journal*, unfavourably comparing the schoolmaster's oppressive conditions of life with those of Spike island's 'galley slaves'. It was a judgement apparently shared by the penurious poet himself, who was so despondent that he actually envied Mitchel's fate. He taught later in the Cork workhouse, dying obscurely in

74.   *Dublin University Magazine*, vol. 16, no. 96 (December, 1840).

75.   Mr and Mrs S. C. Hall, *Ireland: Its Scenery, Character, Etc* (London, 1841–3), p. viii.

76.   See for example her *Sketches of Irish Character* (London, 1842) and *Lights and Shadows of Irish Life* (London, 1838). There is an appreciative note on her by C. J. Hamilton in *Notable Irishwomen* (Dublin, 1909), though David J. O'Donoghue, never the most devoted fan of the Halls, refers to her 'monstrous and sickening repetition of the same emasculated verbiage' (*Life of William Carleton*, vol. 2, p. 135).

77.   See Thomas Moore's letter to her of 31 May 1831, in response to her offer to assist in caring for their sick child Russell. The Moores, perhaps wisely, declined. (Wilfred S. Dowden [ed.], *The Letters of Thomas Moore* [Oxford, 1964], vol. 2, p. 128.)

1850. Declan Kiberd describes him as 'probably the most brilliant and neglected translator of the last century'.[78] Jeremiah Callanan eked out an equally faceless existence, so much so that there is some doubt over his first name. Like Walsh, he survived precariously for a spell as a schoolteacher, indeed put in a stint at Maginn's father's school; but he lived for the most part a reclusive life on an islet in Clonakilty bay, communing with Nature, cocooned in frustrated nationalist visions and collecting legends and historical manuscripts. His English-language poetry swerves between the natural and the national with a minimum of mediation. His only foray beyond this bleakly constricted world was to Lisbon, as tutor to the child of a Cork merchant; but he fell ill there, struggled to board ship so as to die in Ireland, and failed in this venture as he had done in most others.[79]

Callanan's life, wrote one critic, 'seemed to him objectless and vain', and he was 'wayward and careless in his conduct'.[80] Robert Welch remarks on his fissured subjecthood: 'while his imagination drew him to West Cork, his literary ambitions and the expectations of the literary Corkman turned his eyes to London'.[81] There seems no doubt that these lives of noisy desperation are coloured by a peculiarly colonial hopelessness. Indeed taken en masse, the careers of the Cork literati of the day manifest an astonishingly consistent wretchedness, fecklessness and misfortune. These blighted, vagrant existences, marked by a kind of extravagant aimlessness, speak of blocked desires and spiked ambitions, which cannot be divorced from the barren milieu of provincial life in the colonies. Samuel Forde, a painter of genuine talent, led a stifled, shadowy existence in his native city, taught briefly in the Mechanics' Institute there and died at the age of twenty-three.[82] Thomas Davis thought him Ireland's greatest artist. Joseph O'Leary, editor of the Cork Mercantile Chronicle, began as a strolling player in Ireland, left for London in 1834 and stumbled into parliamentary reporting; possibly an early Punch contributor, he drowned himself some time in the 1840s.[83] Like almost all Cork writers of

78.   Declan Kiberd, *Synge and the Irish Language* (London, 1979; reprinted 1993), p. 68.

79.   For some sensitive analysis of Callanan, see B. G. McCarthy, 'Jeremiah J. Callanan: Part 1: His Life' (*Studies*, vol. 25, no. 138), and 'Part 2: His Poetry' (*Studies*, vol. 25, no. 139).

80.   *Journal of the Cork Historical and Archaeological Society* (vol. 1, 1892), pp. 57–8.

81.   Robert Welch, *A History of Verse Translation from the Irish* (Gerrards Cross, 1988), p. 70.

82.   See John Francis Maguire, *The Industrial Movement in Ireland* (Cork, 1853), for a note on Forde's contribution to the Cork National Exhibition of 1852. Forde was the son of a failed Cork tradesman with possible Jacobin leanings. Jane Elgee called him the 'Angelo of Ireland' (*Dublin University Magazine*, vol. 35, no. 205 [January, 1850], p. 77).

83.   O'Leary left behind a lively, well-executed account of his early acting days, dedicated to the Cork patron of the arts William Crawford. See *The Tribute* (Cork, 1833). There is a note on him in David J. O'Donoghue, *The Poets of Ireland* (London, 1892), p. 193.

the time, he penned the obligatory poem in praise of whiskey, and – again *de rigueur* for Cork poetasters – had it translated into Latin, in his case by the minor Corkonian hell-raiser Jack Sheehan.[84] Another scapegrace was John Boyle, editor of the scabrous Cork periodical *The Freeholder*, wit and literary benefactor but also shiftless and spendthrift. Since the charge of shiftlessness was made by Joseph O'Leary,[85] hardly a paragon of prudence himself, it no doubt has some force. Boyle apparently lived in the insouciant style of Castle Rackrent, landed in the Marshalsea for debt, and may have met with a sticky end when one of his readers belaboured him with a mallet.

Richard Milliken, wastrel, failed lawyer and *bon viveur*, was another middle-class drop-out, the grandson of a Scottish Quaker linen manufacturer who became a dilettante-about-town and salvaged himself for posterity only by writing 'The Groves of Blarney'. A London print, no doubt to the chagrin of Young Ireland, referred to this piece of semiotic pointlessness as the 'National Irish poem'.[86] An abominable poet and prominent Volunteer in 1798, Milliken dabbled in Cork drama as an amateur stage designer at the Apollo theatre, and though with 'little merit as an Actor, yet it never deterred him from taking a part'.[87] He was, however, the moving spirit behind the Fine Arts Society.

Perhaps the most extraordinary career of all, however, was that of Edward Kenealy, lawyer, scholar, *habitué* of the Cork Fraserian set, obituarist of Maginn and later religious maniac. In 1845 he published *Brallaghan, or the Deipnosophists*, a feebly roistering set of sub-Maginnian squibs and parodies which includes some (real or imaginary) table talk by John Boyle, snatches of plodding stage-Irish wit ('What is an Irishman but a mere machine for converting potatoes into human nature?'), and a few heavy-handedly carnivalesque anecdotes of a literary 'fun club' in the Cork of his youth. The whole aberrant project is a strained attempt at spontaneity, a laborious exercise in the orgiastic. The book is a kind of lame parody of Corkonian parody, a botched mimicry of skilful literary botchers. Mahony, Kenealy has the gall to remark, 'has squandered away in Epicurean idleness, hours that might have been made of inestimable value to the literary world'.[88]

84.   Sheehan, a Fraserian hanger-on, knew Mahony well, and contributes an informative memoir on him to *The Final Reliques of Fr Prout* (London, 1876).

85.   O'Leary, *The Tribute*, pp. 203–12. O'Leary characterises Boyle as 'a mere creature of impulse, [who] indulged all his sentiments, but overlooked the obligations by which society is bound together' (p. 205).

86.   *Poetical Fragments of Richard Alfred Milliken* (London and Cork, 1823), p. xxlv. The poem is not in fact reprinted in this collection. There is a special irony in 'The Groves of Blarney' being assigned this august status in Irish culture, since a case can be made that it is really a satire of those Irish writers whose imperfect knowledge of English led them to try to sound impressive by stringing together resonant sounds and random classical allusions. There is also a tradition of portentous nonsense in Irish-language writing.

87.   ibid, pp. xxll–xxlll.

88.   Kenealy, *Brallaghan*, p. 107.

It comes as something of a surprise, then, that in the same year that Kenealy published *Brallaghan* in London, he delivered an edifying inaugural address to the Cork Temperance Institution of Literature and Science, of which he was vice-president. Whereas *Brallaghan* links alcohol and erudition in Fraserian style, the Cork lecture insists upon the unity of temperance and knowledge, and records its author's horror at 'how frequently the world has seen lamentable examples of the disunity of [the two]'.[89] Kenealy proceeds to illustrate his point by graphic portraits of celebrated literary drunks, Maginn passing tactfully unmentioned but no doubt held steadily in mind. This florid performance concludes with some fulsome praise of England ('The English have approached nearer to the highest pitch of perfection [of the intellect] than any other people',[90]) and announces on the eve of the Famine that 'in a very short time every substantial cause of difference between Englishmen and Irishmen will be removed'.[91] If Mahony and Maginn, as we shall see later, delight in a kind of anti-plagiarism, Kenealy is clearly a specialist in anti-prophecy.

Despite his belief that the English are 'the noblest, the bravest, and richest, and wisest, and most intellectual race upon which the sun of heaven ever shone',[92] Kenealy was finally to fall foul of them. As the defence attorney in the Tichborne claimant case, his obstinate trust in the legitimacy of his client drove him into professional ruin and disgrace.[93] Works like *The Book of God*, an immense farrago of mythopoeic claptrap, suggest an unsoundness of mind. It is as though the pedantry of a Mahony or Maginn has cut loose from their ludic irony, to petrify into madness. Knowledge, having given the slip to temperance of mind, is now spawning into a monstrous form of unreason. Like Callanan, Kenealy would seem one of colonialism's fractured subjects, but now to the point of derangement: if one part of him consorts with the decorous Halls and Crokers, frostily disdaining Francis Mahony as living 'in utter defiance of decency and morality',[94] his *Brallaghan* persona suggests a

89. Edward Kenealy, *Inaugural Address to the Members of the Temperance Institution of Literature and Science* (Cork, 1845), p. 18.

90. ibid, p. 29.

91. ibid, p. 51.

92. ibid, p. 51.

93. See the apologetic biography by his daughter, Arabella Kenealy, *Memoirs of Edward Vaughan Kenealy LLD* (London, 1908). The work contains Kenealy's own autobiography, which passes diplomatically over his boisterous Cork years, and is described by his daughter, with what some might see as a Corkonian flourish, as 'one of the most interesting human documents ever presented to the world'. Kenealy was charged by the legal profession with having 'described the Tichborne family as Hampshire hogs, the priests as infamous night owls, the teachers and governors of Stonyhurst as wilful corruptors of their pupils...' (*Memoirs*, p. 271).

94. Quoted by Arabella Kenealy, *Memoirs of Edward Vaughan Kenealy*, p. 101.

Maginn clone or bohemian wannabe. His volume *Poems and Translations* translates Irish into Greek, a sure mark of Cork literary rakishness.[95] And like Oscar Wilde, though in quite a different way, he was finally brought low by the British legal system, of which (unlike Wilde) he had been a devoted servant. The schizoid fragments of *Brallaghan* became, in the end, the paranoid systematising of his commentaries on the Apocalypse and other arcane texts.

The final category of Cork artists, those who were in some sense inside and outside the metropolitan culture simultaneously, is inevitably harder to define. John Hogan was admitted in Rome to the most prestigious conclave of artists in Europe, but met with uncertain success at home. Unable to support his family on the irregular returns on his work, he died desolate and impoverished. William Carleton saw him as a companion in misfortune, though Carleton's biographer comments with brutal realism that 'Hogan really was a martyr to national apathy, while Carleton merely fancied himself as such'.[96] Jeanne Sheehy suggests that his religion and nationalist politics may have counted against him,[97] though while still in Cork he was the recipient of Protestant patronage. The poet John Augustus Shea moved from a clerkship in Beamish and Crawford's counting house to one at West Point military academy in the USA, where he began a long friendship with Edgar Allen Poe and became a newspaper editor in Philadelphia. He also wrote for the *Catholic Magazine* and the more profanely entitled *The Knickerbocker*.[98] John Wilson Croker attended Shea's father's school in Cork to have his stammer cured, evidently unaware that this defect was a sign of genius.[99] The poet was present at O'Connell's Mullaghmast meeting, and presented the Liberator with his atrocious poem *Clontarf* as Hogan crowned him with the Repeal cap.[100]

95. See Edward Kenealy, *Poems and Translations* (London, 1863).
96. David J. O'Donoghue, *Life of William Carleton*, p. 217. Carleton wrote a furious letter appealing for a state pension for Hogan's family. For a perceptive analysis of Hogan's work, see Thomas MacGreevy, 'Some Statues by John Hogan', *Father Mathew Record* (August, 1943). MacGreevy describes Hogan's statue of O'Connell as 'probably the greatest piece of sculpture executed by an Irishman since the High Cross at Monasterboice' (p. 5).
97. Jeanne Sheehy, *The Rediscovery of Ireland's Past* (London, 1980), p. 56.
98. See S. A. Allibone, *Dictionary of English and American Authors* (Philadelphia, 1859), vol. 2.
99. See *The Correspondence and Diaries of the Late Rt Hon John Wilson Croker* (London, 1884), vol. 1, p. 6.
100. See John Augustus Shea, *Clontarf* (New York, 1843), and *The Lament of Hellas* (London and Cork, 1826). John Augustus O'Shea, apparently Shea's son, was a journalist who published letters from the Paris Commune and was well acquainted with the Irish colony in Paris, including James Stephens. See his *Leaves from the Life of a Special Correspondent* (London, 1885), in which he refers to Francis Mahony's courage during a cholera epidemic (p. 117). There is a note on O'Shea in the *Irish Book Lover*, vol. 7, nos. 9–10 (April/May, 1916).

Shea, mystifyingly enough, seems to have enjoyed a distinguished literary career, which was never quite so unequivocally the case with the Cork playwright James Sheridan Knowles. The second cousin of Richard Brinsley Sheridan, Knowles was the son of a respected Cork lexicographer, wrote an opera and a tragedy at the age of fourteen, and having moved to London as a child was taken up by William Hazlitt. Part Three of Hazlitt's *Liber Amoris* is addressed to him, and a note tacked on to the end of *The Spirit of the Age* rashly declares him 'the first tragic writer of the age', despite the fact that '(h)e has hardly read a poem or a play or seen anything of the world'.[101] This carries the cult of natural genius perhaps a little far. Having qualified as a medical doctor, Knowles acted in Belfast with Kean, taught for a while alongside his father at the Belfast Academical Institute, and made his name with his play *Virginius*.[102] He also helped to found a Whig newspaper in Glasgow, and while living in London got to know Dickens, Browning, Wordsworth and Lamb. Driven for a while to the USA, he ended up with a small state pension and the curatorship of Shakespeare's house in Stratford. Astonishingly, he was considered alongside Tennyson for the Poet Laureateship on the death of Wordsworth.

Knowles paid a visit to his native Cork in 1862 and was graced with a public reception, dying in the same year in the unhistrionic setting of Torquay. According to his son, he never made much money from his plays,[103] which are lamentably threadbare and jejune, 'inharmonious in rhythm, trivial in dialogue, and often turgid in passion', as one critic puts it.[104] Apart from the scenery, this doesn't leave a great deal. Maginn, who denounced Knowles as a Whig, declared rather cryptically that he was to Beaumont and Fletcher what they were to Shakespeare, perhaps an elaborate way of calling him third-rate. He was also evidently an appalling actor, 'noisy, ranting, violent', with 'a face of rather fat intelligence'.[105] Unlike Daniel Maclise, he apparently abandoned his Irish accent, though perhaps with more professional justification. Hazlitt remarks in a classic backhanded compliment that '(h)is most intimate

---

101. P. P. Howe (ed.), *The Complete Works of William Hazlitt* (London and Toronto, 1932), vol. 11, p. 184.

102. Included in James Sheridan Knowles, *Dramatic Works* (London, 1847), 2 vols. With arresting candour, the editor of this work describes the child Knowles in his Preface as an 'incorrigible dunce' (p. vi).

103. See Richard Brinsley Knowles, *The Life of James Sheridan Knowles* (London, 1872). Mrs Oliphant's note on him in *The Literary History of England* (London, 1882, vol. 3) suggests that some of his plays were still popular in the late nineteenth century.

104. W. Bates, *The Maclise Portrait Gallery* (London, 1883), p. 399. Knowles, however, is admired by a minor character in Irish fiction, Harry Thomson in Shan F. Bullock's novel *By Thrasna River* (London, 1895), who holds that 'his language rivals that of the sweet swan of Avon himself' (p. 120).

105. Quoted by Leslie Howard Meeks, *Sheridan Knowles and the Theater of his Time*, p. 40.

friends can see nothing in him, by which they could trace the work to an author',[106] as though the fact of his having written his plays was as astounding as if they had been composed by a cocker spaniel. Split between Cork and London, Knowles preserved his provincial roughness and simplicity of manner in the fanciest of drawing rooms, a walking cultural contradiction but seemingly unperturbed by the fact. It was this stolid self-identity, persisting through his cultural conflicts, which no doubt proved as useful in real life as it was a disaster on stage.

With Mahony, Maginn and their Cork Fraserian *confrères*,[107] the situation was rather more complex. In one sense, these men moved from the margins to the centre; but Cork, the margin in question, was itself already doubled in this respect, a provincial periphery with metropolitan pretensions and a history of genuine global significance.[108] Indeed the very idiosyncrasy of the place, its wayward uniqueness, paradoxically endowed it with a certain centrality. If it was not the capital of Ireland it was at least the capital of the south, which may explain why the Cork artists looked not to Dublin but to London. Moreover, their journey was less from margin to centre than from a colonial periphery to a metropolitan one. What they did was to translate a certain colonial aimlessness, spiritual eclecticism, pointless pedantry, intellectual fragmentation and wry self-ironising to the underworld of Grub Street, where these marks of colonial frustration and *ennui* proved eminently saleable commodities.

It is this, surely, which accounts at least in part for the extraordinary invasion of the London journals by this Munster Mafia. Their literal eccentricity to the metropolis could be converted into a literary and political dissidence within it, as a passed-over, petty bourgeois colonial intelligentsia gave vent to its envy and rancour in the form of an engagingly flamboyant backwoods Toryism. By shifting to the by-ways of literary London, these inauthentic colonial mimic men could become, as it were, authentically inauthentic, centrally

106. *Complete Works*, vol. 11, p. 184.
107. Along with Maclise, and Crofton Croker, these included a number of lesser luminaries, among them Gosnell the surgeon, Frank Stack Murphy of the Cork brewing clan, who was (conveniently enough for this bunch of spendthrifts) the commissioner for bankruptcy, John Sheehan, and one Moriarty, lawyer brother of the celebrated anti-Fenian bishop of Kerry. According to Elizabeth Tully, the magazine became a model for the *Dublin University Magazine* ('Changing Culture in the *Dublin University Magazine*', unpublished paper, 1997), and was later to be edited by another, rather more politically progressive Irishman, the poet William Allingham. See John Hewitt (ed.), *Poems of William Allingham* (Dublin, 1967), p. 13.
108. John Wilson Foster writes of the Cork of Daniel Corkery's novel *The Threshold of Quiet* as a city 'betwixt and between – a bustling regional capital for the summer visitor, a provincial town of quiet suburban hillsides for the residents among whom Corkery sets his novel' (*Fictions of the Irish Literary Revival* [Syracuse, 1987], p. 183.)

peripheral, diverting their blighted lives and baulked talents to an arena of political importance. The protean spirit engendered by a colonial uncertainty of identity could feed directly into the literary promiscuity Grub Street demanded: as Maginn comments of his role as magazine editor, 'all times and tastes are catered for with a commercial keenness equally dexterous, practised, and profitable'.[109] What began as an enclave of ambitious, down-at-heel artists in the colonies ended up as a nonconformist rump of Tory satirists askew to middle-class Benthamite Britain. John Gross describes Maginn as the 'last of his breed. By the 1840s the kind of raffishness which he represented was being driven steadily underground.'[110]

From another viewpoint, this mass infiltration of some of the commanding organs of metropolitan public opinion can be read as the unconscious *rassentiment* of the repressed, as the sidelined exact their vengeance on the dominant powers not by scrambling from margin to centre but by marginalising the centre itself, trifling with its forms, trivialising its knowledges and dismantling its canons. In one sense, the Cork Fraserians brazenly sell out to the British cultural establishment, to be denounced later by Daniel Corkery as constituting a 'shameful tradition' of stage-Irish exiles along with Lever and Lover.[111] In another sense, these rollicking Corkonians can be seen as infiltrating and contaminating English culture with their local feuds and obsessions, deconstructing it from within. Mahony and Maginn were classicist hacks, apologists for the ancients who paradoxically harnessed modernist techniques to that end, and who, like the Swift of *A Tale of a Tub*, pressed these Grub Street forms to a limit where they satirically undermined themselves.[112] Their calculated trifling, textual bastardy and semiotic sportiveness may have lent new life to the London journals, but they also wickedly parodied the culture to which they belonged.[113]

As jokers in the pack, licensed jesters to the London literary scene, Mahony and Maginn uncover something of their own colonial non-self-identity installed at the very heart of the established cultural system they occupy from within. They constitute a kind of internal edge or colony within the centre itself, contemptuous of literary crawlers and obsequious *parvenus*, fêted literati themselves, at least in the case of Maginn, but maintaining somehow the fierce, lonely integrity of their obscure starting-points. As *flâneurs* with faith, both men curiously combined an integrity of principle with their aesthetic shape-changing, a blend bemusing to those in the English moral-cum-

109. William Maginn, *Works*, vol. 5 (New York, 1857), p. 15.
110. John Gross, *The Rise and Fall of the Man of Letters* (London, 1969), p. 18.
111. See Daniel Corkery, *Synge and Anglo-Irish Literaure* (London, 1931), p. 10.
112. For the classicism of William Maginn, see W. B. Stanford, *Ireland and the Classical Tradition* (Dublin, 1971), pp. 170–1.
113. It is interesting that the Irish Fraserians share this textual sportiveness with another Gael, Thomas Carlyle, who was probably a strong influence on Maginn's political thought.

literary tradition for whom ethical and artistic integrity are indissociable. For all his parodies and shifting personas, Maginn maintained a fierce respect for truth, and was impeccably even-handed in his swingeing polemic, rigorously indifferent to political interest or personal friendship. *Fraser's* even sent up some of its own regular contributors. Mahony pointedly wore his clerical garb to Fraserian booze-ups, and Maginn's political principles never swerved from his early Orangeism. Both loathed time-serving opportunists, and both preserved much of the unworldliness of the provincial outsider.

But there are connections, even so, between their protean artistic selfhoods and the periodical press. A colonial uncertainty of identity breeds just the kind of quick-change artistry or play of masks which Grub Street could use,[114] while the quirky, shapeless, esoteric learning of the isolated colonial scholar could be easily translated into the intellectual *pot pourri* which the London journals liked to serve up. In the notorious scurrility of publications like *Fraser's Magazine*, an insulting rag crammed with doggerel and brutal burlesque, the minor malices of a claustrophobic colonial culture could be projected onto the larger screen of metropolitan literary politics.[115] The contentious political milieu of the day demanded men skilled in abusive rhetoric and sectarian wrangling, and the overcharged ethos of Cork, along with the fertile Irish tradition of cursing, served Mahony and Maginn admirably in this respect. William Maginn claimed that he kept the detested *Edinburgh Review* alive simply by mentioning it in his own columns, a striking instance of the creative word.

There may also be in the Irish Grub Street hack a dim memory of the medieval *scholaris vagrans*, just as the Fraserians' nonchalant mixing of literary genres recalls the *mélange* of history, mythology, folklore, biblical and classical materials of such early Irish texts as the *Leabhar Gabhala* or Book of Conquest. Robin Flower draws attention to the medieval Irish writer's literal preoccupation with marginalia, their habit of 'setting down in the margins and on blank spaces of their manuscripts personal memoranda, invocations of saints, little fragments of verse, and all the flotsam and jetsam of idle fancy'. This 'marked characteristic of the Irish scribe at all ages', so Flower claims, is not to be found in other writers of the time;[116] but it is certainly to be found flourishing in the hybrid, fragmented forms of Mahony and Maginn.

114. Robert Browning considered Mahony protean to the point of multilocational, since he seemed to run into him everywhere he went in Europe. See Leonard Huxley (ed.), *Elizabeth Barrett Browning: Letters to her Sister, 1846–1869* (London, 1929), p. 60. As far as Irish role-switching goes, no finer example could be given than the great Abbey theatre actor Michael MacLiammoir's performance of Oscar Wilde, an Englishman playing an Irishman playing an Irishman playing an Englishman.

115. Thomas Carlyle considered *Fraser's* 'a chaotic, fermenting dung-heap hill of compost' (quoted in Gross, *The Rise and Fall of the Man of Letters*, p. 16). Carlyle was one of the journal's most eminent contributors.

116. Robin Flower, *The Irish Tradition* (Oxford, 1947; reprinted Dublin, 1994), p. 36.

The careers of most of these Cork artists were tightly interwoven, in what might be derogated as tribalism or clientelism, or respected as a sort of dialogism or mutual solidarity. Daniel Maclise sketched for Prout's *Reliques,* Anna Hall's *Sketches of Irish Character* and for an edition of Crofton Croker's *Fairy Legends*, a work which was a composite of Croker's own writings and those of Maginn and Samuel Hall. Crofton Croker, who supplied airs to Thomas Moore, contributed sketches to the Halls' *Ireland: Its Scenery, Character, Etc.* Callanan had a hand in translating the material in Crofton Croker's *Popular Songs of Ireland*, while Anna Hall published a volume of songs with William Forde, brother of the painter Samuel. John Windele edited a poem in Irish by the Blarney antiquarian Matthew Horgan[117] which was translated by Edward Kenealy, and also compiled Callanan's literary remains. Mahony added some notes to a travel book edited by Crofton Croker,[118] and Mahony, Croker and Maginn all wrote for John Boyle's *The Freeholder*. Maclise may have attended Maginn's father's school, and his brother-in-law, Perceval Banks, was one of the Fraserian clique.

James Dufforne, who edited a collection of Maclise's sketches, was Hall's editorial assistant, and John Hogan executed a bust of Francis Mahony. Richard Milliken wrote for *Bolster's Magazine*, which also published Callanan. Frank Mahony, John Sheehan and Frank Stack Murphy all attended Clongowes together. There was a good deal of mutual patronage too: Maginn introduced Callanan to *Blackwood's Magazine,* and both Crofton Croker and Samuel Hall supported Maclise when he first arrived in London, as Croker had himself been aided by Tom Moore. Maclise, Hall and Croker were all sons of soldiers, which might have helped. While some of this may well be seen as Cork clannishness, as well as the anxious hanging-together of émigrés, it is nonetheless an impressively intricate network, and presses at points towards the kind of collaborative or dialogical authorship which, as with Mikhail Bakhtin's own productions, is one aspect of the carnivalesque overturning of the isolated writing ego.

To move from a colonial culture to a metropolitan one is bound to raise questions of precedence, originality, mimicry, derivativeness, belatedness, translation.[119] Jeremiah Callanan was pronounced by the Celtic scholar George

117. Horgan, a cleric and notable Irish scholar, was an important figure on the Cork literary and historical scene; there is a note on him in S. C. Hall's *Retrospect of a Long Life*, pp. 463–4.
118. T. Crofton Croker (ed.), *The Tour of the French Traveller M. De la Boullaye le Gouz in Ireland* (London, 1837).
119. These concerns are not of course only post-colonial. One might risk the proposition that the theme of originality and derivativeness in its broadest philosophical sense – the irony that one becomes an 'original' individual only by participating in signifying systems which always precede you – runs from the great European Idealist and Romantic thinkers to Marx, Freud, Wittgenstein,

Sigerson to be the first Irish poet to have captured in English the distinctive rhythms of Irish, though his colleague Edward Walsh is a strong competitor for the title. Callanan's work, like Mangan's, preserves a certain strangeness or sense of cultural distance, a dislocation of signifier and signified, which according to Robert Welch 'prevents him from giving the impression that that [Gaelic] world is readily exploitable for a civilised English market that has developed a curious taste for Celtic *frissons*'. Having grown up 'between two worlds – the Anglicised life of Cork and the Gaelic life which enclosed the city on every side',[120] his language joined these spheres dialogically, inscribing an alien voice inside a familiarised tongue. Such dialogism is formally speaking an aspect of the carnivalesque, however sombre in content Callanan's and Walsh's work may be.[121] The intriguing point, one highly relevant to the parodic pranks of the Cork Fraserians, is that we do not always know quite what Irish originals Callanan's nine English translations are translations of. They are, as Welch puts it, translations not of particular Irish poems but 'of a certain *kind* of Irish poem',[122] and some of them may well be composites.[123] They are, in short, imitations without an original, like many of James Clarence Mangan's exotic 'translations' from languages with which he had not the slightest acquaintance. As such, they make a telling contrast with one of Callanan's major English-language poems, 'The Recluse of Inchidory', which indeed imitates an original (Byron's 'Childe Harold') and is all the worse for it.

Michael Cronin has argued that early Christian Ireland was dialogical in just this sense. Free from military humiliation at the hands of the ancient empires, its hospitable response to pagan cultures was uninhibited by the experience of defeat.[124] It confronted in any case a well-embedded tradition of pre-Christian learning within its own shores, with which it learned confi-

---

Lacan and others, as well as lying at the root of some of the major anthropological, sociological and historicist inquiries of modernity.

120. B.G. McCarthy, 'Jeremiah J. Callanan: Part 2: His Poetry', p. 387. Sean O'Faolain points to the clash between the Gaelic Callanan and Callanan the early author of a poem in praise of George IV (*The Irish,* Harmondsworth, 1980 [first published 1947], p. 125).

121. See Michael Holquist (ed.), *Mikhail Bakhtin: The Dialogical Imagination* (Texas, 1981), and M. M. Bakhtin, *Rabelais and his World* (Cambridge, Mass., 1968). The latter work is the prime theoretical treatise on carnival of the century, on which I have drawn implicitly in this essay.

122. Robert Welch, *A History of Verse Translation from the Irish,* p. 7.

123. B. G. McCarthy, p. 399.

124. J. E. Caerwyn Williams makes a similar point in his *The Irish Literary Tradition* (1958, reprinted Cardiff, 1992), p. 3. For translation in the Irish Revival, see chapter 6 of Philip O'Leary's splendid study *The Prose Literature of the Gaelic Revival, 1881–1921* (University Park, Pennsylvania, 1994).

dently to interact. It was this self-assurance, so Cronin claims, which enabled Irish society to absorb other cultures through the practice of translation. Far from figuring as some solitary outpost of Europe, it became the site of several languages, a semantic cross-roads or polyphonic space.[125] It was to do so again later with Joyce, an author who has no style of his own to speak of. It is perhaps not fanciful to detect some continuity between this condition and the carnivalesque heteroglossia of the Fraserians, whose robust classicism and ramblings through a range of European cultures represents, like James Joyce's, a return of medieval Ireland in a new guise. Indeed John Sheehan refers to Mahony's 'medieval quaintness of mind'.[126]

A tradition of free renderings, so Cronin points out, had in Ireland long shadowed a rather more rigorous lineage of strict translation. From the middle ages onwards, there was a custom of translations richly expanding and elaborating on their source texts, 'a willingness to experiment that is a feature of one strand of Irish translation activity from Stanihurst through Maginn to Ciaran Carson in the twentieth century'.[127] Maginn's description of his translations as 'free and easy' is both an aesthetic and an ethical category, as textual and moral license become hard to disentangle. Translation begins to border here on joke, transgression, licentiousness, free play or parody, as the original text is bent and manipulated to the expectations of the host culture. In one sense, this privileges the translation over the original; but in another sense, a translation which was scrupulously true to its source would merge into it and risk displacing its priority. The more humbly subservient a translation is, the more it secretly subverts its original by threatening to oust it; the more accurate to the source you are, the more you can pretend to be the source yourself, like a Borgesian copy which merges into what it mirrors. And if the original can be displaced in this way, then how original it was in the first place becomes a troubling question. A work which can be translated must have been always already translatable, must somehow have borne the inscription of the translating tongue within itself, and so was always belated in relation to itself. By contrast, a freer rendering at once exerts authority over the original and permits it its autonomy.

So it is that Mangan can mischievously dub the Irish poet John Anster, translator of Goethe's *Faust*, the 'real author of *Faust*',[128] just as his own autobiography is a cunning fabrication which invents his life far more than it reflects it. Mangan had hardly any Irish, working up his Irish-language 'translations' (or 'perversions', as he called them) for the most part from literal transcriptions by his Ordnance Survey colleagues John O'Donovan and Eugene O'Curry; but it is always possible that by being creatively unfaithful to a literal

125.   Michael Cronin, *Translating Ireland* (Cork, 1996), ch. 1.

126.   Blanchard Jerrold (ed.), *The Final Reliques of Father Prout* (London, 1876), p. 8.

127.   ibid, pp. 121–2. Seamus Deane has some comments on the theme of translation in Irish culture in 'Joyce the Irishman', in Derek Attridge (ed.), *The Cambridge Companion to James Joyce* (Cambridge, 1990).

128.   Quoted by Welch, *A History of Verse Translation from the Irish*, p. 105.

transcription one can be more 'accurate' a translator than the transcriber.[129] In any case, the concept of intertextuality means no more than that an original text is itself already an imitation, and not necessarily consciously so; William Maginn well grasped the distinction between intertextuality and conscious influence when he remarked that many a jest in *Tristram Shandy* harks back to the Talmud, which is not to say that Sterne had ever read it.[130] Maginn also claims that Coleridge's 'Christabel' remained for twenty years unpublished though not unknown, so that, having given rise to various derivative texts before it saw the light of day, it then appeared in the eyes of the reading public as an imitation of its own progeny.[131] In one of his intertextual frolics, Maginn solemnly treats Byron's 'Mazeppa' as an imitation of Cowper's banal ballad 'John Gilpin', contrasting the former censoriously with the supposed beauties of the latter.

Seamus Deane comments of Mangan that 'all his original work is, in some sense, translated'.[132] No work could be intelligible if we had not in some sense already encountered a version of it, which is what we mean by literary codes and conventions. James Sheridan Knowles, terrified of lapsing into plagiarism, responded by the breathtakingly simple strategy of never reading anyone else.[133] But equally a translation may be at least as good as the original. The publisher of the eighteenth-century Irish translator Thomas Franklin presented his version of Sophocles as 'equal, in every respect, to the original',[134] and Thomas MacDonagh claims in his *Literature in Ireland* that certain English versions of Irish poetry are in a way finer than the originals.[135] Indeed for MacDonagh modern Irish poets succeed by a kind of creative misreading of the old Irish myths: 'Their vision is a mistranslation; not for the first time has the world owed a beautiful thing to a mistranslation of genius'.[136] Aesthetically speaking, a translation can outdo its source ('Vienna' will serve as an example), just as an impersonator, by dint of streamlining and highlighting, can come to resemble an impersonatee even more closely than he does

129. As far as Mangan and imitation goes, it is perhaps worth pointing out that the bust of the poet in St Stephen's Green in Dublin bears a remarkable resemblance to one of Lady Morgan a few hundred yards away.
130. William Maginn, *Works* (New York, 1856), vol. 3, p. 342.
131. See Miriam H. Thrall, *Rebellious Fraser's* (New York, 1934), p. 96.
132. Seamus Deane (ed.), *The Field Day Anthology of Irish Writing* (Derry, 1991), vol. 2, p. 6. In the Penguin edition of Francis Stuart's novel *Black List, Section H*, the word 'republican' is at one point misprinted as 'republication'. The Irish republic has certainly been republished a number of times.
133. See James Sheridan Knowles, *Dramatic Works*, vol. 1, p. v.
134. Quoted by Cronin, *Translating Ireland*, p. 76.
135. Thomas MacDonagh, *Literature in Ireland* (Dublin, 1916), p. 101. The Trinity wit Robert Tyrrel said of Browning's translation of the *Agamemnon* that the original helped to clear up some of the obscurities. See Davis Coakley, *Oscar Wilde: The Importance of Being Irish* (Dublin, 1994), pp. 149–50.
136. MacDonagh, *Literature in Ireland*, p. 120.

himself. What is secondary in time may be primary in quality, as the aesthetic does battle with the chronological. In a similar way, the source text can be seen as secondary for the translator, mere raw materials for her own discourse, but may figure as primary for her reader, who may use the translation simply as a form of access to it.

It is not clear, anyway, quite who has the edge over whom, with translation as with colonial power. Is the obedient mimicry of the colonial subject submission or subversive parody, mockery or flattery? Who actually has priority here, if the coloniser always arrives belatedly, to find that his political authority must negotiate the native culture simply in order to flourish? The Irish are a kind of pastiche of the British, yet shape their identity to its roots. The novelist James Stephens observed of his great English mentor William Blake that he was 'good to steal from; and let it be conceded that theft is the first duty of man'. Stephens's biographer comments that many a passage in his *Irish Fairy Tales* sounds like a translation of a twelfth-century original, while conversely some original texts which Stephens quotes sound much like his own work.[137] A nation can also become a kind of inauthentic parody of itself, as Marcel Proust notes: 'The human plagiarism which is most difficult to avoid', he writes, 'for individuals (and even for nations which persevere in their faults and indeed intensify them), is self-plagiarism'.[138] Writers like Mahony and Maginn are self-confessed parasites who need a 'host' culture to feed upon, yet are also quirkily independent spirits who castigate that culture without fear or favour. Ireland, a land of noble ruins, is also in a way secondary to itself, yet it is just this sense of a fractured heritage which will stir the nineteenth-century nationalists to claim autonomy for it. For both nationalism and classicism, all authenticity derives from a repetition of the past, but both at their most persuasive view that rehearsal as a creative transformation. John Dryden wrote in praise of the Irish translation theorist Wentworth Dillon, but rationalised this celebration of a colonial subject by pointing to Dillon's English ancestry. Dillon, after all, is himself just a translation from the English, so that the pre-eminence of Ireland can be unmasked as itself derivative.[139]

To restore Irish culture in the English tongue, in the manner of Walsh and Callanan, meant paradoxically to strengthen the language which had helped to subdue it, reversing the relations between primary and secondary, or vehicle and tenor. Thomas Moore was accordingly relieved when John MacHale of Tuam translated his Celticising English verses into Irish: the poems, he announced, had discovered their native language.[140] MacHale had somehow transposed Moore's poems into what they covertly were all along. The Young

137. See Hilary Pyle, *James Stephens: His Work and an Account of his Life* (London, 1965), pp. 5, 96.
138. Marcel Proust, *Remembrance of Things Past* (Harmondsworth, 1983), vol. 3, p. 443.
139. See Cronin, *Translating Ireland*, p. 47.
140. ibid, p. 115. Joyce in *Finnegans Wake* (Part 1, vii), describes *Ulysses* as a forgery

Ireland poet Denis Florence McCarthy marked the death of Francis Mahony with an elegy modelled on Mahony's 'Bells of Shandon', so that the unique occasion of Mahony's death is solemnly memoralised in a medium plagiarised from himself.[141] The one case of cultural plagiarism which Mahony and Maginn never quite confront, however, is the one nearest to them: Anglo-Irish relations. But it is this, no doubt, which lies at the back of their minds. Just as Ireland mimics Britain, so the British, at least since Thomas Moore, have now taken to stealing Irish culture too. It is a two-way plagiarism, but without that equitable exchange or mutual enrichment which, as we shall see, translation at its finest represents for both men. What is possible at the linguistic level can only serve as a utopian image in the light of actual politics.

The 'anti-plagiarist' poem, as we shall see in a moment, denies its own belatedness, dressing itself up in antique guise and displacing derivativeness instead onto its rival; and it is not hard to discern in this an allegory of Ireland's relations to Britain, conscious of its secondary, 'invented' status but also of the noble past in the light of which it is the British who can be made to appear as newcomers. To avoid the unwelcome consequences of yielding priority to the English language in the act of trying to salvage Irish texts, you can, like Mangan, allow the medium to be estranged by the message, bent out of true by the sheer otherness of the materials it seeks to negotiate. This at once underscores the ultimate impossibility of any equitable interchange of cultures, given the asymmetry of the power relations between them, and allows you to invert those priorities within language itself. In Cronin's splendid formulation, John Synge allows 'the language of the coloniser to be colonised in its turn by the language of the colonised'.[142] Synge's dramatic language is doubled and dialogical to its core, a sheer semantic in-betweenness which contrives to estrange both of its constituent tongues.

It is some such inversion of priorities, though of a less directly political kind, which underlies the strategy which Mangan calls 'the antithesis of plagiarism', in which the opposition between plagiarism and originality is definitively deconstructed.[143] 'Anti-plagiarism' consists in writing a work modelled on an existing one and declaring the latter to be filched from the former, thus reducing the source text to derivative status and turning another writer into a

and his past style of writing as 'piously forged palimpsests . . . from his pelagiarist pen', which of course is just as true of his present style.

---

141. For McCarthy's poem, see D. O. Crowley, *Irish Poets and Novelists* (San Francisco, 1893), pp. 423–4.

142. Cronin, *Translating Ireland*, p. 141.

143. See David Lloyd, *Nationalism and Minor Literature* (Berkeley, 1987), p. 103. By 'the antithesis of plagiarism' Mangan meant the writing of a translation without an original, a meaning which can then be extended to cover Mahony and Maginn's rather different elaboration of this technique.

literary pilferer by stealing his work.[144] The supplement, as is the habit with such appendages, comes to supplant what it depends upon. (As far as supplementarity goes, 'Oliver Yorke', the fictional editor of Father Prout's *Reliques*, declares in a remarkable feat of dialectical thought that the book is 'complete, as far as it goes'.[145]) Along with a reversal of 'host' and 'parasite' text, such anti-plagiarism, which adds new meaning to the Wordsworthian dictum that the child is father to the man, involves an inversion of the relations between past and present, in which the present work claims priority over the original one, authoritatively reconstituting it as inauthentic. In this sense, it represents a subversive 'modernist' smack at nationalist antiquarianism, a delegitimising of the past. If an 'original' text can be so fluently translated into Hebrew, Latin or Old French, must it not have already anticipated its own iterability, its capacity for plagiarism being somehow constitutive of its identity in much the same way that a capacity to be appropriated by someone else is constitutive of one's private property?

The politics of anti-plagiarism, however, are interestingly ambiguous. In one sense, the practice involves unmasking the present as a mere repetition of the past; yet since the 'ancient' text which accomplishes this is in fact a construction of the present, it simultaneously affirms the power of the contemporary. The technique thus serves to satirise the modern while impudently stripping the past of its authoritative aura, and so in its Janus-faced nature is peculiarly appropriate for traditionalist peddlers of modern-day ephemera like Mahony and Maginn. It also springs from a culture which is at once erudite and self-ironising – one, like colonial Ireland, which is wryly alert to the value of knowledge as well as to its relative uselessness. It is, then, a typically carnivalesque device, for carnival must posit the very scholastic learning it simultaneously relativises. John Sheehan describes Mahony as one who in Irish style blends fun and argument, 'mock[ing] reason with an appearance of reasoning'.[146] Moreover, if the present can expose the past as derivative, it undercuts in that very act whatever authority it claims, since in doing so it lays itself open to precisely the same operation.

144.   The question of which parts of some copied letters are original and which are forged is central to the plot of Maria Edgeworth's novel *Helen* (1834). There is also a reference to copied letters without originals in James Stephens's *The Demi-Gods* (London, 1914), p. 252. It is said that the poet Patrick Kavanagh, on encountering an American buyer of original poetic manuscripts, decided to write the original drafts of his own poems.

145.   *The Reliques of Father Prout* (London, 1873), p. lx. Mahony was born in Cork in 1804, and educated by the Jesuits at Clongowes Wood College. He later trained as a priest in Amiens, Paris and Rome, and returned to Clongowes as prefect of studies in 1830, to be dismissed under a cloud. He was ordained as a priest in Rome, but not as a Jesuit, in 1832. He worked as a journalist in London, spent nine years on the Continent as correpondent for various newspapers, including Dickens's *Daily News*, wandered aimlessly around Europe and finally settled in Paris, where he died in 1866. He is buried in Shandon church in his native Cork.

146.   *The Final Reliques of Father Prout* (London, 1876), p. 103.

It is even possible to be a self-anti-plagiarist, composing 'translations' which are actually one's own work, and so combining source and derivation in a single text. This is the case with much of Mangan. Fiona Stafford notes that James Macpherson's 'original' poems, in the sense of his non-Ossianic writings, read more derivatively than his supposed Ossian translations: in writing his Ossian texts, Macpherson 'was to produce poetry that seemed more original than his own compositions'.[147] Macpherson considered the oral poetry of the Highlands to be a corrupt version of Scotland's ancient literature, and was reluctant to translate it for fear of English mockery and condescension. In composing his Ossian poems, he was therefore producing his own 'original' ancient song, which was in his view more authentic than the literary fragments which had actually descended from the past. In penning a piece of his own which claimed fraudulently to be the original version of these broken relics, Macpherson represents the Scottish equivalent of the Irish anti-plagiarists. Indeed it could be claimed that his was the great founding act of anti-plagiarism, which the Irish writers then plagiarised. In another ironic twist, some of the Irish scholars who pitched in to the Ossian debate claimed that this 'original' Scottish culture was in fact derivative of their own, the true fount and origin of the Celtic spirit. Hugh Trevor-Roper writes that 'James Macpherson picked up Irish ballads in Scotland, wrote an "epic" in which he transferred the whole scenario from Ireland to Scotland, and then dismissed the genuine ballads thus maltreated as debased modern composites and the real Irish literature which they reflected as a mere reflection of them.'[148] This is in fact simplistic: the materials Macpherson exploited cannot be so neatly divided into Scottish and Irish, sharing as they did a common cultural inheritance.[149] But it is agreeable to imagine that Macpherson stole some Irish material in anti-plagiarising style, and that the Irish, in the shape of men like Mahony and Maginn, then had their revenge by stealing the anti-plagiarist technique from him. The Highland Society of Scotland, concerned by the slurs which Macpherson's poem attracted, appointed a committee to inquire into its authenticity, which delivered a report in which an 'original' for the work was found by piecing together lines and images from a variety of sources. The committee, in short, had come up with a derivative original.[150]

147.   Fiona Stafford, *The Sublime Savage* (Edinburgh, 1988), p. 84. See also Gauti Kristmannsson, 'Ossian: A Case of Celtic Tribalism or a Translation without an Original?' (offprint, Sonderdruck, 1997), and Ian Haywood, *The Making of History* (London and Toronto, 1986), chs. 3 and 4.148. Hugh Trevor-Roper, 'The Invention of Tradition: The Highland Tradition of Scotland', in Eric Hobsbawm and Terence Ranger (eds.), *The Invention of Tradition* (Cambridge, 1983), p. 17.
149.   See Donald E. Meek, 'The Gaelic Ballads of Scotland', in Howard Gaskill (ed.), *Ossian Revisited* (Edinburgh, 1991).
150.   See Malcolm Chapman, *The Gaelic Vision in Scottish Culture* (London, 1978), pp. 41–2.

We may examine these themes more closely by turning to the work of Francis Sylvester Mahony, wit, hack, toper, ruined priest, scholar and satirist, of whose prodigal array of pseudonymns 'Father Prout' is the one which posterity has preserved.[151] It is with this appellation that he has, to quote his own words, come 'floating triumphantly down the stream of time, secure and buoyant in a genuine "Cork" jacket'.[152]

Prout, so he tells us, was the offspring of a secret marriage between Swift and Stella, and was kidnapped at a tender age by the Englishman William Wood, in vengeance for the savaging which he had received in the Dean's *Drapier's Letters*.[153] The villainous Wood left the child exposed on the bleak summit of Watergrasshill near Cork, identifiable only by a locket around his neck containing a lock of his mother's hair and inscribed with the motto *Prout Stella Refulges*, '*Prout*' meaning literally 'to the extent that'. Father Prout, then, is Father-up-to-a-point, an accurate enough description of Mahony's dubious clerical status as a defrocked priest still in holy orders. It was the brutal abduction of the child which was the cause of his father's madness, though the story turned out well enough for the lad himself. Taken into the Cork foundling hospital, the young Prout escaped from the institution hidden in a wooden churn, to end up as the erudite clergyman of Watergrasshill whose papers have descended to us by the good offices of his editor Oliver Yorke, also *alias* Frank Mahony. Prout is hot in defence of his father's reputation, and asserts of the bare-faced political self-promoter Swift that he 'sought not the smiles of the court, nor ever sighed for ecclesiastical dignities' (p. 115). We read all this in Prout's essay 'Dean Swift's Madness, or the Tale of a Churn'.

Prout, then, has an illicit pedigree, like forged literary texts or false etymologies. The word 'kidnapping', so he informs us, is cognate with the word 'plagiarism', since in Cicero's day kidnappers were known as *plagiarii*, after the lash or *plaga* which they could expect if apprehended. (This is itself a false

151. Mahony stole the name from a real cleric, parish priest of Arnagehy, Co. Cork. There are some comments on the real Prout in William Le Fanu, *Seventy Years of Irish Life* (London, 1893), pp. 179–80, a work which also contains some observations on Sheridan Knowles and Sergeant Frank Murphy of the Fraserian circle.

152. *Reliques of Father Prout*, p. 104. All subsequent references to this work are given in parentheses after quotations. There is a reference to 'prouts' in James Joyce's *Finnegans Wake* (New York, 1939, p. 482), followed closely by one to 'the bells of scandal' (i.e. Prout's poem 'The Bells of Shandon').

153. Robert Mahony points out that Prout's defence of Swift as an Irish patriot, in the period of Catholic Emancipation, was quite unusual. It is clearly among other things an attempt to marginalise O'Connell. See his *Jonathan Swift: The Irish Identity* (New Haven and London, 1995), pp. 82–7.154. We have here a version – perhaps even the origin – of the old Irish anecdote about the editorial in the *Skibbereen Eagle* which declared that the newspaper was keeping a close eye on the Tsar, or in another version on the Treaty of Versailles.

etymology: *plagiarius* actually derives from *plagium*, a net to catch game.) To steal an infant is a kind of plagiarism, appropriating what is not your own, rather as Prout's father Swift does with his assumption of literary personae, a tendency inherited by his son. Prout is a protean impersonator, a literary ventriloquist whose 'soul is multilateral, his talk multifarious' (p. iv). He is an odd mixture of the conservative and the carnivalesque, 'a rare combination of Socrates and Sancho Panza, of Scarron and the venerable Bede' (p. 167). The reactionary Prout is one of the 'polished and high-born clergy of the old Gallican church' (p. 5), deeply contemptuous of the vulgar herd of petty-bourgeois Corkonians with whom it is his lot to mingle. These, in his essay 'The Watergrass Carousal', include a down-at-heel fashion journalist who though not well-dressed himself is the cause of dress in others, and who, as the editor of a local newspaper, keeps an eye on Russia in his columns vigilant enough to annoy the Tsar.[154] There is also a dentist who finishes his dinner parties with especially hard nuts, thus profitably converting his guests into patients.

Despite his conservatism, however, Prout is a kind of cultural studies exponent *avant la lettre*, whose chief field of scholarly inquiry, so he tells us, is popular song; indeed Mahony himself has survived on the strength of one such ballad, 'The Bells of Shandon'. It is true that the Cork Fraserians practised along with their anti-plagiarising a kind of anti-popularising, translating ephemeral works into more durable linguistic media, as with William Maginn's rendering of 'Old King Cole' in Hebrew. Maginn's persona O'Docherty dreams of landing the office of Embalmer General, commissioned to turn living languages into dead ones for their better conservation. The danger, he reflects, would be to beautify the original to the point where it would be made better than itself, and so encourage readers to value inferior modern products by the allure of the linguistic wrapping he lends them. In his essay 'The Songs of France', Prout gives us a commendable French version of the anonymous eighteenth-century Irish verse 'The Night before Larry was Stretched'. But since the point of this project is to help preserve the ephemeral as well as antiquate it, it could be said to be popularising enough in its perverse way.

A supposed correspondent to *Fraser's Magazine* (in fact Mahony himself) describes Prout as being a 'rare combination of the Teian lyre and the Tipperary bagpipe . . . of the Ionian dialect blending harmoniously with the Cork brogue; an Irish potatoe (*sic*) seasoned with Attic salt, and the humours of Donnybrook wed to the glories of Marathon' (p. 66). Or as another commentator has it, 'a piquant mixture of toryism, classicism, sarcasm and punch'.[155] Mahony, in short, is the very essence of carnival, with his abrupt

154. We have here a version – perhaps even the origin – of the old Irish anecdote about the editorial in the *Skibbbereen Eagle* which declared that the newspaper was keeping a close eye on the Tsar, or in another version on the Treaty of Versailles.

155. Quoted in Ethel Mannin, *Two Studies in Integrity* (London, n.d.), p. 149.

lurchings from the erudite to the everyday, from pokerfaced pedantry to knockabout humour. In his essay 'The Painter, Barry', the Cork artist James Barry, painting at dead of night in the Vatican for fear (significantly enough) of snooping would-be plagiarists, is disturbed by a shadowy figure who, once wrestled to the ground, turns out to be the pope.[156] The two then proceed to conduct a learned conversation. Dinner-table conversation, of which there is much in Mahony's writing as well as in his life, is itself a carnivalesque mode, combining the intellectual and biological, semantic and somatic, while exploiting the comic tension between the two.[157]

Mahony, who was kicked out of the Clongowes seminary because of a gargantuan bash which got grotesquely out of hand, was never actually suspended from the priesthood – he was, as his editor Blanchard Jerrold remarks, 'a half-pay soldier of the Church, minus the half pay'.[158] Though he was a pious right-wing Catholic, his notions of temperance, as a friend put it with exquisite diplomacy, were 'too liberal for the Church'.[159] Ironically, however, he was a close friend of Father Mathew, commissioned a bust of the friar, and was commended by Mathew for the selfless courage he displayed while attending the poor as a young curate during the Cork cholera epidemic of 1832. As Mahony himself commented of his priestly status, he flirted openly with all nine Muses, since his vow of celibacy prevented him from forming a permanent liaison with any one of them. He was a bohemian backwoodsman who moved with aplomb from Horace to claret, a polyglot of enormous erudition who seemed with deliberate perversity to trivialise his own talents and cultivate an assiduous hackery.

In carnivalesque mode, Mahony deranges the proportions between central and peripheral, with a multifunctional style of writing like 'the proboscis of an elephant, that can with equal ease shift an obelisk and crack a nut' (p. 33). His art, so he informs us, is 'to magnify what is little, and to fling a dash of the sublime into a two-penny-post-communication' (p. 134); and this upending of literary hierarchies, this scrambling of the mighty and the myopic, can be seen as the aberrant colonial's smack at the literary categories of the metropolis. Indeed he and William Maginn were such superlative hacks that they seemed to raise that lowly status to the second power, and so to transcend it. Like Oscar Wilde, Mahony is a major kind of minor writer, so doggedly, brilliantly peripheral that he ends up troubling the very distinction between that and centrality, as one might claim that the O'Connellite politics

---

156. Mahony might have been influenced here by Samuel Ferguson's knockabout piece 'Father Tom and the Pope' (*Blackwood's Magazine*, May, 1838), which Yeats misattributed to William Maginn. See Peter Denman, *Samuel Ferguson: The Literary Achievement* (Gerrards Cross, 1990), p. 53.

157. There is today a Father Prout restaurant in Cork's Watergrasshill.

158. *Final Reliques of Father Prout*, Preface. Jerrold was the son of Mahony's friend Douglas Jerrold, editor of *Punch*.

159. Mannin, *Two Studies in Integrity*, p. 150.

of his day did in their own way too. There is a cross-grained, perverse streak in his writings, as in those of Maginn,[160] which is evident elsewhere in Irish letters, and which is closely linked to colonial eccentricity.

The line between the trivial and the substantial, then, is as hair-thin for Prout as the border between madness and sanity, or drunkenness and sobriety. He has some Foucaultean reflections on madness in the case of Swift, or should one say Swiftian reflections, musing that the frontier between the sane and the crazed is utterly indeterminate, not least for want of a 'really solid sensible man' to act as a norm by which to measure deviations. In similar spirit, he is fascinated by the precise metaphysical point at which sobriety passes over into inebriation. As far as authenticity goes, was Mahony himself entitled to be called 'Father', suspended as he was in some limbo between orgy and ordination? His very existence was liminal, his authority undecidable, his identity aporetic. The whole odious, gimcrack world of Benthamism and Whiggery struck him as hollow, parasitic, entirely intertextual: 'all I read now', writes Prout, 'strikes me as but a new version of what I have read somewhere before . . . I'm sick of hashed-up works' (p. 137). This of course is pretty rich, coming as it does from a master plagiarist whose whole selfhood is merely a recycled version of a derivative fiction. As with the practice of anti-plagiarism, the Tory Prout deplores the death of authenticity at the very instant that he saps away at the whole illusion of it. Fearful lest forged Prout papers, or a 'false paper currency', might begin to circulate, his 'editor' Oliver Yorke solemnly gives notice to his readers that 'no "Prout paper" is the *real* thing unless with label signed "OLIVER YORKE"' (p. 232). We are not told how we are to determine whether this signature itself is forged or genuine. One is reminded of the man in Ludwig Wittgenstein's *Philosophical Investigations* who bought extra copies of the morning newspaper in order to assure himself that what the first copy said was true. What, in any case, is an original signature, since a signature can be authentic only by virtue of being a repetition? That a piece of writing can be fraudulently detached from its authorial source is constitutive of the act of writing, for both Jacques Derrida and Andrew Prout: 'nothing so truly serves a book', as the latter (though it could be the former) remarks, 'as the writer's removal from the sphere or hemisphere of his readers' (p. x).

Enraged that Thomas Moore ('this Anacreontic little chap') has accused Henry O'Brien of plagiarism in his study of Irish round towers,[161] Prout turns the charge back on Moore himself, a detestable self-publicising Whig in any case in Mahony's eyes. He does so by himself composing the French

---

160. Maginn remarks himself how he is accused by some of 'maintaining always the untenable side of any question', just to demonstrate his logical dexterity (*Works* [New York, 1856], vol. 3, p. 155).
161. There are some comments on this controversy, and on Prout's part in it, in Joep Leerssen, *Remembrance and Imagination* (Cork, 1996), pp. 121–6.

troubadour ballads of which, so he maintains, Moore's *Irish Melodies* are imitations, thus constituting them as a brand of 'petty larceny'. For good measure, he also arraigns Moore for having transmogrified his own 'Bells of Shandon' into his 'Evening Bells', and claims that some lines from Moore's 'Lalla Rookh' originally appeared in the Mogul language over the audience chamber of the king of Delhi. As it happens, Prout's own anti-plagiarising tactics are themselves plagiarised: he derives them, as he admits, from a French Jesuit who held that Horace's odes were written by a twelfth-century Benedictine monk. Generously enough, however, he acknowledges that some of Moore's 'translations' are very nearly as fine as the originals. The real-life Mahony, if that is not too strong an epithet, finds his fictional equivalent in the literary dilettante Joe Atlee of Charles Lever's novel *Lord Kilgobbin*, whose delight is 'to write Greek versions of a poem that might attach the mark of plagiarism to Tennyson, or show, by a Scandinavian lyric, how the laureate has been poaching from the Norsemen' (ch. 4). With Atlee, this textual dialogism is turned against the most revered figure of the English literary pantheon.

The poet Beranger's father was a tailor, so Prout informs us, whereas Tom Moore's 'juvenile associations were of a grocer sort' (p. 259) – the reason why his compositions, with their 'mock-turtle pathos', are so highly spiced. This kind of word-play is second nature to Mahony, who likes to pronounce the word 'morale' as 'more ale', claims that 'Jupiter' is a corruption of 'Jew Peter', ruminates on the female root of the name of a fish ('Ann Chovy'), and finds in the Latin *dignitate* an inescapable echo of 'diggin' taties'. Etymology concerns the exchange-value of words, and one of Mahony's most abiding metaphors is that of exchange-value/commerce/translation, a constant analogising of signs and commodities. This, in its own muted way, is a carnivalesque tactic, deflating the idealist pretensions of the spirit in Swiftian style by stressing its kinship with humdrum material life. It is also an appropriate metaphor (literally: transport, traffic) for one who sells words as commodities on the metropolitan market.

It is no wonder that the materiality of the signifier should have been a popular theoretical doctrine on Grub Street. Both Mahony and Maginn were fascinated by the material circulation of texts, the happenstance of literary transmission and reception. Translation, like the trade between colony and metropolis, involves a sort of unequal exchange, 'the interchange in vocabulary showing at times even a balance in favour of the substitute [language], as happens in the ordinary course of barter on the markets of the world' (p. v). (One is reminded that for the poet Mangan the link between commerce and translation could be embarrassingly direct: he occasionally translated on the spot for cash in John O'Daly's shop in Dublin.)[162] There can be no exact translation, so Prout maintains: 'the *tradottore* differs from the *traditore* only by a syllable'

162.   See C. P. Meehan (ed.), *Poets and Poetry of Munster* (Dublin, 1906), p. xxv.

(p. 396), ringing a variation on the familiar Irish cognates of tradition, translation and treason. The Irish, one might say, are a kind of translation or mimicry of their colonial masters, but the line between this and political treachery is never well-defined. All translation for Prout is a kind of false etymologising, just as all tradition is a sort of illegitimacy and all meaning contaminated. As he stoically puts it, 'there is ever a cankerworm in the rose; a dactyl is sure to be mixed up with a spondee in the poetry of life' (p. 7).

As a cosmopolitan conservative, Prout is in favour of intellectual free trade but commercial protectionism, a universality of the spirit but a nationalism of the economy; and this, one might note, was a fairly unique position in the Ireland of his day, offensive at once to Irish cultural nationalism and British political economy. His translations are a way of 'promoting the interchange of national commodities': by translating from the French he has 'enriched England at the expense of her rival, and engrafted on her literature the choicest products of Gallic culture', so that the inhabitants of these islands may now whistle his 'Songs of France' 'duty free', in their native language (pp. 201–2). In translating Homer, Alexander Pope 'works the mineral ores of Greece with the abundant resources of English capital' (p. 395). William Maginn writes in his turn of translation as a kind of imperialism, admiring the poet who 'having explored the mines of foreign intellectual ore, devotes himself to the glorious task of enriching his country's treasure of words and thoughts – HER LANGUAGE – with the brightest and the rarest gems, the diamonds which his own hands have raked from their native beds, and washed in the streams of Helicon'.[163]

Maginn approvingly quotes from one of Pope's letters which argues that 'A mutual commerce makes poetry flourish; but then poets, like merchants, should repay with something of their own what they have taken from others'.[164] Translation, in other words, is at once purchase and sale: by extending your own language with a foreign engraftment, you enrich the translated language too, disclose a depth within it, so that your profit can seem like payment. Dryden, claims Maginn, is right to hold, in his *Essay on Dramatic Poesie*, that Ben Jonson 'invades authors like a monarch, and what would be theft in other poets, is only victory in him'. It is a kind of genius which according to Maginn 'does but assert its own prerogative in rendering the intelligence of past ages tributary to its success'[165] – an excellent *résumé* of anti-plagiarist practice. The problem lies in the undecidable distinction between this form of 'creative' borrowing and the petty pilfering of a Moore, who, Maginn believes, says nothing which has not been said before but does not say it half so well.[166] When does inspirational influence become plain theft? Perhaps,

163. William Maginn, *Miscelleneous Writings,* vol. 5 (New York, 1857), p. 145.
164. ibid, p. 146.
165. ibid, p. 132.x
166. See his essay 'Poetical Plagiaries: Thomas Moore', *Miscelleneous Writings*, vol. 5, p. 145. Moore considered challenging Maginn to a duel over this article.

Maginn considers, genuine imitation consists in so mixing the gold of the ancients with one's modern materials that the difference between them disappears; but how is this not just to claim that the finest poem is the most deviously derivative, the most cunningly plagiaristic? The conservative in Maginn wishes to enforce a distinction between authentic and inauthentic which his own metaphors unwittingly deconstruct.

Mahony, who rambled aimlessly as far as Asia Minor, rejects all provincialism of the mind in the name of exchange, hybridity, cosmopolitan cross-breeding; yet he denounces any economic version of such spiritual *laissez faire* as injurious to the poor and unprotected. Free trade, then, is for him just a cultural trope; but since Mahony, along with Maginn no doubt as a stout Tory, endorses imperialism as a fact as well as a literary strategy, this would not be wholly compatible with the economic protectionism he also favours. The distinction can only be kept in place by insisting on the purely figurative force of one of its terms (imperialism), which threatens nonetheless to intrude its 'literal' meaning and so to undercut the protectionist case. Mahony, in any case, is like his colleague vehemently opposed to economic *laissez faire*: if you're going to dismantle protective commercial barriers, why not, he enquires, do away with the quarantine laws while you're at it and permit a free trade in plague?

Moore steals supposedly from the French troubadours, but there are built-in security devices against such expropriation: 'Unfortunately for such attempts, the lays of the Norman troubadours, like the Government rope in the dock-yard at Portsmouth, have in their texture a certain twist by which they are recognised when they get into the possession of thieves' (p. 247). Writers who pillage foreign produce are really smugglers, as opposed to those who pay the custom duty of acknowledgement. The god Mercury derives his name from *merx* or merchandise,[167] and he is also of course, so Prout reminds us, the god of wit, messages, eloquence, mediation, highways, commerce, diplomacy, mobility, secrets, translation, interpretation – and robbers.[168] (He might have added: borders.) Mahony's own work is entirely mercurial and hermetic – though he notes the oddness of this deity of locomotion and rapidity being also the protector of fixtures, milestones, permanence, and – an unfortunate phrase for a cleric – 'monumental erections' (p. 401).

Maginn also observes that Mercury, said to be the inventor of written characters, was the patron of thieves, and explains this connection mock-pedantically by claiming that Mercury was the prototype of Moses, also associated with letters and in Egyptian eyes a thief. 'He who could make a pun would pick a pocket', he quotes Dr Johnson as proclaiming.[169] As a conservative quick-change artist or antiquarian modernist, however, Mahony resolves this

167. Perhaps another false etymology; the point is evidently controversial.
168. Susan Mitchell describes George Moore as 'a born literary bandit' (*George Moore* [Dublin, 1916], p. 103).
169. Maginn, *Miscellaneous Writings*, vol. 5, p. 223.

apparent conflict of change and conservation in his own person. Like Maginn, he was the best sort of reformist Tory, the Johnsonian variety who believes that Whiggish liberalism will simply injure the poor. O'Connell – the 'bog-trotter of Derrynane' – was his predictable *bête noire*, a man who, so he scathingly remarks, never put a Latin hexameter together in his life. In his late reports from Italy for Dickens's *Daily News*, in which the land of Sardinia figures as a thinly veiled allegory of Ireland, O'Connell appears as Dandelone, the champion of 'immaculate emancipation', and Thomas Moore as Thomaso il Moro.[170] The Whigs are 'Perukes', and the Irish Famine the great chestnut rot. But Mahony's anti-Connellite animus is less red-neck reaction than the old canard that the Liberator was ripping off the poor.

Indeed in his own tongue-in-cheek or tongue-in-glass way, Mahony was a kind of nationalist. His 'Poetical Epistle from Father Prout to Boz' admires Dickens's concern for the poor but urges him also to 'Think of the poor / On t'other shore, / Poor who, unheeded, perish, / By squires despoiled, by "patriots" gulled, / I mean the starving Irish'.[171] His 'Apology for Lent' commends the 'Celtic and Eastern races' (which mysteriously includes Greeks, Arabs and Irish) for the lightness of their diet, in contrast to the Teutonic craving for heavy meat, or the 'gross, carcase-eating propensities of John Bull' (p. 16). 'We are in truth a most abstemious race' (p. 25), he comments without twitching an eyebrow, casually poking his finger through an anti-Irish stereotype. When he adds later that the Irish are 'the most ill-fed people on the face of the globe' (p. 25), one registers the political animus lurking behind the bland iconoclasm. It is curious, Prout reflects, that no monument exists to that demographic hero Sir Walter Raleigh, who by importing the potato has fed more families and provided a greater impulse to procreation than any other benefactor of humanity.

What Prout is up to in this essay, in fact, is a kind of dietary theory of history,[172] one centred like so much from Swift to Samuel Beckett on the body, and the starving body at that. Ancient Rome having 'burst of its own

170. See, for Mahony's correspondence from Rome and Paris, *Final Reliques*. Like James Joyce, Mahony when abroad was interested in what was afoot in Ireland, and was proud of the tombs of the exiled earls O'Donnell and O'Neill in Rome, which John Hogan took it upon himself to repair.

171. *Final Reliques,* p. 234. If one is to judge by Dickens's satirical portrait in *Bleak House* of Mrs Jellyby, busy with overseas charity but careless of want at home, he would not perhaps have responded to this appeal with wholehearted enthusiasm.

172. As opposed to the tobacco theory of history expounded in 'A Tavern in the Town', in James Stephens's *Here Are Ladies* (London, 1913). Stephens speculates that our ancestors' lack of pockets, and consequently of the ability to carry around tobacco, was responsible for their diverting their energies into wars, revolutions and the like. He also reflects that what is unique to the human animal is brewing and shaving. There is much of Mahony's pokerfaced mock-erudition in Stephens's soberly expounded metaphysical fantasies.

plethory', it was fasting which, in a kind of culinary version of the Freudian doctrine of sexual sublimation, 'originated civilisation and commerce'. This theory of the rise of an ascetic anti-materialism is, like Freud's, a thoroughly materialist one. 'In the progress of maritime industry along the shores of southern, and subsequently northern Europe', Prout maintains, 'we find a love for freedom to grow up with a fondness for fish' (p. 20). Indeed it is Lent, of all things, which cements the union between Britain and Ireland, since if fasting were abolished in Ireland the natives would eat rather than export their meat, and Repeal of the Union would quickly follow. Conversely, were Lent to be revived in England, the consequent fall in the price of cattle and the flourishing of the fishing industry would 'eventually harmonise the jarring interests of agriculture and manufacturing industry' (p. 24). Mahony adds for good measure a few notes on the pig-based parallel between the Irish and the Israelites: in both cultures the pig is a sacred object, and the mass export of the creatures from Ireland resembles nothing quite so much as the rush to the sea of the Gadarene swine. Shortly after these musings, Prout expires on Shrove Tuesday, having consumed a particularly indigestible pancake.

Prout describes British rule in Ireland as 'oppressive', and is not slow to sing the praises of Irish history. In 'A Plea for Pilgrimages', he lectures Sir Walter Scott, who has come to kiss the Blarney stone, on that object's venerable pedigree. It was, so he claims, brought to Cork by the Phoenicians, who cleared the pillars of Hercules and landed with it in the Cove of Cork. (Carthage, he informs us, is 'Tarshish' in Hebrew, which means 'valuable stone'.) The Blarney stone beggars all rivals: 'the long-sought *lapis philosophorum*, compared with this jewel, dwindles into insignificance' (p. 50), along with the Luxor obelisk, the treaty-stone of Limerick and the Elgin marbles. Without the eloquence and 'splendid effrontery' which it affords, how, he asks, could Dan O'Connell have come to con the world? But Irish history extends back still further: the Nile was so named after the tribe of O'Neills, its aboriginal inhabitants, who threw up a few pyramids before they set sail for Ireland. The poet Richard Milliken's 'The Groves of Blarney', so Prout has ascertained through his researches, was originally an ancient Greek lyric, and the industrious cleric has compared Greek, Latin, Norman-French and Irish manuscript versions of the poem, all of which, apart from the Irish, he duly gives us, while rejecting as spurious the Arabic, Armenian and Chaldaic fragments which survive.[173] Moreover, since it was the Irish monks of Bobbio who counselled Dante not to write his *Divine Comedy* in Latin,[174] the Irish can take credit for the whole of Italian literature.

173. W. J. Mc Cormack has some illuminating comments on the political subtext of Milliken's poem in *The Field Day Anthology of Irish Writing* (Derry, 1991), vol. 1, p. 1102. 'Groves', he suggests, may be a family name. Mahony's father, a prosperous wool merchant, moved his factory to Blarney from Cork. Prout himself plans a university of Blarney, which would combine 'cultivated fun and the genial development of national acuteness' (p. 65).

174. There is apparently no evidence for this claim.

Mahony's antiquarianism is of course a send-up, but his backward glance is also genuine conservative nostalgia. Is the homesickness of 'The Bells of Shandon', with its ritual denigration of foreign exotica in favour of provincial Cork, straight, tongue-in-cheek or poised more likely at some undecidable in-between?[175] Bakhtinian revellers like Mahony and Maginn were in one sense free cosmopolitan spirits, heretically at odds with a chauvinist, parochial culture, their writing shamelessly mongrelised and macaronic in a way which constitutes a silent rebuke to the linguistic purism of a narrowly conceived Irish nationalism. But like the great nationless modernists who were to follow them, they paid the price of this deracination too, forced to cobble together styles, forms and idioms in the absence of a vigorous set of native English-language traditions. They are drudges, parodists and *bricoleurs* adrift between cultures, shuttling from one (sometimes) invented tongue to another, gifted wastrels who squander their extraordinary philological talents on poems in praise of port, wicked burlesques of Wordsworth and a pathology of punning.

This inbred, fragmentary form of writing then gives off all the resonance of a directionless, self-involved colonial society, not least in its virulent literary sectarianism. Though Prout loftily proclaims that there is no place for religious or political differences in the realm of Parnassus, he also characterises the *Edinburgh Review* as 'that ricketty go-cart of drivelling dotage' (p. 163), and brutally traduced a friend in print. He also writes that Attila king of the Huns, and Leigh Hunt king of the Cockneys, have both spread 'havoc and consternation' in Italy (p. 318). William Maginn almost lost his life for writing a vicious review, called Sheridan a 'buffoon' and Macaulay a quack and moral beggar. As with the great modernists, one needs to recall the pains of exile as well as the pleasures of the polyglottic, the oppressive as well as emancipatory aspect of colonial identities which are unstable, self-fashioning, intertextual. Mahony, like Wilde, died as a lonely expatriate in Paris. He was a potentially major writer striving very hard to become a minor one,[176] and brilliantly succeeded.

William Maginn, son of an eminent Cork schoolmaster who died as a victim of road rage, is reported to have entered Trinity College, Dublin, at the age of eleven,[177] won his doctorate at the age of twenty-four, and in addition to the

175. The disastrous effects of taking the poem entirely straight are betrayed in the earnest academicist comments of Cleanth Brooks and Robert Penn Warren in their *Understanding Poetry* (New York, 1938), pp. 133–6. I am grateful to Dr Timothy P. Foley for this reference.

176. The protagonist of Graham Greene's *Travels with my Aunt* declares that he would have been content to be a poet in a quite humble station, like 'an English Mahony'.

177. According to Oliver Goldsmith, the Irish poet Thomas Parnell entered Trinity at the age of thirteen, so Maginn beat him for precociousness by two years. (See Arthur Friedman [ed.], *Collected Works of Oliver Goldsmith* [Oxford, 1966], vol. 3, p. 407–8).

major European languages is said to have been familiar with Latin, Greek both ancient and modern, Irish, Hebrew, Syriac, Sanskrit, Basque, Swedish, Turkish, Assyrian, Portuguese and Magyar, though nobody ever caught him actually reading.[178] He was sometimes so drunk that he did not know what he was writing, and nobody has scribbled so much and so devotedly on the subject of alcohol, which might almost be said to constitute his major theme. He claimed to review all books dedicated to 'the great two sister sciences of eating and drinking', but declared 'THE BOTTLE, and all that pertains to it, [as] my proper concern'.[179] The spirit of liberal disinterestedness he saw as most finely exemplified in a catholic taste for all wines, and in a review of a history of wine he urges the reader to taste each vintage commended by the author, thus drinking his way through the volume. At one point in his work, Maginn informs us that he has paused to mix a glass of grog, writing to the moment in Shandyesque style. He spent most of his latter years on the run from his creditors, lurking in wretched hovels with his long-suffering family and dashing off pieces for *Fraser's* in the Fleet prison. He died, a burnt-out alcoholic wreck, in 1842 in Walton on Thames, though he would doubtless have preferred to expire in some less prosaic spot.

A labour historian *avant la lettre,* Maginn believed that there was a great work yet to be written entitled 'The History of the Lowest Order from the earliest times'. It would, he remarked, prove 'of far more importance, of deeper philosophy, and more picturesque romance, than all the chronicles of what are called the great events of the earth'.[180] His awareness of the lowest orders was more than theoretical: he frequented a number of louche dives in London, was familiar with the passwords to criminal haunts, and used his knowledge of the Irish language to move among the Irish hovels of London's St Giles area. On arriving in a new town, he made a habit of seeking out the foulest slums. He was a particular favourite with children, and was known 'to spend himself as freely and gayly for a street *gamin* as for a parliamentarian'.[181] Though chronically down on his luck, he was a tirelessly generous patron to struggling Irish writers in London, especially those from Cork.[182]

As a reforming Tory hostile alike to Wellington and Peel, Maginn thought society was to blame for crime and poverty, clamoured for the protection of

---

178. For this latter claim, see Edward Kenealy, *Brallaghan,* p. 333. I have examined the work of Fr Prout elsewhere, in *Irish Studies Review,* no. 16 (Autumn, 1996).
179. William Maginn, *Miscellaneous Writings,* vol. 1 (New York, 1855), p. 250.
180. *Miscellaneous Writings,* vol. 3, p. 35.
181. Miriam H. Thrall, *Rebellious Fraser's,* p. 164.
182. Maginn helped out the Limerick novelist Gerald Griffin, securing him an introduction to the *Literary Gazette* before he had even met him. The Irish poet William Allingham, who edited *Fraser's Magazine* after Maginn, reports a visit with Thackeray to Francis Mahony in Paris, when they discovered that he had taken into his apartment a penniless young man from Cork (*A Diary* [London, 1907], pp. 77–8).

labour against capital, and inveighed in Ruskinian style against the Benthamite quantifying of human needs. He opposed capital punishment, child labour and debtors' prisons (the latter, perhaps, with a mild touch of self-interest), and held that Britain could never adequately hold down an O'Connellite Ireland. He was also an implacable Orange opponent of Roman Catholic rights, a supporter of the landed interest who praised Burke for having rescued Britain from the revolutionary demon. In Maginn's politics, the values of a largely pre-industrial, patrician-governed Ireland, with only a minority middle class and a consequent dearth of liberal ideology, are transmuted into a critique of British bourgeois Utilitarianism of a classical 'Culture and Society' kind.[183] What appears in Ireland as a defence of Protestant Ascendancy privilege is radicalised in its shift to the industrial-capitalist metropolis.

This ambivalence crops up in Maginn's attitudes to both nations. He writes in a reverent obituary notice of Walter Scott that 'all those who love their native land must be more or less Tory in soul',[184] but it is not quite clear which of his own possible native lands Maginn himself has in mind. The fact that Scott's is Gaelic does not necessarily entail that Maginn's is too. In a savage review of a novel by the Scot Grantley Berkeley, which issued in a bungled duel between the two men,[185] he lauds the English aristocracy as 'the first body in the world' and snobbishly defends them against Berkeley as 'a class of which he knows as little as the scavenger who sweeps their crossing'.[186] This is Maginn the English insider anxiously parading his superior knowledge of London against his fellow-Gaelic blow-in. A similar stance is assumed, to begin with at least, in a piece on 'Irish Genius', which starts by proclaiming that 'really, in England, less is known about Ireland than about any other country of the same importance in the world'. The country is one dreary catalogue of massacres and assassinations, and even Caliban would disdain O'Connell for a god. 'All these things', Maginn comments, 'do and should deeply prejudice and incense us against impracticable Irishmen'. The 'us' here clearly includes the author among the English. But Maginn then proceeds to provide a lengthy list of distinguished Irishmen, all the way from the Wellington he detests ('the very topmost man of all the world'), to John Wilson Croker ('the creator of your periodical literature'), the flower of the

183. See the English tradition of radical-humanist criticism of industrial capitalism recorded in Raymond Williams's *Culture and Society 1780–1950* (London, 1958). One of Maginn's novels, *John Manesty, the Liverpool Merchant* (London, 1844), has the staid, dissenting capitalist Manesty as its villain. His other surviving novel, *Whitehall; or George IV* (London, 1827), is equally poor stuff.

184. *Miscelleneous Writings*, vol. 5, p. 179. Scott has a glancing compliment for Maginn as an editor in *The Private Letter-Books of Sir Walter Scott* (London, 1930), pp. 40, 47.

185. It also nearly issued in the death of James Fraser, the proprietor of the journal, who was beaten senseless by Berkeley and never fully recovered.

186. *Miscelleneous Writings*, vol. 5, p. 289.

journalistic wits ('the brighter monuments of your literature'), and Edmund Burke, responsible for 'the finest orations ever yet composed, in any language, with the solitary exception of the orations of Demosthenes'. The pronouns have now significantly shifted, from 'us' to 'your'. All the English comedy worth reading except Shakespeare has been produced by the Irish, he declares with only a mild degree of inaccuracy, and he even has the barefaced cheek to throw in the odious creep Thomas Moore, 'a song-writer second only to Beranger'.[187] The semantic slipperiness of the passage is the sign of an intriguing problem of identity. It is perhaps not entirely surprising that on his death-bed Maginn asked for a book on Cork.

It would seem, then, unclear to Maginn just what constitutes his native land. On the one hand he can pen a fulsome ode on George IV's visit to Ireland, with some grotesque imagery of the very bogs rising up and travelling long distances to address their monarch.[188] On the other hand he can assail popular Irish songs, some of them penned by Celtophile English authors, as despicably ignorant of the country in their allusions or turns of phrase. Maginn certainly acted the stage-Irishman, bullyingly accusing the Celtic-feminised Moore of lacking his own rollicking Gaelic virility; but he had a keen nose for Irish kitsch as well.

There are other connections between Maginn's Irishness and his Toryism. 'There is', he writes, 'an easiness, a suavity of mind, engendered by Toryism, which it is vain for you to expect from fretful Whiggery or bawling radicalism'.[189] Toryism is an enemy of moral earnestness, and so is the émigré Maginn, a writer who like Oscar Wilde is devoted to surfaces and distinctly wary of depths. 'There is not a truer saying in the world', he comments in Wildean vein, 'than that the truth lies on the surface of things . . . Nothing that is worth having or knowing is recondite or difficult to be discovered . . . I therefore take things easy'.[190] If this is in one sense the doctrine of the hard-pressed hack, it is equally a kind of conscious colonial perversity, a snook-cocking dismissal of portentous English moralism and an insistence on the

187. ibid, pp. 197–200. 'Odious creep' refers to Maginn's judgement on Moore, not mine.

188. There would seem something of a minor tradition in Irish literature about moving bogs. A shifting bog figures centrally in Bram Stoker's novel *The Snake's Pass* (London, 1890), and there is also an Irish ballad by the present author entitled 'The Moving Bog of Mayo', which contains some imagery strikingly akin to Maginn's, though composed without an awareness of his own verse. This would seem a plain case of unconscious plagiarism. Patrick Brontë, father of the Brontë sisters, also penned a poem about a bog which suddenly erupted near Haworth. See 'The Phenomenon, or, an Account in Verse, of the Extraordinary Disruption of a Bog' (1824), in *Bronteana* (Bingley, 1898), p. 201, a poem offered by Brontë as a prize for Sunday school pupils.

189. *Miscellaneous Writings*, vol. 1, p. 247.

190. ibid, p. 148.

triviality of metropolitan metaphysics ('the zeal about nothings, the bustle about stuff')[191] in comparison to such weighty matters as how to toast cheese, discovering the best way to support your drawers[192] and tossing off pseudo-Japanese lyrics. 'What is an old roofless cathedral', he muses, 'compared to a well-built pie?'[193] Just as the colonial expatriate finds the priorities of the insiders ridiculously self-important, so the genteel Tory insider is he who refuses to hierarchalise, savouring trifles with a Sterne-like or Beckettian digressiveness, disturbing the conventional order of bourgeois normality with a programmatic eccentricity.

As with Wilde, this is both radical and patrician together. Maginn's contempt for English middle-class moralism is nowhere plainer than in his coruscating parodies of Wordsworth, author of 'My Great Poem on My Own Life', whose leaden, portentous prose style he wickedly mimics. An 'Irish' laid-backness thus consorts with a complacent Tory pragmatism, just as a certain Gaelic distaste for the abstract fits well with an English conservative nervousness of ideas. In carnivalesque style, Maginn stubbornly refuses to acknowledge the reality of anything beyond the sensuous body; what is real is what he can drink. Indeed for William Hazlitt this sluggish confinement to the immediate circuit of one's sensations was more or less definitive of Toryism. It is not hard to detect beneath Maginn's free-booting *carpe diem* style a touch of hedonistic nihilism, a profoundly superficial sense that nothing really matters, which carries with it echoes of colonial futility.[194] His brief fable 'A Story without a Tail' turns out to be, in Sterne-like mode, entirely phatic or self-referential, all to do with some dinner-table conversation which everyone present is too drunk to remember. Maginn is rarely so hollow as when he is swashbuckling: the stage-Irish persona, lived out with impeccable consistency, has an air of masking an abysmal non-identity.

It is ironic, then, given his upending of norms and taxonomies, that Maginn was like Mahony a dedicated classicist of rare distinction, committed to notions of order, truth and centrality.[195] This shameless subjectivist is profoundly allergic to Romantic subjectivism, which he never ceases to guy. Shel-

191.   ibid, p. 248.
192.   This seems a peculiarly Irish dilemma: George Moore has some suavely malicious comments on William Yeats's inability to keep his trousers up in *Hail and Farewell*.
193.   *Miscellaneous Writings*, vol. 1, p. 150.
194.   In a novel by a later rebellious Irish writer, the tormented protagonist, contemplating the metaphysical pointlessness of human existence, cries out: 'Oh hell, now I understand Rabelais!' See Liam O'Flaherty, *The Black Soul* (London, 1924), p. 88.
195.   The classicism of both men had been anticipated by the great Cork painter James Barry, who harnessed it to national motifs. See Luke Gibbons, 'A Shadowy Narrator: History, Art and Romantic Nationalism in Ireland 1750–1850', in Ciaran Brady (ed.), *Ideology and the Historians* (Dublin, 1991).

ley's *Adonais* becomes in his hands 'Weep for my Tomcat! All ye Tabbies, weep. . .', full of lush, vulgar hyperbole. Like Mahony, Maginn is at once intensely intellectual and vehemently anti-idealist, scornful of Tom Moore's ethereal blandishments and determined in Swiftian fashion to deflate them by crude materialist travesty. Moore's last rose of summer becomes in Maginn's send-up the last lamp of the alley in an inebriated stagger home. What has happened is that Tory satiric classicism has now itself become marginal, deviant and eccentric, its situation at odds with its own beliefs. It is left with the kind of carnivalesque blending of sensualism and intellectualism which Maginn finds exemplified in the figure of Falstaff: 'sensuality in the lower features of his face, high intellect in the upper'.[196] Knowledge, if it is to be authentic, must keep contact with the body and with common life, so that in his riposte to Richard Farmer's denigration of Shakespeare's learning, Maginn deploys his own vast erudition to mock Farmer's nit-picking academicism.

Maginn himself is not an academic but a man of letters, a more capacious, sociable, popularising role.[197] His translation of Homer into popular ballad form rather than traditional pentameters – a carnivalesque move in itself – made his versions read more like parodies than serious renderings, though they were rated highly by Matthew Arnold.[198] As the editor of the Homeric ballads comments, he was a classicist who nevertheless 'addressed himself to the great body of the reading public'.[199] Miriam Thrall maintains that some of his anti-Whig articles were reprinted as pamphlets and sold in tens of thousands,[200] and Francis Mahony had his own fifteen minutes of fame too, when his Italian version of 'The Groves of Blarney' was lustily sung by Garibaldi's troops.[201] Maginn is hostile at once to academicist pedantry and Romantic

196. *Miscelleneous Writings*, vol. 3, p. 40. Maginn's translations of Horace were likewise greeted as 'at once genuinely classical and unmistakably Irish' by Michael Monahan, *Nova Hibernia* (New York, 1914), p. 252.

197. See, for the contrast, John Gross, *The Rise and Fall of the Man of Letters*, T. W. Heyck, *The Transformation of Intellectual Life in Victorian England* (London and Canberra, 1982), and my own *The Function of Criticism* (London, 1984). For London periodicals of the day, see Walter Graham, *English Literary Periodicals* (New York, 1966).

198. See W. B. Stanford, *Ireland and the Classical Tradition* (Dublin, 1977), p. 170. Maginn's Homeric translations can be found in volume 4 of his *Collected Works*. Matthew Arnold has some comments on them in his *On Translating Homer* (London, 1862).

199. Maginn, *Miscelleneous Writings*, vol. 4, p. 7. Maginn was not entirely free of the taint of academicism. See his essay 'Did Hannibal Know the Use of Gunpowder?', ibid, vol. 5, which suffers considerably from not being a parody.

200. Thrall, *Rebellious Fraser's*, p. 117.

201. See Charles A. Read, *The Cabinet of Irish Literature* (London, 1880), vol. 3, p. 302. Read describes Mahony with some justification as 'entitled to a place among the great masters of comedy' (p. 303).

naturalism or libertarianism; if he has the colonial's distaste for formality, he shares the Tory's suspicion of spontaneity. Too sceptically rationalist to trust to the impulses of the heart, he is equally scornful of cold-blooded scholarship. If he knows more than the academics, he values it less. His erudite derision of learning is a typically carnivalesque feature, more Irish-European than English. It involves what Maginn calls 'despising the rabble of the wise',[202] and relates to his Nietzschean call for a philosophy of laughter ('To all, therefore, who do not wish to remain in ignorance . . . we recommend a loud, a hearty, a continuous roar').[203]

Maginn enjoyed an enviable reputation in the nineteeth century. One critic claims extravagantly that Swift fell far short of him,[204] while Edward Kenealy wrote in his obituary in the *Dublin University Magazine* that he was the most universal scholar of his time, a Rabelais shorn of the grossness and obscenity. A biographical note in the *Irish Quarterly Review* found that he could be compared only to Lucian, Rabelais and Fielding.[205] For William Jerden, Scottish editor of the *Literary Gazette,* his career was 'devious, zigzag, coruscating',[206] while Miriam Thrall hails him as 'the greatest magazinist of the nineteenth century' and 'among the best parodists of the English language'.[207] Byron, whose biography was offered to a still unknown Maginn but finally went to Thomas Moore, lavished praise on his work. The stuff-shirted Mrs Oliphant was as usual rather less affirmative when it came to the Irish: for her Maginn was the 'crystallised Paddy', whose history was 'never written at any length or deserving to be so'. Thackeray's portrait of him as Captain Shandon was in some respects too good for him, and 'it is almost immoral to be sorry for him'.[208] The Irish Fraserians aimed at no patriotic goal and added nothing to the honour of their country. Indeed it would be useful, she reflects, if engineering science could move 'that uneasy Erin out into the wide Atlantic'.[209] D. E. Enfield, in a monograph on Maginn's probable lover Letitia Landon, who killed herself in a messy imbroglio involving the Corkman, remarks that Maginn was as incapable of 'carrying out any long-continued labour as the aborigines of Central Africa'.[210]

202. *Miscelleneous Writings,* vol. 3, p. 71.
203. *Miscelleneous Writings,* vol. 5, p. 121.
204. John Timbs, *Anecdote Lives of the Later Wits and Humourists* (London, 1874), vol. 2, pp. 152–3.
205. *Irish Quarterly Review,* no. 7 (September, 1852), p. 622.
206. William Jerden, *An Autobiography* (London, 1832), vol. 3, p. 82.
207. Thrall, *Rebellious Fraser's,* pp. 5, 235.
208. Mrs Oliphant, *Annals of a Publishing House,* pp. 362–4.
209. Mrs Oliphant, *The Literary History of England* (London, 1882), vol. 3, pp. 265, 251.
210. D. E. Enfield, *A Mystery of the Thirties* (London, 1928), p. 101. There is a brief personal memoir of Maginn by Mrs K. Thompson, *Recollections of Literary Characters and Celebrated Places* (London, 1854), which mentions his great admiration for Swift (p. 7). See also Rev Peter Webster, *The Closing Years of William Maginn* (Cork, n.d.)

If Samuel Hall and Crofton Croker could be said, from the viewpoint of their fellow Corkonians, to have risen without trace, both Mahony and Maginn have today met the opposite fate. Yet Thrall's judgement on Maginn as one of the greatest parodists of the language is probably just, and Mahony is a wonderfully rewarding wit. A university of Blarney of which they were patrons would not be out of place.

Carnival is by no means as attractive a world as it sounds. It is full of aggression, male bravado and coarse buffoonery, and the rugby-club-like Fraserians were no exception. Their swaggering sub-culture, boisterous and misogynist, could apparently deconstruct every opposition but gender.[211] Even Miriam Thrall, one of their most steadfast fans, is constrained by her gender to note that Maginn's writing 'smacks of the tavern and the drunken braggart'.[212] There is a strain of calculative, self-fashioning roguery here, a kind of carnival raised to self-consciousness, which will pass straight into the stage-Irish rollickings of Samuel Lover. Perhaps the debauchery of the Cork Fraserians reflects something of their background: Ian d'Alton describes the Cork Ascendancy of the 1830s and '40s as 'as publicly dissolute as any in the United Kingdom'.[213] For Maginn, civilisation and intoxication were well-nigh synonymous: with his customary eye for the sliding signifier, he suggests that the latter is how the former is pronounced when drunk.[214] Textual experiment and inebriation are both forms of semantic slurring. Michael Monahan, who rates Mahony and Maginn as 'the two wittiest Irishmen of the last century', sees them both as belonging to an 'Age of Drink' in English culture, which he dates with suspicious accuracy from the mid-eighteenth century to the early nineteenth.[215] Yet it could also be claimed that the carnivalesque is a major Irish genre, remarkably persistent in the national culture over several centuries, and that the Cork Fraserians belong in this sense to a distinctively Irish lineage.[216]

211.   Though Maginn has some unexpectedly acute remarks on Shakespeare's women in his *Shakespeare Papers* (London, 1859), defending Lady Macbeth (who did it all for the love of her husband) and claiming that there is only one fallen woman in the entire *oeuvre*. He also insists that Latin literature sadly produced no female character of the faintest memorability, and speaks out against misogyny (pp. 142–87). Maginn has in general some shrewd insights into Shakespeare, salvaging Bottom from the condescension of posterity, perceiving that Timon's altruism is really a monstrous egoism, and remarking of Romeo that 'the sorrows which we can balance in such trim antitheses do not lie very deep' (p. 71).

212.   Thrall, *Rebellious Fraser's*, p. 126.

213.   Ian d'Alton, *Protestant Society and Politics in Cork*, p. 232.

214.   *Miscelleneous Writings,* vol. 1, p. 150.

215.   Michael Monahan, *Nova Hibernia*, p. 205.

216.   For Irish carnival, see Vivian Mercier, *The Irish Comic Tradition* (Oxford, 1962), especially chs. 2 and 3. Mercier has some brief comments in his book on Mahony and Maginn (pp. 221–5).

The reasons for this persistence are no doubt legion. Carnival is part of the popular culture of most European societies, and it is arguable that Irish writers, deprived for the most part of a full-blown literary institution insulated from society as a whole, preserved by and large more popular roots than their British counterparts. Daniel Corkery argues a vaguely Bakhtinian case of this kind in *The Hidden Ireland*: Renaissance art, for him as for Bakhtin, is an essentially artificial, unpopular construct, but in Ireland it encountered an already mature vernacular culture which was able to resist being suppressed by it.[217] Whatever the truth of this speculation, Irish writers sprang from a society with only a slim, fairly recent middle class, and were thus in general less straitjacketed by an entrenched bourgeois morality than the metropolitan nation. The amorphousness of colonial life, its want of clear linear direction and self-identity, its relative lack of tightly autonomous individual subjects, also lent itself to the sprawling collectivism of the carnivalesque.

Ireland's heteroglossia, as a nation in which distinct tongues were closely interwoven and sometimes politically at odds, made it a natural home for dialogism and polyphony.[218] Carnival, moreover, is a notoriously violent affair, and so was much of Irish society. 'It is hard to look at some of the manifestations of Irish collective violence', writes Charles Townshend, 'especially the clearly structured faction fight and sectarian riot, without seeing in them some element of carnival'.[219] A scandalous mingling of the sacred and the profane easily took root in a culture which was at once profoundly religious and replete with pagan residues.[220] The carnivalesque relativises all values in reaction to oppressive ideological absolutisms, and clerical Ireland was an obvious breeding ground for such anti-foundationalist high jinks. Mahony and Maginn, as we have seen, were both absolutists and relativisers together. Carnival mocks the ruling class, inverting high and low, and there was plenty of motivation for that in a nation where the governors were palpably alien. A Maginn short story turns on a question of mistaken identity between a noble lord and a domestic servant, both of whom are known as 'Butler'.[221] Some echoes of Goldsmith's *She Stoops to Conquer* can perhaps be detected here.

217. Daniel Corkery, *The Hidden Ireland* (Dublin, 1925), pp. 153 f.
218. W. B. Stanford (*Ireland and the Classical Tradition*, p. 176) points out that Mahony's macaronic use of so-called bog Latin, which combines Latin words with English grammar and syntax, harks back to Swift and the Norman period, and passes on to Carleton and Joyce.
219. Charles Townshend, *Political Violence in Ireland* (Oxford, 1983), p. 45.
220. For a fascinating account of this Irish *mélange*, see S. J. Connolly, *Priests and People in Pre-Famine Ireland* (Dublin, 1982). Maginn has a short story which figures a drunken underworld assembly of Irish saints chaired by St Patrick, a kind of celestial equivalent of the Fraserian drinking club. See 'A Vision of Purgatory' in his *Ten Tales* (London, 1933).
221. See 'The Two Butlers of Kilkenny', ibid.

An iconoclasm of learning is an essential trait of carnival, and a tradition of mock erudition goes back a long way in Ireland.[222] A medieval text like *The Vision of Mac Con Glinne* is a blasphemous parody of clerical scholarship. A nation with strong lineages of scholastic learning, but also with a poverty-stricken material life, is likely to be acutely aware of the (tragi)comic tensions between high and low, the sublime and the ridiculous. Indeed one might claim that the figure of bathos is one of the most recurrent of all Irish comic tropes.[223] 'If the Irish have a highly developed appetite for the magical and the marvellous', writes Vivian Mercier, 'their sense of the ludicrous has reached an equally high pitch of development.'[224] Francis Hutcheson pivots his theory of comedy on just such an oscillation: 'If any writing has obtained a high character for grandeur, sanctity, inspiration, or sublimity of thoughts, and boldness of images', he writes, 'the application of any known sentence of such writings to low, vulgar, or base subjects, never fails to divert the audience, and set them a laughing.'[225] Freud, who regarded all thought as a form of sublimation, would no doubt have explained this in tems of the sudden unbinding of psychic energies which have been invested in the labour of thinking and can now be expended instead in laughter. Even Patrick Pearse, not usually considered the most rib-tickling of Irish figures, speaks up for the therapeutic value of laughter in his essay of 1913, 'From a Hermitage', and throughout his writings displays flashes of a dry sardonic wit quite at odds with the popular image of him.[226]

Part of what the original Dublin audiences found most offensive in Synge's *The Playboy of the Western World* – its mixture of tragedy and burlesque – was not in fact a sullying of some pure Celtic spirit, but was derived by Synge from the oral tradition on which his story was founded.[227] Douglas Hyde notes that in Irish folk song 'the most beautiful sentiments will be followed by the most grotesque bathos', and attributes this to the fact that the texts are often composites, replete with borrowings, interpolations, improvisations.[228] Two traditional aspects of carnival – the mingling of discourses and a veering from high to low – are here brought interestingly together. As far as bathos goes, the Irish nationalist George Russell (AE) writes to a friend that 'The gods have returned to Erin and have centred themselves in the sacred mountains and blow the fires through the country . . . Can you tell me some moderate priced hotel (in Sligo)

222.   See Robin Flower, *The Irish Tradition*, pp. 75–6.
223.   The first published work of Bram Stoker, author of *Dracula*, was sensationally entitled *The Duties of Clerks in Petty Sessions in Ireland*.
224.   Mercier, *The Irish Comic Tradition*, p. 12.
225.   R. S. Downie (ed.), *Francis Hutcheson: Philosophical Writings* (London, 1994), p. 53.
226.   See *Collected Works of Padraic H. Pearse: Political Writings and Speeches* (Dublin, 1917–22).
227.   See Leerssen, *Remembrance and Imagination*, p. 220.
228.   Douglas Hyde, *Language, Lore and Lyrics* (Dublin, 1986), p. 144.

to put up at?'[229] The very style of J. M. Synge seeks to fuse lofty idealism and everyday life, while his dramatic actions often rip them apart. In post-Revival Ireland, writes Seamus Deane, 'the discrepancy between mythological grandeurs and quotidian pettiness [became] so severe that it became impossible to incorporate them satisfactorily in fiction'.[230]

The urge to debunk and disfigure, which is not wholly separable from the belligerence of a colonised culture, runs deep in Irish letters, and the impulse to cut savagely down to size is not perhaps surprising in a country which felt that something of the kind had been done to itself. It is an impulse apparent all the way from Swift's crassly materialist suspicion of idealism, or Tristram Shandy's empiricist scepticism of his father's high rationalist insanity, to the conflict between Stephen and Bloom in *Ulysses* and Flann O'Brien's reduction of humans to bicycles. This is less the epistemological scepticism of Humean England than a farcical sense of the overweeningness of learning in a socially devastated society. There may also be a Christian sense of the futility of such scholarship for salvation, in a 'holy fool' tradition which is central to the carnivalesque. The severe asceticism of Irish monastic culture runs up against an intellectual aestheticism, a delight in words and concepts for their own sake. Few moves are more crucial to Irish comedy than a self-ironising double-take on imposing intellectual notions, a pitting of clown against priest, sometimes in the same body. And there may even be a dim resonance here of a Gaelic cultural tradition which is nervous of the abstract and wedded to the sensuous particular.

That sensuous particular, in classical carnival, is generally the body, and it is remarkable how often in Irish writing the body intervenes to bring low Reason's hubristic schemes. Yahoos against Houyhnhnms, Mangan's decaying members at odds with his German metaphysics, Bloom *contra* Stephen, Yeats's Crazy Jane cheeking the bishop, O'Casey's hopeless male topers versus his morally idealised women, Lucky's hat as against his mumbled shards of scholasticism, the libidinal at war with the theological in Kavanagh or Austin Clarke: much of this is already foreshadowed in *Tristram Shandy*, the most typical novel in Irish literature,[231] where as we have seen already biological accident, a slip of the signifier or sheer senseless material process loom up to disrupt Walter Shandy's paranoid projects. Maginn, along with a host of others, dubbed Sterne 'the British Rabelais',[232] and his favourite reading matter was Rabelais and an Irish song-book.

But the body in Irish literature is not always of the riotous variety. There is nothing erotic about the Yahoos, or about Beckett's poor forked creatures. Those hairless balls and squatting skeletons in Beckett are a form of extreme

229. Alan Denson (ed.), *Letters of AE* (London, 1961), pp. 17–18.
230. Seamus Deane, *A Short History of Irish Literature* (London, 1986), p. 202.
231. To adapt the celebrated slogan of the Russian Formalist Victor Shlovsky, for whom Sterne's anti-novel was 'the most typical in world literature'.
232. *Miscelleneous Writings*, vol. 5, p. 200.

epistemological scepticism, but to no emancipatory end. Mockery does not foreshadow here a fresh creation, as it does in carnivalesque art. It was the body which destroyed both Wilde and Parnell. The Irish body is famished as well as festive, and there was in the end nothing funny about Maginn's descent into dipsomania. So much is clear from the career of James Clarence Mangan, who can be seen as a kind of tragic version of the Corkonian jesters. Intertextuality, the play of masks and modes, the digressive, derivative and dissolute: all these are at work with him too, but there was little joy in them, and he was to die a solitary, squalid death.[233] There are lethal as well as liberatory forms of non-identity, and a colonial history is likely to know both, in curious combinations.

Canon Sheehan, himself a Cork man, complains in his novel *The Graves at Kilmorna* (1915) that 'For sixty years we have not produced a decent artist – that is, since Maclise died; nor a single sculptor, since Hogan died; nor a single architect, since Barry died' (ch. 33).[234] In fact, roughly around the time of this utterance, Cork was experiencing something of a second renaissance, greeting the birth of the twentieth century with something of the panache with which it had seen in the nineteenth. Under the tutelage of Daniel Corkery, a man of cosmopolitan cultural interests, Sean O'Faolain and Frank O'Connor were to emerge as major writers, and the Cork Dramatic Society, for which Corkery was a writer and Terence MacSwiney a director, was a seed-bed of cultural growth.[235] There was an active Gaelic League branch and the Literary and Scientific Society lived on, to provide yet another forum for artistic debate. Just as politics and letters had fused in the early nineteenth century, so they did once more in one of the country's most militant republican centres. An unusual number of Irish nationalist figures sprang over the years from County Cork, from Thomas Davis to Michael Collins, and Tom Garvin has shown how southern Munster, with its small-scale production, fertile agricultural land and low-profiled industry, was the kind of 'developmentally intermediate' zone from which nationalism classically stems.[236] As far as literary production went, the county was to witness a new efflorescence with Somerville and Ross, Peadar Ua Laoghaire, Patrick Sheehan, Lennox Robinson and Elizabeth Bowen. Cultural Cork had come alive again, though

233. See David Lloyd, *Nationalism and Minor Literature*, especially chs. 3 and 4.
234. Sheehan seems to have overlooked the great Irish sculptor John Henry Foley (died 1874). There is a note on Foley in Sarah Atkinson, *Essays* (Dublin, 1896).
235. A valuable account of these cultural energies can be found in Patrick Maume, *Daniel Corkery and the Search for Irish Ireland* (Belfast, 1993). Vivid cameos of the Cork of the day are to be found in Sean O'Faolain's novels *A Nest of Simple Folk* (New York, 1934) and *Bird Alone* (London, 1936). See also Corkery's own grim fictional portrayal of the city as a place of frustrated yearnings and tormented souls in his novel *The Threshold of Quiet* (Dublin, 1917).
236. Tom Garvin, *Nationalist Revolutionaries in Ireland 1858–1928* (Oxford, 1987), Conclusion.

the resurgence should not be idealised. As with its earlier flowering, the city's artistic life was a secret to the great majority of its inhabitants, and most of its writers escaped as soon as they could, as they had done a century before. Half of the city's houses had no water closet, and the place was ridden with small-pox, enteric fever and tuberculosis.[237] Cork is 'a most cultivated centre of the arts', John Aloysius O'Sullivan insists to an impressionable foreigner in Sean O'Faolain's story 'The Old Master', lying strategically through his teeth.

237.   See Maurice Harmon, *Sean O'Faolain: A Life* (London, 1994), p. 16.

HOME AND AWAY
Internal Émigrés in
the Irish Novel

Jane Austen wrote *Mansfield Park* only once, whereas Maria Edgeworth wrote it several times over. The heroines of Edgeworth's novels of English high society are more lively than Austen's dull, dutiful Fanny Price; but like Fanny they court the suffering and solitude involved in upholding moral standards in a society where most other people flout them. The irony of this is clear: to be an outcast in this world is not to trangress common moral norms but to stay faithful to them. Fanny is an outsider who adheres to the aristocratic ideal more conscientiously than the nobility themselves, and as her surname suggests must reckon the cost of this contradiction. It is surely no accident in this respect that both Austen and Edgeworth have an ambivalent relation to English high society, inside and outside it simultaneously: the former as a gentlewoman of modest means, the latter as part of a provincial and thus second-class gentry.

So it is that the stylish but dissipated Lady Delacour of *Belinda* (1811) casts off the virtuous heroine, suspecting her of an affair with her drunken sot of a husband. Belinda will finally redeem her frivolous, nihilistic but essentially good-hearted protectress, but not before she has endured the victimage of the innocent. Lady Delacour represents art, fiction, scheming, theatricality, in contrast to Belinda's untutored transparency, and one character in the novel remarks that 'half the miseries of the world arise from foolish mysteries – from the want of courage to speak the truth'. But if Edgeworth was true to her own precept, her fiction, which like most realist novels trades in secrets, revelations, misinterpretations, would never get off the ground, so that the artist and the moralist are to this extent at odds. As with Austen, one must steer a precarious course between artfulness and gullibility, as virtue finds itself unable to promote its ends without negotiating the deceitfulness of others, and so risks being contaminated by it. If Lady Delacour is all too cultural a creature, the Rousseauesque young Virginia, who we are asked to believe has never laid eyes on a man, is all too natural. Nor is the mischievous iconoclasm of the cross-dressing Harriet Freake any true alternative to social falsity, alluringly postmodern though she may appear. Idiosyncratic insiders like Harriet are allowed to kick over the traces from time to time, whereas the vulnerable Belinda needs the conventions for her own protection.

So does the saintly protagonist of *Leonora* (1805), who loses her husband for a while to a considerably more vicious version of Lady Delacour. The novella, a kind of cross between *The Golden Bowl* and *Les Liaisons Dangereuses*, is all about how to win back your philandering spouse by being so supremely self-possessed about his indiscretions that you outshine your rival and end up by securing his admiring homage. Henry James's Maggie Verver may just be a squalid schemer beneath an appearance of sainthood, which is not of course true of Leonora; but Edgeworth's heroine is nonetheless forced by social propriety into just the kind of deceit – the concealment of her jealousy – which she and her author most abhor. Her very refusal to storm is turned against her as emotional frigidity, propriety misread as insensibility. Once again, to uphold the ethical ideals of one's culture is to be forced to its edge as an internal émigré; to conduct oneself with righteousness is to be travestied, marooned, traduced. Just the same is true of the excellent *Helen* (1834), in which Lady Cecilia's duplicitous conduct ends up by exposing the principled young protagonist to scandal and disgrace.[1]

Since Leonora's rival, the manipulative, self-theatricalising Olivia, is Parisian-bred, and since the French cannot believe that a wife can still love her husband after eighteen months of marriage, Leonora herself is bound to appear false in her very authenticity. The French, in Edgeworth's Anglo-Irish eyes, are not only vain, cynical, corrupt and coquettish, easily bamboozled by the metaphysical and tiresomely given to political turbulence. They are also full-blooded sentimentalists, emotional deregulators who hold, transgressively, that the realm of feeling should be free of social considerations, whereas propriety for Edgeworth as for Austen means shaping your emotional life in accordance with certain public codes in order not to damage others. If the affections are not rational then they wax violent and egoistic, a threat to the unprotected in their very seductive intensity. Olivia and her cronies are 'novel-bred ladies' (bred on or by novels?) who are living in a filigree French romance folded within Edgeworth's own stoutly bourgeois-English text. Edgeworth for her part disdains such contrivances, preferring unlike the equally frenchified Oscar Wilde that art should imitate life rather than *vice versa*; but the irony of this is that only her own novelistic art will bring justice to wronged women like Belinda and Leonora. Just as French passion is a manipulative game, so moral realism must raid the resources of literary artifice to validate itself. To affirm your values is thus also to betray them, in that maladjustment of means and ends which is the novel as moral fable.

If this is a structural irony, it is one which Austen seems to appreciate more than Edgeworth. Austen sees what is alluring as well as degenerate about stylishness, and wins her battle not to be seduced by flashy *beaux* she

1. For an account of the novel, see Marilyn Butler, *Maria Edgeworth: A Literary Biography* (Oxford, 1972), ch. 9. For Edgeworth more generally, see Tom Dunne *Maria Edgeworth and the Colonial Mind* (Cork, 1984), and James Newcomer, *Maria Edgeworth* (Lewisburg, 1973). See also Michael Hurst, *Maria Edgeworth and the Public Scene* (London, 1969).

fashioned for damnation. The point about Fanny Price is that she really *is* dull, as the creator of an Emma must have known, but that for the reader to say this outright is to risk colluding with the unscrupulous social order which makes Fanny's piousness entirely necessary. Edgeworth, by contrast, presses the moral ambiguity of a Maria Crawford to positively Laclos-like limits in the monstrous Olivia, so that even if the very act of writing about an hysterical French hedonist is a way of having your sensationalism and decrying it, the moral conflict in question remains essentially unequivocal. Leonora refuses to regain her husband's affections by art; unlike the novella in which she appears, she is incapable of deploying fiction even for morally honourable ends. Morals and manners, the ethical and the aesthetic, are ideally one; indeed in *Helen* Edgeworth quotes Archbishop Ussher on the need to make goodness agreeable. But she instantly goes on to distinguish such amenity from vulgar fun, and insists that the truth must be told whether it is agreeable or not.

Edgeworth's most ambitious orchestration of English high society, *Patronage* (1814), will also need to resort to a palpably literary device to restore the fortunes of the virtuous but victimised Percy family. Indeed the gambit in question, as often in Edgeworth's fiction, is itself a piece of writing: the mislaid deed by which the Percys will be able to repossess their plundered estates. For all her disdain for romance, Edgeworth must insert a reductive moral fable like a rigid spine through her richly complex realism, so that the good may prosper and the wicked get their comeuppance in just the way that they would not in real life. *Patronage*, a disenchanted liberal-rationalist critique of aristocratic corruption and abuse of power, is a curious blending of Jane Austen and George Eliot, combining something of the moral vision of the former with the broad social canvas and complex totalisations of the latter. If it deals with the domestic sphere with Austen-like acuity, it also ventures *à la* Eliot into legal, political and diplomatic issues beyond Austen's compass. Like *Middlemarch*, it is now families as much as individuals who stand at the centre of the narrative, as the upright Percys, doughty refusers of patronage, counterpoint the self-promoting, overreaching Falconers who fawn on the favours of Lord Oldborough. Here as elsewhere in Edgeworth, to be principled is to risk becoming socially deviant, a prey to the depredations and misreadings of the powerful. Morality and society, it would appear, go together only in fiction. The virtuous must be at once more and less rational than the vicious: more wise and prudent, yet less callously calculating. But if the price of rectitude is an eternal vigilance to evil, how can such vigilance not risk undoing one's innocence?

Some of the great figures of Irish fiction are rootless or reclusive souls, all the way from Swift's Gulliver, who can be homeless anywhere, not least at home, to Charles Maturin's Melmoth, Sheridan Le Fanu's Uncle Silas, Hardress Cregan of Gerald Griffin's *The Collegians*, Bram Stoker's Dracula and James Joyce's nomadic Stephen Dedalus and Leopold Bloom. It is no wonder that the short story has bulked so large in Irish writing, tailored as it often is to the consciousness of an alienated individual. But though exile is one of the most central of all Irish experiences, as characteristic of the culture as hearing mass or planting potatoes, what preoccupies Irish fiction in English is less literal expatriation than the plight of the internal or metaphorical émigré – less the dislocations consequent on mass emigration, than the inner fissures of the society which those fugitives leave behind. One recurrent type of internal exile, as with the ludicrously romanticised hero of Charles Maturin's *The Milesian Chief* (1812), is the Gaelic nobleman usurped by the English landlord, a figure also much in evidence in the novels of Lady Morgan. Maturin's protagonist O'Morven is ideally at the centre of his society but in reality an outsider in his own land, and to this extent, if to no other, his plight parallels that of Edgeworth's heroines. The novel describes him as 'this fugitive, this outcast, this rebel' – a rebel, ironically, because he regards himself as a true native in contrast to the false insiders who are no more than English blow-ins. His lover in the novel is Armida Fitzalban, a society belle afflicted by *Weltschmertz* who joins him in his rebellion and thus places herself outside the social order of which she is so fine a flower. More careless than unfortunate, Armida has to be snatched from death twice by O'Morven in the space of a few pages.

The Irish novel returns recurrently to those who are both home and away, present and absent simultaneously. Its most definitive condition is that of a misfit, idealist or outsider trapped within a claustrophobic social order. Formally speaking, this structure involves a paradox: the more the oppressive power of this order is imaginatively realised, the more the ideals of its hounded antagonist are both endorsed and struck ineffectual. In one sense, one might claim, this opposition is no more than a structural requirement of literary realism. For such narratives to get started, something must be fractured or displaced, if only for the sake of triumphantly restoring its integrity at the conclusion. The realist novel thrives upon some form of aberration, which is part of what Georg Lukács meant by describing it as the epic of a world abandoned by God. The picaresque, in which the picaro is prised loose from some originary settlement and thrust out upon the road, is in one sense a fundamental trajectory of realism itself. A community entirely at one with itself generates not narrative but mythology – one reason, no doubt, why romantic nationalism in Ireland could portray the struggle to achieve its goals but not, in novelistic form, those goals themselves.

Some Irish writers try to circumvent this restraint by depicting a self-identical community which is blighted by forces external to it. Charles Kickham's *Knocknagow* (1873), one of the most popular works of Irish fiction of all time, is a celebrated case in point. But the exigencies of realism demand that the forces in question are dramatically realised, which then tends to interweave them with the social order they undermine. Even so, in a *gemeinschaftlich* society like traditional rural Ireland, the estrangement of the lone individual from common mores might seem hard to realise on any dramatic scale – one reason, perhaps, why some of William Carleton's plots are notably thin, or why the essentially unfallen world of a James Stephens finds it hard to launch a consistent storyline. It may also be a reason for the relative absence of tragedy in such writing, which even in cases of well-nigh pathological alienation such as John Banim's *The Nowlans* (1825) feels the need, as a Hardy or an Ibsen would not, to gather such waywardness into a final communal settlement.

There are good reasons, however, why the fiction of internal exile nevertheless thrives in Irish society. For one thing, a burdensome social reality is bound to breed its clutch of aliens, *schöne Seele* at odds with the censorious or monotonous life around them. And since writers, not least in Ireland, are themselves prime examples of such 'unhappy consciousness', it is hardly surprising that it forms the substance of much of their work. Tales of baulked idealists, scapegoated outsiders or quietly desperate dissenters are thus almost always coded commentaries on the relationship between the artist and Irish society. For another thing, since the Irish novel naturally takes Ireland itself as its subject matter, and since that social order is haunted by the experience of a mass flight from the country, the two converge imaginatively in the figure of the internally displaced protagonist, lost, unhappy and at home. A novel set in Ireland can record the leaving of émigrés, but not their actual experience of uprootedness; one which attends to the plight of the emigrant-at-home can explore, metaphorically, something of the condition of actual exile while staying put in the country and so portraying at the same time some of that exile's domestic causes. 'If the Irishman abroad became a rootless colonist of alien earth', writes Sir Horace Plunkett in his gem of well-meaning condescension *Ireland in the New Century*, 'the lot of the Irishman in Ireland has been no less melancholy. Sadness there is, indeed, in the story of "the sea-divided Gael", but, to me, it is incomparably less pathetic than their homelessness at home.'[2] Just as in Dickens's later fiction there is a sense in which everyone is orphaned, so it is possible to see Ireland as populated by nothing but outsiders: on the one hand, a culturally and ethnically foreign governing caste; on the other hand, a Gaelic people which lives its condition as a form of dispossession. Quite who is a 'native' in such a situation is then difficult to say.

No two Irish novelists could be more bizarrely dissimilar than the Protestant Ascendancy landowner Maria Edgeworth and the zealous Catholic nationalist Canon Patrick Augustine Sheehan.[3] Yet what we have seen in

2. Horace Plunkett, *Ireland in the New Century* (London, 1904), pp. 55–6.
3. I should perhaps make it clear that what governs my rather heterogeneous selection of authors in this essay, apart from the question of whether they lend themselves to my theme, is a desire to avoid for the most part writing again on those novels I have already examined in my *Heathcliff and the Great Hunger* (London, 1995, ch. 5), along with a wish to retrieve a range of interesting but neglected Irish authors. Hence the exclusion of writers like Joyce, Beckett, O'Brien and other luminaries, otherwise obvious instances of the theme in question, who in my view have been attended to to the detriment of other Irish authors.

Edgeworth as the social sidelining of the moral idealist emerges in different guise in some of Sheehan's extraordinarily popular fictions in the form of the Irish nationalist who is at once spiritually central and practically washed-up. Myles Cogan, hero of the bitterly disillusioned *The Graves at Kilmorna* (1915), fights in the botched '67 uprising, languishes for ten years in Dartmoor prison, and returns to Ireland as an antediluvian militant disdainfully at odds with what he views with Fenian purism as the sordid materialism of the land agitation. His final act is to take to a political platform and be done to death by the mob, a conclusion well in line with Sheehan's vanguardist contempt for constitutional politics. Cogan represents the true Ireland, but has an élitist contempt for democracy and an aristocratic disdain for the peasant masses. He is thus ideally 'typical' but in fact pushed to the periphery.

Much the same is true of the priggish young clerical protagonist of *Luke Delmerge* (1901), an overbred snob corrupted by high culture who is torn between his Catholic distaste for secular culture and his urge to integrate with the civilised English. One of Maynooth's *crème de la crème*, Luke is contaminated in England by humanism, evolutionary meliorism and dreams of imperialist grandeur, mixes with the upper classes and finds himself estranged from both his native and adopted cultures. Returning to Ireland to a poor parish, his stiff English manners alienate the plain people of Kerry, who respond to his campaign to implant metropolitan habits among them by running him out. Luke will finally shed his absurdly idealist attempts to improve his own people and come instead to embrace them as they are, striving for the kind of pragmatic tolerance represented by Father Dan in Sheehan's most successful novel *My New Curate* (1900). *The Blindness of Dr Gray* (1909) reveals a similar conflict between the austere otherworldiness of Gray, the parish priest, and the humanist proclivities of his curate Henry Liston.

Luke Delmerge's progress is thus the reverse of Joyce's Stephen Dedalus's, one deeper into his homeland after a treacherous cosmopolitan interlude. But the intellectualist Luke whom the novel finally writes off could have written the book himself, whereas the Delmerge whom it approves, a man content not to probe too deeply, probably could not. Sheehan is himself an internal exile, torn between a crudely xenophobic religiosity hostile to secular humanism, and the promptings of a sensitive cosmopolitan spirit pained by parochialism.[4] Since his values are just as anti-aesthetic as Edgeworth's, if for entirely different reasons, his project as a novelist is, like hers, something of a contra-

4. For Sheehan's acquaintance with European culture and philosophy, see Terence Brown, 'Canon Sheehan and the Catholic Intellectual', in *Ireland's Literature* (Dublin, 1988). Some of the fruits of Sheehan's philosophical reflections can be found in his *Under the Cedars and the Stars* (Dublin, 1903). For biographical accounts, see Francis Boyle, *Canon Sheehan* (Dublin, 1927), and M. P. Linehan's hagiographical *Canon Sheehan* (Dublin, 1952). A more recent study is Ruth Fleischman, *Catholic Nationalism in the Irish Revival: A Study of Canon Sheehan, 1852–1913* (London, 1997).

diction in terms. The most surprising aspect of Sheehan's writing is that it reveals a degree of talent. The current aversion to his stridently nationalist fiction overlooks a number of undoubted strengths: his robust popular feeling, his compassion for the dispossessed, his vigorous critique of both industrial capitalism and mindless Whig progressivism. Like Ruskin or Carlyle, Sheehan has all the radical impulses of a full-blooded reactionary, able to satirise the success ethic precisely because he is so benightedly anti-modern. And *Luke Delmerge* is a well-wrought novel, which is more than can be said for the lamentable *Graves at Kilmorna*.

It is more, too, than can be conceded to *The Triumph of Failure* (1898), which partakes in a literary genre – the novel of ideas – notably rare in nineteenth-century Ireland, but only at the cost of serving up great chunks of undigested German metaphysics. For all that, it is interesting that Sheehan is one of the most resolutely intellectualist of Irish novelists, given his clericist scorn for secular culture. Geoffrey Austin, a solitary, spiritually tormented, unemployable scholar at odds with the world, is the very model of the Irish internal émigré, a bohemian who graduates to Kantianism but can never quite reconcile his religious faith with his Germanic philosophy. Austin has a homoerotic hero-worship of the fiery reforming Catholic preacher Charlie Travers, and rediscovers his own faith through him. Travers is falsely imprisoned and dies of tuberculosis, spurned by the rich but beloved by the poor, conjuring spiritual triumph out of worldly failure. Austin himself consummates his estrangement from society by joining a Carmelite monastery. His final rejection of humanistic culture as a Faustian pact with modernity springs from his author's religious chauvinism, but also from a shrewd awareness of the class basis of culture and philosophy, which are fine for the armchair enthusiast but of scant help to the suffering masses. 'One act of kindness is better than all the speculations of Plato', muses Austin, a view which may be controversial but is not necessarily philistine.

Another aberrant idealist is Ralph O'Brien of Gerald O'Donovan's *Father Ralph* (1913), a courageous indictment of a venal, self-serving Catholic church which has betrayed its redemptive mission.[5] O'Brien, the sensitive product of a middle-class Dublin family, is rapidly disillusioned in his priestly vocation by the loutish anti-intellectualism and worldly ambition of the Maynooth seminary, and later by a parish in which the power-hungry clergy are hand-in-glove with the gombeen men. Ralph, who dreams as a boy that Catholics too might produce works as fine as *Robinson Crusoe* and *David Copperfield*, is attracted to theological modernism but falls foul of the hierarchy and abandons the church, cast off by his fanatical mother. The novel ends with his literal exile. As with Maria Edgeworth's heroines, those who take moral values seriously will quickly find themselves on the margin of this materially-minded world. The journalist Fergus O'Hanlon of William Patrick

5.   For O'Donovan, see Peter Costello, *The Heart Grown Brutal* (London, 1977).

O'Brien's *The Plough and the Cross* (1910) is a similar misfit, a romantic-nationalist loner of cosmopolitan cultivation whose dreams are grotesquely at odds with a drably philistine Dublin. Arthur O'Mara in the same novel is a failed priest, rootless and faithless, embroiled like Ralph O'Brien in the modernist theological controversy; and one symptom of the difficult relation of ideas to Irish society is the work itself, a painfully static 'novel of ideas' in which very little happens except talk.

There runs throughout nineteenth-century Irish fiction a kind of political *Bildungsroman*, in which a socially displaced protagonist, alienated from the culture for one reason or another, may finally integrate with it through a nationalist conversion. The outsider thereby becomes an insider, but one politically at odds with the established social order, trading an anti-social solitude for a collective disaffection. Maria Edgeworth's *The Absentee* (1812) is the earliest specimen of this genre, though her hero is 'national' rather than nationalist. A more full-blown version is John Banim's *The Anglo-Irish of the Nineteenth Century* (1828), in which the superior Cambridge-educated aristocrat Gerald Blount, an Irish Anglophile ashamed of his low-bred compatriots, finds himself shipwrecked on the shores of his native land, encounters a fictional version of Daniel O'Connell, and ends up by marrying a mere Irishwoman. A somewhat similar evolution occurs in Gerald Griffin's novella *The Half-Sir* (1827), whose hero Eugene Hammond is both an orphan and a squireen or semi-gentleman, and thus doubly dislocated: 'a mock man . . . not a born gentleman . . . Betwixt and between, as you may say. Neither good potale, nor yet strong whiskey.' Rebuffed by polite society, Hammond turns from it in disgust to become an embittered nomadic radical, finally returning to Ireland to be stirred by its poverty and embrace the nationalist cause.

This, to be sure, is a classic case of what Raymond Williams has termed 'negative identification',[6] as Hammond discovers in political revolt a collectivised image of his own misanthropy, one which moreover proves entirely compatible with gaining an upper-class wife and social respectability. No such integration, however, is available to the transgressor Hardress Cregan of Griffin's *The Collegians* (1829), a genteel insider who puts himself beyond the social pale first by marrying a peasant and then by murdering her. Griffin's story *Suil Dhuv, The Coiner* (1827) turns upon a more literal kind of alienness, dealing as it does with a conflict between Gaelic society and the immigrant Palatine community, in which Denny MacNamara, seeking vengeance on the Palatine Isaac Segur, becomes like Cregan a social outcast.[7] But the most haunting nineteenth-century portrait of the outsider is undoubtedly John

6.   See Raymond Williams, *Culture and Society 1780–1950* (Harmondsworth, 1958), pp. 178–80.

7.   For Griffin, see Thomas Flanagan, *The Irish Novelists 1800–1850* (New York, 1959), pp. 205–51. Biographies are to be had in Daniel Griffin, *The Life of Gerald Griffin* (London, 1843), and John Cronin, *Gerald Griffin* (Cambridge, 1978).

Banim's *The Nowlans*, a powerful if patchily melodramatic study in social transgression, in which the clerical student John Nowlan elopes to Dublin with his lover Letty to become a prototypical internal exile: 'a renegade, a giver of dreadful scandal, a blasphemer, an outcast, a marked sheep' (Part 2, ch. 3). Hounded like Hardy's Jude Fawley and Sue Brideshead from one wretched place of refuge to another, the tragedy gathers to a head when Letty dies in childbirth and John takes to the hills as a deranged hermit. After a period of literal exile in Newfoundland, he returns to Ireland, and as the novel closes is set to resume his clerical studies.[8]

There are twentieth-century versions of this political *Bildungsroman*. George Birmingham's *Benedict Kavanagh* (1907) is one such example, as the protagonist, the illegitimate son of a Parnellite agitator, moves from a shiftless, sceptical existence to a dramatic nationalist conversion. A later version of this turnabout can be found in Francis Stuart's morbidly Romantic *The Coloured Dome* (1932), in which the spiritually rootless hero Garry Delea abandons his cheerless life as a Dublin betting-shop clerk to become a sacrificial republican victim. His lover is Tully McCoolagh, a charismatic revolutionary leader who turns out to be a woman in a bowler hat. The genre is satirised after a fashion by Eimar O'Duffy's somewhat feeble fiction *Printer's Errors* (1922), in which the run-of-the-mill protagonist, oppressed by his dreary career as a printer, gets caught up with the snobbish literati of the Literary Revival.

If the Banim brothers can lapse into melodrama, it is because they parody realism without really intending to, inflate the form beyond what it can decently bear while never abandoning its tenets. It is as if the generic split in Irish fiction as a whole between fantasy and realism reproduces itself within particular novels as the conflict between an unstable individual consciousness and its all-too-material environment. What resolves this ambivalence is so-called Protestant Gothic, which in the hands of a Maturin or Le Fanu can transcend realism while still incorporating it. A novel like *Melmoth the Wanderer* harnesses a fantastically intensified realism to its metaphysical narrative, blending the social and the supernatural in a startlingly new form of literary art. This is not the fiction of the emergent Catholic middle class, which, anxious and alienated though it may be, still manages to contain those broodings within a robust world which is recognisably its own. It is rather the art-form of a class no longer even assured enough to distinguish fact from fantasy, seized by an unreality which now infiltrates the texture of its most commonplace experience. Society for an Edgeworth may occasionally be unreal in the sense of artificial, but it is not ontologically so; in Gothic fiction, by contrast, there is a creeping doubt as to the very reality of identity and experience themselves. What figures in the work of middle-class Catholics like Griffin

---

8.   For the Banims, see Patrick Joseph Murray, *The Life of John Banim* (London, 1857), and Mark D. Hawthorne, *John and Michael Banim: A Study in the Early Development of the Anglo-Irish Novel* (Salzburg, 1975).

and the Banims as the febrile psyche of the disinherited individual, pitched between alternative social identities which are nevertheless solid enough in themselves, has now been as it were collectivised, generalised to a whole social universe in which dread and disorientation are alive even in the weather and landscape and architecture, in the very physiognomy of a seedy Ascendancy culture in which nothing is quite what it seems.[9]

This is true too of the most brilliantly unnerving narratives of Sheridan Le Fanu, of *The House by the Church-yard* (1863) and *Uncle Silas* (1864), though in Le Fanu's inferior work – in a creaky, improbable fiction such as *The Wyvern Mystery* (1869), or in some of the more laboriously spine-tingling short stories – the social and the sensational are more maladroitly intermingled.[10] Le Fanu is superb at capturing the idiom of the uncouth, avaricious minor gentry, but his novels suffer from a dearth of ideas, for which a spurious metaphysical spookiness too often has to do service. Social discourse is narrowed to a kind of bluff, rollicking male sociability, a rattling good yarn whose superficiality is then counterpointed by a pseudo-deep supernaturalism.

Rattling good yarns and jovial male *camaraderie* are also the stock-in-trade of the younger Charles Lever,[11] editor of the *Dublin University Magazine* and (according to his own account) honorary brave of a native American tribe,[12] whose reputation never really recovered from such over-boisterous early efforts as *Harry Lorrequer* (1839) and *Charles O'Malley* (1841). These young army bloods on the loose in a quaintly caricatured Ireland are in one sense exiles, but the soldier on foreign soil is deracinated rather than alienated, since he derives a secure enough identity from his corps. Even when the later Lever presents a considerably more disturbed society, his clubman's wisdom and readily consumable style, skilled but depthless, is the mark of a writer rather too comfortably at home with his materials, churning out one loosely

9.   For Maturin, see Dale Kramer, *Charles Robert Maturin* (New York, 1973), and David Punter, *The Literature of Terror* (London, 1980).

10. See, for an account of Le Fanu, W. J. Mc Cormack, *Sheridan Le Fanu and Victorian Ireland* (Oxford, 1980).

11. For Lever, see Christopher Morash, 'Reflecting Absent Interiors: The Big-House Novels of Charles Lever', in Otto Rauchbauer (ed.), *Ancestral Voices: The Big House in Anglo-Irish Literature* (Hildesheim, 1992). See also ch. 5 of Julian Moynahan's *Anglo-Irish: The Literary Imagination in a Hyphenated Culture* (Princeton, 1995), and the three essays on Lever in A. N. Jeffares, *Images of Invention* (Gerrards Cross, 1996). Charles Gavan Duffy's celebrated assault on the novelist is to be found in 'Mr Lever's "Irish" Novels' (*Nation*, vol. 1 no. 35 [June, 1843]). A weighty Victorian biography of Lever is W. J. Fitzpatrick's *Life of Charles Lever* (London, 1884); for a more accessible account, see Lionel Stevenson, *Dr Quicksilver: The Life of Charles Lever* (London, 1939).

12. This seems to have been something of an Irish tradition. Lord Edward Fitzgerald was also adopted as an honorary native American in Detroit. See Thomas Moore, *Life of Lord Edward Fitzgerald* (London, 1831), vol. 1, p. 147.

discursive novel after another with scant sense of literary tact. If Samuel Beckett writes finely about very little, Lever, much less consciously, does much the same.

Even so, for all their well-bred, laid-back geniality, Lever's novels are awash with rebels, vagrants, eccentrics, misplaced persons, amiable idiots. Man of the world, doctor and diplomatist though he was, his plots, as one critic puts it, 'concern characters who are natural denizens of the periphery, restless, ineffectual, pressurised', and 'his principal characters inhabit wildernesses, inaccessible dwellings, locations far from any centre'.[13] *Sir Brook Fossbrooke* (1866) places at its centre a relic of the old military order. George Grenfell, a genteel English figure in *Luttrell of Arran* (1865), has 'an inordinate liking for those establishments in which a large fortune is allied with something which disqualifies the possessors from taking up their rightful position in society . . . In his estimation, there were no such pleasant houses as those where there was a "screw loose", either in the conduct, the character, or the antecedents of the owners' (vol. 2, pp. 30–1). The Anglo-Irish Ascendancy were to supply Lever with a bountiful source of such material.

The O'Donoghue (1845), in which the wealthy banker Sir Marmaduke Travers has usurped the estate of the ancient O'Donoghue family and exiled them to a dilapidated castle, is keenly aware of a double sort of exile: that of the *parvenu* Ascendancy itself, who are strangers to those they govern, and that of the old Gaelic order who are popular but powerless. It is as though each social group has sidelined the other, to the point where it becomes hard to judge whether the ousters or the ousted are the more marginal. And all this is set in the country's most decayed, peripheral region, the west. The novel centres largely on the O'Donoghues' morose son Mark, a typical internal émigré whose rancour against those who have dispossessed him throws him into the arms of the United Irishmen. Betrayed by his closest colleagues, he flees to France at the end of the novel, exchanging a metaphorical exile for a literal one.

Something of the same conflict can be found in *The Martins of Cro' Martin* (1856), a work in which almost every character seems socially dislodged.[14] The Catholic middle-class *arriviste* Joseph Nelligan, who starts off as a grocer's son and ends up as a Trinity-educated lawyer, suffers the indignities of an outsider in his native Oughterard, caught on the hop as he is between different social classes, but will finally become well-established and socially integrated. Nelligan symbolises a Catholic Emancipation which his liberal-Ascendancy author thoroughly endorses. The landowning Martin family itself, decayed

13.   Tony Bareham, Introduction to Tony Bareham (ed.), *Charles Lever: New Evaluations* (Gerrards Cross, 1991), p. 13, and 'Charles Lever and the Outsider', ibid, p. 105.
14.   For a brief, entertaining account of the actual Martin family of Co. Galway, see Tim Robinson, *Setting Foot on the Shores of Connemara* (Dublin, 1997), pp. 63–5.

gentry saddled with a disastrously encumbered estate, moves in the opposite direction, as the secluded, washed-up old Tory Sir Godfrey and his heartless snob of a spouse meet their nemesis at the hands of new social forces. Sir Godfrey's son is a gambling rake who pledges his estate to a social outsider, the Jewish Merl, while the flashy upstart lawyer Maurice Scanlan skulks in the background brewing mischief. Only young Mary Martin, an idealised Lady Bountiful, upholds the feudalist traditions in her solitary way, dying in devoted service to her tenantry; but though her ethic is admired, it is also anachronistic.

Sir Godfrey loses an election to Jack Massingbred, a carpetbagging young blood who as his name suggests has the edge over the feudalist Martins in his blend of populism and gentility. Massingbred, like Joe Atlee of *Lord Kilgobbin* (1872), is one of Lever's footloose dilettantes, the kind of swashbuckling opportunist who combines canny self-promotion with the shrewd percipience of the detached observer. Such figures in Lever are *parvenus* with no real homeland, sophists who cynically adapt to the local wisdom, and Lever himself is by far the most cosmopolitan of modern Irish writers before Joyce. As an émigré himself, well-versed in the ways of Continental diplomacy and political intrigue, he can bring to bear on Irish society the experience of a seasoned European onlooker, and so does for Ireland in distinctly more minor key what Henry James was to do for its colonial proprietors.[15] Lever's late novel *Luttrell of Arran* (1865) presses the motif of exile to a well-nigh parodic extreme, taking as its protagonist the broken ex-United Irishman outcast John Luttrell, marooned as a haughty, reclusive stranger on Inishmore, and so, as a marginal figure within a marginal society, a kind of upper-class version of Liam O'Flaherty's Skerrett. *Lord Kilgobbin* ends with the elopement of two outsiders, the displaced daughter of a Greek adventurer Nina Kostalergi, and the Fenian rebel Daniel Donogan, for whom the anti-nationalist Lever displays a surprising degree of sympathy. For all its social range, it is a work which is all periphery and no centre.[16]

If displacement seems a common condition in some of Lever's works, much the same can be said of Somerville and Ross's *The Real Charlotte* (1894). The novel's most obvious outlander is the petty-bourgeoise Dubliner Francie Fitzpatrick, but those who represent the Irish upper-class community, and so symbolise the endpoint of Francie's aspirations, are hardly less spiritual vagrants themselves. They include the half-lunatic Sir Benjamin Dysart, a traditionalist relic in a wheelchair; his abstracted artistic son Christopher, 'an acrostic in a strange language', who doesn't quite fit into local society; the English outsider Miss Hope-Drummond at the big house; and Charlotte

---

15. Walter T. Rix explores the international theme in Lever in 'Charles Lever: The Irish Dimension of a Cosmopolitan', in Heinz Kosok (ed.), *Studies in Anglo-Irish Literature* (Bonn, 1982).

16. A point well made by Tony Bareham in 'Charles Lever and the Outsider'.

Mullen, the boldfaced schemer trapped between peasant and gentlewoman. Julia Duffy, a *faux*-genteel, semi-witch-like recluse, ends up in an insane asylum, while her servant Billy Grainy is a former tramp. The novel dramatises various forms of madness, not least the obsessive love for Francie of the social climber Roddy Lambert, as the jovial bluffness and winsome idiosyncrasy of a more innocent Anglo-Irish culture harden into something a good deal more predatory and sinister. This grimly disenchanted fiction offers a world in which those who represent official values are as spiritually derelict as the tricksters and chancers who try to muscle in on them. If the novel itself, in classical realist style, explores the complex intermeshings of a whole social order from top to bottom, what this totality lays bare is the solitude and solipsism of most of its members.

Seumas O'Kelly's novel *The Lady of Deerpark* (1917) also presents us with a gatecrasher into the Ascendancy class, this time in the form of the sinister Kish Massy, a freebooting gold-digger who marries the gentlewoman Mary Heffernan for her money and comes to a sticky end.[17] But there is also a major piece of Irish fiction which deals with the theme of internal exile at the level of the poor Gaelic tenantry. Hurrish O'Brien, the worthy peasant protagonist of Emily Lawless's *Hurrish* (1886),[18] accidentally kills his rival Mat Brady and is consequently alienated both from official society and from his own people, distressed as they are that he did not actually murder the farm-grabbing Brady. The novel's true pariah, however, is not O'Brien but Brady's brother Maurice, who commits the unpardonable trespass of informing on Hurrish to the police, ends up by killing him, and is thrust out by his community to experience literal exile in the United States. From the standpoint of the Burren poor, in a deftly managed irony, the real outsider is not the 'murderer' himself, but the informer.

There is a spirit of ironic dissociation, more typical perhaps of English rather than Irish culture, which reflects the stance of the insider/outsider, and which is the dominant tone of the novels of the Westport-based Church of Ireland minister James Hannay (George A. Birmingham). Birmingham's wry, middlebrow stories centre on the detached pragmatist who believes little or nothing himself but is skilled in mediating the raucous conflicts around him. His various fictional alter egos are a cross between Arnoldian ironist, slick middleclass operator and Gaelic trickster, committed to consensus for its own sake

17.   See for a critical account George Saul, *Seamus O'Kelly* (Lewisburg, 1971).
18.   Lawless died in Surrey, a lethal county for Irish writers. Shan Bullock died in Cheam, Gerald O'Donovan in Albury, Eimar O'Duffy in New Malden and the theologian George Tyrell in Storrington. Bournemouth was also fairly risky, claiming both AE and John Eglinton. The south of England as a whole was a dangerous spot for Irish authors: Kate O'Brien died in Faversham, Kent, Standish O'Grady on the Isle of Wight, and Frederick Ryan in Crawley, Sussex.

and expert in soft-soaping truculent opponents into peaceable coexistence. It is an appropriate posture for a liberal Unionist, whose novel *The Northern Iron* (1907), set in 1798, celebrates the virtues of radical Presbyterians and ecumenically-minded United Irishmen in contrast with later, more sectarian brands of nationalism. Hannay was a Belfast-born Unionist but an associate of cultural nationalists, and in a notorious fracas was banished from the Gaelic League. Something of this political even-handedness is apparent in *Benedict Kavanagh* (1907), a work which lavishes praise both on the loyalist Ulster temperament and on romantic nationalism. Kavanagh, son of a nationalist but reared as a Unionist, is a cultural hybrid, a displaced figure who becomes rebel, sceptic, bohemian, and finally a true heir to his patriotic father. *The Adventures of Dr Whitty* (1913) records in light-hearted style the rivalries and machinations of the quarrelsome western town of Ballintra, with Whitty himself as a wily behind-the-scenes diplomatist who is at once a marginal consciousness and an effective fixer. In *General John Regan* (1913), this role is assumed by the charming, crisis-managing crook Dr Lucius O'Grady, a genial sceptic who spins fibs and fictions in order to get things done, and so is a type of his detached, manipulative author. In *Spanish Gold* (1908), a stiff-upper-lip fable of Spanish armada treasure-hunting in the west of Ireland, the same plot-function is assumed by the Rev Joseph Madden, another ironist, blarney-specialist and man-manager who displays sterling qualities of British leadership among the benighted Irish.

As with most brands of ironic dissociation, Birmingham's is not quite as jovially uncommitted as it seems. His suave, spectatorial amusement at small-town Irish imbroglios is never far from patronage, and his fictional alter egos are a good deal too delighted with their own middle-class ability to run rings round anyone with more conviction and less urbane banter than themselves. All of this comes to a head in *The Red Hand of Ulster* (1912), a fine, extraordinarily clever novel written during the Ulster resistance to Home Rule, when Birmingham could not have known its historical outcome. The narrator is Lord Kilmore, amateur historian and west-of-Ireland grandee, yet another of Birmingham's bland operators who lurks sardonically on the margins of political history but ends up, almost by an oversight, in orchestrating that history from the sidelines. If the vagrant is on the edge of society, so in his own lesiurely way is the gentleman. Kilmore is widely perceived throughout the province as a Liberal, though he is in fact too liberal to be anything of the kind, remarking that moderation never got you anywhere in Ireland and certainly not in Belfast. With his epigrammatic style ('At my time of life even good news ought to be broken to me gradually'), it is as though P. G. Wodehouse had penned a novel about Unionist militancy. Kilmore's whimsical tone, as usual with Birmingham, has the effect of craftily defusing political conflicts, while at the same time concealing his own political prejudices beneath a pose of droll detachment. A civilised irony is Kilmore's chief weapon against the hard-headed money-makers of Belfast, who 'never at any time appreciated paradox', but in the end he is on their side against both the imperial British and the nationalist Gaels. Kilmore is in fact just as opposed to Home Rule as the Belfast philistines he disdains, and sits on political platforms with militant extremists; so that the novel, in liberal Unionist style, succeeds at once in satirising red-neck Unionism through the eyes of this debonair dilettante, and in pressing an anti-Home Rule case. Indeed it goes further, ending up in an ironic reversal by espousing an independent Ireland spearheaded by a militant Ulster anti-Britishness. This is an ingenious way of stealing the Irish nationalists' clothes, presenting Protestant Ulster in a familiar Unionist ambivalence as at once more loyal yet more practical, militant and independent-minded, than its Catholic counterparts. It is they who are the true rebels and activists, in contrast to a tamely constitutional nationalism, so that the novel manages to trump the spineless nationalists while preserving a form of Ulster Protestant hegemony over them. At the same time, true to Birmingham's ecumenical impulse, it satisfies the Catholic nationalists too by achieving in its utopian fantasy the all-Ireland independence which they, or at least some of them, desired.

The Ulster anti-Home Rule movement stages a mutinous meeting in Belfast, which Kilmore watches amusedly from his club window; but once the British fleet sails into the harbour, opens fire on the loyalists and is shot up in return, Kilmore's balance of English irony and Unionist commitment tilts notably towards the latter. In an audacious fantasy, he is sent to Downing Street as plenipotentiary of the Ulster provisional government, and persuades the Prime Minister that he must either mow down Ulster loyalists or grant a wholly independent nation. Once more, it is the insouciant aristocrat, lounging satirically on the sidelines, who turns up trumps when the going gets rough, just as it is the plain burghers of Ulster who can be trusted to sort out a spot of trouble. A new dispensation is secured by upper-class sang-froid, as the rumpish aristocracy become, in a Yeatsian fantasy, the harbingers of a transfigured Ireland.[19] The novel is politically astute and extravagantly farfetched, yoking a gung-ho yarn to some serious political content which nonetheless refuses to take itself wholly seriously. To this extent, it demonstrates at least that the notion of Ulster romance is not an oxymoron. On the

19.   In his essays *Irishmen All* (1913), Birmingham reveals his sympathy for the Ascendancy landlords, with their 'joy in desperate adventure' and toughness of fibre, and hopes wistfully that the Irish farmers may one day turn back to this class for their 'disinterested' leadership. This is perhaps as much a fantasy as imagining an Irish-American Catholic funding an anti-Home Rule movement. For an impressively detailed biography of Birmingham, see Brian Taylor, *The Life and Writings of James Owen Hannay* (Lewiston, NY, 1995). See also Andrew Gailey, 'An Irishman's World', *Irish Review* no. 13 (Winter 1992/93), and the brief comments by Patricia Craig in 'The Liberal Imagination in Northern Irish Prose', in Eve Patten (ed.), *Returning to Ourselves: Hewitt School Papers*, vol. 2 (Belfast, 1995).

one hand, the work is shrewdly realist in probing the contradictions within Ulster loyalism, as law-abiding liberal-Unionist gentry sit cheek-by-jowl with unsavoury Belfast thugs, and foreign adventurers team up with extremist academics. On the other hand, in an outrageous flight of fancy, the Ulster resistance movement is backed by an American millionaire who, as the Catholic child of Famine immigrants, throws his resources behind Protestant rebellion because he is ready to do anything to annoy the British. Since he counts the union with Ireland as a misfortune for the British, he is perversely determined to perpetuate it.

Birmingham's cavalier ironies are also wearing notably thin in *Up the Rebels!* (1917), in which Sir Ulrick Connolly, yet another of his author's plausible, smooth-talking operators, neatly outflanks his daughter Mona's ridiculous attempt to spearhead a rebellion in an Irish town. If Mona (a thinly disguised version of Maud Gonne) suffers from a surfeit of belief, her soft-soaping father suffers from a shortage of it. The novel is thronged with cardboard cut-outs of Irish nationalists and laced with nonchalant patrician wit. Once more, it is tone which gets the better of the hotheads, as the facetious scoffing of Sir Ulrick and the narrator trivialise and defuse the whole portentous affair. Birmingham represents the last outpost of an Arnoldian blitheness of spirit in a belief-ridden society, a spirit which like Matthew Arnold's own is by no means as dispassionate as it would have us believe. His novels are among other things a kind of fantastic compensation for the growing marginality of the Anglo-Irish, as provincial medics and gentlemen scholars turn out with comic improbability to be the stuff of which statesmen are made.

A Gaelic scholar wrote proudly in 1684 that the Iar Connacht region of Galway was free of criminals. What he meant was that there was no law in the district well-defined enough to be broken. The simplest way to abolish alienation is to get rid of the conventions from which you are alienated, and this, in effect, is what happens in some of the novels of James Stephens.[20] In his more fabular writings, Stephens resolves the tension between the anomic individual and a conformist social order by creating an anarchic society, in which spiritual vagabondage has now become a general condition. The police appear, briefly and bunglingly, in *The Crock of Gold* (1912), but the law is more a source of mockery than of fear. Nobody in Stephens is ever really lost, since nobody has ever been at home. His tinkers, tricksters and home-spun philosophers fall below the law rather as Yeats's aristocrats rise above it. Patsy Mac Cann, a tinker who travels with angels in *The Demi-Gods* (1914), 'stood outside every social relation' as a purely natural animal, and the angels themselves, as pure freedom and intelligence, are above all legal or social constraint. Stephens's naturalistic

20.   For critical biographies of Stephens, see Augustine Martin, *James Stephens: A Critical Study* (Dublin, 1977), and Hilary Pyle, *James Stephens: His Work and an Account of his Life* (London, 1965).

ethics pit liberty and loving kindness against any form of social authority, pre-ferring wisdom to knowledge, fragmentary fables to linear narrative, the view-point of a donkey to the rights of property. 'Paris', he writes in his letters, 'is all rather unpleasantly law-abiding'.[21] As far as his view of truth goes, he has little to learn from the post-structuralists: a truth may seem 'round and hardy as a pebble', he writes in *The Demi-Gods*, but in 'the beating of an artery . . . it is split and fissured and transformed'. His anti-hierarchical vision is Blakeian at root, democratically treating the smallest fragments of reality as brimful of cosmic sig-nificance. Stephens has a near-hallucinatory sense of delicate particulars. The energies of his books, he comments in a letter, are to be found in the crevices rather than in the important parts of the plot. If he can write about the Dublin slums, he can also capture the inner being of a fish in 'The Story of Tuan Mac Cairill' from *Irish Fairy Tales* (1920). Indeed his avoidance of grand narratives is in part a prejudice for being ('To Be is to be God', he wrote), as against the fre-netic doing of the literary realists. What he calls in his letters the 'sense of recep-tiveness' which characterises his own work has much in common with Keatsian negative capability and Heideggerian *Gelassenheit*.

This is not, even so, a prelapsarian world, but one shot through with vio-lence and deceit in which sexual relations are often enough power-struggles. If Stephens's characters roam around, it is sometimes in search of food. He himself was set to beg on the streets of Dublin at the age of six.[22] The Stephens who wrote *The Crock of Gold* and the *Irish Fairy Tales* was also the author of the starkly realist *Hunger* (1918) set among the destitute Dublin poor, the realist sexual sketches of *Here Are Ladies* (1913), and a fine eyewit-ness account of the Easter Rising in *The Insurrection in Dublin* (1916). (He notes elsewhere the 'amazing silence' in which the Rising took place.) Myth and naturalism are for him harmonious antitheses, since both escape in dif-ferent directions from the protocols of conventional literary realism. *The Charwoman's Daughter* (1912) unevenly combines both genres in a prototype of magic realism. Stephens's fictions are, in the Benjaminian sense of the term, auratic, resonant like all the best traditional storytelling of a rich, replete world which we have lost, at once vividly present and mythologically remote.

The style of his fables is both humdrum and heroic, astute and naïve, materialist and idealist together. By mixing fantasy with matter-of-factness, his sagas are more tenderly and humanely beautiful than the self-conscious grandeur of, say, a Standish O'Grady. *Deirdre* (1923) strikes a fine balance between fable and realism, humanising and psychologising the Celtic myth while preserving its enchantment. It is no accident that Stephens should rework the tale of an archetypal Irish rebel and outsider, and the work reveals an impressive talent for handling dramatic action. Few Irish writers can blend so adroitly the wondrously otherworldly with the humbly quotidian, or can

21.   Richard J. Finneran (ed.), *Letters of James Stephens* (New York, 1974), p. 71.
22.   See Hilary Pyle, *James Stephens*, p. 5.

match the droll, whimsical charm of his sensibility. Few too are his equal in the creation of beauty. Stephens needs his mundane ironies to toughen his Romantic-libertarian vision, which is otherwise – as in much of his collection of poetry *The Hill of Vision* (1913) – in danger of lapsing into mere breathless apostrophising. So it is that a conversation with an angel in *The Demi-Gods* veers without warning into a brief bout of Marxist analysis.

The full flavour of Stephens's impish wit emerges in his delightful letters, which combine political nationalism with an abrasive critique of Ireland. On the one hand, he thinks Irish history more glorious than any other, and holds that Ireland has never been disloyal to England because she has never been loyal to it. On the other hand he views his country as 'the most comprehensive thug and murderer among the nations, infanticide is her choice pastime, and we who love her . . . should hit her big fat farmery, peasantry (*sic*), gombeeny head with a big stick'.[23] Elsewhere he comments acidly of the Revivalist cult of the peasant that 'every city man goes marching about with a countryman pinned in his hat'.[24] Irish art, he remarks, would be sniffed at in disdain by the average Bushman. But he is also much in favour of the language revival, and close in spirit to the nationalist labours of George Russell. His ambition, he acknowledges, is to write a Balzacian *Comédie Humaine* of Ireland, though he confesses that he doesn't know enough for the project ('I have tons of wisdom but no knowledge' [p. 151]). There is a need for a realist totalisation of Irish culture: 'We lack a mirror, a synthesis, we cannot see ourselves and so we cannot see anything but distortions and nonsense' (p. 154). Joyce has 'the vanity of a peacock and the cheek of the devil', and his *Dubliners* and *Portrait* are 'exceedingly unpleasant' (p. 209); Stephens's own short stories are the best in England, so he impartially observes, but his 'real curse is modesty' (p. 278). 'To all literary men', he reflects, 'words at last cease to be speech and become merchandise' (p. 192) – a view which sits well with the logocentrism of his belief that 'in talk a thing has an air which it loses when a pen is stuck through it' (p. 226).

With Stephens, then, the struggle between the natural and the conventional, individual freedom and social constraint, is transcended by the drastic strategy of collapsing culture into nature. The philosophical problems entailed by such a full-blooded naturalism are blandly passed by, in the manner of creative writers. The all-powerful imagination moulds the material world to its own requirements, rather than encountering it as an obstacle to desire. There is perhaps a faint parallel here with Bernard Shaw's much more

23. *Letters,* pp. 49–50. Subsequent page references are given in parentheses after quotations. For an excellent account of Stephens's work, see John Wilson Foster, *Fictions of the Irish Literary Revival* (Syracuse, 1987), ch. 8. Foster discusses several of the writers under consideration here.
24. Quoted in Brigit Bramsback, *James Stephens: A Literary and Bibliographical Study* (Upsale, n.d.), p. 39.

schematic vitalism, which also discovers a correspondence between human consciousness and the natural world; though if Shaw is a social writer, Stephens's pagan, pantheistic world is essentially pre-social.[25] What has been broken apart in Joyce's *Ulysses* (1922), as Stephen Dedalus's exilic consciousness confronts the placid naturalism of Leopold Bloom, was never riven for Stephens in the first place.

Something of his sensuous lucidity re-emerges in more elaborate form in the novels of Austin Clarke, which are considerably finer than the bulk of his poetry.[26] His sumptuous work *The Bright Temptation* (1932) follows the fortunes of the young scholar Aidan, who wanders from his medieval monastery and falls from innocence to experience, clericalism to eroticism. Aidan is yet another Irish picaro at odds with society, though in Clarke as in Stephens society is only dimly present, yielding place as it does to a bountiful nature observed with evocative affection. Like Stephens too, Clarke's ethic is boldly naturalistic, as Aidan and his lover Ethna stray in Edenic innocence through a lushly Celtic-Romanesque universe rather too virile and robust to be entirely plausible. But this world in Clarke's fiction is always fringed by evil, violence and madness, slipping easily into a subtext of surrealist nightmare; in a later novel, *The Sun Dances at Easter* (1952), the sexually jealous Congal is transformed into a repulsive old goat. When Aidan returns to his monastery it is to find it sacked by the Danes. He is finally united with Ethna, and the novel was banned in Ireland even though the couple high-mindedly refrain from making love until the last sentence.

The Singing-Men at Cashel (1936) deals similarly with an idealised society of hermits and high kings, an enchanted but turbulent world which is afflicted by evil but not by alienation. What rescues it from the estrangements of modernity is style, which recreates the sensuous textures of objects and events in Clarke's characteristic mixture of epic material and largely realist tone. The book opens with yet another Irish internal émigré, the roving poet, satirist and trickster Anier Mac Conglinne, a rebellious libertine whose carnivalesque sexuality counterpoints the priestly asceticism of Cormac of Cashel. The novel's focal character, however, turns out to be not Cormac himself but his wife Gormlai. *The Singing-Men at Cashel*, despite its title, is one of those rare Irish novels in which the disaffected figure is a woman. Gormlai is an intellectual adventurer, a free crypto-feminist spirit who rebels against her unconsummated marriage with the saintly Cormac, abandoning him for the king of Leinster. She then defies her new partner's patriarchal rule and elopes

---

25.   Stephens's essay 'A Tavern in the Town' in *Here Are Ladies* can be read among other things as a mischievous parody of Shavian grand narratives of history. He advances here a kind of tobacco theory of history, as we have noted earlier, and flirts with the idea that humans are 'brewing animals'.

26.   For an account of Clarke's prose, see Maurice Harmon, *Austin Clarke: A Critical Introduction* (Dublin, 1989), ch. 5.

to wed the high king Nial, with whom she finds happiness. In this world of sweetness and repletion, desire conquers the law, and the displacements of the picaresque finally give way to the integration of classical realism.

If Clarke has something of Stephens's *sanitas* without much of his irony, Mervyn Wall's *The Misfortunes of Fursey* (1946) manages to reunite the two.[27] Wall's novel is strongly reminiscent of *The Bright Temptation*, but largely by way of mischievous parody. The saintly simpleton Fursey is expelled from his medieval monastery of Clonmacnoise for his embarrassing capacity to attract demons, though the novel piously insists that 'the chastity of the Irish demon is well-known and everywhere admitted'. He briefly marries a witch, and is tried (defended by the devil himself) for being a somewhat incompetent sorcerer. Beneath this vein of whimsy runs a more embattled critique of clerical oppression: Fursey is a victim who graduates first to being a rebel, setting fire to the bishop's palace, and then an exile, leaving with his lover for Britain in revolt against the wretchedness of life in Ireland. Despite the roguish comedy, this is a brutal society of violence and despotism, and Fursey, a superfluous man cruelly treated, feels the world to be drained of meaning in the manner of the classical picaro. Indeed the novel's humour, a shade too arch and fey (Fursey has a familiar spirit called Albert), is among other things a strategy for defusing the real terrors of religious tyranny, as Wall employs the familiar Irish genre of fantasy for what amounts to a bitter repudiation of the country which produced it.

In *The Return of Fursey* (1948), the hero's charitable monastic colleagues apply for his extradition from England to be burnt, but Fursey, an insider turned alien, joins a Viking ship in an attack on the Clonmacnoise monastery. He ends up on the road again, a forsaken figure in a heartless society. There is a touch of Synge's *Playboy* about his picaresque progress, as he moves from being a gormless victim to a rebel against both Satan and society, and finally flowers into a kind of moral maturity. Like Synge's Christy Mahon, he flirts with murder, but comes to see evil as overrated. Wall's later novel *Leaves for the Burning* (1952), an acerbic, extremely funny satire of the dreariness of life in small-town Ireland, concerns one Lucien Burke, a civil servant of genteel Dublin pedigree pained by the nepotism, puritanism, anti-intellectualism and crude nationalist prejudice of his godforsaken midland town. He and his mates jaunt off on a three-day Lucky Jim-like spree to Dublin, standing idly by when a farmer is thrown to his death through a pub window in a drunken jape. Haunted by nightmares and childhood memories of religious mania, Lucien tries unsuccessfully to redeem a broken relationship with a woman friend, and in a final spasm of savage farce is wounded while trying to defend his office cash box containing all of 1s. 8d. from IRA bandits. The British embassy in Dublin made the novel compulsory reading for its staff as an informative guide to Irish life.

27.   See *The Journal of Irish Literature*, January–May, 1982.

Eimar O'Duffy's *King Goshawk and the Birds* (1926) is another novel in the tradition of whimsical fantasy, in which Ireland applies to rejoin Britain at the end of the civil war, only to have its application firmly rejected.[28] The politician Vanderbags (de Valera) refuses to abide by the decision, truculently asserting Ireland's inalienable right to be part of the British empire. Having declared war on the United Kingdom in its eagerness to become part of it, Ireland is invaded by British troops who re-establish an Irish republic by force. In the midst of these events strays the novel's internal exile, a dissident Stoneybatter Philosopher who visits Tír na nÓg and encounters a Cuchulain reincarnated in the body of a grocer's assistant. The body has first to be purged of its crippling false consciousness to become a fit medium for the ancient hero. In a bizarre blending of heroic epic and Zolaesque naturalism, Cuchulain wanders in bemusement through a dingy, mercenary modern Ireland, observing a Dublin of filth and human squalor and wreaking unwitting havoc as he goes. This creates the opportunity for some effective Swiftian alienation effects, though in a tone more genial than venomous. In this dystopian fable, the world lies in the power of a global Big Brotherhood run by finance capitalists, blowing one's nose is illegal, and two-fifths of the world's literature has been destroyed by the state.

In *The Spacious Adventures of the Man in the Street* (1928), O'Duffy once more plays in fine Swiftian fashion with a satiric reversal of terms, this time of food for sex. In a kind of culinary monogamy, all members of his imaginary society are forced to choose one fruit when young and stick to it for the rest of their lives whether they continue to enjoy it or not. Sex is free and easy, but to speak of hunger is indecent; the greedier inhabitants of Rathe, O'Duffy's socialist utopia, frequent shady restaurants in which illicit eating takes place. Like sex, we are reminded, eating can swell the stomach and lead to a product being expelled from it, but emetics act as an efficient sort of contraception. The people of Rathe worship the powers of darkness, but in hypocritical fashion fail to live up to their own diabolism and are constantly to be found lapsing into guilt-ridden acts of kindness. Those who offend God will be condemned to everlasting life, whereas those who please him may die in full confidence of obliteration. A few crankish members of Rathe, hopelessly utopian, dream of a future society driven by money and market forces.

The Orwellian autocracy of *King Goshawk* is not entirely remote from the Irish Free State, though O'Duffy is in general exceptional for his time in his critique of totalitarianism in portraying a right-wing rather than left-wing brand of it. Indeed he is one of the few Irish writers whose prime satiric target is neither nationalism, imperialism nor the church, but capitalism. The new feudal landlords of *King Goshawk* are millionaire businessmen, and the novel becomes a kind of Voltairean moral fable as the Philosopher and

28.   For O'Duffy, see Robert Hogan, *Eimar O'Duffy* (Lewisburg, 1972), and John Cronin, *The Anglo-Irish Novel* (Belfast, 1990), vol. 2.

Cuchulain's son Cuanduine travel together a world characterised by grotesque inequalities. As newspaper barons bid to buy up Cuanduine as a columnist, the story begins to fall apart at the seams, veering into caricature and slackening into a set of disjointed episodes. It is the familiar problem in Irish fiction of how to sustain a coherent narrative, given the promiscuous mix of genres such writing typically involves. A sequel to Goshawk, Asses in Clover (1933) is a more grievous instance of the same diffuseness, as satire, fantasy and heroic epic are rolled unevenly into another anti-capitalist polemic. The semi-epic style works rather better in The Lion and the Fox (1922), an historical novel set in the Elizabethan era. O'Duffy's work moves easily from sharply focused satire to the broad-brush stereotyping of a poster art; but he is one of the few Irish novelists besides Joyce to deploy the avant-gardist techniques of montage, inserting song, verse and advertisements into his prose and carving up the spurious unities of classical realism in an epoch of global depression, war and revolution.

If one line of literary descent from James Stephens is the novel as fable and fantasy, another is a vein of Romantic vitalism which crops up in very different guises in the work of Liam O'Flaherty and Francis Stuart. Most of O'Flaherty's crudely powerful works centre on the figure of the internal émigré: anguished souls who are by turns brutish, sensual, attractive, half-mad, pigheaded, courageous and terrifyingly violent. They are brooding, inarticulate men in revolt against the universe, and in the less accomplished of the novels – The Black Soul (1924) will serve as an example – this can quickly degenerate into a kind of melodramatic rant. O'Flaherty is at his pseudo-philosophical thinnest when he preaches a slipshod, vaguely Nietzschean or Lawrentian vitalism, lacking in psychological nuance and emotionally histrionic. Sheer force and intensity have then to compensate for his psychological unsubtlety. This is true to some extent of the rather more convincingly portrayed protagonist of The Informer (1925), another O'Flaherty exilic figure in helpless thrall to his own unruly passions; but the displaced character is handled more proficiently in Thy Neighbour's Wife (1923), in which the tormented consciousness of the priest MacMahon is off-set by some stinging social satire of his Aran island community. O'Flaherty seems in general unable to decide quite what he feels about his protagonists, how admirable or despicable he takes them to be; but MacMahon is more effectively detached from his author's own welter of conflicting sympathies. Much the same is true of the almost unbearably graphic Famine (1937), in which a suffering community rather than an isolated spirit stands at the centre of the narrative, and which manages to be at once stark and strictly disciplined.

Something of the same primitive force is evident in Skerrett (1932), in which David Skerrett, another of O'Flaherty's magnificent human beasts, comes to take up residence as schoolmaster on Nara (Aran) only to see his son killed and his wife broken by the disaster. Shedding his religious faith, Skerrett becomes a self-torturing rebel locked in lethal combat with the island's money-grubbing priest Moclair, who provides the novel with an occasion for a superb anatomy of clerical brutality. Nara, far from offering the organic society dreamt of by the Dublin Gaelgeoirs, is a dangerously unstable community obsessed with power and property and ridden with class struggle. Skerrett shifts from being a literal outsider to a brief spell of respectable citizenship on the island, and from there to a state of internal emigration, living as a cantankerous republican with an unhinged wife who hates him. If he starts off as a stiff-necked brute, he ends up as a brave, solitary apostate, a genuinely tragic figure persecuted by a spiteful society and relentlessly hunted by a bullying cleric. An enemy of human society who nevertheless inspires others to thoughts of freedom, he is finally shipped off to an insane asylum on the mainland.

Life on the mainland is hardly preferable to the clannish conformism of Aran, as the reputable *Mr Gilhooley* (1926) testifies. A miserable petty bourgeois trapped in a lonely, futile existence, Gilhooley hangs out with the seedy Dublin *literati* and falls in love with the waif Nelly, who turns out to be less waif than whore. Gilhooley, one of O'Flaherty's mixtures of amateur metaphysician and average sensual man, ends by killing Nelly and drowning himself. He dies, in effect, of *ennui*. Little short of revolution can relieve this terminal boredom, an upheaval which Bartley Madden, hero of *Insurrection* (1950), is fortunate enough to stumble across in the Dublin of 1916. Torn between realistic disgust for the Easter Rising and a naïvely idealist hero-worship, Madden joins the revolt as an outsider on his way home to the west, and so becomes part of a long line of Irish picaros who discovers a fulfilling identity in the patriotic cause. The novel is typically ambivalent about its own central character, a frenzied Romantic who will nonetheless end up as a self-sacrificial hero. If some of O'Flaherty's heroes have an excess of consciousness, the troglodytic Madden has all too little. As usual with his author, he is a heady brew of animal instinct and vacuous poeticism, full of blowsy clichés about the 'divine ecstasy' of fighting. War for him is a quasi-erotic form of mysticism, and he dies in a self-squandering *acte gratuit* of an assault on British forces, motivated more by a sublimated homoerotic love for his level-headed officer Kinsella than by any political doctrine. For much of the novel, the formal focusing of the narrative on Madden lends him a centrality undercut by the negative way he is characterised; like many of O'Flaherty's heroes, he is an ordinary man caught up in extraordinary circumstances, so that the text seems as bemused about his true value as the reader is. Finally, however, it steps in to endorse him, however much it may also dislike him; and from a stagey, threadbare beginning it progresses to a powerful dramatic climax.

O'Flaherty's novels, rather like Irish fiction as a whole, are split down the middle between an outer world of oppressive monotony and an inner life of extravagant fantasy. In an endless dialectic, each presses the other towards caricature: the more shabby the material world appears, the more morbidly introspective or luridly self-theatricalising grows the world of consciousness.

But the more consciousness retreats into its solitary reveries, the more recalcitrant it finds the world to be. This conflict corresponds in O'Flaherty's work to a political contradiction, as his novels swing between celebrating the robust animal energy of the people and despising the bestial masses. Just as a seedy realism is the reverse side of a callow idealism, so a certain nihilism is never far from his vitalism.[29]

An Irish sense of alienation would seem particularly pronounced in the city of Cork. Daniel Corkery's deeply morose *The Threshold of Quiet* (1917) opens with a suicide in the river Lee, hardly an unreasonable action given the fate of the characters left alive.[30] Finbarr, the brother of the suicide, is destined for the priesthood but runs off to sea; Martin Clancy, a despairing lost soul, is hopelessly in love with Lily Bresnan, who has to care for an alcoholic father and finally enters a convent; Stevie Galvin is a broken eccentric with intellectual pretensions whose life is blighted by a quarrel with his brother. The novel, as John Cronin puts it, 'resounds with the tormented cries of lonely men'.[31] Once more, marginality and isolation are presented, ironically, as a general condition, and emigration is a central concern: Cork is an excellent city to get out of. Sean O'Faolain's *Bird Alone* (1936), a diffuse, rather too rollicking narrative couched in an overstimulated style, concerns the Parnellite rebel Corney Coney, grandson of a Fenian, who has an afffair with the rather more socially respectable Elsie Sherlock and gets her pregnant. Elsie tries to kill herself, a common fictional occurrence in Cork, and both she and her baby die as she gives birth. Corney, a loner obliquely involved with the Irish Republican Brotherhood, is ostracised by his community, disdains the conventions and refuses to be reconciled, ending up in ageing solitude in the city. O'Faolain's novel *Come Back to Erin* (1940) also dramatises different kinds of marginality, from St John the romantic returned exile to Frankie the IRA fugitive.

One of the most mordant of all modern Irish portraits of the disinherited self is Brinsley McNamara's *The Valley of the Squinting Windows* (1918), a novel which was publicly burned by the plain people of the author's home town.[32]

29. See for a critical account Patrick Sheeran, *The Novels of Liam O'Flaherty* (Atlantic Highlands, NY, 1976), and ch. 7 of James Cahalan's *Great Hatred, Little Room: The Irish Historical Novel* (Dublin, 1983).

30. For Corkery, see Alexander G. Gonzalez, 'A Re-Evaluation of Daniel Corkery's Fiction', *Irish University Review*, vol. 14, no. 2 (Autumn 1984), and George Saul, *Daniel Corkery* (Lewisburg, 1973). A good account is to be had in Patrick Maume, *Life that Is Exile: Daniel Corkery and the Search for Irish Ireland* (Belfast, 1993).

31. John Cronin, *The Anglo-Irish Novel* (Belfast, 1990), vol. 2, p. 96.

32. For McNamara, see Andrew E. Malone, 'Brinsley McNamara: An Appreciation', *Dublin Magazine* (July 1929), and John Wilson Foster, *Fictions of the Irish Literary Revival*. An account of the witchhunting of McNamara can be found in Padraic O'Farrell, *The Burning of Brinsley McNamara* (Dublin, 1990).

Garradrimna is a village awash with spying and malevolent gossip, where even the children attend school in order to collect spiteful rumours for their parents. The internal émigré of the text is John Brennan, reared for the priesthood, a 'fugitive' within the village whose troubled consciousness is at odds with its mean-spiritedness. His metaphorical exile is shared by the in-coming schoolmistress Rebecca Kerr, who has an affair with the Dublin roué Ulrick Shannon. Ulrick gets Rebecca pregnant and she is hounded out of town; John, also in love with her, kills Ulrick in revenge only to discover in an improbable stroke of melodrama that he is his illegitimate brother. Brennan will now follow his father into drink, his hopes for the priesthood crushed. The novel is so unremittingly bleak and despondent as to border like most untempered pessimism on the comic.

The Clanking of Chains (1919) centres on another baffled idealist, the shop boy Michael Dempsey, an artistic outsider in Ballycullen whose escape from its boorishness takes the form of a poetic Sinn Féinism. Disgusted by the town's shoneenism and Schadenfreude, he is almost never heard to speak in the novel, and despite his republican sympathies is by-passed in his provincial fastness by the turbulent political events of 1913–16. Nationalism is fiercely lambasted as a ruse of the materialist middle classes, who break out into an orgy of phoney patriotism when they get wind of Edward Carson's rebellion in the North; the Volunteers are simply the gombeen men in military dress. But if republicanism is satirised as cynical self-interest, an Ireland empty of idealism is equally impugned. In the manner of Lukácsian realism, the whole book distils the tumultuous pre-history of the Free State in a single microcosmic setting. Dempsey ends up as a republican rebel cast out by a bourgeois nationalist community, and sails finally from Ireland into literal exile. What is striking about McNamara's handling of this subject-matter is the unruffled equability of his style, cool and subdued with a leavening of ironic detachment, and so all the more abrasive.

What cannot be accomplished in social reality can still be achieved in fantasy. The Various Lives of Marcus Igoe (1929) returns to Garradrimna, but now in more avant-gardist literary spirit. The shoemaker Marcus Igoe, holed up in this parochial backwater, lives out various fantastic personae, as all assured identity crumbles into the 'outlandish, ghostly chimera' of a non-self. Igoe is another superfluous man, compensating for his starved social existence with a world of subjunctive identities, refashioning himself in the mind in a town which refuses such possibilities in reality. As with James Stephens, the traditional Irish motif of shape-changing is drawn on as an implicit protest against the rigidities of the present. The experimental form of the novel projects a freedom and plurality grimly denied by Irish society itself, as the protean structure of the book rebels against its drab social content. One text is stacked within another in Flann O'Brien-like fashion, and Igoe comes to read a story in which he himself figures as a character.

A clutch of largely neglected Ulster writers also take up these questions of internal displacement. Shan Bullock's *The Squireen* (1903) is set in his usual Northern landscape around fertile Protestant Gorteen and barren Catholic Bilboa, and like much of his fiction revolves on property-struggles between crafty farmers. The novel opens with two such worthies bartering over a potential wife who is referred to in her hearing as a heifer. Martin Hynes, the down-at-heel squire of Gorteen, wants to buy up Jane Fallon in marriage to settle his debts; but Jane holds out for a while against his imperiousness, defying her sternly patriarchal father before she is finally brought to heel. A defeated rebel, she bows to the law of the father, but her marriage to the squire degenerates after the death of their baby. Hynes tires of Jane and grows increasingly reckless and restive, though the two are reconciled when he dies in an accident. A neglected feminist novel, *The Squireen* reveals Bullock as a vivid chronicler of a proud, mercenary Ulster Protestant community (the local Catholics hardly put in an appearance) which is idealised for its toughness but upbraided for its emotional and imaginative paucity. Work – an eloquent absence in, say, James Stephens – is central to all of Bullock's solidly crafted writing,[33] which displays a quick feel for material process and an enhanced sense of the ordinary.

Much the same is true of *Dan the Dollar* (1905), a sturdily wrought work in its author's familiarly unflamboyant style, which is set once more among the struggling tenant farmers of Fermanagh. The émigré of the novel is Dan Ruddy, son of the somewhat romanticised peasants Sarah and Felix, who returns from the United States to disrupt his parents' traditional lifestyle with his flashy financial ways. Arrogant, work-obsessed and contemptuous of Irish culture, Dan wreaks sexual and material havoc in this impoverished but integral community, returning finally to America and leaving traditionalist Ulster values to triumph in his wake. A tragic version of much the same plot can be found in Seumas O'Kelly's *Wet Clay* (1922), an ill-structured, ploddingly realist piece in which the returned Irish-American Brendan Nilan falls in love with the internal exile Martha Lee, a stylish free spirit who longs to escape from small-town drudgery but becomes trapped in a loveless marriage with Nilan's alcoholic cousin. The novel ends with Nilan's death at the hands of this jealous, grasping small farmer.

It is a sign of the stability of Bullock's society, as well as of its intimately observed monotony, that it needs the interruption of an outsider to stir it into dramatic narrative. His collection of stories *By Thrasna River* (1895), a set of

33. See, for example, his praise of the architect of the Titanic in the brief biography *Thomas Andrews, Shipbuilder* (1912), curiously recorded in *The Field Day Anthology of Irish Writing* as 'his most impressive work'. There are some perceptive comments on Bullock in Patrick Maume, 'Ulstermen of Letters', in Richard English and Graham Walker (eds.), *Unionism in Modern Ireland* (Dublin, 1996), pp. 66–71.

loosely linked tales and episodes, suffers from a similar formal problem: little of dramatic moment can happen in such a fundamentally self-enclosed culture. *The Loughsiders* (1924) is another of his workmanlike fictions, which exploits the structural irony of a protagonist who is outwardly well-integrated but inwardly an alien. The stoutly respectable farmer Richard Jebb is in reality a villainous schemer and hyprocrite, devoted to the destruction of a neighbouring family in order to lay his hands on their farm. This, however, is revealed to us only gradually, with well-handled obliquity; and in this darker work it is the internal émigré who ends up victorious, as Jebb entices his neighbours' son away to the United States so as to marry his widowed mother and possess her property. Bullock is less successful when he forsakes this rural setting for the city, as in his slow-moving, flatly undramatic fable of the London civil service, *Robert Thorne* (1907). His best-known work, quite undeservedly, remains *The Awkward Squads* (1893), a collection of short stories which satirise both Unionist and nationalist zealotry in a hamfisted, largely stereotypical way.

No account of internal emigration could be more authentic than one by a former tramp. Patrick MacGill is one of the few proletarian Irish writers, whose fictionalised autobiography *Children of the Dead End* (1914) tells a harrowing tale of the near-destitute Donegal community of Glenmornan. Dermod Flynn is packed off as a boy to the hiring fair at Strabane, and as a migrant labourer on the hoof in Scotland is plunged into utter solitude as 'an outcast, a man rejected by society'. Part rebel, part vagrant, he endures the brutal plight and backbreaking toil of the Irish émigré worker, in a novel which provides one of the earliest fictional records in the country of industrial labour. Flynn works as a railwayman, reads Henry George and becomes a socialist, an insurgent from his earliest years against religion, convention and class-society. *The Rat-Pit* (1915) recounts much the same narrative from the viewpoint of Flynn's lover Nora Ryan, who is likewise driven by poverty from Donegal, ends up as a sweated seamstress in Glasgow and is finally thrust into prostitution. In a superfluous histrionic touch, her own brother turns up as one of her clients.

MacGill writes a stark, styleless prose, compellingly laconic at its finest and tediously boisterous at its worst. His is a rudimentary, diagrammatic social realism, which swerves from bewailing the rough life of the migrant to celebrating him as a spontaneous Romantic anarchist. *Moleskin Joe* (1923) is a study of the roaming navvy as devil-may-care nonconformist, making a literary virtue of grim necessity. MacGill's somewhat depthless fiction is trapped within his own direct experience and moves easily into a caricatural art, shot through as it is with the image of the migrant as swashbuckling brawler, boozer and braggart. There is something of the same revelling in roguery in Patrick Kavanagh's *The Green Fool* (1938), in which the narrator, fascinated by journeymen shoemakers and tramps ('the blood of tramps was in my veins') finally takes to the road himself in a self-conscious assumption of the role of beggar. The protagonist of Kavanagh's *Tarry Flynn* (1948) is equally askew to his rural community. In MacGill's case, there is an unpleasantly macho quality to much of this delight in the roistering rover, which makes it all the more surprising that he should recast *Children of the Dead End* from a feminine standpoint. If he has his countryman Robert Tressell's fine capacity for graphic realist description, he lacks for the most part his complex political seriousness. What emerges in the English setting as working-class solidarity becomes in the Irish context a maverick individualist revolt. But MacGill evokes the life of the indigent Donegal smallholders with an admirable blend of cold-eyed realism and imaginative affection – not least in the impressive *Glenmornan* (1919), in which the migrant worker returns home in the shape of the novel's protagonist Doalty Gallagher, only to be denounced from the altar and driven once more into exile.

The hiring fair at Strabane also figures in the superb fiction of Peadar O'Donnell, whose *Islanders* (1928) captures the desperately impoverished existence of an Ulster island without either O'Flaherty-like elementalism or Syngean poeticism.[34] This tale of spalpeens and near-starvation is mostly episodic, as befits a tightly bound community in which history is more repetition than evolution. An embryonic narrative flowers around the idealised hero Charlie Doogan, who has a brief sexual entanglement with the middle-class mainlander Ruth Wilson, but the relationship comes to nothing. The finely fashioned *Proud Island* (1975) likewise depicts a society with little historical development. Since there are no real structural conflicts between O'Donnell's island people, the fictions they inhabit cannot be strictly speaking novelistic. The internal exile of the beautifully rendered *Adrigoole* (1929) is Hughie Dalach, who returns to his community after being hired away for six years feeling unaccountably lonely and uprooted. Brigid Gallagher is a kindred errant spirit, who escapes to Scotland from the threat of a loveless marriage. Exile is a ritual part of this society, a culture which O'Donnell loves without too much idealisation, thus worsting both the cynics and the sentimentalists. If he has a Lawrentian feel for work and the land, he is gratifyingly free of Lawrence's portentousness. Hughie is finally imprisoned for brewing poteen, and returns home to discover that his family have died of hunger during his absence.

A late novel, *The Big Windows* (1955), is couched in an opulent, richly figurative English which reads curiously like a translation. The estranging style of the prose thus matches the social remoteness of its content. It contrasts in this way with the muscular spareness of *Islanders*, which clings as tenaciously to the material world as human consciousness, in this society of stern neces-

---

34. For O'Donnell's crowded political and literary career, all the way from anti-Treatyite to anti-Vietnam war campaigner, see Grattan Freyer, *Peadar O'Donnell* (Lewisburg, 1973). See also his own account of his imprisonment as a republican in *The Gates Flew Open* (London, 1932).

sity, must cling to material circumstances. Brigid Dugan of *The Big Windows* is an island woman, and thus already a kind of outsider, who then has to feel her way as a stranger into the mainland community of Glenmore. The work is poetic but not romanticising: Brigid receives some rough treatment from the women of her newly-adopted glenside village, a vindictive, fissiparous community with a tribalist drive to conformity. In what might look to the dewy-eyed visitor like an organic society, even the upper, middle and lower glens turn out to be at daggers drawn with each other. This is a culture which abhors the mark of difference, and Brigid, who wants big windows in her new house according to her island's custom, unwittingly stirs up antagonism by this social deviance. Windows are here a symbol of freedom, as for Brinsley McNamara they are signs of snooping. Men and labour in the book are thrust into the background: it is a novel about women, their networks, rituals, rivalries, intricate negotiations. For all its prodigal richness of perception, this lovingly crafted work borders on a certain monotone vision, just as its ornate style risks a certain cloying and claustrophobia. As with Synge, a profusion of language strangely counterpoints a frugal reality. Once again, there is little plot dynamic, as a plurality of events and episodes are interwoven in a formal experimentalism at odds with the peasant realism of the content. The authorial discourse is pitched on a level with its characters, intimate but not on the whole idealising, refusing an external 'placing' for a companionable consciousness set well inside the working community it observes.

Michael McLaverty's *Call My Brother Back* (1939) is also set on an island off the Ulster coast, a fishing community whose austere conditions are registered in a supple, sinewy language shot through with a delicate sense of natural process. The émigré figure is Colm MacNeill, who leaves the island for a college in Belfast around the time of partition. Most of the work concerns these political troubles (Colm's brother is a Sinn Féiner), but the Belfast portion of the book never really matches for fineness of texture the earlier accounts of island life. McLaverty's writing loses some of its burnished intensity and becomes sparser, more documentary, as the McNeill family move from their magical island to collective exile in Belfast. If the novel's characters suffer a fall from Eden, so too does its prose.

A notably different kind of spiritual exile crops up in the work of the Belfast-born Forrest Reid, whose *Peter Waring* (1937), in what is by now almost *de rigueur* for Irish fictionalised autobiography, portrays the solitary childhood of a sensitive protagonist under the heel of his father's dominion. As in the novels of Elizabeth Bowen, childhood is presented as a form of exile, a region within the present which is also profoundly alien to it. With equal predictability, Waring rebels against the patriarchal power of his family, in a rather tremulous work which cries out for a stiffening edge of irony. Tom Barber of *Uncle Stephen* (1931) is another mutinous youngster, who runs away from home to live in a quasi-erotic relationship with his reclusive great-uncle. The novel presents without comment a fifteen-year-old Tom giving his elderly relative a playful bite on the neck and tickling it with a feather. Much of the rest of the novel, as with the final work in Reid's trilogy *The Retreat* (1936), is devoted to quasi-magical goings-on, pseudo-Gothic psychical landscapes and eerie dreamlike states.

The central form of estrangement in Kate O'Brien's novels springs from the conflict between illicit love and social responsibility.[35] Surprisingly few Irish novels place love relationships at their centre, and O'Brien's *Without My Cloak* (1931) does this while refusing to uproot them from a complex history. Its dense social texture thus contrasts with the sculptured purity of, say, *The Ante-Room* (1934), though it pays a price for this in lacking the stylistic nuance and indirection of her later fiction. It is, for all that, a vastly ambitious first novel, a kind of *Buddenbrooks* of Munster which charts several genera- tions of a prosperous mercantile family, the Considines, the largest forage dealers in the country. This tight-knit web of kinship, evolving over the cen- turies, nonetheless contains its internal secessionists. Caroline, the unhappily married daughter, runs off to London in love with an Englishman, but returns to eke out a dyspeptic existence at home. She is trapped, in the manner of some of George Eliot's heroines, between her personal desire and the com- munal past, which amounts to family culture and tradition; but the fineness of the novel's handling of this tension lies in its reluctance to reduce it, as in so much Irish fiction, to a clear-cut confrontation between the aspiring indi- vidual spirit and a sterile society. On the contrary, the communal tradition in question, for Caroline as for Eliot's Maggie Tulliver, is both disabling and enriching, as a *pietas* of place and inheritance wages war with the impulse to individual fulfilment. Just as the Floss is for Eliot a river symbolically freighted with this ambiguous heritage, so for this novel is the river of Mel- lick (Limerick).

The narrative focus then shifts to Denis Considine, yet another of the Irish novel's oversensitive, artistic young social misfits, who falls in love with the illegitimate working woman Christina Roche. A classic Irish rebel against social and religious convention, Denis denounces the priest-uncle who ships Christina off to New York out of harm's way, and sails there in search of her. But the relationship fails, and Denis returns to Ireland as a displaced figure still strongly tied to his home. Mellick proves stronger than desire, and love offers no simple escape. Denis has now exchanged literal exile abroad for metaphorical exile at home: locked in a deeply Oedipal ambivalence towards

---

35.   For a brief biography, see Lorna Reynolds, *Kate O'Brien: A Literary Portrait* (Ger- ards Cross, 1987). See also Joan Ryan, 'Women in the Novels of Kate O'Brien', in Kosok (ed.) *Studies in Anglo-Irish Literature*, and Eavan Boland, 'That Lady: A Profile of Kate O'Brien 1897–1974', *The Critic*, vol. xxxiv, no. 2 (Winter 1975). See also John Jordan, 'Some Works of the Month: Kate O'Brien – A Note on her Themes', *The Bell*, vol. xix (January 1954).

his father, he at first theatrically rejects a role in the family business. The dead-lock is resolved by his falling abruptly and conveniently in love with Anna Hennessey, daughter of a Mellick magnate, a device which allows him to combine personal happiness with a loyalty to local tradition. It is not the kind of resolution which will prove typical of O'Brien's later writing.

Agnes Mulqueen of *The Ante-Room* (1934), daughter of an haut-bour-geois family in the *fin de siècle*, is guiltily in love with her brother-in-law Vincent, in a dysfunctional family almost all of whose members are solitary and somehow disabled. There is the dying mother Teresa, the broken-spirited syphilitic brother Reggie, Reggie's fortune-digging nurse, and the unhappily matched Vincent and Marie-Rose. In Chekhovian spirit, it is a world of lonely interlocking fantasies in which most of the characters are outsiders to one another; and they all move in collective isolation from political society at large, which impinges only occasionally on their baffled lives. Though the novel is set in Ireland, it could, in modernist fashion, have been set more or less anywhere. In a supremely powerful scene of renunciation, Agnes finally turns away Vincent for both their sakes, and the novel ends with his suicide. The tragedy reflects a set of stalemates typical of O'Brien's sombre world: you cannot help loving yet you must, you are called upon to act resolutely just when you are least able to do so. *The Ante-Room* is an exquisitely subtle psy-chological study, resonantly atmospheric and delicately wrought; O'Brien at her best reads like Elizabeth Bowen without her self-conscious fastidiousness of perception.

Another such finely wrought work is *Mary Lavelle* (1936), in which Mary, whose chief idea as a child was to be 'free and lonely', becomes a literal expa-triate as a 'miss' or governess in Spain. Spain and Ireland have been long related, once through merchants and now through misses; and since both are patriarchal, honour-conscious, intensely religious cultures, Mellick can be transplanted to Castille without serious damage. Mary falls in love with Juanito, the married son of the family for whom she works, and one is reminded once more that O'Brien writes more powerfully about erotic love – 'at once life's falsest promise and most true fulfilment' – than almost any other Irish author. She is a skilled technician of the tragic joy of illicit desire: sexual love is for her a kind of delicious insanity, a wayward, unmanageable, implaca-ble force which disrupts all settlement and involves an ecstatic casting loose of one's moorings. It is the enemy of communal spirit and social responsibility; and since the novels place a high value on these commitments, their protago-nists live in perpetual danger of being riven apart. Mary returns finally to Ire-land, one of those many O'Brien figures who live in ugly, comfortable, affluent houses in Mellick, torn between these precious bonds and their lonely impulse of delight.

Mary Lavelle had the honour of being banned in Ireland, and so – for the sake of a single sentence – did *The Land of Spices* (1942). (One might claim that *Ulysses* was banned in various places for a single sentence too, though –

in the shape of Molly's final soliloquy – an inordinately long one.) The novel recounts the story of Helen Archer, the mother superior of an order of nuns at odds in its cosmopolitan spirit with Irish nationalism. As an Englishwoman brought up in Europe, Helen is an outsider in Ireland, a 'dark horse' and 'queer fish' who is made to feel her foreignness. In her dealings with her sub-ordinates, she has something of the coolly detached observation of a novelist. As a child, Helen discovers her father's homosexuality and hates him for it, so that in a curious reversal, illicit passion is here part of the paternal establish-ment rather than its antagonist. The novel represents a probing study in female power: by choosing the setting of a convent, at once a face-to-face community and part of a global institution, it succeeds in uniting the emo-tional and the political.

So too does O'Brien's most popular novel *That Lady* (1946), which revisits the oxymoronic condition of a powerful woman, this time in fully tragic spirit. A powerful woman is a classic insider/outsider, central in status but sidelined in gender. The sixteenth-century Ana de Mendoza, a free spirit and the most formidable woman in Spain, offends her friend King Philip by taking a lover and is thrust by his jealousy into internal exile, languishing in prison and dying there. Ana wants to protect what she sees as the private sphere of her relation-ship with Antonio Perez from the public realm of the absolutist state; but the personal world, here as elsewhere in O'Brien, is bound to have its complex social consequences. An illicit love stands once more at the focus of the narra-tive, but O'Brien is remarkable for the way she refuses to sever this eroticism from a wider history. Indeed part of the point of transposing and backdating the novel to a place and period where a woman could indeed exercise politi-cal rule is to refuse the kind of literary modernism for which personal rela-tionships hang in some luminous void. In sixteenth-century Spain, as in twentieth-century Ireland, such an artistic form is hardly appropriate, since in neither case can power and desire be so simply divorced. O'Brien's historical and political shrewdness would be quite beyond the reach of a Woolf. If she has the psychological intricacy of the great modernists, she combines it with the range and social density of the nineteenth-century realists.

Throughout Irish writing, a lonely outcast hungering for freedom revolts, usually unavailingly, against a censorious social order. The rebellion is almost always solitary – one reason perhaps why it is in the short story, rather than on the more communal, companionable terrain of the novel, that this strug-gle is so often staged. The most this anarchic figure can hope for is either a flight to a better world, or a modicum of private fulfilment within a social order which remains stubbornly untransformed. In this Romantic-libertarian tradition, there is almost no notion of collective rebellion, and for an excel-lent reason. For the primary instance of such co-operative action in Ireland is bourgeois nationalism, which figures for the free spirit as at least as much part of the problem as of the solution. The mantle of dissent thus passes to the alienated artist, the displaced intellectual, the victimised woman, the disenchanted idealist, all of whom crop up in some form or another in the novels of George Moore. What reaches its supreme formulation in Joyce's Stephen Dedalus is no avant-garde novelty, but a phenomenon with a venerable pedigree in Irish culture.

One of the greatest modern Irish inheritors of this anarchic-libertarian lineage is Francis Stuart; but Stuart, a professional heretic, is an apostate with respect to this tradition too. Almost uniquely among Irish writers, he understands that individual dissent is impotent unless it secretes the germ of a new community at odds with the insolence of official power. Hence his recurrent exploration of those microsocieties in which a group of deracinated individuals, torn and wounded but not without hope, come together in comradeship to form what might just prove the spiritual nucleus of the political future. Stuart has a claim to being the greatest revolutionary writer of modern Ireland not because he is in the least politically astute – on the contrary, his hair-raising political naïvety led him, in the Nazi period, into the criminal folly of lending his voice to the murderers of Jews – but because his fiction proclaims the disruptive radicalism of the Christian gospel. As one reared in the Protestant tradition, he is able to cling to this insight without, like so many of his ex-Catholic compatriots, turning from it in disgust to some politically less subversive creed because of the oppressive reality of the Roman Catholic church.

At the core of Stuart's great trilogy – *The Pillar of Cloud* (1948), *Redemption* (1949) and *The Flowering Cross* (1950) – lies just this Christian insight that only through a revolutionary self-abandonment scandalous to orthodox society can new life have a hope of flourishing. So it is that his narrators consort with prostitutes, psychopathic killers, the crippled victims of war, in what must surely constitute the most uncompromising nay-saying to official society which modern Irish letters have ever witnessed. Stuart's characters are the last word in nonconformist denial, enthralled by an otherworldliness so radical that it is a wonder how they still manage to eat and talk. It is a stylistic refusal too, as the 'stark and uncivil beauty'[36] of his painfully honest prose, disclaiming all superfluous elegance, gropes with a quasi-Lawrentian intensity for the spiritual subtext of the realist world, nervously responsive to the psychic networks and fragile epiphanies which thread their way through everyday speech and conduct. The form of human communication he is searching for is one represented by the pigeons in his bizarre juvenile fantasia *Pigeon Irish* (1932), who speak to one another in emotions rather than words.[37] Art,

36.   The phrase is Hugo Hamilton's, in his article on Stuart in *Writing Ulster*, no. 4 (Jordanstown, 1996), p. 71.
37.   Terence Brown notes that carrier pigeons were among the means of communication stringently controlled by the Emergency Powers Act in Ireland of 1939. See his review of Donal Ó Drisceoil, *Censorship in Ireland 1939–1945*, in *Irish Studies Review*, no. 20 (Autumn, 1997).

like the gambling with which Stuart is so obsessively concerned, is a matter of instinct and self-risking, as well as of decoding subliminal signs.[38] Like Lawrence, Stuart's art aims to prise open the ordinary befeathered ego to articulate the transindividual depths which sustain it. The point is to present doing in a way which elicits being, and here Stuart's post-war trilogy has something formally in common with *Women in Love*, a response to an earlier military carnage. In both cases, a group of lost individuals, stripped of their social history, assemble together on the brink of political apocalypse, searching for tremors of new life in a social void which presses their inner lives to an intensity well beyond realist bounds. But Stuart is not thereby breezily impatient with the material world, as Lawrence too often is; if he is a Romantic fantasist to the core, his fiction also moves paradoxically at the level of extreme physical states: torture, blindness, starvation, mental collapse. His theme is the triumph of failure, and his guiding doctrine is that only that which has been rent can be whole.

All this in Stuart has its own dark underside. Few Irish writers have trod such a hairthin line between their vices and their virtues. His Romantic anarchism can also be a squalid cult of the artist as demonic immoralist, a superior form of slumming in which the need to place oneself always at the extreme edge, in the midst of the most brutalised of human conditions, led him to set up home for a while in the Third Reich. The narrative is recorded in lightly fictionalised form in his *Black List, Section H* (1971). There is a fine line between solidarity with the suffering, and a daredevil bohemianism which is allured by 'extreme' conditions regardless of their moral content. In the teeth of all historical triumphalism, Stuart understands that suffering is in some sense what is most real about humanity; but this unflinching insight is never far from an élitist contempt for common social life, which refuses this revelation. In his flirting with the perilous doctrine that only extreme states will disclose the truth, this moral maverick is in fact a thoroughly conventional modernist. Stuart's self-destructive urge to put himself beyond the social pale, his masochistic wallowing in self-abnegation, can be simply the reverse side of the artist as state lackey, which is just what he became for a while in Nazi Germany. His patronising scorn for mere suburban living is among other things an overreaction to his own privileged upbringing. Magnificent though his trilogy is, there is something morally offensive about a man offering his own experience of imprisonment as a source of wisdom, when that brief interlude happened in the aftermath of his quiescence in a regime which butchered and incarcerated so many more. Along with this adolescent callowness, subtly self-dramatising for all its authentic humility, runs a sexist idealisation of women as suffering spiritual redeemers – not only in the trilogy, but in such later works as *Memorial* (1973), which nostalgically

38. The connection is noted by Robert Welch in ch. 8 of his *Changing States* (London and New York, 1993).

recreates the wartime situation of the trilogy in terms of a 'criminal' sexual relationship between an elderly bohemian and a young woman in the context of the Northern Irish Troubles. Herra, the woman in question, is killed by British troops, but the protagonist conveniently discovers a new lover almost immediately.

Like much of Stuart's fiction, *Memorial* is at once embarrassingly naïve and impressively powerful. If the Troubles are central to its action, it is because Stuart's chief characters need a context of political turmoil – and any old turmoil, it seems, will suffice – as a background against which they can live out a sort of private revolution of the spirit. The violation of others close at hand, a political situation to which Stuart's protagonists are neither committed nor non-committed, would thus appear an essential condition of one's personal salvation. The infantile egoism of this attitude does not prevent Stuart's novels from offering some of the most tender, moving accounts of loving kindness in modern fiction, just as his morbid fascination with the detritus of modern civilisation sits cheek-by-jowl with a profound insight into the condition of victimage. There is a lethal innocence about his writing which is at once the source of his lyrical beauty and of his dangerous delusions.

Stuart's flight to the Third Reich sprang in part from his naïve romanticising of the victim: he believed at the time that Germany would be defeated. Since this was more folly than crime, some of his more emollient Irish commentators, who would have little relish for defending the politics of, say, John Mitchel, have been quick to absolve him from charges of fascist sympathies, and equally eager to upbraid his critics as self-righteous moralists. It is true that in one sense arraigning Stuart's actions as disgraceful is beside the point, since disgrace, humiliation and social ostracism were precisely what he was seeking. Stuart holds that art is fashioned in the gutter and the margins, a Baudelairean banality from which he nevertheless conjured some magnificent fiction. But it is also the case that he went to Berlin at a time when Nazi persecution of the Jews was common knowledge, and in one of his radio broadcasts for the Germans praised Hitler and denounced international finance, a thinly coded piece of anti-Semitism. According to his biographer, he never subsequently condemned Hitler for the Holocaust.[39]

It can be said in Stuart's defence that like a good many others at the time he mistook Hitler for an anti-capitalist radical. In fact, in a familiar lineage of Romantic libertarianism from Blake to Lawrence, Stuart's politics are less anti-capitalist than anti-*bourgeois* – a stance which can always tilt ambivalently to either far left or far right. In rejecting middle-class society, the Romantic libertarian tends often enough to include democracy, liberalism, industrialism, rationality and political organisation as such in the baggage to be contemptuously discarded. The revolution of the spirit he desires is one which cuts much deeper than the political: it is a form of pre-political radicalism which

---

39.   See Geoffrey Ebourne, *Francis Stuart: A Life* (Dublin, 1990), p. 143.

can then end up in the arms of extreme forms of populism, individualism or anti-democratic élitism. Stuart's politics are in this sense classically modernist. But he is also a genuine revolutionary in the way that few modernist artists are. If he can be suspicious of democracy, denouncing *das Mann* of suburban society and hankering instead for the excessive, the abyss, the *acte gratuit*, he is also free for the most part of the authoritarianism to which such modernist politics rapidly led. Like Lawrence, he finally rejects fascism as just another dreary form of social regimentation; but the same *caveat* can apply just as easily to socialism, leaving the Romantic radical with nothing to pit against political barbarism but a change of heart. It is a politics so utterly uncompromising and absolute that it disappears from the light of common-or-garden society and leaves everything exactly as it was.

Reading this body of fiction, it is hard to resist the impression that Ireland drove in on themselves almost as many people as it drove out. Every national novel-form is replete with rogues, misfits, dreamers, rebels – characters who, as one critic of modern English literature puts it, are 'groping, puzzled, cross, mocking, frustrated and isolated . . . a-social rebels, martyrs, misfits, minor prophets'.[40] But it is perhaps significant that the critic in question is the Irish writer Sean O'Faolain. The encounter between the dislocated soul and a recalcitrant society is the stuff of *Middlemarch;* but it is a compulsively repeated formula in the Irish novel, where it rarely ends up in the mood of wry acceptance which marks the conclusion of George Eliot's novel. There are literal expatriates, returned natives, spiritual nomads, migrant labourers, frustrated rebels, epicene sons, insurgent daughters, tricksters and tramps, idealists who are spiritually central but practically washed-up, characters who conceal an alien identity beneath their social respectability. A remarkably high proportion of the novelists discussed in this essay endured or enjoyed some form of personal exile.[41] Again and again, this fiction dramatises the plight of figures who are absent from their own surroundings, unable to belong to their own experience. It is a condition summed up in an epigraph borrowed from Montaigne by Brinsley McNamara's Marcus Igoe: 'We are never present with, but always beyond ourselves.' Seamus Deane writes of the Irish exile who 'remains at home but in a state of deep disaffection from it. Such immobility has all the characteristic features of underdevelopment, of being removed from history – poverty, provincialism, submissiveness to authority, a regressive investment in religion and its consolations, fear of the world beyond . . . To complete the circuit, within such immobility there is a longing to escape that is regularly

40.   Sean O'Faolain, *The Vanishing Hero* (London, 1956), pp. 17–18.
41.   The modern Irish literary emigration reverses an early-modern influx of English writers into Ireland: Edmund Spenser, Walter Raleigh, John Harrington, Barnaby Rich, John Davies and others. See Andrew Hatfield and Willy Maley (eds.), *Edmund Spenser: A View of the State of Ireland* (Oxford, 1997), p. xiii.

thwarted by the fear of leaving . . . The text which specifies most fully the relation between immobility and exile is *Dubliners*.'[42] What sounds like an
unchanging keynote through all of this anomie is the sheer meagreness,
monotony and spiritual blightedness of ordinary Irish life. This is partly the
effect of a tyrannical clericalism and a stifling patriarchy; but it is also just as
plainly the upshot of a colonial condition of political powerlessness and economic backwardness.

That this is one primary cause, rather than any inherent defect in the Irish
populace themselves, is testified to by a single fact: the existence of this literature itself. The more ferocious a nation's self-satire, the worse things clearly
are with them – but also, of course, the better. Satire is a credit to the very
culture it lampoons. And to sit loose to a culture may be a mark of distinction as well as alienation. Jorge Luis Borges observes that 'the Irish have been
outstanding in English because they act within that culture and at the same
time do not feel tied to it by any special devotion'.[43] To be at once home and
away is not always an unenviable condition. If there is rancour and tedium in
traditional Irish life, there is also imaginative flair, ironic intelligence, a haunting sense of beauty. The literature is where these two dimensions meet in
deadlock. If the theme of Irish writing is often enough the slow death of the
spirit, the fact of Irish writing is its refutation.

42.   Seamus Deane, *Strange Country* (Oxford, 1997), p. 167.
43.   Quoted by Declan Kiberd, 'Post-Colonial Ireland: "Being Different"', in Daltún
      Ó Ceallaigh (ed.), *Reconsiderations of Irish History and Culture* (Dublin, 1994),
      p. 110.

THE RYAN LINE

Despite being denounced by an outraged canon as the most dangerous man in Ireland, Frederick Ryan is almost unknown today, either a blank or a curiously fleeting reference in most histories of Irish labour or the Revival.[1] Even in his lifetime he was something of a shadowy figure, present at the making of history but always discreetly in the background. He seems to have been cursed with the virtues of a good committee man, prepared to do the donkey work while others stalked the boards or the hustings, and became secretary in turn of the Irish National Theatre Society, the Dublin Young Ireland branch of the United Irish League, and the Socialist Party of Ireland. He was also for a while treasurer of the fractious Abbey Theatre. More lecturer than orator, lacking the panache of a Larkin or the charisma of a Connolly, he published only one book, a compilation of pieces which had already appeared elsewhere, and bequeathed to posterity almost nothing of his personal life. Yet this reserved, retiring man was also one of the most remarkable thinkers of early twentieth-century Ireland, combining a whole range of identities: socialist, internationalist, anti-colonialist, free-thinker, cultural critic, libertarian, social philosopher.

1. Ryan's disappearance from the historical record is really quite remarkable. As far as his cultural activities go, Stephen Gwynn refers to him simply as 'a writer of socialist tendencies' in his *Irish Literature and Drama* (London, 1936, p. 156), and there is no note on him in the bibliographical appendix to Ernest Boyd's reasonably comprehensive *Ireland's Literary Renaissance* (New York, 1922). Declan Kiberd is equally silent about him in his broad survey of the Revival, *Inventing Ireland* (London, 1995). Lady Gregory makes no allusion to his secretaryship of the Irish National Theatre Society in her *Our Irish Theatre* (New York and London, 1914), though she makes one or two brief mentions of his Abbey play *The Laying of the Foundations*. Despite his close co-operation with James Connolly, there is no allusion to Ryan in most studies of Connolly; see for example Austen Morgan's *James Connolly: A Political Biography* (Manchester, 1988). Wilfred Scawen Blunt, for whom Ryan did sterling work, has a mere three or four glancing references to him in his *My Diaries* (London, 1932), including one to Ryan's dining with him and Hilaire Belloc, and another to Ryan's death at Blunt's home in Sussex. Elizabeth Longford's study of Blunt, *Pilgrimage of Passion: The Life of Wilfred Scawen Blunt* (London, 1979), has two cursory references to Ryan, while a memoir of Blunt by his grandson the Earl of Lytton, *Wilfred Scawen Blunt: A Memoir by his Grandson* (London, 1961), makes one brief mention of Ryan and William Maloney as co-editors of the journal *Egypt* (p. 124). Edith Finch's *Wilfred Scawen Blunt 1840–1922* (London, 1934) has a passing reference to Ryan as 'an intelligent young Irishman' (p. 332).

Ryan was born in 1874 into what sounds like a middle-class, left-intellectual Dublin family. Padraic Colum describes his family as 'fairly well-to-do'.[2] His father was a member of the Free Literary Union, along with Jim Connell, author of the socialist anthem the 'Red Flag'. Ryan senior was said to have taken the 'utmost pains' to turn out young Fred as a militant agnostic, a task at which he triumphantly succeeded.[3] As a young nationalist, Fred Ryan joined the Celtic Literary Society, from which Sinn Féin was later to evolve, and delivered a paper to it in 1896 on the 'Social Side of the Irish Question'. He was thus already at the age of twenty-two pressing the kind of political agenda which would later be more militantly and publicly promoted by Connolly and Larkin. His speech to the Society also discloses the seeds of his internationalism, setting the Irish question in the context of Europe and the USA. He has, he announces, a vision of Ireland as a country where the persecuted of all nations might find a refuge.[4] He was close for a while to Sinn Féin and wrote for its journal the *United Irishman*, but fell out with Arthur Griffith, who was later to write him a notoriously churlish obituary.

Ryan became secretary of the Irish National Theatre Society in the days before it took over the Abbey Theatre, helping to stage its productions in small halls in dingy backstreets and writing a letter to Yeats asking him to launch the project with a lecture.[5] Shuttling between culture and politics in a manner typical of the period, he also became an early member of James Connolly's Irish Socialist Republican Party. Connolly was present at his 1896 Celtic Literary Society lecture, in which Ryan is said to have endorsed some of Fintan Lalor's ideas.[6] There is also a record of him chairing an ISRP lecture three years later and delivering an eloquent exposition of political economy.[7] But his old comrade William O'Brien thought that he was not wholly at one with the party's policy, or especially active within it; and in 1902 he drifted away from the organisation to launch the rationalist Dublin Philosophical Society, along with Francis Sheehy Skeffington and the poet James H. Cousins. In 1909 he was to respond to William O'Brien's call for a unified socialist organisation by establishing the Socialist Party of Ireland, of which

2.   Padraic Colum, *Arthur Griffith* (Dublin, 1959), p. 75.
3.   See Desmond Ryan, *Remembering Sion* (London, 1934), p. 53. The two Ryans were not related.
4.   See Minute Book of the Celtic Literary Society, National Library of Ireland, MS 200, pp. 152–3.
5.   See John Kelly and Ronald Schuchard (eds.), *The Collected Letters of W. B. Yeats* (Oxford, 1994), vol. 3, p. 219n.
6.   See C. Desmond Greaves, *The Life and Times of James Connolly* (London, 1961), p. 81.
7.   See William O'Brien, 'Frederick Ryan Remembered', in Manus O'Riordan (ed.), *Socialism, Democracy and the Church* (Labour History Workshop, Dublin 1984, p. 59). This, along with its companion pamphlet *Sinn Féin and Reaction*, is an invaluable compilation of writing by and on Ryan.

he became national secretary. According to O'Brien's diary, it was Ryan who proposed the motion for the party, fashioning it into an ecumenical outfit which set its face against sectarianism.

Before that, however, Ryan had left Ireland for two spells abroad. As a lowly species of civil servant, he endured a year in a government office in London as a second division clerk, but resigned out of what seems a combination of boredom, ill-health and literary ambitions, and returned to Dublin to support a literary career by working with a firm of chartered accountants in Dame Street. It is possible that while in London he saw plays by Ibsen and Shaw and attended some meetings of the Fabian Society. A colleague of his in the Dublin accountancy office was Frank Fay, later of Abbey Theatre celebrity, and Ryan's cousin Maire Davis believes that it was Ryan who introduced Fay to W. B. Yeats, with whom, so Davis declares, Ryan had 'for a long time been particularly intimate'.[8] Davis also reports that Ryan was the first to enter the pit of the Abbey, and opened the door to the theatre's first patron. He detested the sectarian bickerings of the theatre, and considered that Fay should be replaced by a new manager.[9] There is some evidence that he was used as a broker in the split between the company's nationalist members and their critics,[10] though he seems to have been part of the former group himself.

Yeats, Synge and Lady Gregory evidently valued Ryan's administrative expertise: a letter from Synge to Yeats of 1906 refers briefly to the wisdom of postponing a discussion of theatre business until they can get Ryan's advice.[11] He was clearly something of a fixer, respected by those of rival persuasions. But he was uneasy with the Abbey's Celticist agenda, speaking up after a lecture by Padraic Colum to the National Literary Society in 1906 to voice his disquiet with this new form of national drama 'in which so many curious themes are developed'. It is not possible, he claims, 'to give human interest to the problems of kings and warriors in the form of Irish drama of mythical times', and he calls instead for a new dramatic realism.[12] He was worried by the Society's political bent too: in an article in the United Irishman he criticises Yeats's ethical view of literature as the 'principal voice of the conscience', and defines it himself more aesthetically as 'any piece of writing which in point of form is likely to secure permanence'. 'Fine writing', he observes, 'is not always on the side of the true and the just',[13] though Yeats weighed in by cannily

8.   Maire Davis, 'Memoir of Frederick Ryan', in The Irish Independent (January 14, 1955). There is no corroboration of the suggestion that Ryan introduced Fay to Yeats in R. F. Foster's official biography W. B. Yeats: A Life, vol 1: The Apprentice Mage (London, 1997).

9.   See Robert Hogan and James Kilroy, The Abbey Theatre: The Years of Synge 1905–1909 (Dublin, 1978), pp. 98, 102.

10. See Ann Saddlemyer (ed.), Collected Letters of John Millington Synge (Oxford, 1983), vol. 1, p. 141n.

11. ibid, p. 197.

12. Hogan and Kilroy, The Abbey Theatre, p. 121.

13. 'Censorship and Independence', United Irishman, November 23, 1901.

brandishing the example of Ibsen, knowing his colleague to be a devout Ibsenite. Colum writes that Ryan's role in the Revival 'was to pierce with the rays of rationalism the Celtic twilight years of Yeats and AE when it became too druidic'.[14]

Ryan also upbraided Yeats for kow-towing to popular opinion by seeking credentials from Catholic theologians for his officially blasphemous play *The Countess Cathleen*.[15] The National Theatre Society seemed to him in the end a 'flash in the pan' which provided a vehicle for already established writers but brought no unknown ones to the fore; he disliked its partiality for the 'mystical and semi-supernatural', and wanted to see a genuinely popular theatre in its place.[16] Despite his misgivings about the mystical, he apparently played the part of a monk in Yeats's *The King's Threshold*, a role which no doubt suited his ascetic temperament, and Stephen Gwynn claims that he appeared in the first production of George Moore's *Deirdre* in 1902.[17] Frank Fay had doubts about his acting ability, just as Ryan had doubts about Fay's management skills.[18] J. M. Synge thought Ryan's performance in *The King's Threshold* 'dreadful'.[19]

Ryan's only play, *The Laying of the Foundations*, was produced in the Antient Concert Rooms in Brunswick (now Pearse) Street in 1902, and according to William O'Brien was 'one of the things that led to the formation of the Abbey theatre'.[20] Lady Gregory reports that the play toured the USA, along with three pieces by Yeats and one of her own, and was well received there.[21] The script was lost during the tour, but the second act turned up among Fay's papers some decades later.[22] Stilted and lifeless in its dialogue, it reads like a poor translation of Ibsen and takes as its protagonist Michael O'Loskin, a fiercely idealistic city architect encircled by graft and corruption who wants to rebuild *Cathair-Tabhairairedhuitfein* (the city of Lookafteryourself) on sound foundations, but discovers that his own father is a slum-owner and jerry-builder. A cardboard cut-out of James Connolly appears as the labour agitator Nolan. The piece was given a second showing at the Rotunda

14.   Colum, *Arthur Griffith* (Dublin, 1959), p. 76.
15.   See his letter in the *Irish Independent*, May 11, 1899.
16.   'Has the National Theatre Failed?', *United Irishman*, November 9, 1901.
17.   Gwynn, *Irish Literature and Drama*, p. 157.
18.   See Yeats, *Collected Letters*, vol. 3, p. 311n.
19.   Ann Saddlemyer (ed.), *The Collected Letters of John Millington Synge*, vol. 1 (Oxford, 1983), p. 82.
20.   O'Brien in O'Riordan, *Socialism, Democracy and the Church*, p. 59.
21.   Lady Gregory, p. 38.
22.   The play was rediscovered by Robert Hogan and James Kilroy, who reprint it in their *Lost Plays of the Irish Renaissance* (Dixon, California, 1970). It is also reprinted by John Kelly in his 'A Lost Abbey Play: *The Laying of the Foundations*', *Ariel*, vol. 1, no. 4 (3 July 1970). Kelly prefaces the play with what, along with Manus O'Riordan's work, is the fullest biographical account of Ryan to date.

in 1903. There is some evidence that Yeats wanted to revive it in 1913, the year of its author's death, only to discover that there was by then no trace of the manuscript. Yeats's views of the play varied from calling it 'excellent . . . a really very astonishing peice [sic] of satire' to describing it somewhat less enthusiastically as 'a very witty though slightly rambling attack on municipal corporation of a slightly socialistic tinge'. Frank Fay, never a fan of Ryan, dismissed it as 'a drama of drain pipes after the Ibsen model'.[23]

William O'Brien records *en passant* that Ryan was 'very friendly' with James Joyce, and even suggests that he may have introduced the young Joyce to the work of Ibsen.[24] Ryan crops up in chapter nine of *Ulysses* in a passage which refers to the fact that Stephen Dedalus is the only paid contributor to the journal *Dana*: 'Fred Ryan wants space for an article on economics. Fraidrine. Two pieces of silver he lent me. Tide you over.' 'Fraidrine' might just be an imitation of the way Ryan pronounced his own name, and the allusion to the two pieces of silver is to the five shillings Joyce is reputed to have tapped him for when setting sail for Europe. Hence the ambiguity 'Tide you over'. Ryan was also a good friend of George Moore and most of the literary and political luminaries of the day, though his closest associate was Francis Sheehy Skeffington, whose pacifist doctrines no doubt appealed to his temperamental aversion to violence.[25] As a lifelong apologist for women's rights and a worker in the suffrage movement, Ryan probably absorbed much of his feminism from Hanna Sheehy Skeffington.[26] Francis remarked in his obituary of Ryan that he favoured the extension of the franchise to women at a time when such an idea was merely derided. The *Irish Review* of August 1912 carried a powerful plea from Ryan for women's suffrage, under the title 'The Suffrage Triangle'. In 1906 he proposed to Sheehy Skeffington the idea of a National Democratic Committee, which Michael Davitt was prevented from chairing by his death. The committee fell gradually apart, but out of it sprang the journal *The National Democrat*, which Ryan and Sheehy Skeffington co-edited throughout 1907. He had previously co-edited the remarkable cultural journal *Dana* (1904–5) with John Eglinton, a periodical which had the distinction of turning down a very early draft of Joyce's *Portrait of the Artist as a Young Man*.[27]

23.   See Yeats, *Collected Letters*, vol. 3, pp. 232, 623, 277n.

24.   O'Brien, in O'Riordan, *Socialism, Democracy and the Church,* p. 60. I can trace no reference to this in any account of Joyce's life.

25.   See Leah Levinson, *With Wooden Sound: A Portrait of Hannah Sheehy-Skeffington* (Syracuse, 1983), p. 93.

26.   Ryan is described as an 'ardent supporter of the suffrage movement' in an obituary in the *Irish Independent*, 9 April 1913.

27.   Stanislaus Joyce reports in his diary that the draft was rejected 'because of the sexual experiences narrated in it . . . Jim thinks they rejected it because it is all about himself, though they professed great admiration for the style of the paper' (quoted in Richard Ellmann, *James Joyce* [New York, 1959], p. 152). The

Ryan's second spell out of Ireland was in Cairo, which he visited in 1907. As Frank Sheehy Skeffington acidly remarks in his obituary of his friend, he was a fine journalist who could never make a living at the trade in Ireland since 'he never wrote a line which he did not believe'.[28] In 1907, Ryan had published in his *National Democrat* an essay by the Egyptian nationalist leader Mustafa Kamil, who in 1900 had established in Cairo the journal *The Standard* as the chief organ of Egyptian nationalist opinion. Kamil later launched English- and French-language versions of his newspaper under the title *The Egyptian Standard*, and hired an Irishman, William Maloney, to edit them for him. Maloney was an old comrade of Ryan's from the Young Ireland branch of the United Irish League,[29] and Ryan, in dire need of journalistic employment and reputed to speak perfect French, went out to Cairo to co-edit the paper. While he was there he also published a translation of Kamil's letters.

The *Egyptian Standard* folded after Kamil's sudden death in 1909 and Ryan returned to Dublin, where he reinvolved himself in radical politics. James Connolly, returning to Ireland in 1910 after seven years' absence in the USA, is said to have gone straight to Ryan's house in Rathmines. The house still stands, a pleasant, modest-sized Georgian residence. Gratified by the progress of the Socialist Party of Ireland, Connolly became one of Ryan's close collaborators, and accepted the post of national organiser of the party. One year later, however, financial straits forced Ryan to leave for England again, this time to edit Wilfred Scawen Blunt's anti-colonialist newspaper *Egypt*. Blunt describes him in his diaries as 'an intelligent young man of the same Irish type as Malony [*sic*], good, modest and sincere'.[30] It is a pity that Blunt was unable to spell the name of one of his most important adjutants. Ryan remarks in a newspaper article that Blunt believed that the British decision to coerce Egypt in 1882 was due in some degree to their anger at the Phoenix Park assassinations.[31] Living in London again, he worked for the electoral victory of George Lansbury, later leader of the Labour Party. He died of appendicitis in 1913 at the age of thirty-nine while staying with Wilfred Blunt, and is buried near

offending editor would seem to be more likely Eglinton, who remarked that he could not understand the piece, than Ryan himself. Joyce got his own back later by sending the poem 'My love is in a light attire' to the journal and becoming the only contributor to be paid (Ellmann, p. 171).

28.   Francis Sheehy Skeffington, 'Frederick Ryan – The Saint of Irish Rationalism', *Irish Review* (May 1913).

29.   Maloney seems to have been a long-standing colleague of Ryan's, having been involved with him in the Dublin Philosophical Society and the National Democratic Committee. See Sheehy Skeffington, 'Frederick Ryan – The Saint of Irish Rationalism'.

30.   Wilfred Scawen Blunt, *My Diaries* (London, 1932), p. 657. For a brief account of Blunt, see N. Jeffares's essay 'Blunt: Almost an Honorary Irishman', in his *Images of Invention* (Gerrards Cross, 1996).

31.   'Ireland and Egypt', *Irish Nation*, 25 September 1909.

Blunt's home in Crawley in Sussex. James Larkin, embroiled in that year in the great Dublin lock-out, wrote a glowing notice of his life, Francis Cruise O'Brien proposed a vote of sympathy after a lecture in the Abbey,[32] and Blunt commemorated his death with an atrociously bad sonnet.[33]

Francis Sheehy Skeffington called Ryan a philosophical descendant of the French eighteenth-century Encyclopaedists, praising his 'calm, incisive reasoning' and 'relentless logic'. There is indeed an Enlightenment crispness and lucidity about his prose, which manages to be at once cool and committed, equable and sardonic. He is an intriguing combination of Marxist and liberal rationalist, Morris and Mill, suggesting in his own person the way in which any authentic socialism must be an extension of classical liberalism as well as its critique. Something of this tough, well-tempered reasonableness is captured in his only book, Criticism and Courage (1906), a selection of his pieces from Dana on the topic of freedom of thought. Ryan was a formidable champion of intellectual liberty and a relentless scourge of clerical censorship, scorning the 'mental and moral cowardice' of a provincial torpor which refuses to submit its beliefs to critical scrutiny. Ireland was a culture profoundly afraid of intellectual conflict, 'warped and injured by lack of political freedom', the prevailing tone of its religious establishment 'a cultivated ignorance, as ludicrous as it is contemptible'.[34] Evasion and insincerity typified its theologians' response to scientific humanism, with their absurd claim that those who disagreed with them were morally degenerate. An admirer of Mill, Morley, Darwin, Comte, Spencer, Tyndall and Huxley, Ryan has great fun with the quaint clerical notion that one reads these weighty thinkers in order to dig out a licence for moral laxity. How many of those charged in our police courts, he gravely inquires, are students of positivism?[35]

The game is up, Ryan somewhat sanguinely considers, for dogmatic religion, and the problem now is to place morality on a sounder basis. He speaks with high Victorian zeal of the 'positivist and scientific ideal', and in Comtist vein urges a recognition of the 'supremacy of humanity'. Sectarianism is to be countered not by 'boycotting, by intimidation, or by abuse', but 'by science

32.   See Irish Independent, 9 April 1913.
33.   Larkin's obituary of Ryan appeared in The Irish Worker for 12 April 1913. Blunt's sonnet can be found in his My Diaries, p. 825.
34.   Criticism and Courage (Dublin, 1906), pp. 15, 37.
35.   There is an interesting subcurrent of positivism in nineteenth-century Irish thought, of which Ryan is one of the last inheritors; the creed's upbeat scientific progressivism was not to survive the first world war. John Kells Ingram was a disciple of Comte, visited him in 1855, and dedicated his Outlines of the History of Religion to him. Ingram was a key influence in the Trinity College of his day, and something of his Comtism passed into the earlier work of the rationalist, secularist, sociologically-minded W. E. H. Lecky. See Donal McCartney, W. E. H. Lecky: Historian and Politician 1838–1903 (Dublin, 1992), p. 12.

and by moral appeal',[36] of which national self-government is the first step. In the face of a moral code which sees humanity as naturally prone to evil, he affirms in benevolist style, in a tradition we have already examined, that 'sympathy is as natural to the heart as that purely self-regarding feeling on which the dogmatist solely bases his "moral" appeals'.[37] He has, in short, a rational-progressivist view of human nature, and even throws in a reference to Kropotkin's *Mutual Aid*, that bible of libertarian faith in human virtue. Like most advocates of a naturalistic ethics, he avoids the more embarrassing corollaries of this doctrine, such as why not torture toddlers if one feels a natural impulse to do so, by loading his sense of human nature in favour of the more morally admirable qualities.

But Ryan is finally a radical rationalist rather than a liberal one. He is not an Irish Matthew Arnold, promoting an ironic disinterestedness over the crudities of political conviction. 'Whenever anyone calls for a cessation of the political warfare and a "union of all classes" ', he observes in most unArnoldian fashion, 'we know at once that he is a reactionary, well-meaning or otherwise.'[38] He even sails as close as he dares to justifying the Phoenix Park murders, which he describes with surprising boldness as 'excusable even if regrettable'. A passionate faith in intellectual freedom does not entail that any view is as good as any other. It is rather a way of discovering which views are to be promoted and which combated. To cultivate the free play of the mind as an end in itself is an alternative to the bigotry of the Catholic Truth Society only for those privileged souls for whom there is nothing of great moral or political significance at stake.

'I am not so enamoured of any reform or any opinion', Ryan writes in an article on 'The Economic Future of Ireland', 'as to blind myself to what can be urged against it; and I can hardly compare in value an intelligent critic and an unintelligent supporter.'[39] It is not that his open-mindedness sits incongruously with his Marxism and nationalism, but that these views actually deepen his liberalism. The clergy, he observes, call for the suppression of newspapers advocating class hatred, but they always seem to have in mind labour journals pressing for higher wages, not capitalist ones clamouring to cut them. 'The capitalist press, in the view of minds like Father McEnerney's, never stirs up class against class. It never abuses trade unions or denounces the working men's leaders. It only preaches in dulcet terms the love of social order to the often sweated victims of social injustice.' Unafraid to take on a body as august as the Local Vigilance Committee for the Suppression of Immoral Literature in Sligo, Ryan notes that the clergy's training has 'unfitted them to discriminate between actual immorality or indecency and any rational dissent from

36.   ibid, p. 33.
37.   ibid, p. 49.
38.   ibid, p. 11.
39.   *The Harp* (July 1909).

the views which they favour in religion and politics'. He quotes the great English liberal John Morley's dictum that 'no possible evil of freedom is half so grave as the demonstrated evils of suppression', and condemns 'self-elected committees of ignorant busybodies'.[40] In the Ireland of 1912, this was fighting talk.

Ryan has an extraordinarily keen nose for cant, and turns the full blast of his urbane satire against it. He reports in his journal *The New Democrat* on the essay of a monsignor who detects a danger to faith and morals in public libraries: 'Newcastle West in all its bookless glory was contrasted with vile places like Dublin and Cork which possess Free Libraries, and where even Protestants are tolerated on municipal bodies without bringing about the end of the moral world'. The same cleric attributes a growing insecurity on the streets of Ireland's cities to the malign influence of public libraries. All this 'nauseous cant' about immoral books, Ryan remarks, is not at all about obscenity: 'Shakespeare himself has made murder, adultery, jealousy and lust the object of his inimitable art.' It is about preventing people from reading works which run contrary to the views of the church, but which the priests are too ignorant to refute. 'Assuredly', he writes with impressive *gravitas*, 'if there is to be a bandying of charges of "immorality", I do not know against whom that charge could more properly be brought than against those who use their influence to slander men who give their honest thought to the world, or those who impute vice to men whose arguments they are too indolent to refute.' The programme of the *New Democrat* will thus be to fight the 'twin tyrannies which oppress Ireland – the British Government and the Catholic Hierarchy' – by fostering free speech and opinion, educating the people and enabling them to 'develop character' by opening its columns to all kinds of viewpoints, 'if courteously expressed'.[41] The editors were to put this pluralism into practice by running in the first number of the journal a hostile review of Ryan's *Criticism and Courage* which brands him as a survivor of the middle ages.

Independence of thought was also the hallmark of *Dana*, which Ryan edited with John Eglinton from 1904 to 1905. Their range of material was strikingly varied: poems by Joyce, Roger Casement and George Russell, essays on France, Jane Austen, religion, colonialism, education, prose pieces by George Moore, R. B. Cunningham Grahame on Parnell, Padraic Colum on creameries, Jane Barlow on Irish literacy, Eglinton on Nietzsche or Brian Merriman. Synge detested the journal, denouncing Eglinton 'as a fearful instance of pedantic degeneration', and announcing that there was 'no hope' for the publication.[42] Secularist, rationalist and humanist in bent, the journal announced chin-leadingly in its first issue that 'people are not accustomed to

40.   'The Labour Crusade', in *The Irish Review* (January 1912).
41.   *New Democrat,* vol.1, no. 1 (February 1907).
42.   Saddlemyer, The *Collected Letters of John Millington Synge*, vol. 1, p. 88.

think in Ireland', and declared war on the pietism of Canon Sheehan and his ilk. Eglinton remarks acerbically in the second number of the journal that 'Dante had a place in his Inferno for the joyless souls, and if his conception be true the population of that circle will be largely modern Irish.' 'It is a sad truth', comments George Russell, 'that in Ireland every cause is injured more by its adherents than by its opponents.'[43] An essay by Ryan entitled 'Political and Intellectual Freedom' denounces the 'rival bigotries' of Orangeism and Catholicism, but sees the winning of national self-government as an essential first step beyond this sterile antagonism. His anti-sectarianism is of a radical rather than liberal brand, seeing political and intellectual independence as allies rather than opposites. Colonialism breeds intellectual torpor and conformity, so that 'a people long suffering from political servitude have the vices of slavery, lack of constructive political faculty, lack of initiative, lack of the wise compromise that comes of action'. The Irish, Ryan adds, 'have shown at least as much political sagacity as the English',[44] but 'trampled by alien and unsympathetic rule, [they] have looked with aching eyes to a heaven of bliss, and they have, more or less contentedly, lain down in their chains soothed by the hope of after-reward'. In short, he gives as little comfort to the colonialists as he does to the chauvinists, boldly unafraid to round upon his compatriots but clear too that their spiritual inertia has its roots in material oppression.

Dana both berates the Irish and affirms their right to political autonomy. Its pages are unswervingly *engagé* yet hospitable to conflicting views. Ryan is rigorous, hard-headed, dryly ironic; Eglinton is less nationalist and more suavely Arnoldian, putting in a good word for the British Empire and even for the penal laws, which were apparently a valuable source of discipline.[45] Whereas Ryan is terse and pointed, Eglinton is discursive and generalising. The spiritually individualist Eglinton enthuses over the spirit of humanity, while Ryan is more preoccupied with anti-Semitism. If *Dana* is that rare article in early twentieth-century Ireland, a quasi-Comtist organ promoting the religion of humanity, Eglinton is hotter on the religion and Ryan keener on the humanity. A contributor calling himself 'Ossian' waxes lyrical over the virtues of imperialism, rhapsodically claiming that Britain has established the 'most perfect freedom of action and thought . . . ever known under any government',[46] only to be rapped smartly over the knuckles by Fred Ryan in a subsequent number. Ryan himself puts in a highly qualified word for Sir Horace Plunkett's *Ireland in the New Century*, while Maurice Moore remarks in

43.   'Physical Force in Literature', *Dana*, vol. 1, no. 5, 1904.
44.   *Dana*, vol. 1, no. 1, May 1904. The journal was republished in a single volume edition by the Lemma Publishing Corporation in New York in 1970.
45.   Eglinton's slim volumes of prose, with their humane, disinterested intelligence, are still well worth reading. See in particular *Two Essays on the Remnant* (Dublin, 1894), *Pebbles from a Brook* (Kilkenny and Dublin, 1901), *Bards and Saints* (Dublin, 1906), and *Anglo-Irish Essays* (Dublin, 1917).
46.   'Imperialism II', *Dana*, vol. 1, no. 2, 1904.

the second issue of the journal that 'my view is not that Sir Horace Plunkett is a dishonest thinker, but that he is not a thinker at all'. 'Dissent and heresy', Ryan writes, 'are really the very salt of the intellectual life',[47] yet he is no maverick individualist either, toeing as he does an orthodox anti-imperialist line to magnificent effect. In a coldly eloquent response to Ossian's comfortably generalised apologia for empire, he notes that he has 'no eye for the Jameson Raid, the Transvaal War, the age-long tragedy of India, prevented from developing along her own lines and taxed to famine point by English officialdom, and the age-long tragedy of Ireland, kept in a state of perpetual smouldering civil war and bleeding to the point of extinction'.[48]

In our own day, this kind of impassioned discourse is one thing, while the language of irony is quite another. Dismantling this stale antithesis is not the least of Ryan's virtues; as his colleague Tom Kettle observes, political struggle is a two-edged sword, 'with enthusiasm for one of its edges and irony for the other'.[49] Ryan's writing manages to be at once tolerant and partisan. Those uncomfortably specific allusions to the Jameson Raid and the Transvaal are typical of his bent for practical politics, a preference which he combines unusually with a strong philosophical penchant. To raise fundamental 'questions of humanity', to open up suppressed theoretical conflicts, is part of the journal's critique of a narrowly based nationalism which seeks to promote 'an artificial and sentimental unity in Irish life' by burying contentious issues.[50] Young Ireland, Ryan considers, largely evaded such far-reaching philosophical issues of democracy, republicanism, monarchy, land reform and the like, as a literary and idealist rather than 'scientific' and realist movement. In Arnoldian fashion, he chides its failure to enrich its politics with intellectual reflection. As a result of this philosophical dearth, 'Nationalism to the majority of people in Ireland means mostly the hoisting of the Green Flag in place of the Union Jack over a society resting on a basis of competitive capitalism differing in no vital or essential particular from any other such society or from our own condition now'.[51] The whole tenor of the journal is one of intellectual confrontation, the nailing of romantic evasions and the fostering of vigorous dialectic. Such pluralism is not an alternative to political commitment, as it might be for some today; on the contrary, the nurturing of intellectual vitality is *Dana*'s contribution to the national movement, and only political independence will yield the material conditions for true freedom of thought to flourish. Ryan is admirably open-minded, but a zealot too for clarity and concision: in a piece in the *National Democrat* he defends his desire for 'definite convictions', as hostile to the woolly-minded as he is to the doctrinaire.

47.   'Church Disestablishment in France I', *Dana*, vol. 1, no. 10, 1905.
48.   'Empire and Liberty', *Dana*, vol. 1, no. 4, 1904.
49.   T. M. Kettle, *The Philosophy of Politics* (Dublin, 1906), p. 16.
50.   'Introductory', *Dana*, vol. 1, no 1, May 1904.
51.   'Young Ireland and Liberal Ideas', *Dana*, vol. 1, no. 2, 1904.

Throughout his career, Ryan savaged Irish chauvinism as a libertarian, a nationalist and an international socialist. The struggle against British colonialism could not be divorced from matters of social class: 'William Murphy, running his tramwaymen twelve or thirteen hours a day, with one day off in ten, gaily tells us that he is a patriot! . . . This is ideal nationality, this which shouts in one breath against the music hall and the gutter Press, and in the next clamours for the very conditions to be multiplied which have bred the music hall and the gutter Press in every manufacturing country under the sun.'[52] Dialectical thought becomes textual irony here, in a materialist perspective beyond both middle-class liberal and bourgeois nationalist. As a socialist, Ryan sets his face firmly against one of the nationalists' leading demands, tenant proprietorship of the land. If land can be no more a private possession than the air, then it cannot be right to claim it as one's own, 'even though the "owner" be called Farmer Murphy instead of Lord Tomnoddy'. His critique of nationalism, in other words, is far more fundamental than that of those anti-nationalist liberals, of his time and our own, who are entirely at one with the philosophy of possessive individualism.

What is the point, Ryan scoffs, of creating a lot of little landlords in place of a few large ones? What about the landless labourers, whom this 'solution' to the country's agrarian ills hardly touches? Why should the state advance money to farmer Murphy to enable him to become 'a master over Pat?' The Land Bills, he declares with heretical boldness, are just palliatives: peasant proprietorship means the 'manufacture of little outposts of capitalism', and will probably make socialism harder to achieve than the presence of a few big landlords. Legislative independence is worthless without economic autonomy: 'a starving man can't eat a parliament nor a homeless man get lodgings in Westminster Hall . . . I am not an enthusiastic Home Ruler in order to set up a talk shop in College Green to rival the talk shop at Westminster or provide a stage on which the Justins, and Timothy's, and John's and Willie's can perform the same farce and burlesque in which the Balfours and Harcourts excel at St Stephens.'[53] He is, in short, obedient to the tradition of Fintan Lalor and Michael Davitt in his belief that the liberal critique of national chauvinism is simply not radical enough; and like those men, he urges this case as a nationalist. The *National Democrat* saw itself as consciously continuing the heritage of Davitt, who was only recently dead, and Ryan could be dubbed a disciple of Davitt quite as much as a comrade of Connolly. Davitt, wrote Sheehy Skeffington in the first number of the journal, was 'the greatest National Democrat Ireland ever produced', a politician who 'had no toleration for that narrow insularity which is the Irish form of Jingoism, and which runs into extravagances of economic and intellectual protectionism'.

52.   'Capitalism and Nationalism: A Socialist View', *United Irishman,* 29 December 1900.
53.   'The Economic Future of Ireland', *The Harp* (July 1909).

Ryan is adept at embarrassing conservative nationalists by pointing out, for example, that their portrayal of socialism as 'red ruin and savagery' is just as much a caricature as the English view of Irish nationalism as 'Phoenix Park murders and Kerry moonlighting'.[54] Sinn Féin, he points out, did not devise the Gaelic Revival, the industrial development movement or the national theatre: 'I respectfully decline to give "Sinn Féin" credit for everything that was done in Ireland by anybody for ten or fifteen years before it was heard of'. One should not behave as though one discovered the notion of national self-reliance single-handedly, and as though all previous Irishmen and women had been 'poltroons and knaves'. Nor can one alter the fact that Britain is meddling in Ireland's affairs by pretending not to recognise it, as in Sinn Féin's abstentionist tactics. There has been, he considers, 'a notable tendency to substitute for the wide sweep and generous idealism of the United Irishmen a narrow and purely racial idea of Nationalism, divorced from all large or permanent principle, and moving in an atmosphere of petty animosity'. A pseudonymous contributor to the fourth issue of *Dana*, possibly Ryan himself, speaks dolefully of the emergence in Ireland of a new spirit of nationality which is ignorant not only of Molyneux and Grattan but also of the Renaissance, the Reformation and the French revolution. Socialists like himself and Connolly support nationalism 'just as we would have wished success to the French *bourgeoisie* in 1780 in overthrowing the Court, and would have done nothing to thwart them, nor anything to save the Bourbons. Perfectly – perhaps one might say brutally – clear as to the immediate results of the political fight, and to the social outlook of many of the men who are waging it, we would yet support it.'[55]

So it is that Ryan contributes an angry, eloquent piece entitled 'Against the Anti-Semitism of Arthur Griffith' to Sinn Féin's own journal the *United Irishman*, remarking with the Limerick pogrom well in mind that 'it ill becomes Irishmen – themselves persecuted as a race for centuries – to join in a race-vendetta against others'.[56] Such racist nationalism, he comments elsewhere, will take up the anti-colonialist cause in struggles outside Ireland only if the colonialist in question happens to be Britain. The general attitude is that 'we must never take the liberal or humanitarian side for fear of playing the British game', and that 'everyone who protests against the maltreatment of the Congolese is engaged in a British intrigue'. His internationalism, in short, actually makes him a more fervent supporter of national independence than those in Ireland who are most vociferously patriotic. Challenging Griffith's 'puerile

54. 'The Discussion of Socialism', *Irish Nation*, 4 September 1909.
55. 'Mr Connolly's Brilliant Work', a review of James Connolly's *Labour in Irish History* in the *Irish Nation*, 19 November 1910. Ryan writes here as elsewhere under the pseudonym 'Finian', possibly a conflation of 'Fenian', the Irish name Finian and 'F. Ryan'.
56. *United Irishman*, 28 May 1904.

bombast' on the national question, its 'barefaced and shameless playing to the forces of reaction, within Ireland and without', he writes that he 'can easily conceive a "subject" people with freer and robuster spirits than a nominally "free" people that had bought its freedom by some miserable bargain'. What would Wolfe Tone ('who has been quietly removed from the present-day Sinn Féin pantheon') say, he who was the friend of the French revolutionary leaders, were he to witness the 'ignorant mediaevalism of Mr Sweetman or the feudalist sympathies of Mr Griffith?'[57] Once again, Ryan criticises nationalism from the standpoint of international socialist republicanism, not from the viewpoint of a middle-class liberalism which is complicit with the social and economic system of the colonialist. From that perspective, ironically, there is little enough to choose between nationalism and its liberal-minded critics. The struggle against Britain is for him essentially 'a branch of the democratic conflict', which is to say that he views it in political rather than ethnic terms;[58] national self-determination and socialist self-government are twin applications of liberal Enlightenment. It does not follow from this, however, that every nationalist is a democrat. Too many of them, Ryan considers, see political independence as an end rather than a starting-point.

Such a one was Arthur Griffith, who contributed a classically backhanded obituary of Ryan to the journal *Sinn Féin*. Griffith characterises Ryan's mind accurately enough as that of the 'English mid-Victorian philosophical Radicals', a phrase in which 'mid-Victorian' is probably the only term Griffith himself would consider inoffensive. Trusting to the 'cant' of the Brotherhood of Man, the idea of the nation seemed to him 'a small thing – even an obstructive thing – to the apotheosis of man, and the suffering Egyptian had not less claim on him than his own countrymen'. What would be a compliment from anyone else is a rebuke in the mouth of Griffith, though he does have the bigheartedness to acknowledge that few intellectuals could have served Ireland better than Ryan if he had turned his back on a 'frozen cosmopolitanism' and 'succumbed to the Gael in him'. He was, Griffith graciously concedes, 'honourable, generous and fearless', as well as being 'the only man in Ireland who ever drifted into the cosmopolitan heresy in our time who was a real loss to Nationalism'.[59] In a gallant defence of his dead comrade, Francis Sheehy Skeffington enquired of Griffith why one who advocated the complete independence of the Irish people should be denied the title of nationalist, to which Griffith riposted that the nation for Ryan was just a collection of human beings rather than a 'soul', and that Ryan 'loved Ireland as a geometrician might love an equilateral triangle, but he loved half-a-dozen other countries in equal fashion'. In Griffith's eyes, Ryan's sin was to be both frigid and promiscuous. The nationalist Stephen Gwynn writes rather grudgingly of

57.   'Sinn Féin and Reaction', *Irish Nation,* 13 November 1909.
58.   *New Democrat,* vol. 1, no. 1 (February 1907).
59.   Arthur Griffith, 'The Death of Frederick Ryan', *Sinn Féin,* 12 April 1913.

Shaw that 'logic made him international';[60] and much the same could be said of Fred Ryan. As for the soul of the nation, Ryan himself had written in the third issue of the *National Democrat* that he was 'a little suspicious of a philosophy which would save the "soul" of a nation whilst the tyrant rode roughshod over the body. Soon there would be very little "soul" left to save.' What some of his critics saw as a clinical, bloodless quality to his thought (even Sheehy Skeffington's warm-hearted obituary speaks a little edgily of his remorseless logic and the 'limpid coldness' of his prose style) was in fact the coolly demystified vision of the materialist.

Like every orthodox materialist from Marx to Morris, Ryan held that the highest ends of human life were spiritual, but that most men and women were currently prevented from achieving them by material want and the excessive demands of labour. The point of political transformation was to create the material conditions in which they could cease to be so distracted by these needs, and be free instead to live predominantly by 'culture'. 'The most spiritual work today', Ryan writes, 'is material: what use is it to tell a man who has to work thirteen or fourteen hours a day for mere subsistence wages that he ought to cultivate his mind?' Moral values are equally dependent on a material infrastructure: how can virtue and modesty flourish, he asks, when whole families are forced to live in one or two rooms? There are some of us, he observes, 'who think intellectual, moral and, in the highest sense of the word, spiritual progress is of prime importance, and ought to be, in the last analysis, the goal of all our effort. Yet it will be admitted that all these questions are secondary for the moment to the problem of poverty and overwork.' 'For the moment' is a vital Marxist emphasis: the point of stressing the primacy of the material over the spiritual here and now is so that it can be historically reversed. The poor are those who are deprived of leisure and eduction as well as of material necessities, and Ryan shares Walter Benjamin's view that every monument of civility secretes a subtext of barbarism: 'Whole districts are desolated and thousands of hearts are broken so that a Clanricarde or a De Freyne can squander themselves in dissipation in London or Paris.'[61]

Those who try prematurely to live by culture in the present fail to grasp the necessary conditions for 'culture' becoming available to all, and among these for Ryan are the cultural nationalists. 'The desire for political independence is admirable', he writes in a piece on the Irish language in *Dana*. Only a nation of slaves would contentedly resign themselves to be governed by another nation. 'But the mere desire to speak another language does not of necessity correlate at all with the active desire for political freedom.' To make the Irish language the test of nationalism would be to shut out some of the best who have served the cause of Irish liberty in the past. The revival of

60.   Stephen Gwynn, *Irish Literature and Drama*, p. 147.
61.   'The Economic Future of Ireland', *The Harp* (July 1909).

Gaelic culture, while valuable in itself, can also be a form of political dis-placement: 'If the Irish people could be lulled to rest with a new toy, in the shape of a new tongue, their English governors need not grieve . . . And if the people are content to let the substance of liberty go, for the gew-gaw of a new grammar, so much the better – for the reactionaries.' The Gaelic League, he contends, contains its fair share of culture fetishists and neo-medievalists, and Ryan is properly sceptical of its popularity: how, he inquires, can any move-ment which appeals to both Cardinal Logue and the *United Irishman*, W. B. Yeats and *The Freeman's Journal*, not arouse suspicion, since if it realised the objectives of some of these men and organs of opinion it certainly could not realise those of others.

Unlike the liberals, Ryan sees that an all-inclusive pluralism can thrive precisely on its lack of definitive content. Even so, with characteristic even-handedness, he praises the League as well: it has 'brought a spirit of study into the country', along with 'a great amount of self-sacrificing work', and has stimulated an indifference towards England that is 'a needed variation on the traditional Irish attitude towards England of appeal, apology and abuse'.[62] 'When the prowess and glory of England are sung to us in every key', he adds with mock humility, 'it is well occasionally to frankly admit that we have nothing in our own history to exactly compare with the England of Clive, of the Chinese Opium War, of the African Concentration Camps and the Peace-ful Mission to Tibet.' Yet even this tart response must in turn be qualified, in Ryan's typically dialectical manner: Ireland has indeed no such shameful record of imperial oppression, but 'a nation is not morally raised by dwelling on its own past glories or its neighbours' present sins; it is raised by increas-ing its ability to deal with its present problems, political, economic, and social, in a spirit of equity and a spirit of knowledge'.[63]

Ryan returns to this topic in a subsequent issue of *Dana*, rebuking both the urge to imitate English culture and the desire to 'aimlessly differentiate ourselves from other nations'. 'It is an ignoble thing to be a sycophant; it is a foolish thing to be a factious antagonist'. Neither pure difference nor pure identity is a sufficient response to Britain's overshadowing influence. It is pointless to vilify the neighbouring island just for the sake of it, and unwise to abandon some well-tried method or custom simply because 'another nation which we dislike has it too'. 'When the hurricanes of national and racial antagonism die away', he concludes, 'we must always come back to equity, to utility, and to righteousness.' He is himself a 'lover of Ireland', though by Ireland, he adds, he means not some mystical entity but 'the peas-ants in the fields, the workers in the factories, the teachers in the schools, the

---

62.   Ryan's judicious attitude to the Gaelic League is reminiscent of J. M. Synge's, who mocked and praised it simultaneously. See Declan Kiberd, *Synge and the Irish Language* (London, 1979), ch. 9.

63.   'Is the Gaelic League a Progressive Force?', *Dana*, vol. 1, no. 7, 1904.

professors in the colleges. . .'. To privilege Gaelic culture over political independence is to claim that 'a nation, miserably poor, without political status,
without education, oppressed by another nation, taxed to extinction-point, is
to be preferred to a free nation, politically mistress of her own destinies, educated and prosperous, speaking a language not "her own" only in the sense
that it is spoken by the great majority of her people at a later date than the
previous one'. Ryan castigates ethnic and cultural nationalism; but he does so
in the name of political transformation, not simply as a liberal who finds ethnic chauvinism unsavoury. His habit is not to dismiss the struggle for national
independence, but to look through and beyond it.

'That everyone, physically and mentally capable of doing so', Ryan writes,
'should contribute his or her share of useful work to the Commonwealth, is a
proposition that may excite the spontaneous distrust of dukes and drones of
all kinds, but the ordinary people will easily survive the shock.' Those who
prate of the right to private property, he notes in the first number of the
National Democrat, forget that 'slavery was one of the forms of private property,
and it has disappeared amidst the protestations, no doubt, of the slaveholders
that their "rights" were being infringed'. Socialists are accused of violence, but
what of the 'vast armies and fleets, paid for out of the sweat and blood of the
peoples, largely to maintain the existing order?'[64] Even-handedness is here on
the side of the radicals, not the liberals. Ryan was not in fact himself an advocate of physical force: he was a social but not a political revolutionary, believing in 'rational persuasion of the majority' and critical of Sinn Féin's
'anti-Parliamentary dogma'. If he was socially at one with James Connolly, he
was politically to the right of him; the United Irish League to which he briefly
belonged was to the left of the Irish parliamentary party but certainly not
insurrectionary.[65] Desmond Ryan sees him, a little misleadingly, as a political
loner: 'One Fred Ryan, returned from Europe, wars upon all physical force and
Gaelic Leaguers and clergymen and Marxian Socialists with the utmost courtesy and persuasiveness . . . "Irial" is his pen name as all the world knows . . .
The Gaels like him not . . . The Socialists bristle weekly and hurl shibboleths
at him.'[66] In fact, Ryan is fairly clearly a Marxist, though not of the revolutionary stripe. 'No considerable body of sane men', he comments, 'with the vote
ready to their hands for seizing political power, will seriously or permanently
turn to 'revolutionary' methods.'[67] As a positivist, evolutionary Marxist typical
of the Second International period through which he lived, he held that a grad-
ualist approach to socialism was the only scientifically tenable position in view
of what he saw as the painfully slow nature of all social growth. He was also
an implacable critic of ultra-leftist purism, holding that one should keep one's

64. 'The Discussion of Socialism', *Irish Nation*, 4 September 1909.
65. See Andrew Malone, 'Frederick Ryan', *The Voice of Labour*, 28 April 1923.
66. Desmond Ryan, *Remembering Sion*, p. 53.
67. 'Socialism and the Parliamentary Method', *Irish Nation*, 24 July 1904.

ideals 'as high as may be, but . . . not despise any clean expedient or peevishly turn from any instrument however clumsy, if only they seem to bring your ideal nearer'.[68] As the voice of a rational yet radical humanism, he also untiringly denounced 'sectarian rancour and abuse'.

Ryan was a full-blooded internationalist, a position at odds with nationalism only for those who reduce the latter to mystical claptrap about the spiritual destiny of a privileged *Volk*. This includes both Arthur Griffith and most modern-day revisionists; it is just that the former rejoiced in the notion while the latter quite properly revile it. Since nationalism, for Ryan as for say Nelson Mandela today, was a matter not of ethnic purity but of democratic self-government, it was naturally a principle which transcended any particular nation. He was a cosmopolitan because he was a nationalist, not in spite of it. 'Are we to acquiesce,' he asks in an essay in *Dana*, 'in base and ignoble wars against the liberty of small communities?', and proceeds as usual to pinpoint the bland hypocrisy of the case he opposes. For the British imperialist, 'any people who do not delightedly welcome political slavery – when the brand is English – are . . . morally inferior beings, with a double dose of original sin. But if the slavery be other than English – Turkish, or Russian, or Austrian – then the people who resist it are patriots and heroes.' Hungarians, Bulgarians, Poles and Italians are noble freedom-fighters, but not Boers, Hindus or Irish. The Irish, he argues, are not a naturally mutinous people: 'Time after time British statesmen had only to be moderately honest in translating their professions into practice to be hailed as deliverers.' Indeed the comment is at least as much a smack at Irish deference as an apologia for his compatriots. He is typically impervious to idealist cant when it comes to the philanthropic rationales for imperialism: 'The unvarnished truth is that no nation interferes from motives of philanthropy in the affairs of other nations, and the ideal of world-rule is itself fundamentally vicious, since the rule of communities by themselves is infinitely better in the long run than the most wise and benevolent outside despotism.'

In an essay on Ireland and foreign affairs, Ryan writes witheringly of Arthur Griffith that 'he has enthused over the Kaiser and applauded the Czar. He has told us that Mr Chamberlain is a true patriotic Englishman, and he thinks the Labour Party of England a pack of tricksters. He thinks King Leopold should be allowed to torture the Congolese to his heart's content, and that the working classes of Spain . . . ought to be court martialled and shot.'[69] The Irish, Ryan considers, should not unthinkingly conclude that England's enemy is their friend, in a mere inversion of colonial prejudice. Even so, 'who is it wishes Ireland to be sympathetic with the massacres of the Matebele or the Tibetans, the robbery of the Boer States, the ignoble and costly farce in

68. Review of Jean Jaures's *Studies in Socialism*, *New Democrat,* vol. 1, no 1, February 1907.
69. 'Ireland and Foreign Affairs – What Should Be Our Attitude?', *Irish Nation,* 30 October 1909.

Somaliland, or the never-ending "frontier expeditions" in India in which human beings are slaughtered in order to keep the Indian Army efficient in the art of man-slaying?' The 'best Englishmen', after all, abhor these enterprises too. To say 'Englishman' in Ireland, Ryan observes, too often evokes not Mill, Cobden, Morley, Spencer, Arnold and Ruskin, but Disraeli, Balfour, Chamberlain and Curzon, the England of Kipling and the music halls. Chauvinist nationalism abominates England as such; liberal anti-nationalism tends merely to invert this racist judgement; Ryan's socialism, by contrast, discriminates amongst the English on a political basis, in a genuine rather than nominal pluralism. The idea of empire must fade, he concludes, if humanity is to grow 'in political science and moral feeling', and he summons the English socialist Edward Carpenter to his banner.[70]

Ryan's editorial contributions to the *Egyptian Standard*, which he edited from Cairo, reveal him at his most satirically combative. A controlled anger at British imperial hypocrisy is blended with his customary dry, analytical logic. In an editorial entitled 'A Question of Character', he mercilessly lampoons the Western view that colonised peoples lack the character for self-government. The apologists for imperialism, he writes with an eye to the playing fields of Eton, 'are always romancing about "developing character" – developing it, one may add, by playing the despot and encouraging subservience. But when real "character" presents itself, character which is not to be cajoled or browbeaten, which is not prepared to play the sycophant, and which demands its rights in no cringing tones, then a new note is struck. That is not the "character" the school-master wanted to develop at all, and so he turns round and denounces and misrepresents and belittles those who exhibit it. Yet its existence confutes his case. For the most striking proof that can be afforded of a subject people's capacity for freedom is that they strenuously demand it.' Ryan understands that the capacity for self-government can be fostered only in the process of being exercised, just as (so he comments) infants can only be taught to walk by being given an opportunity to do so. Colonial governments weep crocodile tears over their subalterns' incapacity for democracy while vigorously quelling every move they make to achieve it. The truth is that 'there is no honest desire that there shall ever exist in Egypt the capacity for self rule, as long as the growth of such capacity can be hampered'.[71]

70. 'Empire and Liberty', *Dana*, vol. 1 no. 4, 1904. The most definitive piece of extended work on Edward Carpenter, since the only one, is T. F. Eagleton, 'Nature and Spirit: A Study of Edward Carpenter in his Intellectual Context' (unpublished PhD thesis, Cambridge, 1968).

71. *Egyptian Standard*, 23 January 1908, Ministry of Culture National Library and Archives, Cairo. The Library appears to hold only the second volume of the periodical, which runs from 1 January to 9 April 1908. The paper, whose masthead slogan is 'Freedom at Home, Hospitality towards all', had been founded one year earlier, in March 1907. Ryan's editorials are unsigned, but can be fairly accurately identified on both stylistic and thematic grounds.

The Western powers, Ryan observes, assume that 'the whole non-European world is morally inferior to all Europe and is sunk in a barbarism from which it is the duty of Europe to rescue it. The methods of "rescue" generally consist in shooting down the people with all the ingenuity which immense attention to the arts of destruction has begotten in Europe, and then introducing every vice that the more moral side of Europe denounces and deplores.' With his usual dialectical turn of mind, he then goes on to renounce any sentimental romanticising of such technologically less advanced societies, of the kind displayed by some more credulous post-colonial theory today. There is no point in assuming 'the extra-European world to be an innocent sphere where moral turpitude is unknown or where the normal deflection of moral judgements, inseparable from humanity itself, are absent'. It would be absurd, he comments, 'to deny that there are great gains to the non-European nations from European contact. The great gift which Europe brings is knowledge, scientific and technical knowledge, financial and political knowledge, and a literary heritage built up by the labour of centuries.' But there is of course no reason why the vehicle of these benefits should be imperialism; and if a people are to have their vices, it is better that those vices should be indigenous rather than imported.[72]

What enrages Ryan most is imperial double standards: 'Everyone is continually engaged in ignoble and under-hand plots but the virtuous diplomats of the Imperialist's own country who having entered Egypt for instance temporarily, for the purpose of restoring order, have remained for twenty-five years, or who having begun the South African war to the cry of: "We seek no territory", ended by annexing the South African states.' On what grounds, he inquires, 'should it be outrageous for Mehemet Ali to claim a "right" in Syria and not outrageous for the English in India to claim a similar "right"? . . . the "right" of the sword and of sea-power . . . are valid when England is concerned whilst it is flat blasphemy for anyone else to hint at similar claims.' English newspapers denounce the tyranny of Russia with virtuous indignation, 'whilst England taxes the Indians to famine-point, gags the native press, and even "shadows" Englishmen, if they are suspected . . . of being friendly to the native cause'.[73] The imperialists are quick to label as 'fanaticism' any resistance to their rule, but 'what is the whole Imperialist cult but a gross fanaticism? This egoistic feeling that the East is uncivilised and needs to be "led forward", if one can assume it to be sincere, which is a severe strain, what is it but a gross superstition?'[74] Ryan is writing in the era of Kipling, Henley and Conrad; what makes him sound like a precursor of Edward Said is among other things the fact that he is an Irishman.

Indeed Ryan uses a good few of his editorials for the *Egyptian Standard* to report on the political situation in Ireland, sometimes in rather more detail

72. 'East and West', *Egyptian Standard*, 27 January 1908.
73. 'Fragments of History: Imperialistic Ethics', *Egyptian Standard*, 19 January 1908.
74. 'Fanaticism', *Egyptian Standard*, 29 February 1908.

than his Egyptian readers perhaps required. One editorial gives a crisp account of the debate on Irish Home Rule, a measure which Ryan fears may be subject, like Egyptian independence, to a degree of shuffling and feet-dragging. 'The new method of shelving awkward and obviously just causes', he writes, 'is not to declare against them; it is to declare *for* them, but to add that the time is not ripe or the moment propitious. Lord Cromer thinks Egypt ought to have autonomy – but not now; he is not in favour of British annex-ation, only for the present and as far as the eye can reach the British occupa-tion must continue.' Irish Home Rule will no doubt only become a matter of urgency once more when one of the British parliamentary parties needs to achieve office. 'Until that day arrives we fear it will remain a matter of pious profession for Mr Asquith and vain regret for Mr Birrell. It is merely one more instance which Oriental nations should note of the high moral level on which these transactions are conducted in the enlightened West.'[75] Elsewhere, Ryan berates his old ally William O'Brien for gullibly trusting to British Home Rule promises. 'Fighting like a devil for "conciliation", Mr O'Brien's immoderate enthusiasm for "moderation" became something painful. The most noisy and scurrilous journal in Ireland was that which was ostensibly preaching the virtues of co-operation and good will. Only all the abuse was reserved for Irishmen; all the good-will for the English Governors and their Irish allies . . . When "conciliation" can only be brought about by turning your guns on your own friends to the delight of your and their enemies, it is certainly time to reconsider your tactics.'[76]

It would not be hard to call to mind one or two exponents of this brand of immoderate moderation or sectarian conciliationism in the Ireland of our own day. The Egyptian National party is reproached by its critics as 'extrem-ist', Ryan writes, whereas 'If an active socialist party existed in Egypt they would probably find the program of the National Party quite moderate and suitable to their peculiar mental attitude. These people laud the via media as the royal road to everything desirable. Their policy in fact, if not in declara-tion, amounts to this, that the safest course to follow in the presence of two antagonistic forces is to side with neither. What usually happens in practice is that they . . . add their strength to that of the stronger force. Unhappily the stronger force is not always the morally superior one. The Man on the Ditch[77] may prate about the beauty of indetermination and moderation but the fact remains that he never initiates any movement.'[78] Ryan himself, as we have seen, is no revolutionary 'extremist', but he is alert to the two-facedness of those Western liberals for whom every militant case is extremist apart from their own implicit endorsement of the Western capitalist system. The point

75. 'The Irish Home Rule Debate', *Egyptian Standard*, 8 April 1908.
76. '"Conciliation" in Ireland', *Egyptian Standard*, 10 January 1908.
77. 'Ditch' in Hiberno-English means 'fence'; hence 'Man on the Fence'.
78. 'On Extremism', *Egyptian Standard*, 4 April 1908.

remains quite as valid today, both in Ireland and outside it. Ryan himself condemns both the violence of the 'physical force' tradition in Irish politics, and the violence of the economic system which generates mass unemployment; our own liberal commentators tend to be rather more selective in their moral wrath. When it comes to the conflict between black and white, or (for some of them, at least) women and men, there is no question of the truth lying somewhere in the middle; when it is a matter of market forces versus job security, they reach for their judicious moderation. Ryan is himself a conciliator, committed to rational persuasion rather than force; but he is aware of the spurious uses of this admirable ideal.

The same kind of liberal, Ryan notes, can be found masked in the persona of the 'reasonable imperialist', a brand of high-minded English moralism which clearly sticks in his craw. The 'moral Imperialist' will 'perforce stick to the "white man's burden" – and the swag – through an ineradicable sense of duty . . . It is excellent for the "subject races" to know that "for generations" they will be denied their liberty in their own interest – through the strict application of Christian principles. If the East which cannot understand the West were not governed by Western bureaucrats, there is no knowing but that the dreadful spectre of "Orientalism" might arise to terrify our souls.' Orientalism means among other things acquiescing in despotic rule; it is just that the 'Orientals' are occasionally ill-mannered enough to forget about this ethnic trait of theirs and demand political freedom instead. What this will mean, in the view of the reasonable imperialist, is minority rule by a native clique, a phenomenon which, so Ryan reminds us, is 'obviously Oriental. No one ever heard of such a thing in the West. Imagine England ever having been governed by anything but universal suffrage. Ireland as we know was always governed on the most democratic lines, no minority ever having been allowed to run the country.'[79] 'Why, in order to leave an impress on the better side of human civilisation should it be necessary to take away human liberty? Ibsen, Maeterlinck, Tolstoy, and Spencer have each of them left infinitely deeper marks on modern civilisation than ever the dapper little peer [Lord Curzon] will, though none of them ever "ruled over" 300 millions of human beings and the first two belonged to the smaller nations in Europe.' Nobody but the colonialists themselves recognise their own remarkable disinterestedness; in fact they don't even believe in it themselves, reverting to the language of the bully after playing the philanthropist. Lord Curzon speaks of the empire as having wiped out misery and destitution, and was himself Viceroy of a country [India] where 'the people die in myriads almost every year from famine, where freedom of speech and action are invaded at every turn by the Government of which he was the nominal head, and where "prosperity" as a term to descibe the state of the vast mass of the people is an odious perversion of the truth . . . The nauseous hypocrisy of the whole business, the alternation

79.   'The "Reasonable" Imperialist', *Egyptian Standard*, 6 February 1908.

of shoddy sentiment and brute threat, is disgusting to anyone not brought up
to the business.'[80] This, written in the tradition of Edmund Burke, is hardly
the language of moderation; it belongs rather to one of the most eloquent,
satirically lethal (as well as almost wholly unknown) critiques of colonial arrogance to be broadcast in the heyday of British imperialism.

Since Ryan's death in 1913, a correspondent writes ten years later, 'none has
appeared with his highly critical mind and great moral courage to take up the
work he left unfinished'.[81] One historian of Irish labour calls him 'the ablest
and most energetic advocate . . . of the rights of Labour',[82] while Sheehy
Skeffington, who sees his dominating impulse as 'love of truth', reports that
Ryan actually praised Pius X's benighted anti-Modernist encyclical because it
was at least logical and consistent, as opposed to what he saw as the woolli-
ness of theological Modernism itself. 'He held in scorn', Sheehy Skeffington
declares in a fine flourish, 'the servile truckling to British Imperialism, which
our modern "leaders" of "Nationalism" offer in return for the Asquithian mess
of pottage.' Ryan was in his view the 'ablest contemporary representative' of
the school of Irish democratic nationalism which includes Tone, Lalor and
Davitt . . . the clearest and most convincing advocate of Socialism in Ireland'.
His mind was a 'model of lucidity . . . an infallible touchstone of genuine-
ness'.[83]

   Manus O'Riordan describes Ryan as 'the most outspoken opponent of
Irish anti-Semitism',[84] while many who knew him comment on his fearless-
ness and – despite his candour – his lack of personal enemies. Padraic Colum
comments on his sweet nature and enjoyable company.[85] Reviewing Tom Kettle's *The Day's Burden*, Ryan writes of the author that 'He, perhaps more than
any of his fellows, brought an air of culture into politics',[86] and praises his
humour, intellectual fastidiousness and good sense. The terms are all eminently applicable to Ryan himself, just as his description of the French
socialist Jean Jaures as 'eminently sane' could well be a self-description too.
He was a man of cosmopolitan erudition, as deep in the history of Persia or
Georgia as he was in European literature and philosophy. The mind revealed
in his eloquent yet tersely disciplined prose is tough and wise, coldly demys-

80.   '"True" Imperialism', *Egyptian Standard*, 26 January 1908.
81.   Andrew Malone, 'Frederick Ryan', *The Voice of Labour*, 28 April 1923.
82.   J. Dunsmore Clarkson, *Labour and Nationalism in Ireland* (New York, 1925), p. 259.
83.   Francis Sheehy Skeffington, 'Frederick Ryan – The Saint of Rationalism'.
84.   Manus O'Riordan (ed.), *Frederick Ryan: Sinn Féin and Reaction* (Labour History Workshop, Dublin, 1984), Introduction.
85.   Colum, *Arthur Griffith* (Dublin, 1959), p. 76.
86.   *Irish Nation*, 24 December 1910. The nationalist Arthur Clery praises Kettle as a thoroughly modern, progressive, cosmopolitan nationalist, all epithets that apply to Ryan as well. See his essay on Kettle in his *Dublin Essays* (Dublin, 1919).

tified yet remarkably judicious, that of a formidable opponent who is nonetheless resolved to give his antagonist his due. Impassioned yet rigorous, his arguments never surrender to rhetorical gesture or sectarian point-scoring. Refusing to display 'personality' in his self-effacing attention to the matter in hand, that material is nevertheless enlivened by a dryly satirical wit. If he has some of the defects of high Victorian rationalism – a too sanguine belief in human persuadability, the power of moral appeal and the essentially positive nature of humanity – he also has its virtues of fairness, reasonableness and lucidity. Unlike so many of his Revivalist *confrères*, he combines intellectual virtuosity with a keen sense of *Realpolitik*, and can move from Renaissance art to the politics of the Congo with enviable ease.

Looking back at Ryan from today's political disputes, one is struck by the way that his work puts the current wranglings between revisionists and anti-revisionists into such powerfully distancing perspective. Unwaveringly critical of both bourgeois nationalism and middle-class liberalism, he reveals exactly how much they share in common. Both creeds are finally committed to the exploitative social system against which Ryan himself never ceased to campaign. It is he who is in this sense the most full-blooded revisionist. If today's revisionists find him hard to take, it is not because he demurs from much in their critique of nationalism, but because his vision is in the end too radical for them. Ryan throws our own rather schematic categories into disarray: he is both civilised and committed, reasonable and radical, a champion of the marginal and dissident who sees no reason not to include marginal nations in this category, a pluralist who scornfully rejects the view that all points of view have their value. Scrupulously fair-minded, he never doubts that the truth is ultimately one-sided. He sees no conflict between supporting women's rights and workers' self-government; since both currents stem for him from the democratic impulse, he would no doubt be baffled by those liberal feminists today for whom socialism is almost as objectionable an affair as sexism. Because he is an Irish anti-colonialist, he regards himself as a citizen of the world. He places a high value on culture, but sees social justice and material well-being as more fundamental. Few idealists have been so quick to detect high-minded humbug. He has an unflinching intellectual seriousness, but admires the way Michael Davitt constantly told stories against himself. If Ryan is relevant today, it is because we have yet to catch up with him.

YEATS AND POETIC FORM

Vincent Buckley remarks in his *Poetry and the Sacred* on the touch of genius which inspires Yeats to write 'upon' rather than 'on' in the line 'The riders upon the galloping horses' from 'At Galway Races'.[1] Buckley doesn't elaborate the point, but one might claim that the monosyllabic 'on' would just have fallen dully in the space between the line's two phrases, failing to bridge them, whereas 'upon' inserts a sort of lilt into the line, rather like a dance-step shuffle, which lends it fresh rhythmic impetus just when it is at risk of sagging in the middle. 'Upon the' recapitulates the metrical stress of 'The riders', as 'on the' would not. Rhythm is important to Yeats when he is walking verbally naked, since he has little else to estrange and intensify an otherwise deliberately unremarkable diction. His other chief strategy here is tone. He does not seem to mind allowing such an inconsiderable preposition as 'upon' to take so much of the strain of the line, just as he does not mind following up the line with the colourless observation 'The crowd that closes in behind', which does little more than just close in behind. He has one of his most memorable images coming up in four lines' time, 'Before the merchant and the clerk / Breathed on the world with timid breath', and can afford to free-wheel for a moment.

Similarly, in a line like 'Who beat upon the wall' from 'An Acre of Grass', he is content not to cast around for a more glamorous verb, assured that the unwonted emphasis thrown upon 'beat' will serve to heighten it a shade and momentarily defamiliarise it. In the preceding line – 'Or that William Blake' – he passes up on the chance of a fancy adjective to add colour to a very brief phrase, and boldly leaves the demonstrative pronoun to take the pressure. 'Beat' crops up again in 'While their great wooden dice beat on the board' from 'The Tower', a line which in one sense could have been written by anybody and in another sense by nobody but Yeats. He favours strong, simple verbs like 'trod', 'ran', 'cry', 'sing', 'glitter'. Since Yeats has one of the narrowest vocabularies of any poet of comparable stature, he has to make every word earn its keep. If Keats goes in for epithets like 'cool-rooted', Yeats prefers adjectives like 'great', 'grey', 'mad', while making them do almost as much work. 'Gong-tormented' in 'Byzantium' is unusually complex for him. In 'The Fisherman', he even repeats 'grey' in two consecutive short lines, partly so that the fisherman's own greyness may rhyme, so to speak, with the greyness of his environment, but also because he is uninterested in any more nuanced specification of either.

This aspect of Yeats, what Graham Martin has called his 'simple direct centrality',[2] is there too in his fondness for bluff, Empsonian, honest-to-goodness

1. Vincent Buckley, *Poetry and the Sacred* (London, 1968), p. 191.
2. Graham Martin, 'The Later Poetry of W. B. Yeats', in *The Pelican Guide to English Literature, vol. 7: The Modern Age* (Harmondsworth, 1963), p. 193.

words like 'stone', 'fool', 'bread', terms which are resonant but purged of ambiguity. If one comes across an ambiguity in Yeats's language, it is almost certainly a mistake. The line 'What made us dream that he could comb grey hair?' from 'In Memory of Major Robert Gregory' almost certainly does not mean 'What made us imagine that he could be a barber for senior citizens?' as well as 'What made us think that he might live to be old?' Conversely, it is probably a mistake if any of T. S. Eliot's phrases turn out to have a univocal meaning. Eliot is far too wary of a language which lacks tentacular roots in the visceral regions to pen a line like 'Because of the great gloom that is in my mind' ('A Prayer for my Daughter').

Yeats, however, is not so much ambiguous as ambivalent, placing two determinate terms in tension with one another rather than allowing them cryptically to conflate into a single indeterminate sense. This goes for his way of seeing as much as for his language. Nor does he like Eliot permit such indeterminacies to infiltrate and undermine the very forms of his poetry, which is one thing we mean by modernism.[3] Yeats, one might say, is modernist more in content than in form, so that even when he is perplexed or fearful or sourly disenchanted, the robust integrity of his verse-forms constitutes a kind of oblique transcendence of their profane materials. The ambiguities, so to speak, belong to the subject-matter rather than to the language itself, a distinction which it would be hard to make in the case of the *symboliste* Eliot. There is a touch of the cavalier about Yeats's use of formal devices to rise above anything as petty-bourgeois as personal anxiety or bemusement. Part of the job of his poetic language is to stand over against the unresolved subject-matter, clarifying and defining its complexities in what Robert Graves calls a new understanding of one's confusion rather than (as sometimes with the reader of Eliot) a new confusion of one's understanding.

If Eliot aims in avant-garde fashion to shatter and dislocate common suburban consciousness, which he takes to be no more than false consciousness, Yeats's equal contempt for the middle class takes the form of a robust belief in certain elemental meanings with which they have lost touch. Eliot believes this too, but the elemental for him must be evoked negatively, by churning up ordinary language to expose its archetypal underside. If he seems to speak out, it is just another poetic feint. Yeats, by contrast, has an astonishingly pre-modernist trust in common meanings, even if this trust is mixed up with a good deal of highly modernist mythologising. If there is a Romanticism about his content, there can be an Augustan buoyancy and *sanitas* about his diction, a faith in the ontological solidity of language which is rare

---

3.   Of relevance here is Eliot's notable insouciance about interpretations of the meanings of his poems. Patrick Kavanagh refers in his novel *The Green Fool* to an Irish librarian who thought *The Waste Land* was a work on drainage. But Eliot might not have demurred. One is reminded of the bookseller who categorised a work on the Little Flower under horticulture.

among his contemporaries but one which was wholly shared by his compatriot Joyce. With both Irish writers, one is tempted to speculate that the residues of an oral tradition play their part in this most unEliotic linguistic assurance. Yeats's poetry thus sometimes reads a lot more lucidly than it actually is, whereas the verse of a Hopkins, with its verbal virtuosity but restricted tonal and emotional range, can seem just the opposite. Part of the experience of reading Yeats is the way that a relatively spare poetic texture, in which each item seems to occupy its own luminous space, is paradoxically accompanied by a sense of complex feelings or ideas. This is a version of pastoral in the Empsonian sense, putting the complex into the relatively simple; but Yeats is not spare in the fetishised, neurotically hygienic manner of the Imagists. The fact that his verse is so uncluttered has the additional advantage of helping to fend off some of his more *outré* ideas, which, fortunately enough, are not easily absorbable into its pristine texture.

With Eliot, things slide into each other, perceptions are mutually contaminating, and every item occupies a number of locations simultaneously. Eliot's poetry tempts us to reach beyond the level of language, flashing seductive hints of a real character or coherent narrative or decodable symbol before our eyes, but does this only finally to frustrate any attempt to travel very far beyond the signifier. As Donald Davie once remarked of a critic who wanted to know whether Sweeney in 'Mr Eliot's Sunday Morning Service' was in a bathroom or a church, the point is that he is in a poem.[4] Given Eliot's symbolist aesthetic, his language can't be allowed to stand off from its subject-matter to the point where it could deliver an articulate judgement upon it, since only in a dissociated sensibility would sense and signifier be so cleanly separable. The kinds of judgements Eliot wants to advance, and indeed has no qualms about doing in his coolly Olympian prose, must thus be carried structurally or subliminally rather than semantically – in the way, say, that *The Waste Land* surreptitiously marshalls its fragments, behind the scenes of consciousness so to speak, into mythical configurations pregnant with their own kind of tendentious meaning.

Such 'totalising' meaning can only be conveyed indirectly, in a poetry where the urge to speak out assuredly lapses into failure as surely as sexual arousal lapses into impotence. Prufrock can't formulate his overwhelming question (not perhaps because he lacks the means of communication, but because, lacking those means, he has no coherent question to ask in the first place); the moment of tremulous insight in *The Waste Land*'s hyacinth garden collapses into sensory shut-down; and what the thunder says is not necessarily what Mr Eliot says. The characteristic crabwise strategy of an Eliot poem is to propose a significance it then nervously retracts, as Gerontion's authoritative judgement on history crumbles self-defensively into the

4. Donald Davie, 'Pound and Eliot: A Distinction', in Graham Martin (ed.), *Eliot in Perspective* (London, 1970), p. 81.

untrustworthy thoughts of a dry brain, and *Four Quartets* bounces one unsatisfactory style of discourse off another so that the reader might just glimpse a dim epiphany of the truth disclosed by their mutual cancellation. No sooner have the *Preludes* gained a precious glimpse of some infinitely gentle thing than they advise us to wipe our mouths and laugh. But Eliot pays a price for his studious avoidance of a Yeatsian poetry of proclamation, since he thereby deprives himself of the Irish poet's genius for stunning one-liners (usually cast as rhetorical questions): 'What had the Caesars but their thrones?', 'How can we know the dancer from the dance?', 'Was there another Troy for her to burn?'.

Just as the aristocrat keeps his chin up when confronted with tragedy, so 'Easter 1916' is much more at a loss than it would like to appear. The celebrated oxymoron 'terrible beauty', more ambivalent than ambiguous and so a matter of two clearly defined responses held in antithesis, is among other things a rhetorical strategy which prematurely resolves the poem's real uncertainties. If it is equivocal in content, the form or tone of this ritually repeated grand gesture is altogether more commanding – so that Yeats is involved here in a kind of performative contradiction between what he says and the way he says it. (Another notable example of this is the ending of 'Coole Park and Ballylee', in which the graceful imagery intended to illustrate the fact that Romanticism is dead undercuts that proposition as surely as would a plea for calm delivered in a panic-stricken tone.) The same goes in 'Easter 1916' for the device by which the poem keeps raising insistent questions ('Was it needless death after all? . . . And what if excess of love / Bewildered them till they died?') which it cavalierly overrides, leaving these questions 'rhetorical' (though in fact they are not), and covering its own canny reticence by the implication that, since the martyrs of the uprising are after all dead and done with, there is really no need to respond, right now at least, to these disquieting queries. A kind of tact or courtesy to the dead acts as a rationale for the poem's refusal to follow up its own enormous political doubts, one reinforced by a tight metrical form which leaves space only for gesture or notation rather than discursive reflection.

Something similar takes place in 'In Memory of Eva Gore-Booth and Con Markiewicz', where a political animus against the two women rears its head in the middle of the poem only to be courteously skimmed over, unresolved but undisruptive, by the affirmative conclusion. This graceful evasion is a lot more acceptable than it is in 'The Tower', where the bombast of Part 3 simply evades the questions about old age (banal enough, to be sure) posed by Part 2. Pronouncing the names of the executed rebels in 'Easter 1916' thus becomes as much strategic displacement as prophetic affirmation; indeed what is actually prophesised – that these tragic figures are 'changed utterly' – is in one sense heavy with symbolic meaning and in another sense banally self-evident, since nothing changes you so utterly as being shot. The poem mounts to a confident crescendo which, given the obscurity of the Rising's likely consequences when it was written, delivers much less than it seems to promise. Yeats announces that his task is just to write it out in a verse, a modest circumscription of the poet's role not much in evidence elsewhere in his work.

In this sense, the cautious, hard-headed side of the poet, who cannot yet see how the present will appear in retrospect to its progeny, is in conflict with the brasher visionary whose impulse is to sweep aside these prudent reservations and simply sing out, partly as a guilt-ridden compensation for having himself espoused and then abandoned some of the ideals for which the insurrectionists died. Something rather similar happens with his inclusion in the chant of his old enemy John MacBride, despite his personal dislike of him. 'Yet I number him in the song', he announces with a mixture of moving generosity and grandee big-heartedness, as though he had been furtively contemplating leaving this drunken bonehead out of the roll call altogether. What testifies to the irresolutions lurking beneath the poem's self-assured tone is its imagery:

> The horse that comes from the road,
> The rider, the birds that range
> From cloud to tumbling cloud,
> Minute by minute they change;
> A shadow of cloud on the stream
> Changes minute by minute;
> A horse-hoof slides on the brim,
> And a horse plashes within it;
> The long-legged moor-hens dive,
> And hens to moor-cocks call;
> Minute by minute they live:
> The stone's in the midst of all.

Here if anywhere, in a passage all about blurring and shifting, Yeats seems creatively unsure of what exactly he means, as the narrative falters into these wavering, inconclusive lines. It is as though the poem has momentarily lost its way, dissolving into a series of fragmentary impressions which refuse to add up. The poem, with the semi-oxymoron of 'enchanted to a stone' behind it, seems uncertain of how some of the connotations of 'stone' (cold, impervious, intransigent) pull together with certain others (sturdy, enduring, dependable).[5]

In 'The Second Coming', the apocalyptic anxieties and excitements of the subject-matter can only be kept in place by a rhetoric which is too theatrically pitched, too sonorously inflected. This then makes the poem's language seem oddly to connive in the very impending apocalypse it is supposed to be partly fearing:

5. I have examined these issues more fully in my 'History and Myth in Yeats's "Easter 1916"', *Essays in Criticism*, vol. xxi, no. 3 (July 1971).

> Turning and turning in the widening gyre
> The falcon cannot hear the falconer;
> Things fall apart; the centre cannot hold;
> Mere anarchy is loosed upon the world,
> The blood-dimmed tide is loosed, and everywhere
> The ceremony of innocence is drowned;
> The best lack all conviction, while the worst
> Are full of passionate intensity.

Actually, as long as this set of authoritative pronoucements can be made, the centre is holding with a vengeance, so once more we have a kind of performative contradiction at work. Even so, the vagueness of that drowned ceremony of innocence hints at something less than assurance. The tone of the second stanza then carries over something of the grandly omniscient manner of the first, even though Yeats is by no means as clear about what he feels about the rough beast as this tone would intimate. And the poem's concluding rhetorical question – 'And what rough beast, its hour come round at last, / Slouches towards Bethlehem to be born?' – is a shade too well-informed about the nature of the beast in question to be quite as honestly interrogative as it sounds.

Eliot's syntax flails and fragments beneath its heap of broken images, creating some fine ambiguities in the process. Is it the violet hour, or the typist, who lays out food in tins in *The Waste Land,* and do the breastless creatures of 'Whispers of Immortality' lean themselves backwards or are they 'leaned' in the sense of being propped in position by someone else? Yeats's syntax, by contrast, preserves its integrity even when, as in the opening lines of 'Sailing to Byzantium', one of the great emigration poems of Ireland, it makes a plausible feint of being just about to lose it:

> That is no country for old men. The young
> In one another's arms, birds in the trees
> —Those dying generations—at their song,
> The salmon-falls, the mackerel-crowded seas,
> Fish, flesh, or fowl, commend all summer long
> Whatever is begotten, born, and dies.

The exclamatory excitement of the lines, with their staccato, paratactic phrasing, hints at the possibility of an ecstatic loss of control in the face of these sensuous delights without ever coming remotely close to it. Once we reach the main verb 'commend', all of these apparently breathless phrases fall into place retrospectively as part of an impeccably coherent grammatical structure. Yeats's syntactical breathing-in here is deep enough to allow him a few quick pants. Percy French wrote of Yeats 'french polishing a poem', and he does just that in an exquisitely well-turned verse in 'The Tower' in which the name French actually appears:

> Beyond that ridge lived Mrs French, and once
> When every silver candlestick or sconce
> Lit up the dark mahogany and the wine,
> A serving-man, that could divine
> That most respected lady's every wish,
> Ran and with the garden shears
> Clipped an insolent farmer's ears
> And brought them in a little covered dish.

The stanza is as gleaming and unflawed as Mrs French's tablewear, but a touch too trimly, well-clippedly so, so that there is a slightly shocking contrast between its self-conscious deftness, in which rhyme is notably foregrounded, and the gratuitous piece of neo-feudal violence it rather too suavely records. (The serving-man gets a 'that' rather than a 'who', as though he too is a piece of furniture.) The verse needs to drop a final foot in three of its lines to modulate its rather too polished unity. Here again, the forms of Yeats's verse stand some way off from their more dishevelled content, rather as the ceremonies of the big house of which the verse speaks conceal a rather more rebarbative reality. Later in the poem, however, he will tire of this well-crafted anecdotalising and appear to throw it away in the name of a more personal distress:

> Hanrahan rose in frenzy there
> And followed up those baying creatures towards —
> O towards I have forgotten what   enough!

The metre, even so, continues to tap away with metronomic precision.

Another sort of throw-away gesture happens in the first stanza of 'Coole Park and Ballylee, 1931', with its look-no-hands dexterity in folding a struggling knot of clauses into a smoothly grammatical whole:

> Under my window-ledge the waters race,
> Otters below and moor-hens on the top,
> Run for a mile undimmed in Heaven's face
> Then darkening through 'dark' Raftery's 'cellar' drop,
> Run underground, rise in a rocky place
> In Coole demesne, and there to finish up
> Spread to a lake and drop into a hole.
> What's water but the generated soul?

The verse almost deliberately provokes the critic into belle-lettristic waffle about how beautifully the sinuous curving of the syntax enacts the flow of the stream. Topography is stylised and compressed here rather as in a map. To speak these lines would require a voice which could pause fractionally to register the quotation marks around 'dark' and 'cellar' without losing momentum. Rather similarly, the opening verse of 'Meditations in Time of Civil War' piles line upon line in a precarious-looking syntactical accumulation which is meant to mime the overflowing of a fountain. Like a fountain, the sentence-structure looks ready at any moment to topple under its own weight, but irons itself out finally into a perfectly controlled statement. But in case the total effect of the first verse of 'Coole Park and Ballylee' is one of an *excessive* deftness, subduing all this tumultous flow too easily to a shapely narrative, the last line of the stanza – 'What's water but the generated soul?' – shifts abruptly to a new register, rounding upon what has gone before while sustaining a rhythmic continuity with it. It is one of Yeats's sudden, carefully contrived shifts of tone, pitching a blunt image or observation against his own rather too heady rhetoric, as with 'And there's but common greenness after that' or 'And maybe the great-grandson of that house, / For all its bronze and marble, 's but a mouse' ('Meditations in Time of Civil War').

Yeats is good at knowing when to shift gear, throw a phrase away or appear to falter, as in a line like 'Lion and woman and the Lord knows what' ('The Circus Animals' Desertion') or 'and where was it / He rode a race without a bit?' ('In Memory of Major Robert Gregory'). In 'Among School Children', some high-toned Greek philosophy is suddenly deflated to 'Old clothes upon old sticks to scare a bird'. This belongs to Yeats's carnivalesque impulse, to the cackling scorn of the unadorned body for a lofty intellect whose fascinations the poet knows only too well. The opening of *Four Quartets*, which undercuts an arcane set of speculations with a sudden concrete image – 'But to what purpose / Disturbing the dust on a bowl of rose-leaves / I do not know' – presses this tactic to an unYeatsian extreme. Eliot begins the poem by solemnly catering to his reader's awed expectations of intellectual difficulty, only to appear to throw this whole piece of cerebration away in mischievous Old Possum style. Yeats, similarly, has an intuitive feel for just when he needs to crank a too-enraptured tone down several notches, before proceeding to wind it up again, and how to manage this discontinuity without formal or tonal disruption. The point of some of these gear-changes is to lapse without warning into a sort of disenchanted realism without courting the dangers of bathos. As it happens, the undermining last line of the opening verse of 'Coole Park and Ballylee' is a little too calculatedly rhetorical, a shade too theatrical and *voulu*. Its metaphysical content is rather too ponderous for its tonally modifying function. It is as though the lines which lead up to it have surrendered too whole-heartedly to the autonomy of natural process, which is now rather too hastily re-appropriated for the symbolic. The mind, having let Nature have its way for seven lines, must now reassert Berkeley-style a governing edge over it, posing with a touch too much panache a rhetorical question which it simultaneously answers. In doing so, it risks the blunt riposte that water is in fact the sort of thing the poem has just spent seven lines describing, which seemed at the time precious little to do with the generated soul.

Just as Eliot in the *Quartets* appears to ditch an abstruse discourse for an abruptly specifying image, so Yeats occasionally introduces a sudden image as a convenient sort of shorthand for what might have been a whole complex argument. And just as one feels about Eliot's bowl of rose leaves that this is rather too urbane a ploy, as baffling in its own way as the piece of philosophising it is supposed to undercut, so one can feel about Yeats that these images sometimes only deviously illuminate what they are supposed to clarify:

> Is every modern nation like the tower,
> Half-dead at the top? No matter what I said,
> For wisdom is the property of the dead,
> A something incompatible with life; and power,
> Like everything that has the stain of blood,
> A property of the living; but no stain
> Can come upon the visage of the moon
> When it has looked in glory from a cloud.
> ('Blood and the Moon')

The moon image seems a way of calling a halt to the poet's intellectual reflections, rather than — as it would seem to present itself — offering a resolution to them. Yeats is not at his best with the poetry of ideas, as overdiscursive pieces like 'Ego Dominus Tuus' or the disastrous 'Seven Sages' would suggest, and in any case he believes that discursiveness, like doctrine and opinion, is strictly for shopkeepers. Thus, in the enchanting 'A Prayer for My Daughter', a poem much opposed to intellectual wrangling, what might have been an argument is suddenly short-circuited by a particularised image:

> My mind, because the minds that I have loved,
> The sort of beauty that I have approved,
> Prosper but little, has dried up of late,
> Yet knows that to be choked with hate
> May well be of all evil chances chief.
> If there's no hatred in a mind
> Assault and battery of the wind
> Can never tear the linnet from the leaf.

The concluding image, like, say, 'No loving man can drink from the whole wine' in 'All Souls' Night', has a proverbial smack about it, like a sudden nugget of anonymous wisdom tossed into the flow of the argument to end-stop it. Yeats does this quite often, but one feels that these sudden crystallisations always *could* be unpacked into discourse, and so are far from symbols in the *symboliste* sense of the term. They are rhetorical gambits rather than Eliotic enigmas. If these are concrete images, they are not of the uniquely specified kind favoured by that Leavisian, very English ideology of the concrete which reconstructs authentic English poetry from Donne to Hopkins as a seamless whole of language and lived experience. If this is an 'organic' English smack at rationalist abstraction, Yeats is in his own pseudo-aristocratic

Irish way just as hostile to the abstract; but he does not forsake it *à la* Keats or Hopkins or the Imagists for the lovingly individuated. This flight from the cerebral to the untranslatable *quidditas* of things belongs to a modernist crisis in the relations between individual and universal, to which Yeats himself is largely a stranger. Because the Romantic heritage is still for historical reasons a powerful resource for him, as it is not by and large in Britain, Yeats has a largely pre-modernist sense of the particular, and of its relatively unproblematical consorting with the general. The sensuous world elegiacally portrayed in the first verse of 'Sailing to Byzantium' is more a set of brief notations than an intricately individuated uniqueness, emblematic rather than symbolistic, but this is quite enough for his purposes.

Likewise, in 'Coole Park, 1929', it is sufficient to write 'When nettles wave upon a shapeless mound / And saplings root among the broken stone'. There is no pretence of giving us the feel of the nettles or the texture of the stone: as with some eighteenth-century verse, we are supplied with just as much detail as we need for the moral point to be made. If Yeats wants to suggest human squalor he says something like 'foul ditch', a phrase which merely designates the condition, rather than raiding the resources of language to recreate it. Used recurrently, such phrases then assume the status of a kind of code, accreting complex implications which don't need to be spelled out but are evoked, semi-magically, just at the sight of the word. To this extent they behave rather like Eliot's Tradition, forming a kind of ready-to-hand context for individual particulars, which, in Yeats has the advantage of saving a specific poem some tedious spadework. It can rely instead on certain pre-established patterns and relations on which the particular can then ring a change, providing that particular with a stable background which sustains it without overwhelming it.

Yeats's poetry is at its most boring when the particulars become formulaic, and the myth or system seems to be doing a poem's thinking for it. The concrete for Yeats is less ineffable than elemental, and so belongs to a common language which does not *à la* modernism need to be disrupted, compacted, stripped of its freight of tarnished commonplaces, in order to release its specifying force. He does not bother actually describing his Fisherman in any but the most stereotypical terms, and elsewhere can even slip from time to time into Augustan phraseology such as 'slippered Contemplation'. His is the particularism of folk wisdom, earth-bound rather than sensuously detailed. The peasant girl he mentions in 'The Tower' 'lived somewhere upon that rocky place', a topographical vagueness which one could hardly imagine Edward Thomas permitting himself. Even when he sings the praises of 'one dear perpetual place', with the big house well in mind, that phrase is itself a general one. Indeed politically, if not affectively, one big house is as good as another. Individuals must be grasped as such, but not in a way which dispels their redolence of something broader than themselves. Yeats's poetry keeps the focus wide, not allowing discrete things so to enthral the eye that one can't think one's way around them. His occasional Wordsworthian use of the word 'image', to mean both the specific object and the general idea of it, is typical in this respect. If the relation between general and particular is unclear or non-existent, he will legislate it arbitrarily into being: "Another emblem there!' ('Coole Park and Ballylee, 1931'), 'I declare this tower is my symbol, I declare / This winding, gyring, spiring treadmill of a stair is my ancestral stair; / That Goldsmith and the Dean, Berkeley and Burke have travelled there' ('Blood and the Moon'). The reader watches, awed by the poet's cool insolence as he stitches his own humble particulars into a bogus tradition.

The point is delicately to 'texture' the poetry in ways which don't distract from its rhetorical thrust. A superb instance of this is the celebrated final verse of 'Among School Children':

> Labour is blossoming or dancing where
> The body is not bruised to pleasure soul,
> Nor beauty born out of its own despair,
> Nor blear-eyed wisdom out of midnight oil.
> O chestnut-tree, great-rooted blossomer,
> Are you the leaf, the blossom or the bole?
> O body swayed to music, O brightening glance,
> How can we know the dancer from the dance?

There is a great deal of busy consonantal activity in this opulent tapestry of sound, as an extraordinarily numerous set of *b* sounds ('blossoming', 'body', 'bruised', 'beauty', 'born', 'blear-eyed', 'bole', 'brightening') weave their way through the stanza, but it is as if the poetry is innocently unaware of them. There are a number of discreet para-rhymes too – labour/pleasure, despair/blear, born/own, out/nut), but despite all this the signifier remains as wedded to the signified as the dancer is to the dance. The aristocratic ethic is to do things so gracefully that nobody notices that you're doing them, stash away your guest's overcoat before he is aware that it is off his shoulders, and this is as true of the form of the stanza as of its theme. Labour is for grocers and realist novelists.

The other side of that ethic is the bluff honesty of those so much in control of the forms that they can afford from time to time to set them aside. This is one, perhaps excessively charitable way of reading some of Yeats's more maladroit effects: 'A humorous, unambitious man' ('In Memory of Alfred Pollexfen'), 'By those that are not entirely beautiful' ('A Prayer for my Daughter'), or, from the oddly erratic 'The Tower':

> Strange, but the man who made that song was blind;
> Yet, now I have considered it, I find
> That nothing strange; the tragedy began
> With Homer that was a blind man . . .

What looks here like a candid stab at spontaneity, catching one's thought on the hop, comes through as merely cack-handed. Yeats, not least in *Last Poems*, is ready to dispense with verbal diplomacy and throw art to the winds for the sake of emotional authenticity (though this is a kind of mask too), but not even this could excuse an atrocity like 'My mediaeval knees lack health until they bend' ('The Municipal Gallery Revisited'), 'And horrible splendour of desire' ('The Tower'), or some of the contrived swagger and slap-dash of the last poems. If Yeats had not been the great poet he was, no editor would have bothered reading past a first line like 'An abstract Greek absurdity has crazed the man' ('Supernatural Songs II').

Yeats does not linger cloyingly over his objects, furnishing his poems rather like the big house with a few dear familiar pieces which you can simultaneously love and take for granted. If he is extravagant in other ways, he is spare and economical in this one. To be really enraptured by objects, you need a sense of their mysterious contingency, which the modernists had in plenty; but Yeats is pre-modernist in this sense too. His 'mature' vision, if that is the right word for it, is by and large a determinist one, in which in Blakeian manner any particular opens out into a cosmic whole and so is locked into place by the entire universe. Yeats prevents this on the whole from interfering with his sense of specific things, as the poet comes to be creatively at odds with the metaphysician; but it nonetheless leaves its mark on the poetry as an interest in rather general categories of objects, sometimes signalled in early-Auden style by the definite article ('The living men that I hate, / The dead man that I loved' ['The Fisherman']). But he is also uninterested in Hopkinsian *haeccitas* because he scorns a mimetic art, as slavishly dependent on reality as the clerk on his employer. Yeats finds such naturalism English and low-bred, terms which might well be synonymous in his book, and wants a poetry which like the aristocrat lives only from its own self-delighting resources. Miraculously self-generating fountains are one symbol of this among several, though Yeats has to suppress the underground pipework which lends them their air of self-containment. The task of poetry is not to express the world, or even directly to express the self – the theory of the mask provides an alternative to that – but to take up a stance towards the world, a stance which will fashion a particular self as well as a particular reality.

This is another reason why the language of the poem has to separate itself somewhat from its content, so as to open up an enabling gap which allows it to go to work on it. Yeats's poetry is typically performative rather than constative, blessing, spurning, summoning, denominating, listing, exhorting, bequeathing and the like. There is no doubt a trace here of an Irish tradition of the poet as magician, social functionary and political activist. Performative art of this kind allows you to combine transcendence and worldiness, the saint and the swordsman, in the very forms of your poetry, issues which in Yeats are equally germane to its content. The poem is worldly because it makes a rhetorical intervention into reality, but transcendent since this intervention springs not from reality itself but from the creative imagination, which for a Romantic like Yeats is radically self-grounding. You could not dig beneath this imaginative baseline, since you would need another act of imagination by which to do so, and so on *ad infinitum*. The self must be transcendental in the sense that anything which might seem anterior to it would have, just to be intelligible, to be the product of its own interpretative act, of the word that existed from the beginning.

This is a consoling epistemology for Anglo-Irish gentlemen whose mundane selves seem less and less essential. As an aesthetic doctrine, it is merely the reverse side of mimesis: if language does not button down upon the world, then it must float free in its own space. If not Zola, then surely Mallarmé. But if language is not rammed close up against the world, neither does it stand off from it. One inadequate spatial metaphor here merely replaces another. The doctrine fails to grasp the point that a performative act is as much motivated by historical conditions as a reflective one – that language does not have to be a mirror in order to be part of what it signifies, that a stance towards a situation is as much part of it as a reflection. Even so, regarding his art as performative allows Yeats to escape the greatest modernist cliché of all, the fear that language can never quite live up to its object. It is a queasiness which Joyce escaped too, if for rather different reasons. Yeats may tell us that his tongue is a stone, but it does not stop him from talking. His language is never hollowed out by the silences and terrors of which it may speak. Since there is no question for him, when the transcendent fit is upon him, of a correspondence between word and thing in the first place, of an empiricist fit between concept and reality, there can be no question of a breakdown between them either. A curse or a celebration plainly does not 'reflect' what is being cursed or celebrated, in the sense that one might mistakenly imagine that the word 'glittering' is supposed to capture the essence of a certain perception. A gnarled, densely material language such as the early Seamus Heaney's does not capture the gnarled, densely material nature of a tree trunk; it is just that, by a process of metaphorical transposition which is really a sort of *trompe-l'oeil*, one form of (semantic) materiality puts us in mind of another (ontological) form of it. But Yeats is for the most part outside these sorts of questions, just as, in his later, Berkeleyan phrase, there can be no point in worrying about the fit between mind and world if the former creates the latter in the first place.

Yet this out-and-out idealism is only one of Yeats's moods. Something *does* in a sense precede the creative mind, which is to say the collective mind or *Anima Mundi*. It is here that his images loiter around waiting to be conjured up, inhabiting some limbo between being solid objects and mere figments of the individual imagination. Thus when he announces in 'In Memory of Major Robert Gregory' that 'that enquiring man John Synge comes next', the verb makes it sound as though Synge stands in some given pecking order, has a particular place in the queue of wraiths standing by to be summoned, though we know in fact that it is up to Yeats in what order he chooses to recall his dead companions. The fisherman, in the poem of that title, has been lurking around for years on the edges of Yeats's vision even before he is evoked, rather as Berkeley's tree continues to exist when I am not looking at it because somebody else, perhaps God, is. The piece ends with a resolve to write the fisherman a poem some day, so that we have here the curious spectacle of Yeats writing a verse to one of his own images. The fisherman is fashioned by the performative evocation of the poem, but seems as blithely indifferent to his creator as to anyone else, so that content neither escapes the governance of form nor is purely a function of it.

At another level, though, true correspondences between mind and reality do matter to Yeats. Whereas full-blown symbolist poets like Eliot merge symbol and reality into one, Yeats is sometimes to be found anxiously checking off a symbol against a reality, wondering whether it will quite do. The distinction he enforces between things and emblems in 'The Circus Animals' Desertion' – 'Players and painted stage took all my love, / And not those things that they were emblems of' – would make any self-respecting *symboliste* shudder. A fully-fledged exponent of the creed would not be able to peer behind his symbol to the experience which grounded it, but Yeats is to be found in the same poem doing precisely that: 'I must lie down where all the ladders start, / In the foul rag-and-bone shop of the heart'. In 'Nineteen Hundred and Nineteen', he declares himself 'satisfied' with the image of the soul as a swan, while in 'Blood and the Moon' he sets up his symbols in full view of the reader ('I declare this tower is my symbol. . .'), baring the device and letting us in on the act of symbol-constitution rather than just presenting us with the finished product. One admires the candour of this, while noting the lordliness of it.

He is doing something like this in 'The Fisherman', anticipating the cultural conditions in which the fisherman will be able to become one of his symbols, provide the subject of a poem, because he represents the ideal reader of a more propitious future. This is a wan sort of hope, since the fisherman's admired indifference to the present degenerate Dublin mob also comes through as an indifference to his author too. He would not care whether Yeats wrote him a poem or not, which is precisely why Yeats might get round to doing it. In 'A Dialogue of Self and Soul' Yeats acts as his own critical commentator, annotating his symbols for us, drawing up one-to-one correspondences between emblems and realities in a way utterly foreign to the creator of the Marabar caves or of the Ramsay family's lighthouse. (Forster's caves and Woolf's lighthouse are symbols of a symbol, a device to tempt the literary tenderfoot to write 'Symbol' in large letters in the margin of the text.) To write 'And therefore I have sailed the seas and come / To the holy city of Byzantium' ('Sailing to Byzantium') is Yeats's way of letting us know that he has just erected a new symbology. He puts his bits and pieces of symbolism forlornly on show in 'Meditations in Time of Civil War', a meagre clutch of totems to shelter him from the military storms. And these conflicting epistemologies, in which a mind-created universe seeks to compensate for one all too solidly given, are reflected in the vicissitudes of the word 'dream' in Yeats, which is used in his poetry almost as many times to mean dangerous illusions as it is to signify creative imaginings.

Another sense in which form and content can pull against each other in Yeats is the way in which the beauty or assurance of the verse may tempt us into endorsing attitudes which are really a good deal more bizarre, bathetic or offensive than they appear. The form, in other words, may have a quality of unruffled, impersonal wisdom about it, picked up often enough from ballad or song, which deflects our attention from the crankiness or even farcicalness of its content. A famous instance of the farcical is his grave description of Lionel Johnson as 'much falling' in 'In Memory of Major Robert Gregory', where the elegance of the verse makes it hard to credit that this is an allusion to Johnson's penchant for tumbling drunkenly off bar-stools. Something similar happens with his account of Florence Emery in 'All Souls' Night', a poem which reads like a poor parody of 'In Memory of Major Robert Gregory':

> On Florence Emery I call the next,
> Who finding the first wrinkles on a face
> Admired and beautiful,
> And knowing that the future would be vexed
> With 'minished beauty, multiplied commonplace,
> Preferred to teach a school
> Away from neighbour or friend,
> Among dark skins, and there
> Permit foul years to wear
> Hidden from eyesight to the unnoticed end.

The ridiculous vanity of Ms Emery, who seems to assume that blacks cannot spot ageing in whites, goes unremarked, in a grotesque failure of a sense of proportion which happens from time to time in Yeats. It is not as though he has noticed this vanity but is courteously not saying so, rather that he seems not to have registered it at all. The verse bears much the same relation to his more accomplished writing as the untidy mess of stitches on the back of a tapestry does to the fine embroidery of its front. Later in the same piece he has an unwittingly hilarious couple of lines about the philosopher MacGregor: 'I thought him half a lunatic, half knave, / And told him so, but friendship never ends'. Lines like this remind us of just how devastatingly unself-critical Yeats can be, hinting as they do at the skewedness of vision which can be felt lurking as a just-avoided catastrophe beneath even some of his most superb writing. His immoderate respect for the minor philosophical eccentric MacGregor is itself a token of this astigmatism.

A parallel lack of emotional tact leads him occasionally to inflate his own experience out of proportion:

> I am content to live it all again
> And yet again, if it be life to pitch
> Into the frog-spawn of a blind man's ditch,
> A blind man battering blind men;
> Or into that most fecund ditch of all,
> The folly that man does
> Or must suffer, if he woos
> A proud woman not kindred of his soul.
>
> ('A Dialogue of Self and Soul')

There is a touch of bathos in those concluding lines, as the reader's expectations of some unspeakable human degradation come down to the bald fact of being jilted. Yeats has an impressive way of offering his own biography as microcosmic of a whole history, converting himself into a kind of concrete universal in a way which, like Wordsworth at his best, is the very opposite of egoism; but he can also get the relations between particular and general wrong in the case of his own life, too eager as he sometimes is to pluck a sententious maxim out of his own contingent biography:

> Get all the gold and silver that you can,
> Satisfy ambition, animate
> The trivial days and ram them with the sun,
> And yet upon these maxims meditate:
> All women dote upon an idle man
> Although their children need a rich estate;
> No man has ever lived that had enough
> Of children's gratitude or woman's love.
>
> ('Vacillation')

The fifth and sixth lines of the verse are so plainly false that they undermine almost everything around them. It is similarly absurd to assert, as he does in 'In Memory of Eva Gore-Booth and Con Markiewicz', that 'The innocent and the beautiful / Have no enemy but time', but the plangent simplicity of the words deflects our attention from the spurious sentiment.

Yeats has in common with the modernists a certain philosophical extremism: his scenarios are often violent, histrionic, unbalanced, even savage; but the very stability and well-temperedness of the verse-forms can succeed wonderfully well in concealing this, intimating that he is a good deal more 'mainstream' than he actually is. Graham Martin's word 'centrality' is accurate in one sense, since Yeats has a quick eye for sorting the substantial from the marginal; but in another sense he is much more weird and deviant than the term suggests. If his poems are for the most part beautifully well-made, this is not entirely true of his mind – a claim he would probably not have regarded as an insult, since he was not particularly keen on being considered sane. The splendid closing stanza of 'A Dialogue of Self and Soul' seems to argue that the poet isn't in the least sorry for anything he has ever done, and that the supremely heroic event of saying so at the top of his voice will so transfigure the world that everything we look upon, including presumably cholera and cot deaths, will be blessed. But the rhetorical power of the language does not incline us to read the lines so harshly. A milder case in point is this stanza from 'A Prayer for My Daughter':

> Considering that, all hatred driven hence,
> The soul recovers radical innocence
> And learns at last that it is self-delighting,
> Self-appeasing, self-affrighting,
> And that its own sweet will is Heaven's will;
> She can, though every face should scowl
> And every windy quarter howl
> Or every bellows burst, be happy still.

This recommends that his daughter should do what she wants in the confidence that she has divine backing for it, not quite the kind of advice that a parent interested in a carefree future should pass on to a child. Similarly, what sounds like tender parental solicitude in the fourth section of 'Meditations in Time of Civil War', where the poet worries about the vigour of his progeny, has, in the context of his thought as a whole, an unpleasantly eugenicist subtext.

An earlier stanza of the poem advances an equally dubious proposition under cover of its perfectly achieved observation:

> O what if gardens where the peacock strays
> With delicate feet upon old terraces,
> Or else all Juno from an urn displays
> Before the indifferent garden deities;
> O what if levelled lawn and gravelled ways
> Where slippered Contemplation finds his ease
> And Childhood a delight for every sense,
> But take our greatness with our violence?

What this seems to mean is that human civilisation may be built only at the cost of sublimating and thus emasculating violence, and that since violence is part of our greatness, this may be an unwise bargain. The poem was written in 1923, just three years after Freud published his *Civilisation and its Discontents*, a drama of *Eros* and *Thanatos* highly relevant to Yeats's later work. Freud's gloomy thesis is that the more we sublimate the death-drive into the civilisation-building forms of *Eros*, the more we deplete our psychical resources and so leave ourselves vulnerable to the destructive forces of the id. The more we sublimate, the more we tighten the grip of death upon us. Human society is in this sense self-deconstructing. The point about Yeats is that he is not entirely sure which side of this self-cancelling equation to back, and this reflects a fundamental ambivalence in the aristocratic ethic he embraces. The aristocrat would seem the epitome of both *Eros* and *Thanatos*: a bearer of civilised values on the one hand, an anarchic ruffian on the other. If there is Robert Gregory, there is also the wild old wicked man whose indifference to convention is the mark of his spiritual nobility. The two images are secretly akin: to live in a sweetly wilful way, acknowledging in Nietzschean fashion no law other than one's own being, is to become as autonomous as a work of art, and thus to resemble that enclosed, organic order which is the ceremonious life-style of the gentry. The aristocrat lives indifferently, which suggests a kind of cool serenity embodied in his orderly estates; but it is also an indifference to anyone's law but his own, and thus licenses a belligerence at odds with that tranquillity. *Sang froid* and savagery are not so clearly distinguishable.

These two aspects of aristocratism, what one might call the Gregorian and the Byronic, are constantly at war in Yeats's poetry. Because he is essentially above the law, the nobleman resembles no one quite so much as those who fall outside it, the swarm of beggars, rogues, lustful geriatrics and amiable idiots who troop their way through Yeats's stanzas. These are acceptable figures to him because like the gentleman they are radical individualists, and so a very different proposition from the anarchy of the mob. It is alright to lurch wild-eyed around the countryside, but not to stagger wild-eyed around the stalls of the Abbey Theatre. But it is not simple to reconcile this hymning of sheer irresponsible individualism with the sedate, impersonal ethic of a Coole Park. Yeats approves of the impersonal, which stands in judgement on the money-grubbing individualism of merchant and clerk, but also of a form of personal flamboyance which contrasts with their dingy anonymity. 'Personality' is the aesthetically acceptable form of individualism, a selfhood so grounded and resilient that it is prepared to give itself lavishly away, as the gombeen men and Sinn Féin politicians are not. For Yeats as for Nietzsche, unbending or dismantling the self is just another instance of its lordly power, and so ultimately strengthens rather than weakens it. The middle classes, by contrast, give themselves away essentially out of timidity.

There is, even so, a ferocious drive in Yeats to obliterate the self which cannot be rationalised by the belief that this is just the ultimate form of its mastery. The fact that he veers constantly between haughty self-affirmation and a desire to strip himself of identity suggests an ambiguity which cannot be simply flattened out as 'dialectical'. The more the achieved self is celebrated, the more the sadistic fury of the death drive strives to plunge it back into utter non-being. For *Eros* to thrive, which is to say for Coole Park to flourish, the chaos which threatens this order must be violently excluded, and this means for Yeats, among other things, the woman. The woman for Yeats, in a familiar patriarchal paradox, is both the bearer of civility and its anarchic destroyer, both *Eros* and *Thanatos*. This comes to a head for him in the figure of Maud Gonne, who symbolises, impossibly, both unity of being and the political disruptiveness which undermines it. It was deeply unfortunate for Yeats that the woman he loved should have come by sheer historical accident to represent both things together, since this touched him on one of his sorest psychical spots. Falling for a sexually attractive leftist was the last thing he needed for his psychological well-being, even if he plucked some magnificent poetry from it. Maud is the phallic aggressor who signifies the very anarchy against which she also shields him. To idealise the woman is to deploy her as a fetish to plug a certain nameless void in being which she also incarnates.

With this in mind, one can see why the 'terrible beauty' of 'Easter 1916' is no achieved resolution of opposites but an indecipherable riddle. The phrase idealises and defaces simultaneously, projecting on to the Rising the psychic conflict which Yeats feels about Gonne, or perhaps about women as such, and in part using the political event to rationalise and resolve this enigma. Since it is reasonable for the ex-Fenian poet to feel both alarm and admiration in the face of this insurrection, an aporia can be transformed into an antithesis. The oxymoron 'terrible beauty' acts as a kind of compromise formation, compressing idealisation, anxiety, defence and aggression. If it tears at the beauty, it nonetheless lovingly restores it; it remains beauty after all, however terrible it may be. One might even detect a dash of Kleinian ambivalence here, as in a mixture of sadism and remorse the woman's body is both dismembered and left intact. To aestheticise the woman, or to mythologise the Rising, is to defuse something of the unsettling force of both; but just as the mythologising cannot be complete since the event is still too raw-edged, so that 'terrible' intrudes into the very aesthetic affirmation of female beauty. Neither are quite ready to be gathered into the artifice of eternity.

Woman, then, rather like the aristocrat, would seem to be on the side of both life and death. If she stands for form, order, symmetry, she also represents the obstreperous energies which these things have to transfigure. So form cannot just stand off from content: to do so, it needs to draw on the dynamic of content itself, rather as for Freud the force by which the ego represses the id is actually drawn from the id itself. But in doing so, social or poetic form risks depleting the very powers which sustain it, which is what Yeats means by our greatness being taken along with our violence. Woman is civility, in the figure of a Lady Gregory, but also the emasculator who thereby tames a virile turbulence. Order is thus destructive of our destructiveness. But if woman is seen as natural rather than civilised she is on the side of death here too, since Nature is what the death drive wishes to merge with. A place like Coole Park dismantles the distinction between the social and the natural by 'naturalising' certain social forms; but the 'one dear perpetual place' in which one can feel rooted sounds ominously like the grave.

This whole contradiction in Yeats is bound up with his blasphemous attitude to death, one encapsulated in his hair-raisingly triumphalist epitaph. It is typical of the poet that in writing his own epitaph he should try to pre-empt death itself, turn history into a shadowing of his own utterance, as he had previously done from time to time with life. The alarming words on his tombstone repress the reality of death, and so of the ultimate form of human self-renunciation, rather as the theory that the self is only reinforced by being given away evades the real *kenosis* of human self-abandonment. Death just thrusts you conveniently back into a superior form of life, or into a realm beyond such oppositions altogether. *Four Quartets*, by contrast, understands that such self-abandonment, to be authentic, can only be fruitful if one ceases to contemplate its potential fruits. It is true that with Eliot there does not seem to be much of a self to be surrendered in the first place, and that the secular world of his poetry, unlike that of 'Sailing to Byzantium', is one which it would not take a great deal of cajolement to leave behind. Eliot's version of 'Sailing to Byzantium' is 'Ash Wednesday', which is rather more gestural about the sensuous world it is abjuring. But Eliot sees as a Christian that there can be no real death if you die with the ace of eternal life up your sleeve. This is also what the Thomas of *Murder in the Cathedral* has to learn from the last tempter. Otherwise martyrdom or crucifixion become not tragic self-dispossessions to be mourned, but mere stratagems by which one rises triumphantly to immortality.

What Eliot and Yeats have in common, on the other hand, is the fact that for neither of them is self-surrender really a transitive matter, a question of giving the self up for others. On the contrary, it remains for both poets as lonely a business as death itself – though the Eliot of *Murder in the Cathedral* understands that maryrdom is a kind of socialising of one's death. Yeats's pathetic belief that he is unkillable belongs with the most callowly pagan aspects of his work, and betrays its paucity in the sham posturing of 'Under Ben Bulben', as well as in parts of the final section of 'The Tower'. The same paganism is apparent in the bathos by which he agonises so much about growing old, a far less exalted *topos* than he seems to imagine. His ultimate refusal of tragedy, unlike that of, say, Bertolt Brecht, is far from the brave humanist affirmation it can sometimes sound like. It belongs rather to a profoundly anti-humanist fear of human frailty, not least his own. His 'Translunar Paradise', like Pincher Martin's lonely rock, sounds more like the hell of those who value themselves too highly to accept that they are finished.

Yeats's poetry is at its most rhetorically threadbare when he does not appear to be reckoning the cost of what it is renouncing. He sometimes buys his victories too cheaply, concealing this under a cloak of lavish self-expenditure. If 'Sailing to Byzantium' is so persuasive, it is partly because it allows us to feel the losses as well as the gains of chirping away for all eternity on a golden bough. 'Byzantium' also turns the tables on the reader in this way, persuading us to admire a spiritual transcendence which disdains all mere complexities, while in the next breath apparently revelling in the riot of unregenerate images which this art must struggle to subdue. The poem thus refuses to give itself an easy ride. But the tragic joy of the Chinamen at the close of 'Lapis Lazuli', who have climbed stoically beyond the profane scene beneath them, is wholly bogus: if that human scene really means no more to Yeats than the slipshod language in which he describes it would indicate, this transcendence has been bought at a knock-down price. Equally, when 'The Tower' portentously informs us that the poet has prepared his peace with 'learned Italian things / And the proud stones of Greece', it is impossible to believe that he is doing much more than cheering himself up, betraying the triteness of these classical totems in the very act of brandishing them defiantly before our eyes. This is not how one feels about the pathetically hoarded emblems of 'Meditations in Time of Civil War', fragments stored against his ruin whose cobbled-together quality the poem makes us feel. Nor is it of the same kind as the conclusion of 'The Man and the Echo':

> O Rocky Voice,
> Shall we in that great night rejoice?
> What do we know but that we face
> One another in this place?
> But hush, for I have lost the theme,
> Its joy or night seem but a dream;
> Up there some hawk or owl has struck,
> Dropping out of sky or rock,
> A stricken rabbit is crying out,
> And its cry distracts my thought.

This is genuinely anxious and alarmed: its queries urgently require some sort of response, which is not always true of Yeats's questions. The final faltering, as the poet turns from these metaphysical musings to the cry of the rabbit, is one of Yeats's boldest throwaways or self-undercuttings; such a stray particular does not usually distract him from what are literally matters of life and death. But neither is this mere displacement: the rabbit's stricken cry is death brought brutally home to experience, and so a way of querying metaphysical speculations on mortality while perpetuating that very theme.

Death in Yeats is a question of form, indeed is sometimes synonymous with artistic form itself. In his Romantic binarism, form is as still and self-contained as a corpse, whereas content is vital, turbulent, amorphous. But content transmits some of its energies to form, so that form is a kind of death warmed up, something 'dead yet flesh and bone', as he writes in 'The Double Vision of Michael Robartes'. Trees, dancers, streams, mummies, fountains, spinning tops and the like are ways of interpenetrating these two dimensions, objects which seem like art itself ambivalently dead and alive, bounded and overflowing, and so places where passion and precision are at one. The big house, Yeats's most treasured artefact, ideally combines its impersonal (and so deathlike) rituals with a boisterous energy which never quite spills over their limits. (Liam de Paor writes of the Book of Kells as displaying an order 'barely controlling an explosive anarchy'.)[6] The house belongs to tradition, another realm which hovers between life and death. These binary oppositions break apart all the time in the substance of the poetry, but the structure of the poetic utterance itself is meant to gesture to their reconciliation.

It is an imaginary resolution, however, since though the big house can accommodate both Renaissance heroes and Crazy Janes, there is no ultimate way of uniting a respect for custom and ceremony with a relish for anarchic violence. Fascism is a kind of caricature of that unity, yoking rituals which have hardened into mass drillings with a violence which is lethally real. Fascist society is a kind of shoddy artefact, its form too tight and its content too unstable. Its discipline is too blatantly imposed, whereas the discipline of organic form emerges from some inner shaping or reticence in the subject-matter itself. If purely amorphous content suggests democracy to Yeats, mechanically willed form is an analogue of authoritarianism. He was attracted to this kind of despotism, but it is really out of step with his organicism. In this organicist vision, life and death are supposed to be at one; but if wisdom really is 'the property of the dead, / A something incompatible with life', he is espousing a more Nietzschean theory of action and contemplation as mutually at odds, life thriving on a necessary ignorance, amnesia and fiction-spinning. And if it is true that only the dead can be forgiven, then a remorse-torn life will never attain to the deathly perfection of art, and that liberation will only ever come too late to be savoured.

Freud, for his part, has *Eros* and *Thanatos* the other way round: it is *Eros* or the life-instincts which are form-yielding, while *Thanatos* or the death drive is the dynamic content they strive to sublimate. Since in doing so they will ironically end up by intensifying it, death for Freud is in a sense more real than life. The vitalist Yeats cannot allow death to have the edge over life in this way, even if how you shape up to death is ethically speaking the deepest test of your mettle. In his Nietzschean philosophy of tragic joy, shaping up to death is really a matter of spitting proudly in its teeth, a defiance by which death itself is unlikely to be impressed. Yeats can cope with the Freudian notion that the death drive is the content of life only by seeing destructiveness as itself a kind of ecstatic creation, and so reappropriating *Thanatos* for *Eros* rather than, like Freud, viewing the latter as finally in the service of the former. Life and death, then, intermingle on both sides of the form–content equation: if form is a sort of life-in-death in which death has the upper hand, content is a turning of destructiveness to creative ends. By wilfully abnegating the self, and thus stealing a march on death, you can reap the delights of masochism and so remain on the side of *Eros*. Being threatened with extinction, as with the mysteriously unsquashable characters of a Disney cartoon,

6.   Liam de Paor, *Ireland and Early Europe* (Dublin, 1997), p. 38. De Paor also comments on how form in Celtic art is meant to spring somehow from within, rather than being externally imposed – a point perhaps relevant to Yeats's Romantic organicism.

just gives you a chance to show how triumphantly invulnerable you actually are. But since the detached *hauteur* which this involves is itself a kind of living death, it is hard to know whether you have outwitted death or obediently done its work for it, just as suicide for Schopenhauer is less a way of cheating on the Will than the Will's final sick joke at the expense of humanity.

Eliot's poetry becomes memorable after several readings; Yeats's verse is, so to speak, memorable straight away, already recollected when we first encounter it. It is, in Walter Benjamin's sense of the word, auratic, whereas Eliot's poetry is out to destroy the aura of things. There is always a kind of *déjà lu* about Yeats, a sense that what we are reading is at once fresh and monumental, vivid yet framed by distance. It is form which frames the passionate subject-matter into an impersonality which has the smack of a maxim about it, words which resonate in the mind like a phrase we have somehow always known. As a man, Yeats looked at the present with one eye on how it would appear to the future; and another kind of oxymoronic tense is characteristic of our experience of his poetry.

BECKETT'S PARADOXES

One hears from those who knew him personally that Samuel Beckett was a genial enough character, a tolerably good-natured Gael, and this might seem bizarre only to those who took his art to be some form of self-expression. But Beckett does not have much belief in a self, and 'expression' in any case sounds too strenuous an affair for his debilitated world, in which utterance can be a physical pain, a nervous spasm, a quasi-biological process in which words are heaved up like foreign matter from the gut or torn laboriously from the flesh, and where keeping a discourse going can be like rolling a boulder uphill. Just as Proust's enormous sentences can be seen as a consequence of the Paris Commune,[1] so Beckett's parsimonious way with words has an obscure root in Auschwitz. But since he is doing nothing so idly luxurious as expressing himself in portraying this dire condition, it is possible that in real life he was a sentimental optimist with a Panglossian faith in human potential.

In fact he was not, but there is nothing in his aesthetic views to suggest why he should not have been. Beckett's works are not the artistic equivalent of some 'The Way I See It' newspaper column. They are fictional hypotheses, which like the poetry of Mallarmé or the music of Schoenberg work out the immanent logic of their materials with scant regard for anything as arbitrary as an intending subject. Beckett's art takes a set of postulates, and in quasi-mechanical manner lets them run through their various permutations until the process is exhausted and another equally rigorous, equally pointless computation takes over. What is then ironic is that his fingerprints can be detected all over his writing precisely in its laconic impersonality, its austere lack of self-regard. His brand of anonymity is *sui generis*, his facelessness unmistakable. If his work is idiosyncratic, it is not at all subjective. If nobody but he could have produced it, this 'he' is notably elusive. There is a parallel here perhaps with the role of the human body in these texts, which given the snares of memory and the stratagems of language is the only principle of individuation one has left, yet which is also an utterly unspecific assemblage of organs, a kind of dead levelling of human difference.

Yet though everything is contingent, subjunctive, in the work of this man whose most definitive word is 'perhaps', that *oeuvre* itself has an air of

---

1. Proust's mother was pregnant with him during the period of the Commune, and the anxiety she experienced during those events was in Proust's view responsible for his life-long asthma. His extended, fluent sentences have been read by some as an unconscious compensation for his asthmatic breathlessness. See George D. Painter, *Marcel Proust: A Biography* (reprinted London, 1996), p. 4.

necessity. There is, to be sure, nothing necessary *in* Beckett's universe, any more than there is in David Hume's; but that world itself has a smack of ineluctability about it. A reverse image of this is the game, that most Beckettian of metaphors, whose rules are arbitrary when viewed from the outside, but absolute for those players on the inside of it. A necessary work of art, to be sure, is not always synonymous with a great one. Some of the art we feel could not not have existed has a kind of archetypal aura about it, as though we were familiar with it long before we actually encountered it. But there is also a backwards form of necessity in which, reviewing some past phase of artistic evolution or period of cultural history, we can see, with all the conviction of a vision of the future, that *someone* was going to have to take it in that particular direction, break beyond a certain set of constraints, if we were to arrive at where we are today. (Though there was, naturally, no necessity about that either.)

It is as though we can now recognise that, for example, simply because of the sharpening contradictions of naturalistic drama, there would have been a thrust beyond such theatrical realism, even if its names had not turned out to be Beckett or Pirandello or Ionesco. Someone, we feel, would have had to come up with free verse or musical dissonance or showing a face from five different angles simultaneously, just as once you have a variety of liquors it is hard not to think that cocktails were somehow pre-ordained. Every cultural period presents us with a *combinatoire* of possibilities, whose several permutations are, if not predetermined, at least predictable. In late nineteenth-century England, some authors wrote of the new currents of sexuality, a few were preoccupied by rural decline and others by the collapse of Victorian rationalism, but it seems logical in retrospect that the connections between these topics would have cropped up somewhere too, even if Thomas Hardy had never existed. In post-war Europe, there were those authors gripped by a sense of spiritual exhaustion, writers who carved out a niche of anti-heroic debunkery, artistic exiles adrift between languages, and avant-garde experimenters in theatrical form; but there was also, so to speak, a place vacant in the structure of artistic production where all four modes might interlock, and its name was Samuel Beckett. On the other hand, not every place in a structure has the genius of a Beckett, which is to say that the author, rather like the ceaselessly disintegrating but never quite deceased characters of Beckett's own work, is not quite dead.

In another sense, however, if everything in Beckett's world is gratuitous and provisional, then this must also apply to his writing as such, which in a purely contingent world, seems continually astonished by the fact it does anything as emphatic as existing. It must apply also, in some Cretan Liar paradox, to that writing's 'way of seeing'. How can the exclamation 'there is no truth' not fall foul of its own judgement? Nietzsche believed all propositions to be false, in which case the unavoidable question is: false to what? The view that everything is hypothetical is itself a hypothesis, and on pain of self-con-tradition must calculate this fact into its reckoning. How can those bereft of an absolute meaning be sure of that truth, if no certainty can be absolute? Godot's absence from the world may have plunged all into indeterminacy, but that means among other things that there is no assurance that he will not come. If reality is indeterminate, then this must also be true of our knowledge of it, which means that we can never be entirely sure of its indeterminacy. This is not yet another effort to recuperate Beckett for some affirmative humanism, as so many commentators rattled by his implacable bleakness have tried, sometimes a touch pathetically, to do. If it tempers Beckett's cheerlessness to insist that even this must be on his own aesthetic reckoning a sort of fiction, the fact that there is nothing but fiction may itself be the most cheerless truth of all. But even bleakness cannot be absolute in a world without absolutes, however much it is that lack of absolutes which makes things so dismal in the first place. In such a world there can be no salvation, but no absolute need for it either, which is perhaps some meagre consolation.

In any case, if everything is ambiguous and obscure, how can we know that viewed from some other perspective this world of freaks and cripples is not teetering on the brink of transfiguration? Who is to say that there is no all-loving, all-merciful Godot? He does not seem to come, to be sure; but if nothing is certain then this absence might always be a cryptic form of presence, a momentary lull or eloquent silence within some grander narrative of which we can know nothing, an obscure twist in some ultimately translucent tale. How do we know that what we are enduring is not precisely Godot's coming, which may not after all be an advent in the sense of some personage stomping on Fortinbras-like before the final curtain? Perhaps *Waiting for Godot* is not exactly a play in which nothing happens, nor even, as Vivian Mercier maintains, one in which nothing happens – twice, but one in which, to adopt a phrase from Paul de Man, we cannot say for sure whether anything is happening or not. What would count here as an event? Is waiting an occurrence, or the cessation or anticipation of one? Perhaps it is the waiting, not the coming, which is the purpose of Vladimir and Estragon's existence, so that things are adding up before their very eyes even though they themselves glumly defer a totality to the future. Or perhaps they are not really waiting at all, simply feigning to do so to lend some point to their listless presence.

One can also of course wait without knowing it, and – as with desire, which waiting so closely resembles – not know what you are waiting for until it finally heaves into view and retrospectively reformulates the narrative which brought it to birth. The phrase 'waiting for something to happen' captures a relevant ambiguity: any old something, or something in particular? And how can the first not also turn out to be the second? Something in particular is always a disappointment, as desire well knows, and Godot's coming will only avoid this fate if it is as unspecific as the waiting which precedes it, and hence unrecognisable. The alternative to something in particular would have to be everything, which would then be difficult to distinguish from nothing. In what sense it might be possible to wait for nothing is one of the questions the drama poses.

Perhaps when Godot comes we will know exactly what it is that the tramps (though we are not told that they are tramps) are being saved *from*, what it is that is so intolerable to them, which is not much clearer than the nature of Godot himself. Or perhaps it is only Godot's coming which will reveal that there was no need for his arrival after all, that it was mere Protestant false consciousness to imagine that there was one big thing which was crying out for redemption. One might imagine that we have, at least, negative knowledge – that we can give a name to the nature of our malaise, even if the remedy is far from obvious. But Beckett's work casts grave doubt on this most natural of assumptions. How can we know what is awry with us unless we can compare it with something better, or at least different? If Beckett's men and women could rise to a meta-statement about what exactly they hoped to be redeemed from, perhaps this itself would be their redemption, or perhaps they would then have no need of it. Meanwhile, what is so painful is not exactly that there is apparently no salvation in this world, but that it seems on a quick glance the kind of place where there might be. If Beckett is more modernist than postmodernist, it is because his world has shattered into fragments which leave rather at their centre not just a blank, but a hole whose shape is still hauntingly reminiscent.

Ludwig Wittgenstein once remarked that intending is not an experience, and something similar might be claimed of the act of waiting, if an act is what it is. Waiting may well be accompanied by experiences – dread, boredom, anxiety, impatience and the like – but to say that someone is waiting, as with saying that they are promising or intending, is to describe a situation rather than a state of mind. Waiting is in one sense a suspension of experience – of the event or encounter which will bring it to a close – and so has too little meaning in itself, a mere empty passageway to something else; but it also has a surplus of significance, since you can wait and do any number of other things at the same time. This is because waiting is not in fact a distinct action over and above what you do in the meanwhile, any more than intending is a mental act that you tack on to whatever it is you purposefully perform; but the condition seems to hover indecisively between doing and not doing something ('What are you doing, since you seem to be doing nothing?' 'I'm waiting'), and so is a peculiarly suggestive state of being for an artist whose universe is fundamentally ambiguous.

Anyway, if uncertainty is all there is, then a meta-statement to this effect would seem notably vulnerable, which is why Beckett's art, like Wittgenstein's *Tractatus*, can show what it means but not say it, since to say it would be to run headlong into epistemological contradiction. It may also be why there is a problem about characterising his work as tragic, since tragedy seems to involve a more determinate universe than he ever offers us. His work has, to be sure, something of the wretchedness of tragedy, along with its implicit faith in some universal human condition. But there is perhaps a touch of parody about Beckett's exploration of the 'human condition', that singular object which, so we are instructed, is what all accomplished art should be about, just as there is more than a hint of parody in Wilde's rather too self-consciously well-made plays. Beckett's writing is so palpably 'universal', so much in this respect the kind of thing that the bourgeois theatregoer expects from his evening out, that one wonders whether this starkly unspecific discourse of Man, while in one sense entirely genuine, is not in another sense ironic. If it has the scope of the classical humanist vision, it also empties that vision of its robustly affirmative content. It is a humanism turned inside out, so that the denial of ultimate value has all the universality of the world it refuses. Beckett's work has no very uncomfortably specific referent, so we imagine that its referent must therefore be the species as such, thus passing too hastily over the question of in what sense it 'refers' at all. What, for example, does *Breath* represent, other than an answer to the theatrical conundrum: How do you write a play with no dialogue, scenery, plot or characters? Some of his art has a representational look about it, as a circus resembles a theatre; but we would not ask what a liontamer or trapeze artist represents, as we might of an Ibsen symbol. If Beckett is one of the most grandly globalising of writers, he is also deeply allergic to the portentousness of all that, debunking the 'philosophical vision' with a flash of farce or a deflating aside. If there is indeed a tragic crisis in his work, then it is known as the commonplace, of which he is perhaps our foremost poet. 'The fact that "everything just goes on"', Walter Benjamin once observed, 'is the crisis', and Beckett is the supreme literary incarnation of this insight. Protestantism may be the locus of apocalypse, but it is also where the everyday is raised to a certain dignity and ransacked for significance.

What is so shocking about this world is that the extreme is now the dully normative, even if this cannot actually be true, since if it were we would not be shocked by it at all. The fact that we laugh at Murphy or Malone implies a norm from which they deviate. For good or ill, we are not like Winnie of *Happy Days*, blandly accepting the extraordinary as the rule, since if we were we should find nothing striking in her condition at all. Anyway, if there is a 'Gallic' fine-drawnness and asceticism about this *oeuvre*, it also betrays a most unGallic strain of the sheerly humdrum, moving like so much Irish writing between high formality and low farce. Its ludic quality, too, is not quite the high-toned, somewhat cerebral form of play one finds from Mallarmé to Barthes, but a rather more knockabout sort of messing around, more populist than Parisian.

Beckett's world may not be determinate enough to be tragic, but that, one might claim, may be part of the tragedy. Catastrophe exists only if it can be signified, but the instability of the signifier in Beckett's world is perhaps itself a catastrophe of sorts. The puzzle is how reality can be at once so inconstant and so persistently painful. At least Phèdre and Hedda Gabler are up to their tragic roles, carry them off with brio and panache, whereas these pedants and puppets bungle even that, muff even that amount of solid meaning. Does this then undercut the tragedy or raise it to the second power? Is a tragic protagonist who doesn't know he is one – a Willy Loman, for example – more or less tragic than an Othello or Cleopatra who pumps every last drop of pathos from their status? If time is eternal recurrence, and everything will return with some trifling variant on its infinitely enduring identity, is this more or less calamitous than a linear notion of time in which you can always hope for change, but where for the same reason actions can be irreparable? Is a world like Beckett's in which there is no death, no definitive closure, more or less tragic than one in which there is? Something apparently unkillable keeps taking its course, some process with all the implacability of a purpose though quite without a *telos*, but it might be more merciful if it did not.

Perhaps Beckett falls below the tragic because that form depends on a sense of value, and things are now too dire even for that, in which case pessimism pushed far enough reverts to a kind of hope. A society which has moved beyond tragedy may not after all be the most inspiring place to inhabit, since the destruction of men and women may not seem to it worth weeping over. If there is no need for redemption, this may simply mean that there is nothing precious enough to be redeemed. If human subjects are in pieces, then they may not be coherent enough to be the bearers of tragic significance. If they are safely beyond alienation, it may be because there is nothing left to alienate, no interior depth to be confiscated or estranged. Perhaps it is simply a metaphysical hangover to expect the world to be the kind of thing which could be meaningful in the first place, and so to find its apparent senselessness somehow lamentable. 'Isn't there some meaning?', asks Masha in Chekhov's *Three Sisters*, to which Toozenbach dryly responds: 'Look out there, it's snowing. What's the meaning of that?' It is not a deficiency of the snow that it is meaningless, any more than the handle of a cup is a flaw in the pottery.

Beckett's work has this strain of positivism about it, of the world just being baldly whatever is the case, of things resisting signification less because meaning has gradually haemorrhaged away from them than because they never had it in the first place, meaning not being something that a thing 'has' like a certain weight or taste. Nihilism is perhaps just the wish that this were so, and the fury that it is not. But an absence of meaning is not necessarily to be mourned: farce, for example, is action with the meaning switched off, *King Lear* on television without the sound. In any case, Beckett's characters are sometimes far too busy to fuss about anything as high-falutin' as significance, too preoccupied with their hoard of knick-knacks or with the sheer fatiguing business of keeping their heads biologically above water to lose sleep over this rather academic affair. It is good in a way that the body is steadily disintegrating, since otherwise one would have nothing to keep oneself occupied. If this is all displacement activity, it is worth asking what exactly it is supposed to be displacing – just as we can see a sign as a substitute for a thing, but when asked 'what thing?' tend simply to come up again with the sign in question. Perhaps one's pointless, unending narratives are there to dispel the boredom of what Walter Benjamin called empty, homogeneous time; but without such stories we might have no sense of such time in the first place, and thus no medium in which to be bored. The point of this perpetual yarn-spinning may be *pour meubler le vide,* but one cannot rule out the possibility that this void is less something out there that narrating fills in, than a lack it creates around itself as a kind of aura. If Beckett's characters are distracting themselves from some Kurtz-like glimpse into chaos, then this, at least, would be a grand metaphysical condition of sorts, however negative; the rather more mundane truth, however, may be that distraction is all there is, as life for the later Freud is itself just one fruitless deviation on the part of the death drive.

Beckett does not sign on for the currently fashionable view that the body is wholly a construct of the signifier, with its hubristic horror of the given. For him, there is always a residue which escapes the sway of language, and its name is suffering. The body is as radically given as an avalanche, and though there is more than that – there is also language, and always more language where that came from, which is why death or closure is continually deferred – the mystery of the human body, like the enigma of black marks on a page, is how exactly this piece of matter comes to be more than itself, how it some-how keeps crawling or bleating, even if that feeble impulse to self-transcen-dence is persistently exhausted, or takes only the form of articulating how the body is more or less all there is. Suffering in Beckett is fundamental, but it is not unreserved, since language opens up a small space within the body which allows for its articulation. As Bertolt Brecht writes: 'Lamenting by means of sounds, or better still words, is a vast liberation, because it means that the suf-ferer is beginning to produce something. He's already mixing his sorrow with an account of the blows he has received; he's already making something out of the utterly devastating. Observation has set in.'[2] Language is the edge we have over biology, but this in Beckett is a mixed blessing, since language is what keeps us going, and so allows us to suffer more. His signifying has just come loose from screaming, detached itself rawly from the body; but it remains almost as mechanical, and certainly as anonymous, as the body whose traces it still bears; and if the focus of *Not I* is the mouth, it is because there meaning and materiality converge mysteriously together.

Language is the point where the body stirs for a moment from its sluggish self-identity, producing something which travels beyond it and turns it inside out; but this impulse to articulate in Beckett is still not clearly separable from a biological reflex, as words hover somewhere between signs and symptoms. Discourse in his writing can be as much an object as pebbles or bowler hats – chunks of shopsoiled cliché to be fingered like worry beads, reach-me-down tags to be tossed to and fro, crumbling bits of proverb to be stored away like mouldy sweets. One is and is not one's body, just as language is and is not

2.   Bertolt Brecht, *The Messingkauf Dialogues* (London, 1965), p. 47.

material. On the one hand, the self perches inside the body as in a rusty tank, manoeuvring its bulk at long range as one would shift a corpse; on the other hand, this dualism no longer implies à la Descartes a self which is substantial, cleanly separate from the body and in authoritative command of it. Beckett thus inherits all of the embarrassments of Cartesian dualism with none of the benefits.

It would seem, then, that as far as tragedy goes he has the worst of both worlds. Things are either obtusely self-identical, impervious to meaning, or they are freighted with ambiguity, rife with too much significance rather than too little, and so desperately opaque. Something similar can be said of that other fashioner of grotesques, Charles Dickens, whose characters can appear enigmatic either because they are nothing but their appearances, or because these appearances conceal some impenetrable hinterland. With Beckett, it seems that one either falls bathetically below tragedy into the realm of pure facticity, or one cannot say for certain whether anything, let alone anything tragic, is happening or not. Reality is either a rockface which offers no hold for meaning, or is dissolved to a dim flickering of signifiers in which anything can be permutated with anything else. Exploiting the ambiguity of language, and understanding that there is a point where its power falters in the face of the real, are both, one might claim, characteristic of the colonial mind.[3] Those slippages of the signifier, moreover, are not in the least liberating, as they are for a certain euphoric vein of post-structuralism, just as Beckett's infinite deferment is more heart-sickness than an exhilarating play of difference. It is true, as we have seen, that these equivocations let one off the hook of absolute negativism; but they also mean that we cannot even call our suffering our own, cannot even reap the cold consolation of a definitive statement of our misery. There is pain in abundance, but if subjecthood is now just a garbled memory, we cannot be sure quite who is having it, as Wittgenstein asks us to imagine a room in which there is a floating pain which attaches itself to different individuals at different times.[4]

Even so, Beckett never ceases trying to eff the ineffable, which is not to rank him with some vulgar Romanticism or existentialism for which the problem is one of trying to tell it like it is. This way of putting it presupposes what Beckett can be read as calling into question, namely that there is indeed that beyond the signifier to which it must strive to be faithful. But if indeterminacy is our ontological condition, then we cannot assume that there is, though neither of course can we take it for granted that there is not. There is a parallel ambiguity

3. Fintan O'Toole has shown the importance of the motif of linguistic instability, both politically and artistically, to Richard Brinsley Sheridan. See his *A Traitor's Kiss* (London, 1997).
4. Wittgenstein's point in the *Philosophical Investigations*, however, is that this is absurd exactly because pains are not private property. To think that they are involves a confusion between the grammar of 'My pain' and 'my hat'.

in the epistemology of Beckett's own writing, which suspends us in the space it creates between itself and a referent. Is his drama more like circus or documentary, ballet or story? Does it present a real time-stream along with a virtual one, or just the former? The point, anyway, is that Beckett is not a Conrad, full of vague portentous immensities, but an Irish scholastic with a monkish devotion to precision. What, if anything, is mad about his writing is not the swell of some monstrous chaos which laps at the edges of speech, but its crazedly clear-minded attempt at an exact formulation of the inarticulable, its exquisite sculpting of sheer vacancy, the scrupulousness with which it plucks ever more slender nuances from hints and velleities. If one aspect of Beckett is a 'post-structuralist' suspicion of language, the other is a Protestant thirst for truth, or rather for that rigorously formulated scepticism which is perhaps the nearest we moderns can approach to it. Beckett's language shaves away at the inessential, in a universe where there is nothing essential in the first place, with a Protestant animus against the superfluous and ornamental. Each of his sentences has an air of being free-wheeling, reminding us that it might just as well not have existed, at the same time as it seems meticulously deduced from the equally contingent one which preceded it, as a kind of necessary inference or rigorous implication. There must still be a trace of truth in this world, since why otherwise would one be driven to specify one's doubts about its existence so punctiliously?

The temporal equivalent of this striving to know in Beckett is the act of trying to remember – another rich locus of ambiguity, since to recall implies having forgotten, yet if this were really true one would not even know there was anything to be remembered. (Tom Stoppard captures something of this paradox in an exchange in *Rosencrantz and Guildenstern Are Dead*: ' "What's the first thing you remember?" "No, it's no good, it's gone." "You don't get my meaning. What's the first thing after all the things you've forgotten?" ') There is a difference here between a reality-shaped absence and absence pure and simple, as there is in Beckett's epistemological universe more generally. Indeed memory and its lapses become symbolic of the aporias of present knowledge, as characters gaze at an object before their eyes as though it is something they are trying to dredge up from an uncertain past. Memory tells you among other things whether something has happened before, which in Beckett's world is usually the case. That it has happened already is in one sense consoling, confirming testimony of its reality. As Milan Kundera remarks, '*einmal ist keinmal*': anything which occurs just once has an unbearable lightness of being about it, as though it might as well not have happened at all. It is repetition which establishes the reality of things, but which also undercuts it. For the more things repeat themselves, the more tarnished and threadbare they become; if once is nothing in this ontological arithmetic, so is many times over. The more something is recycled, the more its meaning starts to leak from it. The more it happens, the less it does.

One of Kundera's finest illustrations of this is the sexual orgy, which turns out to be hilariously comic in its endless mechanical repetititon of coupling bodies, the supposedly unique nature of erotic love uproariously multipled in a wilderness of mirrors.[5] What was thought distinctive – the individual body – turns out, as in Beckett, to be a realm of identity rather than difference, even if the only sure way of telling us apart. The exchangeability of things is what underscores their existence, but also what threatens to strike them valueless. If something has already taken place a few times, then it sets up a kind of mini-tradition by which you can guide your personal conduct; but nothing happens twice, precisely because it has happened once already, so that 'tradition' is no more of a guide than a dog-eared book of proverbs. Beckett's characters live not by that Catholic sense of history which is tradition, but by that privatised equivalent of tradition which is habit. Habit is automated repetition, a way of ordering your life without having to take action, and thus perhaps the only form of structuring possible in a world in which the very notion of agency may be a mirage. Habit, as a Beckett character famously remarks, is a great deadener, which means that it is both problem and solution, insulates you against wretchedness with a miserable tedium of its own. Habit is a homeopathic sort of defence, both poison and cure.

Remembrance is a way of possessing the past, but even this feeble degree of agency is a luxury in Beckett's world. More usually, it is not quite possible to remember whether something has occurred already or not, a condition which lands you once again with the worst of both worlds. Just as the world seems at once crucifying and evanescent, so the past is continuously airbrushed out but continues nonetheless to exert some relentless determinism. As far as determinism goes, there might be some glum comfort in being able to give a name to whatever it is one is a mere bearer of, and the nineteenth and early twentieth centuries had candidates for this in plenty: History, Will, Reason, will-to-power, myth, evolution, language, the unconscious, the dark gods, the Life Force and the like. At least one could preserve, even intensify some form of subjectivity here, ousting the petty individual ego with some altogether grander and deeper variety of Subject, however aloof or malevolent. And even if some of these processes were altogether without a final purpose, they at least retained the drift and thrust of one, in a negative imprint of teleology.

Beckett's schizoid figures, however, are typically denied even this dubious metaphysical dignity, incapable as they are of giving a name to whatever may be taking its course, and conscious as we readers or viewers are that this death-dealing force may be just another life-saving fiction. The steady decay we call human growth may be only as determined as the blowing of a rose; it is just that this very dreary normality seems so aberrant and intolerable that we seek to explain it in terms of some fatality visited upon us from the outside, preferring a malign metaphysical meaning to a naturalistic lack of one.

5.   See my essay 'Estrangement and Irony', in the special issue of *Salmagundi* entitled 'Milan Kundera: Fictive Lightness, Fictive Weight' (no. 73, Winter, 1987).

Because the past dissolves behind one's back, the amnesiac subject has to fashion itself anew at every moment, improvise some gratuitous identity on the spot; but this, which the existentialist might hail as freedom, turns out to be just enough liberty to discover for yourself a new mode of inertia, rearranging the determinants of one's being into a new sort of prison-cell; and it is possible in any case that this has all happened before and will do so interminably in the future. There is self-invention, then, but no real selfhood to accompany it, since what necessitates this continual remaking is just the fact that one cannot remember who one is, with the consequence that one becomes just a perpetual series of such refashionings, which is to say nobody at all. And the more everything seems provisional, constructed, the more this discloses how brutely given everything really is, since the freedom to make the self up as you go along suggests that reality is a sheer *donnée* which lacks enough immanent meaning (as opposed to mere dead weight) to constrain this purely negative liberty. Once more, Beckett's world is cusped between too much meaning and too little, a place which is burdensome because it is both too capricious and too torpid.

There are all sorts of responses, some more plausible than others, to the question of whether there is value in Beckett's world. The query itself springs most commonly from the unnerved liberal humanist, and so in a sense begs the question, since one might claim that much of Beckett's value consists precisely in its remorseless demystification of what passes for value in that particular camp. The fact that the liberal humanist is forced to raise the question is one answer to the question. It may thus be less a matter of reclaiming Beckett for humanistic value than of appreciating the value of his anti-humanism. The merciless onslaught on the pretensions of Literature, the sardonic refusal of idealist morphine even when in severe pain, the compact with how it is which undermines the rhetoric of achievement, the puristic horror of deceit which nonetheless knows itself to be unavoidably mystified: all of this bears the stamp of the dissident or peripheral writer, along with that ruthless shrinking, mechanising and hacking to the bone which is ironically what has enriched and enlarged us, and which might recall the excoriations of a Swift. Swift, however, is easy enough for the humanist to handle, not despite his 'misanthropy' but because of it: one has no problem in dealing with one's antithesis, and 'misanthropy' is after all quite as intelligible, value-laden an affair as optimism. Love of humankind and hatred for it lie on the same plane, and can easily be translated into one another. Beckett is a harder case for liberal humanism because of his apparent lack of effect, his mechanising and externalising of the psyche, his indifference to human difference, his scepticism of narrative, the unwaveringly positivist tone which seems not to register how humanly devastating his scenarios are, his embarrassing habit of being distressingly downbeat while falling short of the grandeur of tragedy, his refusal not just of splendidly vigorous characters – liberal humanism has no trouble with that – but of 'character' as such.

Alternatively, as far as the question of value in Beckett goes, we might just remind ourselves that he is very funny. It is not that one can still laugh despite the disaster, or in Yeatsian style laugh proudly in its teeth. It is rather the disaster itself which is so hilarious. There is something funny about meaninglessness or absurdity, which Freud would no doubt explain as the pleasurable release which comes from no longer having to invest our energies in the laborious business of sense-making. It is never quite possible to decide whether a world without sense is the ultimate in tragedy or the transcendence of it, and there is something comic in itself about this ambivalence. Absurdity is funny, and the fact that it is is also funny. Or, as far as the issue of value goes, one might try instead an Adorno-style response: if Beckett's stylised, balletic forms mime a grievous alienation, their shaping intentionality suggests a constructive spirit which that alienation has not wholly succeeded in banishing.

Or one might venture, finally, a semiotic sort of answer. The bedrock for Beckett, beyond all theme, story or idea, is the bare fact of the *énoncé*, the pure trace of the act of utterance, void of all end and substance. This impulse to communicate may be no more a matter of value than a tendency to sweat or an urge to yawn. But it bears an interesting relation to what the linguists have dubbed the phatic: linguistic contact as an end in itself, devoid of all content, as in 'Well, here we are!' or 'Fancy speaking to you!' These are in one sense the most empty and banal of utterances, the mere time-filling or occasion-marking allusions of language to itself before the properly referential business of discourse gets under way. In another sense, however, they represent the very consummation of language, whose most creative modality after all is not the conveying of information, but that of establishing human sharing and solidarity as a radical end in itself. The scrupulous banality of Beckett's discourse, its depleted, fruitlessly self-referential condition, reminds us in its very hollow formality of the fact that what matters in the end – though the end never quite arrives – is not the content of the stories we tell, but the act of telling them to one another.

REVISIONISM REVISITED

It is a bad time to write on Ireland. The politically overcharged climate of the country – one might, for example, find the word 'country' a source of contention there, for how many countries or bits of them are there on the island? – has had its warping effects on intellectual debate, however dispassionate such discourse might strive to be. This conceptual space has felt the distorting tug of material reality as surely as planetary space is curved out of shape by the bodies it contains. Those who recall the horrors of the Famine are rebuked by some Irish commentators for whingeing, unlike those Britons who commemorate their two world wars without standing accused of morbidity. There has even been a fashion in the country for shifting the blame for the Famine to the gombeenish Irish themselves. To praise the courage and imaginative flair of the United Irishmen; to find the nationalist heritage not universally bigoted and bankrupt; to suggest that the record of British colonialism left much to be desired, to use the term 'colonialism' at all rather than some anodyne alternative: all this in the eyes of some sails perilously close to lending comfort to those who commit murder in the North, and is unlikely to land you a post in quite a few academic history departments in these islands. An eminent Irish historian goes on radio to criticise a nationalist Irish film he has not seen, while an English author who begins an academic work with a reference to his Irish provenance is accused by a reviewer of Nazi-style racism. English newspapers hire Irish correspondents skilled in well-bred sneering at the Gael. The British can now confidently rely on the Irish themselves to produce the kind of anti-Irish sentiments which they had previously to disseminate themselves. A brilliant blockbuster celebrating the Irish Literary Revival is ritually slaughtered by a whole raft of Irish reviewers. The Easter Rising, that relatively bloodless affair, is treated by some as though it outstripped the Jacobin Terror in violence and the Charge of the Light Brigade in folly. To urge respect for aspects of traditional Irish culture is to brand oneself in some quarters as morbidly nostalgic, a diehard opponent of that most vacuous of all sociological movements, 'modernisation'. To regret that the political deadlock known as Northern Ireland was ever legislated into existence is to unmask oneself as a Gaelic triumphalist and red-neck Anglophobe. It begins to seem somehow logical that those who admire Fintan Lalor should take little interest in feminism, or that devotees of the Liberator should be unenthused by gay liberation. And for many such admirers and devotees this is indeed the case, in contrast to a pluralism which would encompass the most creative currents of them all. One has to confess, however, that appreciating both Daniel O'Connell and gay rights is not notably common among those who call themselves pluralists in Ireland today.

To be sure, all this dyspeptic irritation or overcivilised irony about Gaelic culture is a perfectly understandable overreaction to a more long-standing orthodoxy in Ireland, one which is xenophobic, parochial, patriarchal, anti-modernist, philistine, sentimental and corrupt. For the apologists for this mind-set, those who point out that, say, evicting, rack-renting and absenteeism were far less common among the Irish landlords than has been popularly imagined, or that some currents of Irish nationalism have been virulently chauvinist, or that Irish history has come packaged in a good deal of glossily romantic wrapping, are treated as agents in the pay of the British government – which indeed some of them are, though for the most part as academics rather than as intelligence officers. To propose to such apologists that territorial unity, in Ireland or elsewhere, means precious little in itself, or that Northern Protestants have had genuine reasons, along with patently disingenuous ones, for fearing Catholic hegemony, is probably as pointless as proposing marriage to the pope. (As far as the disingenuous reasons go, those who purport to fear that the opposite of Unionist dominion is Rome rule should recall Edmund Burke's refusal to believe that 'discourses of this kind are held, or that anything like them will be held, by any who walk about without a keeper'.)[1] But if the Protestant community in the North had not been under permanent military assault for the past few decades, it is morally certain that cultural and historical discourse in Ireland today would be less full of cheap anti-Gaelic gibes, knee-jerk reactions to 1916 or disingenuous defences of Unionist privilege. The Provisionals have certainly played their part in the rise of revisionism, a truth which neither party would presumably be keen to acknowledge.

Even so, on paper at least, some sort of *rapprochement* between the nationalists and revisionists does not seem beyond question. In theory, there is plenty of room in Ireland for intellectual, as for political, negotiation. If the nationalists were prepared to concede that the British did not gather round a table in 1845 to plan the systematic extermination of the Irish race, the revisionists might in turn acknowledge that some aspects of the British government's relief policy during the Famine probably resulted in thousands of needless extra deaths. If the nationalists would only confess that the penal laws were not the most fiendishly oppressive apparatus ever to have emerged on the planet, the revisionists might show a mite more sensitivity to the insult and indignity which their very existence inflicted on the Irish people. Much the same goes for the English destruction of some Irish manufacturing industry, which may not have been as economically disastrous as was once believed, but was certainly ideologically so. If the traditionalists would only admit that the Catholic church in Ireland has blighted the lives and damaged the psyches of countless numbers of its adherents, the modernisers might be

1.   Edmund Burke, 'A Letter to Sir Hercules Langrishe, MP', in Matthew Arnold (ed.), *Letters, Speeches and Tracts on Irish Affairs by Edmund Burke* (London, 1881), p. 249.

able to bring themselves to concede that without the church's precious work over the centuries, millions of men and women in Ireland would have gone uneducated, unnursed and unconsoled. If the nationalists could bring themselves to see that a good many young people in the republic find talk of roots and martyrdom and patriotism not only boring and irrelevant but positively nauseating, the liberal modernisers might concede that, when these young people land in Britain to experience anti-Irish racism at first hand, they are on the receiving end of a phenomenon about which the Irish nationalist tradition has had something valuable to say. (For anyone brought up in Britain, the revisionist Irish habit of downplaying British anti-Irishness is one of the sickest self-deceptions of all.)

If the traditionalists would only see the value and urgency of so-called identity politics in the republic, the revisionists might allow that such politics have too often been a coded way of forgetting about the North. The traditionalists might be more eager to agree that political martyrdom can be squalidly masochistic if only the revisionists would acknowledge that they are ready enough to praise such actions themselves when it comes to Steve Biko or Martin Luther King. If the revisionists would only sound a little less suavely hard-boiled and emotionally anaesthetised, some nationalists might stop talking as though the point of writing Irish history was to cheer the nation up. We might then all move as one body into a post-revisionist phase, in which many of revisionism's empirical findings could be welcomed, without feeling the need to subscribe to the ideological slantings, sidelinings and silences which so often underpin them. We might recognise that there was no need after all to choose in some rigorously exclusivist way between emphasising the common cultural heritage of Britain and Ireland, and highlighting the excellent reasons why some of the Irish have had a right to feel reproachful about Britain. Liberals may feel that this reproachfulness is unjustifed; but they cannot consistently hold, if they recall, for example, their views of racial conflict, that *any* resentment, social antagonism or reluctance to accept that we are all one mutually interdependent human family is just truculent self-indulgence. The liberal sensibility, which tends to see conflict as destructive in itself, is interestingly at odds with many of liberalism's political positions, not least its strenuous battle against illiberalism.

Hegel once joked that he thought compulsively in threes, no doubt the only joke he ever made, and many intellectual conflicts have a triadic structure. First there is a long-established orthodoxy – say, the belief that suicide attempts are best interpreted as cries for help. This becomes so universally accepted that it is only a matter of time before someone is stirred to challenge it. In the fullness of time, a psychiatric *enfant terrible* arises who pours scorn on this whole complacently unexamined hypothesis. Her colleagues react with scandalised scepticism, but are soon keen enough to climb on her bandwagon – partly because the counter-hypothesis looks plausible, partly because it is less boring, partly because it opens up a whole exciting new research programme, partly because it chimes obscurely with the sensibility of the age. The new conjecture promises to resolve all sorts of conundrums which the cry-for-help hypothesis could not, and promises moreover to cast some light on why it could not. Then, after a while, the anomalies of the new theory gather to the point where someone is driven to articulate the unthinkable: the old hypothesis *was true after all*. But we could only have come to see this because we quite properly left it behind, probing its internal inconsistences, its built-in biases, the mass of evidence it failed to account for. Having gone beyond the old theory in this way, we can now return to it and do it the justice we withheld from it before, extracting the kernel of truth from its mystified shell. We can now acknowledge its truth because we have more than accounted for its untruth.

It is thus, by sublations rather than once-and-for-all subversions, that intellectual development usually comes about. In a first stage, feminists protest that women are slaves. In a second stage, the claim is dispassionately scrutinised by the historical scholars, who judge it to be flawed and intemperate. Modern women may be free labourers in the capitalist market place, but they are in no literal sense slaves, legally owned by a proprietor, and many of them do not sell their labour-power at all. The scholars spend some time feeling quietly satisfied with their demolition job, until stage three sets in, in which the force of the original claim is disentangled from its hyperbolic wrappings and what truth-value it has is finally acknowledged.

But all this, as far as Ireland goes, is only in theory. What prevents it from happening in practice is the fact that this is not just an academic debate, but a quarrel with its roots set deep in political history. How idealist to imagine that you could resolve all that by a set of intellectual trade-offs! It is because this discourse hooks on to power that it proves so recalcitrant, and must thus be subjected to what the Freudians would call a symptomatic reading. If the knives are out, it is partly because the guns are. The constant misreadings on both sides; the quickness with which the discourse of academics pledged to a sober disinterestedness moves into rhetorical overdrive when these questions come up; the Pavlovian response produced in otherwise judicious men and women by certain taboo words or key phrases: all this is a sign that we are in the presence of the kind of rhetorical conflict which, as Wittgenstein might have said, can finally be resolved only by changing the forms of life which give birth to it.

Anyone who has been involved in a career of writing and lecturing will have picked up a truth or two about the psychology of reception, which requires no heavy-duty German theorising. They will be aware, for example, that a good many readers and listeners are ideologically pre-programmed to hear in one's discourse more or less what they want or expect to hear, even if this involves reading or hearing the very opposite of what is actually said. It appears to be a law of human psychology that if one praises a phenomenon but then proceeds to criticise it, those who are in favour of the phenomenon will tend to hear only the criticism, while those who are against it will tend to hear only the praise. Another such law is that it is fruitless to concede too much to one's opponent's case, since this will only irritate him. He would much prefer that one presented a conveniently clear-cut target, in order, by negation, to bolster his own identity. In Irish debate today, all of these laws are much in evidence. One may confidently predict that some reviews of this book will sardonically register its Romantic belief in the innate *bonhomie* of the Gael, despite the fact that it argues specifically against this view.

To recount an entirely satisfying narrative, then, we must change our forms of life. It is both a Wittgensteinian and a materialist insight that what we say depends in the end on what we do; and in the case of Ireland, this means that it is unlikely that any historical account will be entirely free of either sectarianism or sanitising until the problems in the North are somehow resolved. This is not to say that nothing can be achieved in the meantime. But when a society like the Irish republic is in the first flush of modernity, having struggled laboriously out from beneath a soul-killing traditionalism, it is really not very realistic to expect that it is going to turn an attentive ear to those who recall what is precious as well as pernicious in those traditions – some of whom, from their standpoint in societies which underwent their entry into modernity a long time ago, are perhaps a little better placed to reckon the calamities as well as the benefits of this transition. Men and women in such a society are likely to be too bored by dreary sentimental nostalgia, too disgusted by sectarian violence, too bruised by patriarchal arrogance, too concerned to pick up respectable academic jobs or turn a quick punt in Europe, to hark to such caveats. There is probably as much point here and now in trying to speak of the spiritual riches of the Irish Catholic church to a victim of clerical abuse as there is in trying to impress the genius of the young Marx's Paris Manuscripts on those who have just emerged from ten years in a Siberian psychiatric ward. There is reconciliation in plenty, but not for us, quite here or quite yet. There is still too much pain and anger in Irish society, too many spiritually mutilated women and emotionally autistic men, too many parents of murdered children in the North, to suggest that a euphoric leap into modernity, leaving behind all the old rhetoric about partition and rural values, mortal sin and the indomitable Irishry, may not be quite the answer either. There is not much point in trying to convince a Dublin advertising executive that modernity can be every bit as emotionally devastating and spiritually mutilating as lounging unemployed and sexually guilt-ridden at the country crossroads.

Modernity in Ireland means a range of precious things like feminism, pluralism, civic rights, secularisation. It can also mean being shamefaced and sarcastic about one's historical culture – that cultural specificity which all good postmodernists, except perhaps Irish ones, are supposed to celebrate. Specific cultures in Ireland are acceptable in the eyes of most liberal pluralists when they are gay, but not when they are GAA. Modernity means flexible notions of sovereignty, as opposed to fetishised ones; it also means being just as flexible about working hours, granting employers the right to call on their workers at any hour of the clock and sacking them if they do not come running. Its admirable aim is to get out from under the dead weight of clericalism, patriarchy, patriotism, in order, rather less admirably, to leap suitably streamlined and amnesiac into a Europe which has now swung its big guns to point at the impoverished south rather than at the ex-Soviet east, and which is characterised among other things by racism, structural unemployment, urban barbarism, the uprooting of whole communities, and the abandonment of the Irish working-class and small farmers to a brutal neo-liberal polity. (There are, of course, much more positive aspects to Europe than that, but the modernisers do not need reminding of them.)

Tradition in Ireland means an oppressive church, a stifling patriarchy, dancing statues of the Virgin, Gaelic chauvinism, and the contract for building new roads going to whichever relative of the minister is currently most strapped for cash. It also means a respect for one's cultural particularity, a refusal to surrender without a struggle to advanced capitalist hegemony, a suspicion of the success ethic, a valuing of local habitat and heritage in a global landscape dead-levelled by the transnational corporations. It is curious that the apologists for cultural diversity so rarely speak of *this* particular obstacle to their ideal, no doubt the most intractable on the globe, as opposed, say, to the threats posed to such diversity by ethnic tunnel vision. For some liberal revisionists, it would seem that Ireland will have assumed its distinctive place among the nations when it ends up looking exactly like Switzerland. The point, however, is that tradition versus modernity is a palpably false option. How utterly unpluralist of the pluralists to think that one could simply *choose* here! Why are they so zealously one-sided about the matter?

The tradition/modernity antithesis is ripe for deconstruction in other ways too. Atavistic traditionalism is indeed a hideous affair, as anyone who has spent three decades in Oxford hardly needs reminding. But we are advised these days that trade unionism is also atavistic – that the right of working men and women to defend their livelihood in organised ways is drearily *passé*. There are even some post-feminists for whom the notion of women's emancipation is equally old-hat. Modernity is replete with appeals to tradition, many of them recently invented ones, and the term 'modern' itself descends to us from classical antiquity. The modernist rallying cry to break with the past and make it new has a very venerable history indeed. Enlightenment is among other, better things a kind of mythology, and there seems little point in replacing the myth of the Celt with the myth of Europe. Capitalism is at once highly rationalised and a form of furious unreason which leaves most people hungry and unhappy. Its most virulent political form, fascism, is both an orgy of mythological barbarism and the final triumph of a modernising, brutally instrumental rationality. Local atavisms and predatory universalisms are sides of the same coin, the former a rearguard reaction to the depredations of the latter. The answer to whether our world is becoming more local or more global is surely a resounding yes.

Amnesia and nostalgia, the inability to remember and the incapacity to do anything else, are terrible twins. The genuinely free nation would be one which could recollect its history without fetishing it, praise its popular leaders without canonising them. The fact that some 'emancipated' Irish liberals cannot recall Thomas Davis or 1916 without feeling distinctly queasy just goes to suggest how unemancipated they really are, how negatively dependent they remain on a history they believe they have transcended. All modernity to date has stood in need of metaphysical traditions to legitimate itself, whatever its demythologising impulse, and there is no reason to imagine that Irish modernity is mysteriously immune to this necessity. The modern is not necessarily less sectarian than the traditional: in the mouths of some Northern Irish Protestants, it can be a supremacist way of slapping down the benighted southerners. In any case, the category of modernisation is in itself entirely vacuous, compatible with all kinds of desirable and unsavoury social transformations. It has traditionally been one slogan under which societies seek to perpetuate themselves, face-lifting their social orders while leaving their underlying social relations intact. Who are these forward-looking liberals who wish to perpetuate a set of capitalist social relations which have now been with us for centuries, and which betray unmistakable signs of spiritual exhaustion?

Part of the problem is that 'modernising the nation' is both a tautology and an oxymoron. It is a tautology in the sense that modernity and the nation-state belong together in any case; it is an oxymoron to the extent that the nation represents at the same time a pre-modern residue within that state. As Slavoj Žižek points out, the nation is the modern *Gesellschaft* freed from traditional 'organic' bonds, yet at the same time a kind of 'surplus of the Real' that clings to it, in that national identity must continue to appeal to roots, origins, a common history. 'In short,' Žižek writes, ' "nation" designates at one and the same time the instance by means of reference to which traditional "organic" links are dissolved *and* the "reminder of the pre-modern in modernity" . . . "Nation" is a pre-modern left-over which functions as an inner condition of modernity itself, as an inherent impetus to its progress.'[2] It is not, then, a question of tradition or modernity in the nation, but of the idea of the nation as itself a contradictory unity of the two, a contradiction in which both modernisers and traditionalists find themselves inevitably ensnared. The former want to refurbish an entity part of whose very identity is pre-modern, whereas the latter want to adhere to the organic in a set-up which is inherently a modern idea.

The point, anyway, is that all discourse has its historical conditions, a doctrine once known as the model of base and superstructure, and the conditions for a fruitful interchange on these questions in Ireland have not yet fully

2. Slavoj Žižek, *For They Know Not What They Do* (London, 1991), p. 20.

arrived. It is politics, not academic argument, which will finally fail or succeed in sorting out these matters, distasteful though the suggestion may be to those academics for whom ideas are one thing and material circumstances quite another. But there is another reason why these contentions are unlikely to go away. Historical revisionism usually declares itself free of any political agenda or intent; yet one would not perhaps be entirely deluding oneself to conclude that its scholarly findings tend by and large to support an anti-nationalist politics. This, no doubt, is far from the *intention* of such eminently disinterested authors, since their concern is not of course to do down Wolfe Tone or cast aspersions on the Fenians, but simply to give us the unvarnished facts. Political or ideological considerations, we may take their solemn word for it, never enter their head while shaping a narrative, effecting an emphasis, choosing an epithet or selecting a range of data. Even so, such political considerations can hardly be said to be far from their work's *effect*. Most nationalists have concluded that the effect of this revisionist scholarship is to cast doubt (falsely, in their view) on their own political doctrines, confronting them with a history far too shaded and slippery to fit them at all neatly.

If this is what nationalists conclude, then they are surely mistaken. They are not in the least misguided to believe that revisionism is by and large critical of nationalism; they are simply wrong to imagine that its criticisms could ever really matter. We have touched already on the reasons for this in our discussion of nationalism in 'The Good-Natured Gael'. Nationalism, like any other radical political aspiration, is not independent of historical facts, but it is not merely a reflex of them either. Indeed this is part of what we mean by a moral question. There is no reason why nationalists should not accept many of the findings of revisionist historians, while not feeling the need to adjust their political beliefs one jot. Nationalists do of course want to challenge, sometimes rightly, quite a few revisionist findings; but this is not where battle is most fundamentally joined. It does not make the slightest difference to Irish nationalism to discover that Cuchulain was not all he was cracked up to be, that the Act of Union was not primarily responsible for the nation's economic decline, that there were some genuinely enlightened dimensions of British colonial government, that many agrarian agitators or protesting Gaelic poets had distinctly non-national agendas, or that the rural middlemen were not as predatory as they have been painted. To imagine that any of this could make a difference to nationalist doctrine is at best a kind of category mistake, and at worst simply to misunderstand the nature of radical politics. Are feminist demands invalid because many men throughout history have treated women well? Does being a socialist make sense only in the context of child labour, starvation wages and a twelve-hour working day? Socialists recognise well enough that empirically speaking the profit motive has its advantages; but this does not stop them from rejecting in principle the kind of social order in which I will only be of service to you if it is profitable for me to be so.

Nationalism is a child of liberal Enlightenment, one application among several of the principle that human beings should be as far as possible self-determining. Since this applies to collectivities as well as to individuals, and since in the modern world those collectivities have taken the primary form of the nation state, nationalism is simply the logical offshoot of the democratic principle of self-determination in this particular region. The principle itself, however, is far wider than the nation-state itself, an historically transient affair which has so far meant little but trouble, and which it would be good to see the back of. Nationalism, which is an equally ephemeral current of thought, can either be a constructive step towards this wider self-determination, as socialists have traditionally affirmed of most anti-colonial movements, or it can be a form of festering narcissism which thwarts its attainment. But because it rests upon a moral principle, it cannot be refuted simply by presenting empirical evidence about the nature of the regimes which it opposes, or the character of the movements which incarnate it. This does not in itself suggest that the principle is a sound one, or assume that in contemporary Ireland the meaning of self-determination is luminously clear. On the contrary, Ireland's problem is that more than one group within it desires political self-determination, in ways that seem to constrain the rights of others to the same goal. Nor is it to suggest that the principle is not falsifiable at all, that nothing could count as a criticism of it, which would be much too convenient for nationalists. It is just to claim that it is falsifiable only in the way that moral principles generally are, rather than by claiming that, say, the price of bread in Tipperary in 1871 was not as prohibitively high as the Fenians maintained. A Conservative should not have abandoned his belief in private property and public order simply because Margaret Thatcher redefined these doctrines as greed and state repression, since the beliefs can survive these empirical distortions.

Historians cannot avoid such moral principles, but they cannot feel entirely comfortable with them either. They are biased by their current forms of training towards a full-blooded nominalism which makes them restive with such general concepts. The claim by an eminent Irish historian that the Great Famine was essentially a 'regional' phenomenon is one of the more self-caricaturing instances of this aversion to global notions. (The Nazi bombing of Britain was also a regional phenomenon, in the sense that it affected many different regions of the country.) This methodological nominalism is by no means politically innocent. General concepts, structural analysis and radical politics have a certain natural affinity, so that methodological nominalists are rarely political leftists. 'Essentialism' is the latest mantra by which one can place under censure any attempt to characterise Irish society as a whole, thus cloaking one's common-or-garden liberal pragmatism in fashionable postmodernist dress. When one critic recently described John Toland as an exponent of 'Irish theological rationalism', meaning that he was a theological rationalist who hailed from Ireland, another scholar pounced on the phrase as betraying a quasi-racist belief that there was some essentially Irish form of rationalism. Such is the knee-jerk nature of these contentions. In the present overheated political climate, one had better beware of unguarded phrases like 'Danish bacon', for fear of implying that there is a kind of bacon which distils the very essence of Denmark.

In the case of Ireland, to be sure, this revisionist coyness of general concepts can sometimes be curiously selective: 'colonialism' is far too cumbersome a category to capture the subtleties of Anglo-Irish relations, whereas 'Romantic idealism' will do to wrap up the Young Irelanders. But part of the historian's embarrassment with moral principles is that they are by nature general. It would be odd to pronounce torture to be wrong but in the same breath dispense the Nepalese from this stricture. These principles are of course exceptionally complex and controversial in their application; it is because of this that we are in need of the discourse known as moral philosophy. But stated baldly, they have a kind of blunt forthrightness about them which is bound to be distasteful to the sensibility of those – 'literary' men and women above all – bred to value nuance, intricacy, the pied and dappled nature of things. What is truly scandalous to the liberal intellectual is the essential simplicity of such axioms. What distinguishes the radical from the liberal in this respect is the former's belief that, when it comes to the major political conflicts of our world, it is embarrassingly easy to say who on the whole is in the right of it and who is not. There is really no middle ground – not a phrase the liberal likes to hear – between racists and ethnic militants, patriarchs and feminists, transnational corporations and sweated labour.

What also distinguishes the two groups is the fact that liberals, and certainly most revisionist historians, tend to believe that it hasn't all really been as bad as some moaners and masochists make out, whereas radicals are those for whom it has been very bad indeed for a long time, and shows no underlying signs of improving. It is not in the end a matter of nationalists versus anti-nationalists, but of two divergent readings of human history – the one liberal-rationalist, generously trusting to the civilising forces of modernity, the other materialist, reading the record of humanity to date as largely one of scarcity, exploitation and injustice. It is, in effect, a distinction between what Walter Benjamin termed 'history' – the fable recounted by the governors – and 'tradition' – the narrative of the dispossessed. Revisionists tend to be apologists for history rather than custodians of tradition. Whereas our masters are on the whole fairly sanguine, holding that crises are sporadic and untypical, the dispossessed are those who are aware that states of emergency are as chronic as states of sexual jealousy. Both positions are prone to hyperbole: the dispossessed self-indulgently clinging to their tales of woe, the triumphalistic victors briskly sweeping failure under the carpet. In the end, however, Schopenhauer and Nelson Mandela have more of the truth than Hegel and Bill Gates. If Irish colonial history was indeed less traumatic than has been considered, it constitutes a remarkable exception in the narrative of humanity as a whole. Radicals are those who suspect at the risk of mild paranoia that things are generally worse than the official accounts of them tend to indicate, whereas liberals court the alternative psychological dangers of denial and disavowal, reluctant as they are to credit the brutal truth that a great many human beings in history, perhaps the majority, would probably have been far better off not being born.

It is sometimes thought that the principle of self-determination is empirically falsifiable in at least this sense, that those who abuse it should not enjoy it. This is one distinction between the conservative and the liberal or radical. The conservative's approach to the notion is essentially empirical: if the principle works for the British then it should be fostered among them, but if it proves to wreak havoc in post-colonial Africa it should be abandoned in that continent. Liberals and radicals, by contrast, believe that though human beings may abuse their freedom, they are not truly human without it. This is a necessarily abstract, universal faith in the best traditions of the Enlightenment, quite at odds with those Irish historians who would claim, for example, that there was no good empirical reason for the Irish to launch the Land League or the war of independence. There may be some other reason why these things were bad ideas, but it cannot be of the order that most revisionists seem to assume. Those, whether nationalists or anti-nationalists, who believe that historical revisionism is undermining the nationalist case by demonstrating that some sound economic progress was made in Ireland under British rule, or that the rural tenantry were a deferential class, or that the country was not such a violent place after all, are thus simply missing the point. It is vulgar economism to find it perverse or inappropriate, as some revisionist writers do, that Irish men and women should have continued to press for the abolition of landlordism or the British *imperium* even when things were materially and even politically going their way for a change. Such a view reflects a crudely catastrophist notion of political change, with which no self-respecting radical would wish to be allied. It also forgets the fact that people are on the whole more likely to be politically militant when they are feeling materially more self-confident.[3] Revisionist historians, who are usually eager to stress the non-political, purely scholarly nature of their research, will surely be enheartened to hear that their work can play no significant role in altering nationalist opinion. Or will they?

There is another kind of conflict in Irish debate between the empirical and the deontological (that is to say, the belief that a principle is justified regardless of utilitarian considerations). This concerns the question of how disreputable British rule in Ireland actually was. In a now familiar *pas de deux*, the nationalist will highlight some particularly lurid episode – the eviction in the snow, the hunted priest with a price on his head – while the revisionist will rightly

3.   C. C. Townsend makes the point that the worst violence of the Land League occurred in 1880–1, after the restoration of relative stability. See his *Political Violence in Ireland* (Oxford, 1983), p. 118.

point out that such events were not in fact all that common. But that may not be the point. Once again, the two parties may be occupying incommensurable orders of discourse. The nationalist's point, to employ a Hegelian distinction, may be that such events were not *average* but *typical*. They may not have cropped up often, as the revisionist historian quite properly insists; but when they did occur, they laid bare in peculiarly graphic or symbolic form something of the unloveliness of colonial power, and thus provided the opponents of that authority with a vivid allegorical figure of what they were fighting for. In a similar way, most feminists reject the idea that men are simply creatures resting between rapes, but nonetheless find in that aberrant act something typical of patriarchal sexual relations in general. Hamstrung by his empiricist education, the revisionist historian is sometimes slow to appreciate the symbolic dimension of action, and must accordingly go to school with the cultural critic. No historical event is finally separable from the way it is symbolised in social consciousness; and if this truth had been more surely grasped by a positivistically-inclined historiography, as it is by the historians of *mentalité*, much tedious argumentative spadework might have proved unnecessary.

This tussle between the empirical and the deontological shows up in another way too. Revisionist historiography sometimes seeks to palliate a particular form of political unpleasantness by appeal to its historical circumstances. In practice if not in theory, revisionism tends towards ethical relativism. The relativism, to be sure, is somewhat selective: it is not generally drawn upon to exonerate the shooting of landlords' agents, the assassination of Chief Secretaries or the preaching of ideas of blood sacrifice. As an historian, you can maintain an impartial air on such matters while contriving to suggest by your tone that you find them thoroughly distasteful. Many of those who would baulk at defining the conflict of interests between landlords and landless labourers in clear-cut moral terms would be far less reluctant to characterise the conflict between patriarchs and feminists, or racists and anti-racists, in such ways. But in general revisionism is wary of that moral anachronism – an 'error of novices', as Lecky called it[4] – by which one smugly projects one's own contemporary values on to the very different scenarios of the past. This stricture is sometimes wholly just: we cannot understand the ruling classes of antiquity if we assume that they were secretly ashamed of slavery. Sometimes, however, it is a barefaced evasion. We should not, we are counselled, be too hard on those British officials who refused to let famine relief in Ireland impede the working of market forces, since they were simply acting according to the ideological lights of their own day. In fact, every historical period has more than one brand of ideological wisdom, which are often enough at odds with each other. Pluralism is not just a characteristic of the present. Britain's relief policy during the Famine was censured quite as much by some men and women of the day – Quakers, Irish nationalists, even

4. W. E. H. Lecky, *Historical and Political Essays* (London, 1908), p. 14.

high-placed British civil servants – as it is by modern-day radicals. Should we exculpate those who massacred Indians, force-fed the suffragettes or lobotomised homosexuals on the grounds that they were simply conforming to the moral codes of their time or place? Certainly Ireland's greatest political theorist was not prepared to take this line in defence of Warren Hastings.

Revisionism in any field of thought is something of a self-undoing enterprise, since it must logically apply its own revisionary programme to itself. Its discourse must necessarily fall under its own judgement, if it is not simply to replace one set of myths with another (the Celtic Note with the European Idea, for example). The refreshingly sceptical glance it casts on received historical formulas must also be turned on itself, so that the authority of its judgements must be continually tempered by a sense of their openness to perpetual revision. What it does to the nationalist narrative must always in principle be capable of being done to it; in fact nationalist historiography was itself the first great revisionist school in Ireland, which took what were then the official imperial narratives of native history and rewrote them with breathtaking boldness from below, with all the courageous imagining, false continuism, historical truth, Manichean ethics, generous devotion to the dispossessed and triumphalist teleology which that involved. Some of this nationalist revisionism was in the interests of making Ireland seem more civilised, and hence more palatable, to its Anglo-Saxon neighbours. Some of today's middle-class liberal rather than middle-class nationalist revisionism has much the same effect, making Connemara safe for Camden Town. The one was a colonial symptom, the other a post-colonial symptom.

All history-writing is revisionist, just as all poetry-writing is. It is simply a question of which ideological label a particular revisionist current comes under. For Charles O'Conor and Eoin Mac Neill, it was nationalist and populist; for most of our current batch of revisionists, it is middle-class liberal. What is wrong with these scholars from a radical viewpont is not that they are revisionists, but that they are middle-class liberals. And what is wrong with middle-class liberalism is not on the whole its values, most of which are entirely admirable, but the fact that it obtusely refuses to recognise the depth of social transformation which would be necessary for those values to be realised in universal form. It remains committed to sustaining a socio-economic system which makes a mockery of the very values it promotes. It is this question, not whether you think Patrick Pearse was a masochist or Wolfe Tone a social climber, which ultimately divides socialist republicans in Ireland from everyone else, as it divided Frederick Ryan from both Arthur Griffith and Sir Horace Plunkett. For a radical, what bourgeois nationalists and liberal revisionists have in common is far more crucial than what distinguishes them. We should not exaggerate the significance of their sparrings.

One should remember too that there can be different national revisionisms, not always at one with each other. Some British revisionists of the future, for example, might come to shake up their compatriots' rather complacent notions about the history of their empire, demonstrating that imperial rule was a good deal more noxious than has been assumed, and thus finding themselves at odds with the Irish school of revisionism. This vista of potentially unlimitable self-revision is easy enough to accept as an intellectual proposition, but not so easy to sign up to when there are life-and-death political questions at stake. Indeed in this respect Irish revisionism can be quite often found miming the dogmatic posture of some of its antagonists. It can be a truculent, embattled, sometimes even sectarian sort of liberal pluralism, very unBloomsburyish in tone, which does not usually sound at all as though it might be open to revision.

In another sense, however, revisionism is not empirical enough. If it has conducted admirably meticulous inquiries into Grattan's parliament or the seventeenth-century land settlements, it can scarcely be said to have inquired quite so meticulously into itself. Revisionism can indeed write a history of itself of sorts, but it tends to be couched in purely academic terms, and no significant shift in cultural climate is ever simply that. As has been pointed out often enough, it also has much to do with the war in the North, the emergence of a new liberal middle class in the republic, the transformation of a hitherto stagnant post-colonial enclave into a flourishing if grotesquely inequitable capitalist set-up, the escalating 'Europeanisation' of the country, certain historic changes in its relations with Britain and the like. Revisionists themselves tend to track their origins to a newly professional spirit in Irish historiography, as though the growing specialisation of intellectual labour was not itself a fact of far more than academic import.

Rooted in highly particular social circumstances, some of which it serves to justify, revisionism is among other things quite palpably an ideology. It is the intemperate polemic of its popular commentators, not the carefully neutralised tones of its historians, which lets the ideological cat out of the bag. What also betrays the ideological nature of the quarrel is the consistency and predictability of both positions. It is almost certain that those who think that the Famine was planned genocide are also likely to draw attention to the quasi-fascistic elements of Yeats, whereas someone who considers that the Young Irelanders were a bunch of idealistic hotheads will quite probably admire the poetry of Paul Muldoon. There is of course no logical reason why one should not hold that the Young Irelanders were full of hot air and also believe that Sir Charles Trevelyan set out to deliberately exterminate the Irish people; but almost nobody combines such sorts of opinions, since there is a great deal more at work here than *ad hoc* judgements. Consistency is not always a virtue; one is not over-impressed by a coin which always lands the same side up. If revisionism is as local, empirical and specific in its procedures as it likes to maintain, why do almost all of its political implications point in the same direction? And if it is really in favour of the irreducible particular as against the homogenising universal, why do some of its practitioners appear to find little difference between the politics of D. P. Moran and those of Seamus Deane?

Revisionism is an admirable attempt to recount the true story of Irish history, without myth and macho illusions. It is also the discourse of a post-war professional intelligentsia in Ireland, which needs to affirm its authority and autonomy by emphasising the political neutrality of its scholarship. In this way, that intelligentsia can free itself from its previous rather humiliating role as a blunt instrument of nationalist power, and end up instead as the mouthpiece of a post-nationalist establishment. Much the same has happened with, say, some Chinese literary criticism, which was previously a catspaw of Maoist dogma and is nowadays affirming its independence by becoming an apologist for postmodern market freedom. Such movements only become truly autonomous when they no longer need to affirm the fact, and are thus no longer tied by negation to the set-ups they need to spurn. But to suggest that revisionist scholarship is at one level ideological is not to imply that it does not also contain a good deal of truth. Truth and ideology are by no means simply opposites. Marx considered Ricardo and Adam Smith to be ideologists, but he also endorsed quite a number of their 'scientific' findings. Ideologies are not just forms of false consciousness. Nationalism is self-declaredly an ideology, but it does not follow that what it has to say of the Shanavests or the tithe war is pure self-justification. It is just that one reason why revisionists and their critics cannot agree is that the very proposition that revisionist discourse belongs to certain specific historical conditions, without being wholly reducible to them, itself lies on one side of the debate in question. The two parties cannot achieve consensus on the nature, status and origin of this discourse, let alone on its truth-value, since the most interesting critics of revisionism hold by and large to a materialist view of knowledge, one which must naturally apply to their own forms of cognition as well, whereas most revisionists do not. And a materialist theory of such matters does not mean a pragmatist one. Nobody is suggesting that to claim that not all landlords were bloodsuckers is just a covert way of discrediting the IRA. But neither is it grandly independent of contemporary conditions and ideological assumptions. Historical research, to be sure, is about archives, estate papers, judgements as objective as one can make them; yet who can doubt that the course of Irish historiography over the past quarter of a century would have looked different had there not been a war in the North?

The question of objectivity is one crux of the argument. Some revisionist historians will readily concede that their own historical accounts are to some degree value-laden. To this extent, nationalist claims that all revisionism purports to be value-free are a red herring. There are, even so, those positivistically-minded revisionists for whom they themselves are in possession of the facts while their opponents are in possession of ideology. A sound reading of history is empirical rather than political. The radical will riposte that all historical accounts are at some level political, and that the revisionist's scientificity is as much a myth as Milesius. But one can understand well enough why the empiricist should want to make such an implausible-sounding claim. For it seems to him that if all historiography is political, then there is nothing to choose between one version of the past and another. What appears like a choice between narratives of how it was is secretly a choice between perspectives on how it is. And for many a postmodern sceptic, this is indeed the case. The radical who finds neutrality suspect must accordingly guard her back against a relativism which she finds as distasteful as the empiricist does, if for rather different reasons.

The revisionist is right to resist this free-for-all, but does so on the wrong grounds. For it is not true that there is nothing to choose between one political reading and another. This would only be the case if political value-judgements were as subjective as one's taste in whiskey. An interpretation of, say, the Limerick anti-Jewish pogrom early in this century which assumes that anti-Semitism is a laudable sentiment will deliver a less accurate version of what took place in the city than one which does not. It is not that what actually occurred was an attack upon Jews, to which the historian is then free to take up one or another moral attitude if he is so moved. It is rather that what actually happened was a morally offensive assault on the Limerick Jewish community. The moral indefensibility of the action is part of the situation. If one does not see this, then one is not seeing what actually took place. Similarly, there are material situations which cannot be described at all without drawing upon value-judgements. Imagine trying to explain to an observer ignorant of the behaviour of small children just what is happening when one child snatches and destroys another's toy before its eyes. How could one characterise the facts of the matter without mobilising such notions as envy, rivalry, resentment? An account of nineteenth-century Irish nationalism which assumed that nationalism was merely an irrational phobia would be incapable of adequately interpreting what took place. It is not a choice between the factual and the political, but one between the sorts of political frameworks which allow us access to the facts, and the sorts which do not.

There is another sense in which revisionists and materialists are largely at odds. There are left-wing currents of revisionism, strains of neo-Marxist Unionism and anti-nationalist proletarianism; but for the most part academic revisionists tend to look somewhat askance on radical movements in Irish history. They are not on the whole paid-up fan-club members of the United Irishmen, the Irish Republican Brotherhood or the men and women of 1916. Even though they are supposed to be absolved as scholars from anything as vulgar as political opinions, it is clear (if only, occasionally, from their tone or favoured topics) that Sean O'Faolain appeals to them rather more than John Mitchel. What betrays the fact that these are more than specific scholarly judgements is that most Irish revisionists would almost certainly feel the same way about non-Irish radical movements too. It is hard to imagine many of them becoming dewy-eyed at an allusion to William Morris's Socialist League, or wallowing in maudlin nostalgia for British trade union power in the 1970s. On the whole, they tend not to mourn the waning of the student movement or the fading of the Fourth International.

It is not simply, then, that given their understanding of Irish history they judge Mitchel or Pearse to have been in the circumstances wrong-headed; it is also that most of them think such political views are wrong-headed anyway. Strikingly few revisionists are anarchists or Trotskyists, though if their case is politically neutral it is hard to see why not. Some of their opposition to Irish nationalism is for subtle, historically specific, politically honourable reasons, and some of it is for the kind of reasons you find among pub landlords in the Home Counties who say things like 'Pas de problème, squire' and 'What's your poison, old bean?' Similarly, some of their dislike of what they call 'jargon' is specific to the ways one should speak of Ireland, while some of it is just a commonplace scoffing at cultural theory as such. Some liberal commentators are uneasy with words which only a minority use, like 'signifier' or 'hegemony', as opposed to words which everyone in the local supermarket uses, such as 'allegory', 'agrarian agitator' and 'multiculturalism'. Revisionists, in other words, have their particular, often interesting, sometimes valid reasons for disliking nationalist views; it is just that these reasons would be a mite more convincing if they did not also so clearly dislike left-wing politics and cultural theory as such, like any suburban philistine.

There is one particular way in which revisionism seems oblivious to its own historical conditions, an oblivion which is a common characteristic of ideological thought. This is the fact that it clearly belongs to the more general cultural milieu we call postmodernism, while seeming for the most part quite unaware of it. Since revisionists generally know more about Lyons than Lyotard, they appear unable to place themselves in broader cultural terms. But their nervousness of grand narratives, their preference for pragmatic explanations rather than big ideas, their embarrassment with the ethical, their emphasis on regionality, complexity, ambiguity, on plurality rather than monocausality, on heterogeneity and discontinuity, on the role of sheer happenstance in historical affairs: all of this places them firmly within the postmodern camp whether they know it or not, which for the most part they do not. What a remarkable coincidence, then, that the values and methods which for revisionists are determined simply by the requirements of disinterested academic scholarship, and which must therefore claim a timeless validity, should also turn out to be the reach-me-down pieties of a highly specific cultural movement which rejects the whole notion of disinterested judgement as a political fiction!

Indeed much of the programme of academic Irish studies today is silently set by a postmodern agenda, with some interesting political effects. Nationalism, for example, is not much in favour because it is 'essentialist', whereas feminism is firmly on the agenda because it is not. The truth is that some nationalism is anti-essentialist whereas some feminism is essentialist; but one should not allow such minor considerations to interfere with one's comfortingly clear-cut oppositions. Nationalism is also upbraided for cutting across and concealing other kinds of social division; but then some feminist and ethnic theory can do this too, and for its own purposes quite properly so. The concept of ethnicity is much to the fore in such studies – there are, believe it or not, still essays tumbling from the press on the racialisation of the Celt in Matthew Arnold – since the Irish are of course ethnic. Ethnic for whom, and how many ethnicities there are on the island, are questions worth raising. Ethnic, to be sure, for radical American academia, which thus categorises the much-vaunted 'other' of Irishness in highly *American* terms, terms relevant to its own internal politics, with a touch of the very intellectual colonialism it is most at pains to disown.

Or take the fact that postmodernists, like liberal humanists, are notorious for their scepticism of the concept of social class, a scepticism apparently not shared by Liverpool dockers or Chicano grape-pickers. Social class today is a much less sexy notion than gender or ethnicity, a prejudice which may then determine the way one views such social formations as the Anglo-Irish Ascendancy. If one wishes to deflect a nationalist or socialist critique of them, it is always possible to repress their exploitative role as a landowning or urban class and redefine them rather more glamorously as an ethnic minority, hounded out of existence by a bellicose Celticism. Or take the fact that postmodernism tends to be naïvely enthused by margins and majorities as such, suspecting consensus and solidarity as inherently authoritarian. This, need one point out, is an utterly formalistic prejudice: not all minorities are to be applauded (neo-Nazis? ley line buffs?), and the solidarity which brought down apartheid was not an oppressive one. Applied to Ireland, however, such profoundly questionable theoretical assumptions will generate some well-nigh automatic political consequences. Since the Ascendancy formed a minority, one is likely to feel the kind of sympathy for these poor abused gentlefolk that one might otherwise reserve for, say, the Caribbean community in Britain, even though that community does not own almost all the land in the country it inhabits, as the Anglo-Irish governing class once did. But these minor differences need not be unduly inflated. Those who persist in reproaching the Ascendancy can then be accused of ethnic prejudice rather than socialist principle. Just the same can be said of those who criticise the Northern Unionists; it all depends on whether you are thinking of them as an ethnic or cultural minority or a politically dominant formation. In a postmodern age, the former is rather more visible than the latter, so that theoretical fashions give birth to loaded political judgements. The Northern nationalists are a minority too, but from a postmodern viewpoint adhere to the distinctly uncool policy of wishing to join a majority to the south of them. It is hard to see them as aberrant, any more than one can view the Home Counties as aberrant, and aberrancy for postmodern thought is an index of authenticity.

Postmodernism, as I have argued elsewhere, is also a brand of culturalism, which habitually overestimates the centrality of cultural matters.[5] In this way, too, it licenses certain readings of Irish politics while suppressing others. 'Culture' has been foregrounded as a topic in our time partly because of the growing importance of ethnic minorities in the west consequent on the globalisation of capital, but also because it has become for the first time in history a major force of material production in its own right. It is also a natural stomping-ground of intellectuals, who can find outlets in this field which are denied to them by the political deadlocks of our time, and can thus act as a form of theoretical displacement as well as of political enrichment. But the politics of culture are by no means innocent. One can make rational choices between forms of politics, but not for the most part between forms of cultures, so that to redefine the political in cultural terms – to call Orange marches a celebration of one's cultural heritage, for example – is to render one's politics far less vulnerable to critique. Even some of the South African Boers, architects of apartheid, are now claiming privileged status as a dispossessed cultural minority, in what must surely be the ultimate postmodern irony. For a sufficiently woolly-minded Irish liberal, there need be no massive difference in principle between the Unionists and travelling people. Both, viewed from a perspective long enough to obscure the question of power, can be seen as distinct cultural groupings out to defend their unique inheritance. The conflation of culture and politics is in the service of a particular politics, in postmodern thought in general and in Ireland in particular. To view the conflict in the North as primarily one between alternative 'cultural traditions' fits well with postmodern culturalism in general, and so sounds reasonably persuasive; it is just that it also happens to be false.

What is at stake in Irish intellectual debate is in fact much less a conflict between tradition and modernity, than one between modernity and postmodernity. The clash between Irish nationalists and Irish revisionists is a reproduction *in parvo* of a more global altercation between those for whom modernity is still alive if unwell, and those who believe themselves to be confidently posterior to it. The political discourse of modernity is one of rights, justice, oppression, solidarity, universality, exploitation, emancipation. Nationalism, along with liberalism and socialism, belongs with this world-view. The political language of postmodernity is one of identity, marginality, locality, difference, otherness, diversity, desire. With some important qualifications, revisionism is part of this milieu. There are those for whom the former language is now effectively bankrupt, and there are those for whom the second way of speaking is no more than a disastrous displacement of the first, one consequent on the failure of that discourse to realise itself politically in our time.

5.   See Terry Eagleton, *The Illusions of Postmodernism* (Oxford, 1996).

There are others, yet again, who acknowledge the extreme tension between these different registers, but regard them as ultimately compatible and indeed urgently in need of one another. Within Ireland, the best aspects of what might be called the Field Day case have tried to do exactly this – to argue that genuine identity, true difference and authentic pluralism can finally be established only on the basis of political justice and emancipation. Political justice is essential so that men and women can be free to explore what they wish to become, and confirm one another's autonomy in this regard; but if the language of difference and identity is abstracted from this material context, it will end up short-circuiting the very political conditions necessary for its realisation. There is, on the other hand, a real danger that the drive to autonomy, equality and emancipation will ride roughshod over a need to acknowledge difference and otherness here and now. Cusped as we are between modernity and post-modernity, there is no satisfying theoretical resolution of these questions historically available to us. Right now, the two registers in question are bound to remain to some degree incommensurable, which is to say that nationalists and revisionists will doubtless carry on talking past one another while purporting to be conducting a dialogue.

It may well be, then, that only 'history' will ultimately resolve these matters, and not just the history of Ireland. The coming century is indeed likely to be dominated by a battle between north and south, but on the globe as a whole rather than in Ireland in particular. As the post-colonial nations of the south affirm their rights to autonomy, they are likely to run into headlong conflict with a north whose 'advanced' economic system forms an obstacle to their well-being, and which is already armed to the teeth against their encroachments. It might then become apparent that it is this system above all which is conservatively restricting human freedom, and the post-colonial world which is in the van of human development. In that case, what now seems the latest thing to some Irish liberal modernisers will be shown up in its true reactionary colours, while the Irish colonial history some of them find so acutely embarrassing can be read as prefiguring the shape of the future. The country will then have to decide whether to continue to cast its fortunes with a global capitalism which for many in the impoverished world has overstayed its welcome, thus becoming, so to speak, a good deal too traditionalist, or whether it should draw upon the resources of its own history of dispossession in order to align itself with the coming epoch. The situation would then be reversed: the revisionists would then be those who were prepared to make that forward-looking commitment, while the traditionalists would be those reluctant to let go of the benefits of a Western modernity whose praises they now sing, but which would then already be in the process of being surpassed.

INDEX